FORTRESS OF FREEDOM

THE
DECLARATION OF INDEPENDENCE
AND THE
CONSTITUTION OF THE
UNITED STATES OF AMERICA

DONALD HOLMES

The shrine of the Declaration of Independence and of the Constitution of the United
States in the Library of Congress

Fortress Of Freedom

THE STORY OF
THE LIBRARY OF CONGRESS

BY

Lucy Salamanca

WITH A FOREWORD BY

Archibald MacLeish

J. B. LIPPINCOTT COMPANY
PHILADELPHIA   NEW YORK   LONDON
1792–1942

For

JUDGE AUGUST C. BACKUS,

*who, in a lifetime devoted
to the rehabilitation of the
unfortunate, has recognized
the power and influence of
good books*

The earth belongs always to the living generation.

—THOMAS JEFFERSON

Foreword

It may seem strange to some readers that the first complete history of the Library of Congress should appear at this particular moment. Actually, however, the time has a peculiar appropriateness. The basic propositions upon which our government was established are challenged at this moment as they have never been challenged before. The Library of Congress is in many ways the most expressive symbol of those propositions. Not only is it the depository of the great documents in which those propositions are set down and developed—the Declaration of Independence, the Constitution—it is also an expression in fact and in practice of the underlying reality of those propositions. It is a library of the people, by the people, and for the people; and as long as it exists as a free library and a people's library the intellectual and spiritual freedom which Jefferson and his colleagues proposed to establish will not perish from the earth.

Apart from a factual account, published by the Government Printing Office and now out of print, which carried the history of the Library of Congress to 1864, and aside from a few scattered doctoral dissertations on one or another phase of Library operations, no history of the Library of Congress has been written and no record of the origin and development of the Library exists. It is a source of considerable gratification to me that a history should now be provided and, particularly, that it should be written by a member of the Library staff who, both in the Library and out of it, has had unusual opportunities to familiarize herself with the Library's work. Lucy Salamanca wrote distin-

9

guished articles about the Library of Congress, the Folger Shakespeare Library, and other similar subjects for publications like *The New York Times Magazine* for many years before she became a member of the Library staff. For two and one half years now she has been head of the Congressional Research Section of the Legislative Reference Service of the Library and in this capacity has had peculiar opportunity to observe the Library in action as an agency of effective government. As a government official Miss Salamanca knows that the Library of Congress is a legislative tool of immeasurable usefulness. As a writer she knows that the Library is not only a library for Congressmen but one of the greatest collections of scholarly materials ever assembled in the history of the world.

Her book has been written to make clear that the Library's magnificent collections of books and manuscripts and music and maps, its unequaled concerts of chamber music, its efficient legislative reference service, its service for the blind, its union catalog, its bibliographic and reference work for scholars and schools and others, its photoduplication facilities, its prints, its exhibits, are not in sum total the Library. The Library itself—the Library as Dr. Herbert Putnam left it—is an institution of learning unique among the learned institutions of the world—a library having the educational excitement of a great university; a university having the timelessness and the enduring integrity of a great and ancient collection of famous books. No piecemeal account of the units which compose the Library of Congress can convey a truthful impression of the great department of government which has for its end and aim the active and useful possession, on behalf of the people of the United States and in their interest, of the record of their past and of the works of intellect and art out of which their future may be created.

World events have made the Library of Congress more important now than it has ever been before. Today it is, physiologically speaking, the nerve center of our national life. It is alive with activity essential to the nation's defense, to vital legislation, to the expanded needs and extraordinary demands of a nation at war. Every resource at its command is strained for national service to an extent neither possible nor necessary in the past. It hums with that excitement which hovers over every organization which is keyed to crises and the exactions of superbly concentrated effort.

Therefore it is especially fitting that the story of the Library of Congress should come to the attention of the American people at this time. There are many who will welcome its telling and who will be glad, as I am, that Lucy Salamanca has set it down.

—Archibald MacLeish

Contents

Illustrations

FORTRESS OF FREEDOM

Introductory

Two domes rise on Capitol Hill, the white dome of the United States Capitol and the green-gold dome of the Library of Congress. Each is symbolic. Together they emphasize against the Washington sky the fact that in this country a man's soul is his own and his mind is free.

Only 140 years have intervened since the day John Randolph of Virginia asked Congress to authorize that recently purchased books and maps be placed in the Capitol in a room occupied during the last session of the Sixth Congress by the House of Representatives, and that "the books or libraries which have heretofore been kept separately by each House . . . be removed and set up with those lately purchased, and be numbered and labeled with them, making one Library of the whole."

In those 140 years the Library of Congress has grown to be the largest national library in the world, housing more than six million volumes, one and a half million maps, almost two million pieces of music, more than half a million prints, two million manuscripts and transcripts, and about one hundred thousand bound volumes of newspapers.

The Declaration of Independence and the Constitution of the United States are enshrined in its halls. Its departments and divisions of service touch every human activity; its rich resources are freely extended, not only to the people of America but to refugees from other lands. Its card-catalogue system serves more than six thousand American libraries in the fields of cataloguing and classification; through its Union Catalog it acquaints the public with more than eleven million titles and more than twelve million locations of books in other American libraries. At home it accommodates serious students and investigators in private study rooms; its system of interlibrary loans enables scholars in other parts of the nation to continue their research.

In 1941 more than a million visitors from all parts of the world and from every section of the United States crossed the threshold of the Library of Congress—nearly three thousand people every day. In April, when the Japanese cherry trees were blossoming along the Potomac, more than four thousand visited it daily. It has grown from a one-room library for purposes of legislative reference into a national institution of ever widening scope and influence. In a world fighting desperately against the savage inroads of a philosophy of force, its power is great, its obligation sacred to protect the integrity of the written word. Husbanding and dispensing here at home the fruits of man's culture and the written record of man's past, it finds itself at the same time called upon to offer sanctuary to the driven exiled scholars of other lands. These are obligations it never knew in the past. And who could foresee such incredible necessities?

An indispensable instrument on the American continent for the promotion of learning and increase of knowledge—as the American Council of Learned Societies once designated it—it continues to be. As such, the story of its origins, its struggles for survival, its expanding mission and achievements, presents, surely, a definite and important aspect of our national development.

To appreciate the miracle of the growth of the Library of Congress one has only to compare those first few portable cases "with handles to them for purposes of easy removal" with almost twelve million products of man's mind and talents ranged on 414 miles of steel shelving; or tentative occupancy of a borrowed room with one of the most magnificent library structures in the world, overflowing into a white marble annex across the landscaped square. The relative enrichment of our spiritual heritage may be measured by the Library's expanding fields of usefulness, its continuous rededication to satisfying the intellectual needs of this nation, or by the mounting number of people—eager, curious, inquiring people—who fill out more and more slips, ask more and more questions, turn more and more pages under its friendly dome.

It had its beginnings outside of Washington. And it started life borrowing those reading privileges which a very young nation could not yet afford exclusively to provide. Only the unimaginative or the ill-intentioned would, in the light of history, attempt to fix the limits of its future.

I

THE FIRST CONGRESS
AND ITS FIRST LIBRARY

*I*n the days when New York was
the Capital of the Confederacy and George Washington rode up
from Number One Cherry Street in his coach-and-six to deliver
in person his messages to Congress, the City Hall, which then
stood along Stuyvesant Wall, housed the first library to be used
by members of the Senate and the House of Representatives for
official purposes.

Not that the City Library, as it was known, was in any sense
the private library of the legislators. Nor was it a national library.
Its collections were owned by the New York Society Library and
had been offered as the only reference sources then available to
Congress, which was meeting under the same roof.

That roof had sheltered a curious company in its time, for the
building had housed the city's early fire engines, held imprisoned
its debtors and other offenders against the law, offered harbor to
the Court and Common Council. Until 1764 the cage, the stocks,
the pillory and whipping-post, moved up in 1703 from beside the
Stadt Huys at the water's edge, stood outside its doors.

It was the same City Hall that, for nearly a century, had made
Wall Street the center of municipal and provincial affairs, although the Marstons, the McKevers, the Van Hornes, the Den-
nings, the Buchanans and the Cuylers, by their wealth and position, had likewise invested the area with peculiar attractions. After

the transfer to the Common of the blocks for public punishment, the street's claim as the fashionable residence thoroughfare of New York was definitely established.

Historically, too, the City Hall and its environs had accumulated a tradition prior even to the meeting of Congress under its roof. Within its walls Andrew Hamilton had sounded the defiance of royal authority; thirty years later the Stamp Act Congress had convened there; and one December day in 1773 the City's chief citizens had gathered there hotly to discuss rebellion against a stubborn king's duty on tea. Sons of Liberty, after the news of Concord and Lexington, confiscated arms and ammunition stored in one of its chambers. From the front steps of the building on July 18, 1776, while the fleet of the enemy lay at anchor, the Declaration of Independence was read by the Provincial Congress, eight days after Washington had ordered it read to each brigade of the Continental Army. In the days when the City lay under the heavy hand of the enemy, invading armies looted the building, and the houses lining Wall Street served as quarters for British and Hessian officers.

After New York became the Capital of the Confederacy, in December, 1784, the City Hall, enlarged and embellished for the accommodation of the new Congress, became Federal Hall. The City Library was established in the reconstructed building.

This first library to be used by the United States Congress had its beginnings in 1700. The "Public Library" of New York, founded during the administration of the Earl of Bellamont, had by then acquired considerable importance, and in 1729, when the Reverend Doctor Millington, Rector of Newington, England, bequeathed his library to the Society for the Propagation of the Gospel in Foreign Parts, that Society, in turn, presented it to the "Public Library" of New York.

The combined collection, under the charge of the corporation of the City, suffered for some time for want of proper attention. In 1754 an effort was made toward more efficient management by the organization of an association of interested individuals. The various private collections of the gentlemen members of the association were incorporated with the Public Library, and the whole was placed under the care of trustees.

This institution came to be known as the "City Library" and its collections were regularly increased by purchases of books from 1754 to the outbreak of the Revolution. In 1772 the organization obtained a charter and adopted the name "The New York Society Library."

The war almost marked the end of the library, for events not only prevented meetings of the trustees for many years, but threatened destruction of the stock itself. The proprietors reassembled, however, in December, 1788; an election for trustees took place, and the Society resumed operations. The following year the Legislature of the State of New York confirmd the charter.

The library was deposited in the City Hall and during this period served, unofficially, as the first Library of Congress. Later, as quarters became cramped, it was removed to one of the most conspicuous buildings of the day, erected expressly for its use on Nassau Street, opposite the Middle Dutch Church. It was not again moved until expansion of the city's commerce forced it in 1836 to a building at the corner of Broadway and Leonard Street.

During the days of the Revolution the library contained several thousand volumes, many of which were dispersed by events of the times. When the first Congress was making use of the collections, in 1789, there were probably about five thousand volumes at the disposal of Members. This is the number listed in the first catalogue of the library to be printed after the Revolution in 1793. These early Congresses, made up as they were of the ablest men in the country, must have put the five thousand volumes to good and frequent use.

It was the Library Company of Philadelphia which solved the problem of reference sources for the national legislators when Congress was removed from New York to Philadelphia. At a meeting on January 18, 1791, the directors of the Philadelphia Company, desirous of showing some mark of attention to the newly arrived Congress and to the President of the United States, passed a resolution that "the President and Members of the Senate and of the House of Representatives of the United States shall have the free use of the books in the library in as full and ample manner as if they were members of the company."

This generous offer was acknowledged by Tobias Lear, Secretary to President Washington. Lear wrote to William Rawle, Secretary to the Directors, on Thursday, December 20, 1791:

> SIR:
>
> In obedience to the command of the President of the United States, I have the honor to communicate to you, to be presented to the Directors of the Library Company of Philadelphia, his best thanks for the various polite manner in which they have offered him the use of the books in the library, and he begs they will be assured that this mark of attention has made a proper impression on him.
>
> I have the honor to be, very respectfully, Sir,
>
> Your most obedient servant,
> TOBIAS LEAR,
> *Secretary to the President*
> *of the United States.*

This second library of Congress must have proved a rich source of information to the legislators, for many of its volumes had been selected by no less an authority than Benjamin Franklin. Moreover, the collections were enriched in 1792 by transfer of the Loganian Library, consisting of thirty-five hundred carefully chosen volumes.

26

The Library Company of Philadelphia, established in 1731, owned the oldest library in America. Benjamin Franklin once called it "the mother of all the North American subscription libraries." It had had its origin in the famous "Junto" Club, the first literary association in the province, formed in the fall of 1728 by Benjamin Franklin and others, whose trades and occupations ranged from that of "a copyer of deeds for scriveners" to those of mathematician, surveyor-general, shoemaker, pressman, printer and bookbinder, compositor, merchant's clerk, and gentleman of fortune.

These friends met originally at a tavern, but later at the home of Robert Grace—the "gentleman of fortune." By easy stages the club developed into the Philadelphia Library. Benjamin Franklin gave the story of its origin in his *Chronicle of Events* in 1730:

About this time, our club meeting, not at a tavern, but in a little room of Mr. Grace's, set apart for that purpose, a proposition was made by me that, since our books were often referred to in our disquisitions upon the queries, it might be convenient to us to have them all together where we met, that upon occasion they might be consulted; and by thus clubbing our books in a common library we should, while we liked to keep them together, have each of us the advantage of using the books of all the other members, which would be nearly as beneficial as if each owned the whole. It was liked, and agreed to, and we filled one end of the room with such books as we could best spare. The number was not so great as we expected, and though they had been of great use, yet some inconveniences occurring for want of due care of them, the collection, after about a year, was separated, and each took his books home again.

And now I set on foot my first project of a public nature, that of a subscription library. I drew up the proposals, got them put into form by our great scrivener, Brockden, and by the help of my friends in the Junto procured fifty subscribers of forty shillings each to begin with, and ten shillings a year, for fifty years, the term our company was to continue. We afterwards obtained a charter, the company being increased to one hundred. This was the mother of all the North American subscription libraries, now so numerous.

The instrument of association was dated July 1, 1731, and the price of a share in the Company was fixed at forty shillings. By March of the following year there were more than twenty-five subscribers. It was immediately resolved to send to England for some new books.

On the advice of James Logan—"a gentleman of universal learning and the best judge of books in these parts"—forty-five pounds sterling was sent to London. There one Peter Collinson purchased the books ordered, sending over as his own gift a copy of Peter Miller's *Gardener's Dictionary* and of Sir Isaac Newton's *Philosophy*.

The first importation of books was received in October, 1732, and removed to the Grace home in Jones's Alley, where the Society was continuing to meet. Here the first Librarian, Lewis Timottiée, attended on Wednesdays from two until three o'clock in the afternoon, and on Saturdays from ten to four. He was authorized, under the Society's rules, to permit "any civil gentleman to peruse the books of the library in the library room, but not to lend to, or suffer to be taken out of the library by, any person who is not a subscribing member, any of the said books, Mr. James Logan only excepted."

Contributions to the enterprise took various forms, including real estate and pounds sterling. The library grew; its collections increased; and in 1740 Benjamin Franklin printed the first catalogue.

Franklin took a continued interest in the library. Writing from London on July 7, 1769, he mentioned having forborne purchase of any books but Robinson's *History*, lest he should purchase duplicates, having seen "for some time since that other libraries were about to be united" with that of the Philadelphia Company.

It was a reference collection largely determined by Franklin's tastes that the Congress of the United States later consulted. And, although he sought always the opinions of the directors, the Philadelphian had definite ideas of his own as to what a good library should contain. On one occasion he wrote:

> I think we should have in some of our public libraries all the transactions of every Philosophical Society in Europe, viz., The Memoirs of the Academy of Sciences at Paris; those of Petersburg; of Haerlem, in Holland, of Bononia [Bologna] in Italy, etc., with the continuations as they come out yearly, and also the French *Encyclopædia*. They would be extremely useful to us on many accounts, and are rather too heavy for private collections. But they are in different languages, and [as] the majority of our members are only acquainted with English, I have not ventured to buy them without orders, and in general I wish to have expressed directions, and that as little as possible may be left to my judgment in laying out the Company's money.

The library of the Society was reported to contain on April 30, 1789, about 7,700 volumes. Additions were made subsequently by Franklin from his own library, from increased purchases from abroad and from acquisition in 1792 of the Logan collection, so that many volumes were available for the use of Congress for reference and research. The Loganian Library contained "authors all in Greek, with mostly their versions; all the Roman classics without exception; all the Greek mathematicians. —Besides there are many of the most valuable Latin authors and a great number of modern mathematicians." These were the combined resources of the second unofficial library of Congress.

It became more and more apparent, however, as the nation grew and its problems increased, that Congress needed a reference library of its own. It was unthinkable that legislators in a democratic assembly should not have ready access to books, pamphlets and journals of the day, if they were to keep properly informed of popular opinion, of conditions of progress, of trends and events. No longer content to depend solely upon the generosity of other libraries for their sources of information, Senators and Representatives began tentatively to discuss possibilities for establishing a library for Congress.

II

THE STATESMAN'S WORKSHOP

*F*oremost among the advocates of such a project was Elbridge Gerry, Representative from Massachusetts. As early as the 6th of August, in 1789, he had asked that a committee be appointed to report a catalogue of books necessary for the use of Congress, "with an estimate of the expense, and the best mode of procuring them."

It is doubtful if any other Member of Congress at that time were better fitted than Gerry himself to serve on such a committee, or to judge better of the needs of Congress along this line. His long life of public service, his intimate contact with the stirring events of the day, and his naturally scholarly inclinations had developed a keen appreciation for the products of other men's thinking, and he had learned to set a proper value on contemporary records. Gerry's role in early American history had been an important one. "In measures which dissolved the power of the British Crown over the Colony of Massachusetts; in the establishment of a new government by the people; in the declaration of independence by the United States; in the direction of the civil, military, foreign and domestic concerns of the continent during the War of the Revolution; in arrangements for the cessation of hostilities and in the administration of affairs after the treaty of peace—he was conspicuously concerned," his biographer said of him.

Certainly the part Gerry had played and was destined to play

31

in our history was an active one. He had been a member of the convention which formed the new Constitution for the Confederacy. During the entire period of organization of the Federal Government he served in the House of Representatives. He later took part in those negotiations which terminated in our treaties with France. In the tumultuous days which preceded the second war with England he was at the head of the government of Massachusetts. Throughout most of the war period he presided over the Senate of the United States—probably the only government official of that time who had been a member of the "immortal Congress of 1776." When he died in 1814 he was Vice-President of the United States.

Gerry was made a member of the committee suggested in his own motion. With him were Burke of South Carolina and White of Virginia. On the 23rd of June he submitted their report.

He stated that they had "confined themselves in great measure to books necessary for the use of the legislative and executive departments, and not to be found in private or in circulating libraries." He spoke feelingly of the necessity to which Members of Congress and other government officials had been put at every session "to transport to the seat of government a considerable part of their libraries, it seldom happening that they can otherwise command such books on the indulgence of their friends." The alternative, said Gerry, was for Members to be "deprived of the use of such books when necessary." He expressed the opinion that "a sum not exceeding one thousand dollars" should be appropriated and that "the sum of five hundred dollars should be hereafter annually appropriated to the purchase of books for a public library, and be applied to the purpose by the Vice-President, Chief Justice and the Secretary of State of the United States without confining them to the catalogues reported, until, in the opinion of Congress the books provided shall be adequate to the purpose."

The books suggested by this early committee as the nucleus for a library of Congress related to laws of the states, laws on trade and navigation of European nations with whom the United States might have treaties; the laws of Ireland, Scotland and Canada; the British Statutes at Large, books on the militia system of Switzerland and on the Russian and Frederician Codes; books on the laws of nature and nations, on the privileges and duties of diplomatic bodies; a collection of treaties and alliances from the earliest periods; and a collection of parliamentary books and volumes on the civil and common law.

Nothing came of this report; unless one count its influence upon a body thus made aware of specific needs. At any rate it was not until the seat of government was removed to its new site along the Potomac that any further attempt was made to establish a library of Congress.

During its sojourns in New York and in Philadelphia, Congress had managed in an unplanned way and without bibliographical direction to accumulate certain books of its own. The catalogue of 1802 lists 45 folio volumes, 68 quartos and 130 octavos, or 243 volumes which were acquired before and immediately after removal to Washington.

The first mutual library of Senate and House contained among other books, 21 volumes of the statutes at large; 18 volumes of the journals of the House of Commons; the *Bibliotheca Americana*; Hatsell's *Precedents*; Linders, Heywood, and Fraser *On Elections*; Hogan's *State Trials* and 14 other volumes of state trials; volumes on English law, bankruptcy laws, treaties and laws of nations; geographies and gazetteers; 36 volumes of an encyclopedia; dictionaries; volumes on world voyages; historical works and works on economics; such periodicals as *The New Annual Register*, *The American Museum*, and *The Monthly Review*, as well as Thomas Paine's *Miscellanies* and—concession to the austerity of the other titles—a volume of the poems of Robert Burns.

The Act of April 24, 1800, provided for removal of the Capital to Washington; the establishment of the Library of Congress was accomplished in a section added to this Act on motion of Samuel Livermore, a Senator from New Hampshire and a graduate of Princeton. This section authorized an appropriation of five thousand dollars for the purchase "of such books as may be necessary for the use of Congress" and for "fitting up a suitable apartment for containing them therein." These books were to be purchased by the Secretary of the Senate and the Clerk of the House of Representatives "pursuant to such directions as shall be given and such catalogue as shall be furnished by a Joint Committee of both Houses of Congress to be appointed for that purpose." The following day the House agreed to appoint a joint committee to make out a catalogue of necessary books and to adopt rules and regulations in connection with their use. The House appointed a committee consisting of Robert Waln of Pennsylvania, and Thomas Evans and Leven Powell of Virginia. On April 28th the Senate appointed Samuel Dexter of Massachusetts, William Bingham of Pennsylvania, and William Cary Nicholas of Virginia. Samuel Dexter was chairman of this joint committee.

Dexter, an attorney of note, a graduate of Harvard and a man accustomed since childhood to the advantages and environment of good books, was the member most active in carrying out the provisions of the Act of 1800. His was the responsibility of selecting those books which were to form the nucleus of the new library. He charged Samuel Otis, then Secretary of the United States Senate, with placing the order for them.

A list was forwarded to London to the firm of Cadell and Davies. These booksellers, who played so important a part in supplying the initial stock of books for the Library of Congress, were among the foremost booksellers of the day.

Directly and indirectly this distinguished firm had inherited a long tradition. In 1739, the first Thomas Cadell opened his bookshop and publishing house in Wine Street, Bristol, where he continued in business until 1775. The "elder" Cadell, actually his son, born in 1742 and sent to London as an apprentice to Andrew Millar in 1758, became the famous Millar's partner in 1765, and two years later, on Millar's retirement, took his place. Both names are picturesquely associated with such colorful London literary figures as Johnson, Blackstone, Gibbon, Thomson, Fielding and Hume. Cadell and Davies could reasonably feel indeed that they belonged, as one chronicler put it, "to at least a third generation of the highest aristocracy of the Trade."

A contemporary bookseller summed up Cadell and Davies' career thus:

Messrs. Cadell and Davies commenced business under the most favorable auspices, and a capital and stock unrivaled in this, or perhaps any other country. They continued to carry on trade for many years with high talent and respectability. In addition to all the valuable copyrights they possessed they became almost too adventurous and liberal in expensive and heavy undertakings, several of which, singly, almost required a fortune to bring them forward. Among others were the *Historic Gallery of Pictures,* the *Contemporary Portraits,* Murphy's *Arabian Antiquities of Spain,* and numberless others. The last-mentioned work employed a capital of ten thousand pounds. It was published at forty guineas per copy.

I believe that Mr. Cadell, junior, was left an independent fortune, but it was perhaps the wish of his father, as well as his own, that he should continue his praiseworthy pursuits in the cause of literature, although nothing could well excel in the shape of literary undertakings what was already established. However, being possessed of a stock of almost incalculable value, it would require years to dispose of it to advantage; and being connected with persons of the most distinguished talent and virtue in these realms, in the church, the state, in law and physic, as well as several of the nobility and gentry engaged in literature, and was laudable to continue in such a concern.

Mr. Davies, who was the active and efficient person in the establishment for upwards of thirty years, was considered by some of his brethren in trade as haughty and consequential. This arose, perhaps, from his fine dignified form, and manly and noble appearance. I never witnessed in him any but the most liberal conduct as a friend and a straightforward man of business, in which he was most assiduous and attentive, always ready to give his valuable advice, and acting with the utmost fairness and liberality in the position in which his good conduct had placed him. His connection with authors, artists, and persons of splendid acquirements, in addition to his superior abilities, might have given him that appearance of conscious superiority over some low and groveling characters with whom he had to deal.

. . . Mr. Davies became too adventurous and liberal in his literary purchases, or rather in embarking in such heavy undertakings as the times would hardly sanction, and which his partner, who survived him many years, prudently relinquished, but continued to publish in conjunction with his Edinburgh friends on a more limited scale.

The firm of Cadell and Davies flourished in a period which is often regarded as dull in the history of publishing and bookselling. Yet, marking the close of the pre-industrial age and coming just prior to such rapidly displaced improvements as Macadam's roadbuilding, rapid steam printing and gas lighting, it actually offers us one of the most picturesque eras of the trade, when clerks still labored by candlelight, receiving supplies of books by the frequently delayed coastal sailing sloops and letters by mailcoach or wagon. The upper and upper-middle classes provided almost exclusively the market for Cadell and Davies'

wares, and these wares were still printed on slow, hand-manipu-
lated presses.

This, then, was the firm to whom was entrusted shipment of
the first books purchased for the Library of Congress under the
five-thousand-dollar appropriation provided for in Samuel Livermore's addition to the Act of 1800. Cadell and Davies' invoice,
with its covering letter, was ordered to be printed; the two documents represent the first catalogue of what is now one of the
world's greatest collections. Today, in the Library of Congress,
are preserved nine minor documents connected with this purchase.

It was on December 11, 1800, that Cadell and Davies forwarded to "W. Bingham, Esq., and Robert Waln, Esq.," of the
United States Congress the following letter:

London, Dec. 11, 1800

GENTLEMEN:

We were favored with your joint letter of June 20, inclosing a list
of books for the intended library at Washington, and we instantly set
about executing the order in the best manner we were able.

Inclosed we transmit you the invoice and bill of lading, and we
earnestly hope the books will arrive perfectly safe, great care having
been taken in packing them. We judged it best to send trunks, rather
than boxes, which after their arrival would have been little or no value.

Several of the books sent were only to be procured second-handed
and some of them, from their extreme scarcity, at very advanced prices.

We have in all cases sent the best copies we could obtain, and charged
at the lowest prices possible. We annex a list of a few articles that we
have not been able to procure, but, as we firmly trust that the execution
of the present order will meet your approbation, and that, in that case,
we may and hope to be favored with your favored commands, we shall
continue to search for these articles and send them out with the next
parcel.

Messrs. Baring & Company paid us the amount of the bill the instant
it was presented to them, and we therefore made the usual deduction of
five percent.

We shall esteem ourselves much favored by an account of the arrival of the books, and we beg you to accept our best thanks for your obliging preference of us on this occasion.

We are with sincere respect, gentlemen,

Your very obedient servants,

CADELL & DAVIES

Herodotus, Cæsar, Plutarch, Demosthenes, Tacitus, Polybius, Thucydides, Arrian, Dionysius, and Xenophon were represented in this early shipment. There were histories of Mexico, of British plantations of America, of the Five Nations of Virginia, Massachusetts and New England, of the Roman Republic, of the Roman Empire, of Greece, of France, of China, of the American War, of ancient and modern Europe, of Scotland. There were chronologies and memoirs, De Witt's *Maxims* and Father Paul's *Council of Trent*. There were volumes of voyages and discoveries, journals and travels; maps, atlases and gazetteers; laws, trials and treaties.

Debates, precedents, and parliamentary law, histories of commerce; books of rates and trade and customs; constitutions and governments, were included; the lives of famous men, volumes on philosophy, on moral sentiments and the dignity of human nature.

Altogether 740 volumes were sent, costing £475, 4s., with a discount of £23, 15s. To this were added extra charges for "11 hair trunks, mats and cords"; "a case for the maps"; "paid export duty two percent, customhouse fees and shipping expenses"; and "paid freight."

Listed as "Articles not yet obtained" were Belknap's *History of New Hampshire;* Cousin's *Byzantine Historians;* Bentivolio's *Annals; History of Algiers;* Martin on the *Law of Nations;* Brinkershock "on ditto"; *Grotie Mare Clausum; Dictionnaire Diplomatique;* Boo on the rates of France; Gianoni's *History of*

Naples; De Lisle's maps; *Collection of Maps of America*—this last item with the note "there is no collection but what is included in the American Atlas."

Almost five months later, on May 2, 1801, Samuel Otis, then Secretary of the United States Senate, wrote to President Jefferson:

> I do myself the honor to inclose you a copy of the invoice of books for the public library. The package being perfectly dry, I shall omit opening them until further orders. Whenever they are opened some person should be made answerable for them or in my opinion the volumes will be immediately dispersed and lost. . . .

Evidently there were many individuals eager to "be made answerable" for these and other books intended for the use of Congress. What may be construed as the first contest for the Librarianship of Congress was inaugurated then and there. From Philadelphia, William Duane, editor of *Aurora*, wrote to Madison, Secretary of State, on the 10th of May, that he should be glad to undertake the provision of such books as might be required, drawing attention to the fact that he had resided in England for five years and was thus acquainted "not only with the first booksellers but numbers of the first literary characters in that country" and could "undertake the importation of the books for the public library under advantages that few others possess."

Also from Philadelphia, on December 8, 1801, John McDonald "recently a broker and keeper of a circulating library at 14 South Fourth Street" petitioned the House of Representatives that he might be employed "to superintend the arrangement and safekeeping of the books intended for the Library of the two Houses of Congress; and that he might receive such compensation for his services, in that capacity, as to the wisdom of Congress should seem best." This petition was referred to the Joint

Committee on the Library of Congress. Before it could be acted upon, however, the Library had to be organized.

On December 7, 1801, shortly after President Jefferson—an ardent supporter of the Library—had called upon Samuel Otis to state that $2,200 of the appropriated sum of $5,000 had been expended, the Senate passed a resolution. They asked that a committee be appointed to join with a similar committee in the House for the purpose of taking into consideration Otis' statement respecting the books and maps and that they report on the future arrangements of the new purchases. In the Senate Tracy and Nicholas were appointed; in the House Bayard and Randolph.

Senator Nicholas of Virginia was chairman of this new committee. Of the other members, Senator Uriah Tracy, a graduate of Yale, was from Connecticut; Representative James Bayard, a graduate of Princeton, from Delaware; Representative Joseph Nicholson from Maryland, and Representative John Randolph from Virginia. The following week, on December 18th, the committee reported through Senator Tracy, and three days later through Representative Randolph.

Randolph, one of the earliest friends and supporters of the Library, was actually the author of the report, one of the most notable documents relating to the early history of the Library, and one upon which the Act of January 26, 1802, was largely based. This scholarly gentleman from Roanoke, who had once observed that "a good library is a statesman's workshop," possessed an extensive library of his own, although, according to Nathan Sargent, that library, at his express desire, did not contain a single American book, "not even an American Bible."

That Randolph knew books as only a constant and omnivorous reader and devoted student can know them, and that he was a familiar figure in the library established later in the Capitol, is illustrated by a reminiscence of Josiah Quincy in 1882.

Quincy described Randolph during one of his visits as "the remarkable man whom of all others I most desired to see." Admitted to the Virginia Representative's bedchamber, he saw him "sitting in flannel dressing-gown and slippers, looking very thin, but with a strange fire in his swarthy face. He seemed more like a spiritual presence than a man adequately clothed in flesh and blood. His voice was high but very agreeable, having nothing of the shrillness which I heard at the great race, and afterwards in debate."

On the occasion of another visit Quincy relates that Randolph declared it a "great blunder for a speaker to allude to books which are not familiar to his audience," stating, as an example, that while in the British Parliament, where members are all graduates of Oxford or Cambridge, one might quote Horace or Juvenal, it would be folly to quote the classics to an average American audience.

"I know of only three books," said Randolph, "with which all decently educated Americans are familiar. These are the Bible, Shakespeare, and Milton." He then quoted a passage from Burke, in which he declared the author had used thought or language from these three books in its construction.

When Quincy remarked that he did not remember this passage and asked where he could find it, Randolph said, "go to the Congressional Library, look in the third alcove on the right-hand side, third shelf from the floor, fifth volume on the shelf, Page 336, about halfway down." Making a memorandum of the directions, Quincy did as he was bid, "and found the passage exactly where Randolph had placed it."

This able man drew up the report which proved of such consequence. In that report the Committee resolved that "the books and maps purchased by direction of the Act of Congress passed the 24th day of April, 1800, be placed in the Capitol in the room

41

which was occupied by the House of Representatives during the last session of the 6th Congress, and that the books shall be numbered, labeled, and set up in portable cases with handles to them for the purpose of easy removal, with wire netting, doors and locks. And that the books or libraries which have heretofore been kept separately by each House shall be removed and set up with those lately purchased, and be numbered and labeled with them, making one library of the whole."

The resolutions also authorized the Secretary of the Senate and the Clerk of the House of Representatives "to take charge of the room, books, and maps aforesaid" and to make suitable arrangements for the "library and maps; to procure proper furniture for the room; to procure the cases, number and label the books, and set them up in their places; to procure for their own use and the uses of both Houses of Congress printed catalogues of all books with the labeled number of it and of the maps; to place on each book some proper mark or marks to designate it as belonging to the Congressional Library; to procure printed blank receipts for members to sign them when they take books from the room; and to arrange and hang up the maps; all to be done under the inspection and direction of the President of the Senate and Speaker of the House of Representatives for the time being."

But the responsibility of the Secretary of the Senate and of the Clerk of the House of Representatives did not cease here. They were also in charge of "the safekeeping of the room, furniture, books and maps aforesaid," and were not to permit anyone except members of the House and Senate to take any map out of the room; nor were they to permit any member to remove a book without signing a detailed receipt.

The early form for withdrawal of books from the Library of Congress, as drawn up by Randolph, was as follows:

Received this —— day —— of the keepers of the Congressional Library (here the book and its number is to be described), which I promise to return within —— days from this date or forfeit the sum of —— dollars to be paid to said keepers or either of them or to their successors or either of them. Witness my hand.

The resolution stated further that not more than two or three books could be taken out of the library by any member at one time, and listed the days respectively within which a folio volume, a quarto volume, an octavo volume, and a duodecimo should be returned. Upon their return the receipt was to be canceled, "but in the case of forfeiture the keepers were immediately to collect the penalty."

The keepers or those designated by them were to attend in the library from eleven until three o'clock each day except Sundays while Congress was in session. They were to receive for these services a sum to be determined later, paid out of the annual contingent fund of both houses. Furthermore, they were to "exhibit a statement to each House" at the commencement of every session of Congress, "giving in detail the condition of the room, the furniture, books, and maps; information of the sum of forfeitures, if any, which they had collected, and of the necessary expenses for fuel, etc., in said room." Their accounts were then to be liquidated and approved by Congress and the balance to be paid out of the contingent fund of both Houses. Copies of the resolutions affecting Members were to be pasted up in some conspicuous place in the library room.

No detail was overlooked by Randolph. The Secretary of the Senate was next directed "to make sale of the trunks in which the books lately purchased were imported," exhibiting to Congress an account of the actual proceeds, "including a statement of the actual expenditures incurred under the Act of the 24th of April, 1800, as well by the purchase of books and maps and in-

843

4633674

8666242

426

FORTRESS OF FREEDOM

cidental expenses as for the expense of fitting up the room, procuring furniture, cases, etc." The residue of the $5,000 appropriated by the Act of 1800 was to be "laid out by the Secretary of the Senate and the Clerk of the House of Representatives for books and maps, or books alone, under the direction of the joint committee to be appointed for that purpose." It was further resolved that Congress should appropriate each year a sum to be designated, for increasing the Library's supply of books and maps.

At this period of the Library's development, there was persistent dissension in House and Senate as to its possible future policy. There was a desire upon the part of the Senate to establish a library for the use of Congress alone; the House wished to extend its use to other departments of the government. The Senate wanted liberal annual appropriations for the support of their new library; the House wished to keep expenditures for books down to a minimum. Moreover, the House disagreed with the Senate in the latter's desire to place the library under executive control.

Debate on these issues waxed heatedly. Brought up for consideration in the Senate on the 21st of December, the bill was adopted with amendments providing for an annual appropriation and for the appointment of a librarian by the President of the United States. Two days later, after debate in the Committee of the Whole in the House, it was amended to extend loan privileges to the Attorney General, the Judges of the Supreme Court while Court was in session, and to foreign ministers.

Suggestions for annual appropriations ranged from $1,000 to $10,000. Finally it was resolved to appropriate $1,000 for only one year. In the House Bayard moved that a librarian appointed by the President be substituted for the Congressionally appointed Secretary of the Senate and Clerk of the House serving in this capacity. The motion was lost and the amended resolutions were

44

recommitted to a select committee consisting of Randolph, Bayard, Eustis, Dana and Elmer.

So powerful was opposition during this period that the aid of President Jefferson was finally invoked to bring the dissenting factions together. John Randolph drew up the first bill, along the lines of his previous report. It placed the library under a joint committee of Congress but provided that the Librarian should be appointed solely by the President of the United States; it also fixed the salary of the Librarian at "a sum not to exceed $2 per diem for every day of the necessary attendance."

The Act was passed on January 26, 1802.

In 1800, when only the north wing of the Capitol was finished, the east side of the structure had been occupied by the Senate, the west by the House. The early books brought from Philadelphia and those bought from Cadell and Davies had been stored temporarily in the office of the Clerk of the Senate—a room 22 by 34 feet and 21 feet high, just south of the Senate Chamber. Here they remained until March 3, 1801.

During that year the House of Representatives moved into a temporary structure erected on the south, leaving their previous quarters—a chamber 86 by 35 feet and 36 feet high—unoccupied and free for the use of the Library. By the Act of January 26, 1802, this chamber was made ready for the accumulated books and maps now owned by Congress.

Three days after passage of this Act, which gave the Library of Congress a home, President Jefferson's appointment of his friend, John Beckley from Virginia, the Clerk of the House of Representatives, gave it its first official Librarian.

At the time Beckley was appointed first Librarian of Congress, Washington was a scattered community of a few thousand inhabitants whose homes were built singly, in widely separated

areas, or in occasional groups chiefly near public buildings, over
an expanse stretching from Georgetown to the Navy Yard. The
only pavement was in front of detached houses. Benjamin Tayloe, son of Colonel John Tayloe, said in 1801 that when Members of Congress, living on Capitol Hill, wished to attend President Adams' levee, they found it necessary to send to Baltimore
for hackney coaches to convey them to the President's house.
Moreover, to avoid the swamps of Pennsylvania Avenue they
were forced to travel along F Street and the high grounds adjoining. During Monroe's administration it was by no means unusual to see carriages mired in the mud of Pennsylvania Avenue, even then almost impassable. The City had not less than
10,000 inhabitants at that time. Most of the fine residences of
the day had been built on or near Capitol Hill, although a scattered residential community had also grown up in the vicinity
of the President's mansion. The business portion of the city soon
began to be established along the line which connected the community in the vicinity of the White House with that near the
Capitol. Thus, Pennsylvania Avenue, selected by L'Enfant to
be the grand passageway between the legislative and executive
departments, grew instead into the Capital's first business center.

Although there was more than one newspaper in Washington
at the time that Beckley became Librarian, the one destined to
be most influential in the history of the Library of Congress was
the *National Intelligencer.*

The *Washington Gazette,* first published on June 15, 1796,
by Benjamin More, a bookseller, had recently expired. The *Gazette* had been a semi-weekly paper, issued on Wednesdays and
Saturdays at four dollars a year, and its proprietor seems to have
had a struggle to keep it before the public. It apparently did not
appear after March 24, 1798.

The *Washington Daily Gazette,* however, started life in October, 1800, and the *Washington Federalist,* published for several years in the early part of the century, was likewise a contemporary of the *Intelligencer.* There were several minor publications, none of which proved long-lived or expressed any particular interest in the affairs of the Library. The *Intelligencer,* on the other hand, was perennially concerned with its changing needs and problems, and was one of the first newspapers to recognize its potentialities as a great national center for research and study.

At about the time that the Federal Government was removed from Philadelphia to Washington, the first issue of the *National Intelligencer* appeared in Washington. It came out on October 31, 1800, and was published in a row of buildings on New Jersey Avenue. Samuel Harrison Smith, son of the distinguished Revolutionary patriot, Jonathan Bayard Smith, was editor and publisher. As owner of a printing office on Chestnut Street in Philadelphia, Smith had published in August and September of 1796, morning and evening issues of a newspaper known as the *New World.* The experiment of two daily issues seems not to have been successful, for Smith changed his paper to a daily, which appeared for the first time on October 24, 1796. A few months later, convinced that there was no place in Philadelphia for a fifth daily paper, Smith gave up the enterprise altogether. Mr. Jefferson's new Republican party, then springing into consequence, was, however, feeling the need for a weekly paper in which to express its flowering views, and Smith was persuaded to publish a party organ.

He bought Joseph Gales's *Independent Gazetteer,* changed its name to *Universal Gazette* and issued it as a weekly, beginning November 16, 1797. When the Capital was removed to Washington, Mr. Smith went along and there began publication of the *National Intelligencer* as a tri-weekly. From the first the paper received the support of Mr. Jefferson's party. It sustained his administration and was sustained by it. It served and fared equally fortuitously in the subsequent interests of Mr. Madison. In 1810, Smith retired to live the life of a country gentleman, and sold the *Intelligencer* to Joseph Gales, who had been connected with it for three years. From 1800 to 1870, when it ceased to exist, the *Intelligencer* played an active and important part in the life of the Capital and on more than one occasion lifted its voice in the interests of the Library of Congress, urging, as early as 1815, a separate building for the expanding collections, and consistently upholding the ideal of national service. Despite the criticism leveled against its "interminable diatribes," the description of its editor as "Silky Milky Smith" and of itself as the "National Smoothing Plane," the *National Intelligencer* played a real part in its time in arousing public interest in the Library that was then quietly burgeoning along the banks of the Tiber. Moreover, it was the intrepid Mr. Smith who put up the first valiant struggle for the right to publish the debates in Congress as they occurred. It was the *Intelligencer*, too, that figured more or less prominently at a little later date in the bitter attempts to reinstate the gifted but ill-starred Librarian, George Watterston. Strongly in favor of what today might be called civil-service reform, it refused to tolerate Jackson's system of appointing friends and supporters to political office, and developed into a strong Whig organ.

Because of the necessity for prompt publication of the war news, the *Intelligencer* became the *Daily National Intelligencer* on the first of January, 1813. In 1814 the British, entering Washington, tore up most of the newspaper's office, and as a consequence the paper did not appear from August 24th to October 1st. On the first of October, however, it was back, in reduced form, sturdily denouncing the ones responsible for its suspension and promising to expand to its previous size as soon as it could get its bearings.

On June 5, 1841, the *Intelligencer* became a weekly again. After the death of President Harrison it found itself very reluctant to part company with President Tyler but finally did so, on the ground that Tyler had abandoned those principles upon which he had been elected. In 1844 it fought vigorously the annexation of Texas. Gales & Seaton continued publication until the death of Gales, at the age of seventy-five, in 1860. Four years later Seaton retired from proprietorship and editorial management of the paper. In the hands of its new proprietors the *Intelligencer*, enlarged to a seven-column sheet and later consolidated with the *Express*, did not fare so well. In November, 1869, Snow, Coyle & Company, who had taken it over from Seaton, sold out to Alexander Delmar, erstwhile Chief of the Bureau of Statistics of the Treasury Department. Despite Delmar's announcement that he would elevate it to the front rank of journalism, it did not long survive his managership. On January 10, 1870, he discontinued publication. Although it had been said of the *Intelligencer* that it was "Jeffersonian till Jackson's time, and then Whig till Lincoln's time, when it became rebel Democratic, and went into the lobby under Johnny Coyle," this was by no means a fair estimate of its policies. It was never, as a matter of fact, "rebel Democratic." Its motto always had been *The Union and the Constitution*, and when it seemed contradictorily to uphold the institution of slavery, it was probably more truly upholding the restoration of "the Union as it was," that is, with slavery still unimpaired. History, at any rate, owes it gratitude. Had it not been for the efforts of Gales and Seaton, very few of the debates of earlier Congresses would have been preserved. Gales reported in the Senate, Seaton in the House, and Gales's presence in the Senate saved for all time such great

speeches as those of Haynes and Webster in 1830. As a matter
of fact, posterity is as indebted to these men for preservation
of early Congressional debates as it is to James Madison for the
debates of the Constitutional Convention which framed the Constitution of the United States.

Against this earlier Washington setting Members of Congress
were functioning. Closely bound by the common interest of legislation, and more or less segregated by the difficulty of getting
freely about in the Capital's bogs and mires, the little band living and meeting on Capitol Hill probably depended almost entirely upon the collections under their own roof for the kind of
information which only an especially selected library could give
them. Beckley's job as their Librarian was far more important,
owing to lack of transportation, good roads and paving, than it
might have been had the legislators of that day had ready access to the libraries of friends or to those miscellaneous educational institutions located in almost inaccessible parts of the
sprawling city. They were forced to depend upon their own books
and such aid in their search for information as their own Presi-
dentially appointed Librarian might be equipped to supply.

There is no question that Beckley's long service as Clerk of
the House of Representatives might have proved of great value
to the hard-pressed legislators of that day, had that gentleman
given more liberally of his time and talents to the new post. As
it was, the duties attendant upon librarianship seem largely to
have been performed by the engrossing clerk in the office of the
Clerk of the House at the time, one Josias Wilson King. When
Mr. King rode up from his house on F Street next to Mrs. Reagan's Young Ladies Academy, to his work at the Capitol each
morning, it was to face duties even more multifarious than the
tambouring, embroidery, open work, marking, plain sewing, fili-
gree, painting, waxwork, French, music, dancing, reading and

50

writing required of Mrs. Reagan's enrollees next door. For, in addition to his duties as engrossing clerk, King was called upon to label, arrange, and take charge of the books in the Library of Congress and answer as many Congressional inquiries as he might, betimes.

This might not have been so irksome had King been compensated for his services. But he had, it appeared later, entered into a contract with Beckley which the Librarian was charged with not fulfilling. The arrangement, according to King, was that he was to undertake the duties in the Library of Congress on condition that the combined Clerk of the House and Librarian of Congress, John Beckley, share equally with him the compensation allowed the Librarian by the Act of 1802. That Beckley subsequently failed to comply with this agreement seems evident by a memorial from King presented in the House on February 18, 1806. The Committee of Accounts, to whom the memorial was referred, reported unfavorably upon it, and King was obliged to content himself with his $1,000 a year as engrossing clerk.

Nonetheless, the new Librarian had a good background for his post. He had served at various times as Clerk of the House of Delegates and of the Senate of Virginia. On the organization of the House of Representatives of the United States, he had been elected its first Clerk on April 1, 1789, and had served in this capacity to May 15, 1797, and from December 7, 1801, to October 26, 1807.

Beckley was born in Virginia, a descendant of a Devonshire family known variously as Beckley, Bickley or Bickleigh. John James was probably the son of Sir William Bickley, Baronet, who died in Louisa County, Virginia, on March 9, 1771.

During Beckley's administration and consequent upon the Act of January 26, 1802, a new Library Committee had been appointed. The Senate membership consisted of Baldwin, Clinton and Logan; Representatives Nicholson, Bayard and Randolph made up the membership from the House. Their primary duty was to make purchases of books suitable to the needs of a growing Congress, just as the Committee of 1800, under the direction of Samuel Dexter, had purchased the first books for the Library. And, just as Dexter had been the guiding influence in the earlier task, so was Abraham Baldwin, Senator from Georgia and chairman of the new Committee, an important factor in shaping the Library's subsequent collections. Baldwin was, as a matter of fact, a most excellent choice for this particular task. His brother-in-law, Joel Barlow, owned at this time one of the finest private libraries in America and was much interested in establishing a national university. Baldwin himself, a graduate of Yale and an instructor there, was considered one of the foremost classical and mathematical scholars of the age.

Baldwin was in frequent correspondence with Jefferson during this time, about a bibliographic program for the Library of Congress. On April 14, 1802, Jefferson wrote Baldwin that he had prepared a catalogue for the Library of Congress in conformity with Baldwin's ideas "that books of entertainment are not within the scope of it, and that books in other languages, when there are not translations of them, are not to be admitted freely." Jefferson stated that he had confined the catalogue to those branches of science which belonged to the deliberations of the members as statesmen, and in these had omitted "those classical books, ancient, and modern, which gentlemen generally have in their private libraries, but which cannot properly claim a place in a collection made merely for the purpose of reference."

In history, he confined his list "to the chronological works which give facts and dates with a minuteness not to be found in narratives composed for agreeable reading." And under the law of nature and nations he put down "everything I know of worth possessing because this is a branch of science often under the discussion of Congress, and the books written in it not to be found in private libraries." In law he set down only general treaties for the purpose of reference.

Jefferson's comments here are of interest and value. "The discussions under this head in Congress," he wrote, "are really so minute as to require and admit that reports and special treatises should be introduced. The parliamentary section I have imagined should be complete. It is only by having a law of proceedings and by every member having the means of understanding it for himself, and appealing to it, that he can be protected against caprice and despotism in the Chair."

So precise was Jefferson's knowledge of the book market that he was able to advise Baldwin, "in estimating the amount of an annual selection, folios may be slated as costing 1½ guineas, quartos a guinea, octavos 8 shillings, duodecimos 4 shillings, in England, and in France three-fourths of those prices, in neat but not splendid bindings."

The bibliographical program thus outlined by Jefferson undoubtedly formed the basis for Library of Congress purchases until 1806, for in January of 1806, the Treasurer of the United States, Albert Gallatin, referred to an unexpended balance for which George W. Ewing, Consul at London and English agent, was accountable, and which was to be applied "from time to time in the purchase of several scarce books, agreeable to a catalogue prepared, I believe, by the President of the United States."

Aware of the keen interest Jefferson took in the Library's collections, booksellers in all parts of the United States were accustomed to write to him enclosing their catalogues. On one such occasion, when he had received a catalogue from Dufief, a bookseller of Philadelphia who then owned Franklin's library, Jefferson checked some of the books he considered worthy of acquisition and sent the marked catalogue to Senator Baldwin with the comment that he was not "presuming on the answer of the committee" to Mr. Dufief's proposition that Congress acquire the whole or part of the proffered library. "My dealings with him," wrote Jefferson on February 4, 1803, "give me confidence that his prices would be moderate."

In 1802, a catalogue of new accessions was published; a supplement in 1803; and a new catalogue in 1804. The *National Intelligencer* commented upon the gratifying growth of the Library, publishing in its columns on February 13, 1804, this appreciation:

> This collection already embraces near 1,500 volumes of the most rare and valuable works in different languages. We observe with pleasure that authors and editors of books, maps and charts, begin to find that, by placing a copy of their works on the shelves of this institution they do more to diffuse a knowledge of them than is generally accomplished by catalogues and advertisements.

III

CLASSICS IN THE RAIN

*T*he first catalogue of the Library, issued from the press of William Duane, listed the titles of 212 folios, 164 quartos, 581 octavos, 7 duodecimos, and 9 maps; and these constituted the only library of reference in the national metropolis. This number had been slowly increased in size by annual purchases made with the small available portion of the contingent funds of the Houses of Congress until 1806.

It was Senator Samuel Latham Mitchill, an accomplished physician of New York, who, while chairman of the Joint Committee, made an urgent appeal for increased funds for the Library. Mitchill was held in great esteem for his literary and scientific accomplishments and was so prodigal of his learning that one wit said of him, "Tap the doctor at any time, he will flow." There seemed, indeed, no end to the questions on inventions, discoveries, sciences, projects, and literary subjects that were submitted to his critical opinion. He was one of the most distinguished men ever to serve on a Library of Congress committee.

Dr. Mitchill's political life had embraced a period of twenty-two years. He was elected to the Legislature of New York in 1790, and re-elected in 1797; was a Member of the Seventh, Eighth and Ninth Congresses; was subsequently re-elected to the State Legislature; and finally to the Eleventh Congress. He lived in Washington from 1801 to 1813 and during this period wrote almost daily to his wife in New York, keeping her informed of his own active part in the Capital and of the political and social events that were taking place.

So great was his general fund of knowledge and such frequent practical use did his colleagues in the House make of it, that Thomas Jefferson had dubbed him the "Congressional Dictionary." Fellow members called him the "Stalking Library." A story is told to the effect that after being placed upon a certain committee, of which Dr. Dana of Connecticut—also distinguished for learning—was likewise a member, he was being sought one day by Dr. Dana at the door of the House, where Dana came upon Randolph. "I am looking for our Stalking Library," Dana told Randolph. "Are you?" said Randolph; "I just heard him inquiring for his Index."

In addition to his duties in the House, and later in the Senate, Mitchill edited the *Medical Repository*, a journal of some reputation, and made frequent contributions to other scientific journals. He had been only twenty-eight years old when appointed to the professorship of chemistry, natural history and agriculture in Columbia College. Later he served as professor of chemistry, botany and materia medica in the New York College of Physicians and Surgeons.

His personality was unusually amiable and attractive and he was tenderly attached to his wife and to his two adopted daughters. His daily letters to his wife present charming and intimate pictures of contemporary Washington, with the latest Capital gossip and accounts of social and political events.

In one of these letters, written on January 4, 1802, he described the manner in which all the great paid their respects on New Year's Day to the President:

I rode from the Capitol, and proceeding along Pennsylvania, met many gentlemen on their return. In some of the carriages ladies were to be seen, for the Secretaries of the Treasury, Navy, State, etc., with their families, had sallied forth to pay their homage to the Executive, and so had the foreign ministers.

Arriving late, I met a whole troop of ladies and their attendant gallants coming down the outside stairs and going to their carriages. On passing the great hall and entering the withdrawing room, I found still a large party there. The President was standing near the middle of the room, to salute and converse with visitors. The male part of them walked about or made groups for conversation, while the ladies received the bows and adoration of the gentlemen. Among the ladies were the President's two daughters, Mrs. Randolph and Mrs. Eppes, to whom I paid my obeisance; then to Mrs. Madison and her sister, Miss Paine; then to Mrs. Gallatin and Miss Nicholson, besides a number of others. Beaux growing scarce or inattentive toward the last, I had to officiate myself, and to escort several of the fair creatures in succession to their carriages. . . . After the room was cleared, I went into another apartment with the President, and had a conference with him about the best method of preserving our public ships from decay, etc., and then withdrew.

In describing Thomas Jefferson on another occasion, he wrote:

I have had several opportunities of seeing and conversing with him since my arrival at Washington. He is tall in stature and rather spare in flesh. His dress and manners are very plain; he is grave, or rather sedate, but without any tincture of pomp, ostentation or pride, and occasionally can smile, and both hear and relate humorous stories as well as any other man of social feelings. At this moment he had a rather more than ordinary press of care and solicitude, because Congress is in session and he is anxious to know in what manner the Representatives will act upon his message, and how the communications he expects soon to make to the Senate will be received by that branch of the national legislature.

He has been many years a widower, and has never, that I know of, showed any disposition to form a second matrimonial connection. His children are two daughters, one of whom is the wife of an old fellow student with me at the University of Edinburgh, Thomas Mann Randolph.

Waiting one morning in the parlor for the President, who at the moment of my arrival was engaged with the Secretary of the Navy, Mr. Robert Smith, I amused myself a few minutes in looking at the books which occupied one end of the mantelpiece. There were three volumes—one was a volume of the French *Encyclopædia*, in the original; the second was a tome of the Roman historian Tacitus, with the Latin text on one page and a translation into Spanish on the other; and the third was one of the elegant copies of that celebrated edition of the works of Plato which was printed a few years ago at Deuxponts. Mr. Jefferson had been at Deuxponts, and there had purchased the works of Plato and Aristophanes. He is more deeply versed in human nature and human learning than almost the whole tribe of his opponents and revilers.

Still later he wrote:

I recommend to you Jefferson's *Notes on Virginia*. The work is not large. You may borrow it at the library and read all the parts you will find necessary in a few evenings. I asked Mr. Jefferson some questions about the sublime prospect he has described in that work of the passage of the Potomac through the mountains. My chief object was to be directed to the proper place for observation—the place where he himself stood when there. He told me the place no longer existed, for during the reign of Federalism under Adams' administration, the spot, which was a projecting point of rocks on the brow of the mountain, had been industriously blown up and destroyed by gunpowder! A company of Federal Troops quartered there were several days employed in boring and blasting the rock to pieces, doubtless with the intention of falsifying his account, and rendering it incredible by putting it out of the power of any subsequent traveler to behold the like from the same point of view. What shameful, what vandalic revenge in this!

His letter of February 10, 1802, informed his wife:

Though I write verses for the ladies of New York, and figure in contre danses with the lasses of Washington, do not imagine me an idle legislator, for since the beginning of the session I am and have been on the following committees, viz.: 1. The standing Committee on Com-

merce and Manufacturers. 2. The Committee for revising and amending the Naturalization Laws. 3. The Committee for protecting American commerce and seamen against the Tripolitan corsairs. 4. The Committee on Naval Affairs of the United States. 5. The Committee on the
memorials concerning Perpetual Motion. 6. The Committee on amending the act concerning Patent Rights. 7. The Committee on repealing
the laws concerning the Mint of the United States. 8. The Committee
on the memorials of the American merchants for relief against French
Spoliations.

On March 2, 1813, Mitchill mailed home his customary letter from Washington. He wrote:

> This is the last day but one of the session and of my legislative career.
> My situation resembles that in which I was placed four years ago. Then
> I ceased to be a Senator. Now I shall go out as a Representative. I am
> heartily glad of it, for really there is such a hurly-burly and confusion
> in the affairs of the nation and the times that I can scarcely tell what
> is right or what is wrong in our political course, and certainly, as far as
> I can judge, there is more to blame than to praise in our legislative do-
> ings. How joyfully shall I return to my study, my books, and the dear
> companionship of home!

While he served in Congress Samuel Mitchill exerted a real
influence upon the Library of Congress. On the 20th of January, 1806, as chairman of a special committee considering the
purchase of additional maps and books for the Library, he reported to the Senate:

> Every member knows that the inquiries of standing and select com-
> mittees can not here be aided by large, public libraries, as in New York,
> Baltimore and Philadelphia. Nor has it hitherto appeared that so much
> benefit is to be derived from private collections at the present seat of
> government as in those large cities. Every week of the session causes
> additional regret that the volumes of literature and science within the
> reach of the National Legislature are not more rich and ample. The
> want of geographical illustrations is truly distressing; and the deficiency

of historical and political works is scarcely less severely felt. There is, however, no danger of realizing the story of a *parliamentum indoctum* in this country, especially if steps be seasonably taken to furnish the Library with such materials as will enable statesmen to be correct in their investigations, and, by a becoming display of erudition and research, give a higher dignity and a brighter luster to truth.

Out of this report grew the Act of February 21, 1806, which provided that one thousand dollars yearly, for the term of five years, should be appropriated to purchase books for the use of Congress. This amount was to be expended under the direction of the Joint Committee of the House and Senate. The Committee as appointed was made up of Senators Mitchill, Baldwin and Adams, and of Representatives Clay, Randolph, and Dana. John Quincy Adams wrote in his diary on March 31, 1806:

> Met the Joint Committee on the library, and we made some further progress in our business. We agreed that the principal part of the fund appropriated this year should be expended by Doctor Mitchill, Mr. Clay, and myself during the recess, in collecting books in Boston, New York, and Philadelphia, as the occasion may offer. We are to meet again.

On April 8, 1807, John Beckley, the Librarian, died. The question of separating the office of Librarian of Congress from that of the Clerk of the House, arose. Almost two weeks after Beckley's death President Jefferson wrote Henry Dearborn, his Secretary of War:

> With respect to the office of Librarian, I have thought it best generally to give it to the Clerk of the House of Representatives, who being dependent on the House, is, of course, bound to be complaisant to the Members. In the present case I am strongly disposed to depart from the rule in favor of William Mayne Duncanson. He was in the very worst days of terror one of the four or five who alone stood their ground as Republicans in Washington and Georgetown. He is, I think, a very honest man, came here a very wealthy one, has been swindled out of his whole property, and now is in real distress. He is warm in his tem-

per, and on account of some communications with Colonel Smith in Miranda's affair and perhaps some acquaintance with Burr might, I fear, be rather unpopular with the members. But my confidence is that he would be and has been an honest man in all his purposes. I am a little puzzled, therefore, between doubt and inclination.

Despite the President's interest in the impoverished Duncanson of Georgetown, no steps were taken to separate the offices of Librarian of Congress and Clerk of the House of Representatives. Patrick Magruder had been appointed to succeed Beckley as Clerk of the House, and it was Magruder who, in early November of 1807, was also appointed Librarian of Congress. Like his predecessor, Magruder seems to have left many of his library duties to an assistant.

The Library Committee, under the chairmanship of Dr. Mitchill, was extremely active during this period. Upon them had devolved one of the most important duties of the Librarian's office. While the custody of the Library was conferred upon Magruder, it was the committee which was charged with its bibliographical direction. Between March 25, 1807, and March 11th of the next year, they spent $1,149, and between June 8th and December 8th of 1808, invested $1,133 in books. During this same period many gifts were made to the Library of Congress; thirty-one donations are recorded from Senators and authors. The growing collections now represented general and political literature; topically they were arranged under the captions of sacred history, ecclesiastical history; civil history, including chronology, biography, and antiquities; geography and topography; voyages and travels; ethics; law; theology and mythology; logic, rhetoric, and criticism; dictionaries, grammars and treatises on education; general and local politics; political economy; trade and commerce; military and naval tactics; agriculture and rural economy; natural history; natural and experimental philosophy; medicine, surgery and chemistry; poetry and the drama; fiction, arts and sciences; gazettes, maps, charts and plans. The old system of classification by size was abandoned after the catalogues of 1808 and 1812 were published.

The introduction of general literature into the collections was easy to understand when one considered that the legislators of the day were without academic training in politics and found their precedents for the most part in the poetry, rather than in the legislation, of the past.

Greek and Roman verse offered more ready arguments than the principles of political economy or of constitutional or international law. The general character of the collections was due also to another factor: there was no public library in Washington at this time and there were no sources of amusement. Thus the Library of Congress came to be, before 1814, a meeting place for idlers or casual readers. Here students, politicians, diplomats, claimants and correspondents met on friendly terms; while ladies in favor with certain Representatives whiled away the time among the stacks or turning over the pages of magazines while awaiting adjournment or recess.

One of the most regular visitors to the Library of Congress at this time was Chief Justice Marshall, who exercised and appreciated in full the privileges of the stacks. The Chief Justice was fond of waiting upon himself and it was his custom to browse among the books without calling upon the Librarian for attention. On one such occasion he reached for a law book on an upper shelf, with the result that a dozen ponderous volumes toppled down upon him. One volume struck his forehead with such force that he was knocked to the floor, stunned by the blow.

However, when an assistant hurried to his side, the Chief Justice declined aid. With a twinkle he retorted, "I've laid down the law out of the books many a time in my long life, but this is the first time they have laid me down. I am completely floored!" Whereupon he calmly began to take notes from one of the books, still seated on the floor.

In addition to Members of the Supreme Court, the President and Vice-President of the United States, heads of government departments, the Attorney General, judges of the District Court of the District of Columbia, and foreign ministers were now privileged to withdraw books from the Congressional Library.

The first step toward such an extension of privileges had been taken by the House on February 19, 1806, when it resolved to appoint a committee "to consider the propriety of amending the fourth section of the Act of 1802 so as to extend the privilege of taking books out of the Library to the Secretary of State, the Secretary of the Treasury, the Secretary of War, the Secretary of the Navy, and the Attorney General of the United States. . . ."

The House had consistently stood for enlargement of the sphere of service of the Library, for extension of its privileges; the Senate, on the other hand, had stressed the function of service to Congress, recommending large appropriations for this purpose.

The catalogue of 1808 indicates that the Library of Congress was open during Congressional sessions daily from nine o'clock in the morning until three in the afternoon, and from five to seven in the evening, Sundays excepted. During recess it was open on Tuesdays, Thursdays and Saturdays of each week. Receipts or notes were given for all books issued, and the length of time a book might be kept out was determined by the size of the volume. Fines were determined in the same way. Thus for every day's detention beyond the specified term, a penalty of $3 a day was exacted for a folio; $2 a day for a quarto; and a dollar a day for an octavo. If a book were returned in a damaged condition, the borrower was not permitted to take out another until he had "satisfied" the damage for the first. Books were not issued within a week of the termination of any session of Congress and had to be returned three days before the close of the session, whether the allotted term of withdrawal had expired or not. It was the duty of the Librarian to furnish the Speaker of the House and the Secretary of the Senate with a list of the names of all Members who had not, three days before the termination of a session, returned borrowed books. The list was accompanied by a description and statement of the value of all listed books. The Speaker of the House and Secretary of the Senate were then charged before settling the accounts of delinquent borrowers, with retaining a sum equal to double the value of the books or double the value of the whole set if the volume was one of a set. Fines and forfeitures went into the Library fund, later to be disbursed in the purchase of additional books.

The Library of Congress was uprooted many times during these early years in the Capitol. Its first quarters were claimed as temporary accommodations for the House of Representatives when, in 1805, it was found necessary to replace the temporary "elliptic room" the House had been occupying, with a permanent structure. In the Civil Appropriation Act of 1805, $700 was provided for dismantling the Library room and fitting it up for the accommodation of the House while alterations were under way. At the same time $900 was provided for the removal of the Library to a committee room on the south. In these cramped and unsatisfactory quarters it remained until 1810. After completion of the south wing, work was begun on rebuilding the north wing of the Capitol and the old Library room was no sooner vacated by the House than the Supreme Court moved in, giving way, in turn, to later occupancy by the Senate.

Meanwhile that side of the north wing occupied by the Library was gradually falling into decay. The roof leaked; the floor was in need of repair; books were heaped in rows along the walls and at the base of crowded shelves. In vain the surveyor of public buildings cried aloud for a $25,000 appropriation to extend the Library side of the building and fit it for the reception of books before the 1810-1811 session. In vain he outlined his plan for a main library room to contain 40,000 books shelved along its walls in three gallery stages and for a private reading room for Members and two storerooms for unbound volumes and pamphlets. An indifferent clause in the Civil Appropriation Act of 1809 provided a scant $5,000 for "temporary and adequate accommodations for the Library, in the room now used for that purpose and in the one in which the Senate now sits."

In December, 1809, the surveyor of public buildings had pleaded:

> I again beg leave to call your attention to the west side of this wing. It is intended to contain the Library, and is in such state of decay throughout as to render it dangerous to postpone the work proposed. It is now the only part of the Capitol that remains to be solidly rebuilt. But independently of this consideration, the increasing extent of the Library of Congress induces me to represent to you the necessity of constructing rooms intended permanently to contain it. Should the work be commenced in the approaching season, the books may be removed, and the Library and reading rooms be fitted up for use of the session after next.

It was not until two years later, on January 5th, that these appeals produced any effect. On this date a committee was appointed to provide for the safekeeping of the books which belonged to the Library of Congress. Representative Seybert, whose motion it had been, and Representatives Quincy and Macon were appointed to the committee. On the 8th of January a letter was read to the Senate in behalf of this committee. The books in the Library, it stated, were in great danger of being ruined because of the leaks in the roof. Permission was asked to place the collections for a time in one of the committee rooms of the Senate. When the Senate had heard this petition read they resolved to comply with the request "and assign their largest committee room for the purpose." On the 17th of the same month the Joint Committee was directed to inquire into the expediency of making permanent provision for the safekeeping of the books. Thus the Civil Appropriation Act, about a month later, provided $600 for repairing the roof and fitting up the room on the west side of the north wing of the Capitol and $800 for all contingent expenses of the Library and for the Librarian's allowance.

This niggardly provision on the part of Congress was due not so much to lack of appreciation of their own Library as to the events and portents of the times. Congress was in no mood to appropriate money for new buildings when the possibility of a war grew daily more threatening. The War of 1812 was imminent. It was to have a disastrous effect upon the Library of Congress.

IV

THE SPOILS OF WAR

*D*espite the development of the rich regions of the West, the United States during the administration of Jefferson was still closely bound by commercial ties to Europe, particularly to England, and vast quantities of foodstuffs and manufactured articles still were imported. While Europe was at peace, during part of Jefferson's first administration, this trade pursued a normal course. But with resumption of hostilities between France and England in 1803, the United States found it increasingly difficult to remain neutral and at the same time defend her rights. Pinckney and Monroe had sought, without much success, to effect a treaty with England, a treaty designed to put an end to the impressment of American seamen, to restore West Indian trade, and to secure indemnity for captures made under the *Essex* ruling. Napoleon, frustrated in his efforts to control the high seas, had issued his Berlin and Milan decrees; Britain had retaliated with her Orders in Council, and the plight of American shipping was indeed a sorry one. Ships destined for France or nations controlled by France were in danger of seizure by the English; ships destined for English ports might be seized by the French; and both French and English were enforcing their illegal blockades by captures in American waters. British impressment of sailors from American ships, occurring more and more frequently, was arousing the indignation and bitter resentment of the American peoples.

This was fanned to flame when Britain's *Leopard* attacked the *Chesapeake*. Three Americans were killed during the fray, eighteen were wounded, and four deserters were taken off the *Chesapeake* by the British. While British depredations against American merchantmen had frequently occurred, this attack upon an American national ship was regarded as the supreme outrage.

President Jefferson, seeking to maintain peace, issued his proclamation forbidding British warships to take on supplies in American ports and ordered them out of American waters. He demanded reparations and adequate punishment for the offending British commander. Then he set a date for a special session of Congress, the result of which was the Embargo Act of December 21, 1807, forbidding all ships except foreign ships in ballast, to depart from the United States for any foreign port. Ships engaged in the coasting trade were required to give heavy bond that they would land their cargoes in the United States.

The economic life of the country was completely disrupted; importers and ship owners suffered heavy losses; thousands of shipbuilders, sailors and sailmakers were thrown out of work; imported commodities were no longer available and inferior substitutes of American manufacture were offered at high prices; farm prices dropped precipitately; and the Embargo Act was regarded with increasing disfavor.

The temper of the country changed; Federalist strength was revived. The inevitable repeal of the embargo was brought about. Jefferson signed the bill shortly before turning over his office to James Madison, his successor. The Embargo was replaced by Madison's Non-Intercourse Act, which closed American ports to the ships of England and France and prohibited importation of goods into the United States from France, Britain, their colonies or dependencies. Non-intercourse was to be suspended with

France if Napoleon would withdraw his decrees, with Britain if England would withdraw her Orders in Council.

Britain's envoy, George Rose, had returned from the United States without accomplishing anything, nor could the mission of Erskine, British Minister to the United States, be counted any more successful, since subsequently his agreement with Madison was repudiated and he himself was recalled. These were unhappy examples, followed by another as distressing when Francis James Jackson was sent to America in Erskine's place and proved so offensive that Madison refused to treat with him. A year after the adoption of the Non-Intercourse Act it was conceded to be as great a failure as the Embargo. Macon's Bill Number 2 was a later effort at commercial coercion. It repealed the Non-Intercourse Act and sought to bargain with contending European powers. If England would repeal her Orders in Council, the United States would revive non-intercourse with France; if France would withdraw her Napoleonic decrees, the United States would revive non-intercourse with England. On the first of May, 1810, Macon's bill became a law. The American Minister to France, General Armstrong, shortly received a communication from Napoleon's foreign minister, the Duke of Cadore. Napoleon, taking advantage of the American offer, had stated therein that the Berlin and Milan decrees were revoked as of November 1, 1810, "it being understood that, in consequence of this declaration, the English shall revoke the Orders in Council . . . or that the United States, conformably to the act you have just communicated, shall cause their rights to be respected by the English." Madison was quick to re-institute non-intercourse with England. The wary Napoleon lost no time in laying down new regulations against American shipping.

Napoleon had not, however, deceived the British and they would give no assurance to William Pinckney, the American

Minister to England, that the British Orders in Council were to be withdrawn. The British, moreover, sent no one to take Jackson's place and Pinckney left England in 1811 on instructions from his government. This diplomatic impasse was broken with the arrival of Augustus Foster in the United States to adjust the *Chesapeake* affair and generally to seek to improve relations between this country and Britain. Before Foster's arrival, however, the naval encounter between the American frigate, *President*, and the British *Little Belt*—which had been mistaken for the *Guerrière*—had set the American people rejoicing in the belief that the insult to the *Chesapeake* had been avenged.

Despite the now direct demands that Britain withdraw her Orders in Council, the British refused to accede without the assurance that France had actually withdrawn her decrees. The United States and Britain drifted nearer and nearer to war, although Britain, fighting desperately with Napoleon and already suffering from the loss of American markets, had little heart for the encounter. Thus Castlereagh announced in the House of Commons on June 16th that the Orders in Council had been withdrawn. He spoke at the very time that Congress was pushing through both houses a declaration of war. Madison's war message of June 1, 1812, had been voted on in the House on June 4th and in the Senate on June 18th.

In Washington steps were taken to defend the Capital from possible invasion. "Senior volunteers" had enrolled in the summer of 1812, their companies made up of men over forty-five years of age, who were to aid in defending the city. The *National Intelligencer* reported that there was a great show of military spirit following upon the formation of several companies and the drafting of four hundred members of the District Militia, which, under Major King, had been placed in command of Colonel Carberry of the regular Army. These men were encamped on a hill between Georgetown and the Potomac River above Way's Glass Works. The corporation of Washington moreover had appropriated $5,000 "to aid in the execution of such measures as the President might adopt for the safety and defense of the city."

Late in May, 1813, a dinner was given at Davis' Hotel to celebrate recent American naval victories, and large numbers of citizens from Washington, Georgetown and Alexandria met to drink such toasts as:—"The American people: self-collected in prosperity, undaunted in adversity."—"The Genuine Republican. He that is ever ready to defend his country against her enemies." —"The Mission to Russia. As it is pledged to pacific intentions, so may it prove the precursor of an honorable peace."

The assembled company then drank to "The flag of Decatur. To the lightning of heaven it bows, to British thunder, never."

Great excitement prevailed in Washington on July 15, 1813, when the report was circulated that the enemy's ships were approaching the city and that fourteen sails were moving up the Potomac. Citizens met in Capitol Square to organize patrols to watch over the city. But the British squadron apparently abandoned its designs and volunteers were subsequently disbanded, with only the regular troops and drafted militia remaining near Fort Warburton. Quiet reigned for several months. On the Hill legislators convened in regular session, discussed problems of the day, borrowed books from the Library of Congress or loitered in the halls of the Capitol. Patrick Magruder and his assistants continued to carry on the business of the Library in their cramped, inadequate quarters.

It was late in July when the Librarian of Congress determined to depart for Virginia Springs. For some time he had felt the need of recreation and had been suffering from an indisposition which eventually led to his decision. Leaving the newly appointed assistant librarian, J. T. Frost, in charge, Magruder departed. It

71

was, as it proved, the worst possible moment for him to desert his trust, for whatever reason. Frost had scarcely aired the books when, in the middle of August, the British fleet appeared in the Chesapeake. Along the Patuxent the enemy had already burned the villages of Benedict and Lower Marlborough and descended upon Nottingham. The *Intelligencer* reported that this "system of barbarous warfare" spared nothing, burning buildings and plundering families.

After the retreat from Bladensburg many of the troops of the front line had dispersed and gone back to their homes. The commanding general had openly expressed the belief that it would be impossible to defend the city against the invading enemy. Most of the troops upon whom General Winder had had to depend were raw militia, not disciplined veterans like the soldiers of the British army. For the most part, they had been rapidly called together when the need for defending the city seemed imminent, and subsequent events must have been due in large measure to their lack of training and inexperience on the field of battle.

On the 19th of August, when the whole body of the militia of the District of Columbia had been called out, every clerk in the office of Clerk of the House of Representatives was taken into the field. Owing to the fact that the assistant librarian, Frost, was above the prescribed age limit, he was permitted to remain. For four days, following the calling out of the militia, government departments and certain offices in the Capitol itself were busy removing important papers to places of safety, looking toward possible invasion of Washington by the enemy. Yet no effort was made to transport the books or documents of the Library of Congress. Colonel George Magruder, then chief clerk of the office of Clerk of the House, had requested Brigadier General Smith to furlough his assistant, Burch, who had been drafted for the militia, long enough to aid in removing the Library's treasures to a place of safety. On the 21st of August, Burch was furloughed and returned to the Capitol. Here Colonel Magruder gave him instructions not to begin packing until he received word that the clerks at the War Department had started to move its effects. The assistant librarian and Burch began to collect the books of the Library of Congress. As the work progressed Frost sent Burch out in search of wagons or carriages to transport the books.

It was a scene of the greatest confusion that greeted Burch when he emerged from the Capitol. Wagons and carts were rumbling through the streets laden with the baggage of the United States Army. Every vehicle, in fact, seemed to have been impressed into military service. Occasionally a wagon or carriage that had obviously escaped impressment rolled through the ruts of the highways heaped high with the furniture, the boxes and trunks of families who were fleeing from the city and were taking along household possessions.

Burch stopped as many of these as would heed his urgent calls and offered to hire them for his purpose. But one and all the fleeing families turned a deaf ear to his entreaties. Their concern at the moment was for personal safety, not for the reference books of the nation's legislators, and they urged their horses forward, in terror of the advancing British.

The desperate Burch altered his tactics. Entreaty gave way to command. Up and down the highways he shouted to the rolling carts and carriages to stop, or to submit to impressment. But without the backing of authority or military aid he was helpless. None heeded or obeyed him. "The British are coming!" they called back at him, "Out of the way, the British are coming!" and whipped up their horses.

Burch returned to the Capitol and called together messengers from the depleted staff. He sent them off with orders to go beyond the confines of the city if need be in search of a wagon.

Finally, at the home of John Wilson, some six miles from the Capitol, one of the messengers was successful in obtaining a cart and four oxen.

Night had fallen over the city when the cart finally rumbled up Capitol Hill. Burch and Frost worked feverishly removing the more valuable books and papers, filling the single cart to capacity with the heavy volumes, so that even four oxen must have strained in the harness as they set out for a safe and secret place some nine miles out in the country, where the load was deposited.

Back and forth all night the single cart went, bearing as many of the books as could hurriedly be stacked together on each trip. The trips continued until Wednesday morning, the day of the Battle of Bladensburg. The two men were unable to remove anything further, for the retreat from Bladensburg had by that time cleared the way for the British to enter Washington. The Battle of Bladensburg ended at four o'clock in the afternoon; at eight in the evening the British, under the joint command of General Ross and Admiral Cockburn, had entered the city.

It is possible that the Capitol might have escaped the fate it suffered and the collections of the Library of Congress have been spared for future generations, had not a single shot suddenly turned the course of events into one of vandalistic revenge. From the window of a house along the line of march and in the vicinity of the Capitol, someone fired a shot at the British General as he rode past on his horse. The horse was shot from under him. This apparent intent to kill General Ross so enraged the troops that, after setting fire to the house containing the sharpshooter, they marched forthwith upon the Capitol and fired several volleys into its windows. Streaming into the building they set upon such destruction as rivaled all previous depredations.

A British chaplain, George Robert Gleig—not always a reliable

74

chronicler—who served in the expedition, thus described the results of British indignation in his contemporary narrative of the campaign:

> You will easily believe that conduct so unjustifiable, so direct a breach of the law of nations, roused the indignation of every individual, from the General himself down to the private soldier. All thoughts of accommodation were immediately laid aside; the troops advanced forthwith into the town, and having first put to the sword all who were found in the house from which the shots were fired, and reduced it to ashes, they proceeded, without a moment's delay, to burn and destroy everything in the most distant degree connected with the government. In this general devastation were included the Senate-House, the President's palace, an extensive dock yard and arsenal, barracks for two or three thousand men, several large storehouses filled with naval and military stores, some hundreds of cannon of different descriptions, and nearly twenty thousand stand of small arms. There were also two or three public rope works which shared the same fate, a fine frigate pierced for sixty guns, and just ready to be launched, several gun brigs and armed schooners, with a variety of gun boats and small craft. . . . All this was as it should be, and had the arm of vengeance been extended no farther, there would not have been room given for so much as a whisper of disapprobation. But unfortunately, it did not stop here; a noble library, several printing offices, and all the national archives were likewise committed to the flames which, though no doubt the property of government, might better have been spared. It is not, however, my intention to join the outcry, which will probably be raised against what they will term a line of conduct at once barbarous and unprofitable.

The "noble library" to which the British chaplain referred, was, of course, the Library of Congress. When the British troops poured into the Capitol, bent on destruction, it was not a completed building which they entered. Only the two wings of it were finished, and they were connected by a wooden passageway erected where the rotunda now stands.

Led by Admiral Cockburn of the Royal Navy, the officers

entered the chamber of the House of Representatives. Cockburn seated himself in the Speaker's chair and called the assemblage to order.

"Gentlemen," he shouted, "the question is, shall this harbor of Yankee democracy be burned? All in favor of burning it will say Aye!" A shout of "Aye" went up. "Those opposed will say Nay." There was silence for a moment. Then the voice of the Admiral boomed forth, "Light up!" The cry was carried out through the halls of the Capitol, ran along the lines of troops and provided that authority for which the excited men were waiting.

The British swarmed into the rooms occupied by the Library of Congress, tore volume after volume from the shelves, ripped the pitch-pine boards from the passageway between the wings, cut valuable paintings from their frames, heaped papers and books in high mounds and applied their torches to the combustible mass.

Thus the literary treasures collected with such pains, expense and devotion over a period of years supplied the kindling and fuel for the blazing fires that soon reduced the north wing to charred timbers. Had it not been for a sudden thunderstorm which broke providentially with torrential rains over the city a half-hour after the conflagration began, the entire Capitol would probably have been reduced to ruins.

In a report made later by the surveyor of the Capitol the interior of the west room was described as practically destroyed.

> The whole of the interior of the west side having been constructed of timber, and the old shingle roof still remaining over the greatest part of the wing, an intensity of heat was produced, which burned the walls most exposed to it, and being driven by the wind into the Senate Chamber burned the marble columns to lime, cracked everything that was of freestone, and finding vent through the windows and up the private stairs damaged the exterior of the wing very materially.

76

Government documents, newspapers, and thousands of fine volumes were reduced to ashes in the conflagration. It was a crime comparable to the crime of the Mohammedans when they set fire to the great Alexandrian library in Egypt. Lovers of learning and literature everywhere denounced the deed; even British newspapers condemned it. One Nottingham editor, bolder than the rest, published in his columns that it was "an act without example in modern wars or in any other war since the inroads of the barbarians who conflagrated Rome and overthrew the Roman Empire."

Ingersoll declares that Ross, the British General, continually deplored the tragedy which he said he had to perform and much lamented the destruction of the Library. He is said to have remarked, "Had I known it in time, the books most certainly would have been saved."

The indignation of Congress at destruction of their Library knew no bounds. Their wrath fell most relentlessly on the unfortunate Librarian, Patrick Magruder, who was accused of having deserted his post and of not having made suitable provision for saving the books. They stated subsequently that "the error or negligence consisted not so much in delaying to pack up the effects of the office till the 22nd of August as the neglect to provide the means of transportation, which might have been done by the clerk who remained in the office, or any agent employed for that purpose."

Hurriedly recalled by the unhappy events in the Capitol, Magruder communicated with Congress relative to the destruction of the Library, outlining the experiences of the assistant librarian, Frost, and his helper, Burch, in their efforts to remove the books. Magruder's letter was referred to a committee, which reported on December 12, 1814, through Joseph Pearson, that it "had satisfactory evidence that the Library of Congress, consisting of volumes agreeably to the catalogues herewith submitted, was destroyed by the enemy on the 24th of August, last."

A week after the committee had reported, Magruder forwarded to the House of Representatives a letter written by the assistant librarian on December 17th. The letter read:

> SIR: On examining the report of the committee appointed on the subject of your communication to the House of the 20th of September last, I find that the Committee admit that, after the 21st of August, the difficulty of procuring teams for the removal of the books, papers, etc., from your office was so great as to justify a belief that all was done after that period which could (with the means we possessed) have been expected. But the committee states that measures preparatory for a removal had not been taken. On that head I can only say that on Monday, the 22nd of August last, if carriages for the conveyance of the books, etc., could have been obtained, they were in a situation to be immediately removed; the several loads which were saved were taken from the shelves on which they were placed and deposited in the carts by which they were taken away; they have suffered no injury; and to have procured boxes or trunks to pack them in, if that plan had been preferred, would have been entirely impossible.
>
> Your obedient servant,
>
> J. L. FROST.

That no resistance was offered the British, either in protecting the Library of Congress or any other part of the Capitol seems fairly certain. Those clerks, doorkeepers and officers who were not absent under arms had fled the building. The legislative halls and all their appurtenances were without superintendent, occupant or care. The night before the Battle of Bladensburg, Minor's Virginia regiment bivouacked in the Hall of Representatives. The grounds about the Capitol were completely deserted. It was an easy matter for the invading army to march in and consign the literary treasures of the nation to flames.

Unhappily enough there were destroyed at the same time

vouchers covering contingent expenses of the past year. These were deposited in a small drawer which was overlooked when Frost and Burch were removing important papers from the Library. As a result of the loss, the accounts of the office were brought into question when Congress was considering the matter of Magruder's negligence. Magruder had himself invited inquiry, which led to appointment of a Congressional committee. This committee reported unfavorably to the clerks and also reported that out of $50,000 received on account of contingent moneys, vouchers were produced for little more than $30,000. Account was taken of the fact that expenditures had "always been exclusively under the direction of Mr. Magruder's principal clerk and it does not appear that Mr. Magruder himself had any knowledge of its disbursement, considering it as having been duly controlled by the Committee on Accounts." Because of these circumstances a motion had been made to remove the Librarian "on the ground of neglect in confiding these matters to his deputies." This motion was opposed "on the ground of his unimpeachable character and general good conduct."

The bitter indignation of the legislators at their irremediable loss, vented upon the Librarian of Congress, proved too much for the unhappy Librarian, who felt he could not remain any longer in office. On January 28, 1815, the Speaker laid before the House the following letter:

SIR: It is with a reluctance I cannot well express that I find it necessary again to throw myself on your politeness as the medium of communication to the House, on a subject no less painful to me than it must be to them. This is imposed upon me as a duty, as well by the arguments derived from those inimical to me (as I learn) from silence in regard to the last report of the committee, appointed at my request to investigate the situation of the office under my charge, as by the indications afforded by the recent vote of the House. In regard to the accounts of my office, the correctness of which have been arraigned by a committee of the House, I have nothing to add to what I have said on a former occasion on this subject, except to reassert my entire innocence and ignorance of any misapplication of the public moneys, and to express my conscientious belief that the public money has been faithfully disbursed by my principal clerk to whom it was confided, and that he will be able to account for it at the Treasury; and would have been able to do so at this day, had not the unfortunate conflagration at the Capitol destroyed his accounts, and subjected his conduct to a scrutiny, in which the fact of a deficiency of the vouchers destroyed has been adduced as evidence against him.

Could I presume so far, it might be an easy task to exhibit errors of great importance in that part of the report of the committee on my conduct, which relates to the account of the contingent fund. It is my belief demonstrable, that its errors are not limited to hundreds or to any moderate number of thousands of dollars. Still easier would it be to dissipate almost every argument used in debate on that report, tending by assertion or implication to prejudice the House against me personally; but who is put upon his trial without opportunity to defend himself, from accusations adduced against him, can expect no benefit from an after appeal to those who have already pronounced judgment against him.

Little, sir, did I ever expect to have to answer to this House, on charges affecting my character, at this advanced period of my life. Since I passed the age of eighteen years, have I been in public life. By those who knew me best, I have been selected to fill various public stations, judicial as well as legislative, under both State and General governments and no man had ever before appeared to impute to me malfaisance in the duties of my station. In every situation in which it has pleased my country to place me, I have endeavored to sustain a character more dear to me than wealth; and the attempt to rob me of a jewel more precious than life, to deprive me of that honest fame which I had acquired by a long course of public service, however it may temporarily succeed in this body, cannot eventually depress my character or standing in the eyes of the American people. Truth is great, and will prevail. I court its light, and shrink not from its test. The office of Clerk of this House, arduous and trying as are the duties to be performed during the sessions of Congress, has never been considered by me in a pecuniary point of view, an object.

Two years since I should have resigned it, but for the dissuasions of my friends. I was too proud of the honor conferred by the flattering suffrage I had received from the honorable House. I retained my seat; and how cruelly I am treated for that determination let recent events decide.

But, sir, it is not my intention to weary you or the House by reiterating those unavailing regrets which force themselves on my bosom. It is probable, sir, I might, by resorting to humiliating solicitation, reinstate myself in my former footing in the House; but there is implanted within my bosom a principle much more powerful than the love of popularity or of office. It is the sense of honor which forbids solicitation from, or even association with, those who entertain a suspicion derogatory to my fair fame. That there are such among those whom I have once been proud to call my political friends, the motion now pending in the House, and the manner in which it has been supported, sufficiently indicate. After a struggle between contending feelings, I have therefore determined to resign the office I now hold, to permit those by whom I am persecuted to attain, with greater ease, an object to which they have been willing to sacrifice, not only my family but my reputation. I beg the Speaker and House to accept of this my resignation of the office of Clerk of the House of Representatives. I take this last opportunity to offer to yourself, and the House, the homage of my unfeigned respect, and to those who have stood forth to befriend an injured man, and resisted the accusations against me, the assurances of my eternal gratitude. To my successor in office, let him be whom he may, I wish an easier and happier time in the discharge of his duties than I have had.

I am sir, with respect,

PATRICK MAGRUDER

Thus, with his resignation from the post as Clerk of the House, Magruder ceased automatically to be the Librarian of Congress.

V

MAN OF LETTERS
AND MAN OF THE WORLD

*T*he only public building left standing in Washington after the British invasion was a structure on the crest of the F Street ridge at 7th, 8th, and E Streets, NW. Known variously as Blodgett's, and the Great Hotel, this building, destined to serve as the next home of the Library of Congress, and to accommodate the House and Senate for a time after the burning of the Capitol, had accumulated a colorful history.

It had been designed in 1793 by Captain James Hoban, who had also designed the President's house.

In appearance it was a two-story brick building, with a basement and attic story and a frontage of 120 feet. It presented an imposing appearance in the fields and woods of the infant city. The building owed its existence to the fertile brain of the adventurous Samuel Blodgett, whose name had first appeared in Washington's history in connection with an early effort to negotiate a loan on Capital property to facilitate the construction of public buildings in the new city. Blodgett was one of the most striking figures in the group of early promoters and came to be known variously as a rogue, a scoundrel, and "a capital shot." Latrobe referred to him as "one of the adventurers and swindlers whom the establishment of the city brought hither."

Blodgett, who had acquired considerable property in the Capital, and had found numerous purchasers for city lots, succeeded in interesting the commissioners in a scheme to establish a lottery, the principal prize of which was to be a hotel building to be erected in the city. Advertised as "a lottery by the commissioners appointed to prepare the public buildings, etc., within the city of Washington," the announcement was signed "Samuel Blodgett, agent, for the affairs of the city," and at the start it was officially sponsored. John M. Gantt, clerk of the commissioners, was one of the managers. Samuel Davidson and Daniel Reintzel were requested by the board to prepare and examine the tickets for the drawing, which was scheduled for the fall of 1793, at about the same time as the date of the next sale of city lots. William Deakins, Jr., the Treasurer of the board, and Blodgett, had entire charge of selling the tickets, Deakins assuming responsibility for the sale of 40 percent of the number of 50,000 and Blodgett for all the rest.

The hotel was to cost $50,000 and the cornerstone was laid on the national anniversary. "Fifteen hundred people were present and walked from thence in procession, preceded by a lodge of freemasons, to a dinner, the principal dish of which consisted of an ox roasted whole. A number of toasts were drunk on the occasion and the day concluded with much harmony," reported a contemporary chronicler.

After delays and considerable criticism of Blodgett, the drawing of this lottery was finally concluded in the fall of 1794 and Robert S. Bickley of Philadelphia was found to be the holder of the prize ticket. Although the price of tickets given in the lottery prospectus was eight dollars, Bickley had paid $11 for his chance —an indication that speculation had entered into the enterprise. The hotel was in an unfinished state when Bickley drew it, and it was never completed. Four years after the drawing Bickley began suit in Philadelphia, where Blodgett was living. On December 26, 1801, the supreme court of that state rendered a judgment that Bickley was entitled to the hotel building and to $21,500—the difference between the estimated value of the building as it then stood and the stipulated value of the prize. In the following year a suit was instituted in the circuit court of the District to collect this judgment by the sale of property owned by Blodgett in the District; and there were subsequent suits for the same purpose. Meanwhile the hotel stood, an imposing derelict, conspicuous amidst its primitive surroundings.

It served to shelter, one after another, many a transient enterprise. Public meetings were held there. A tavern set up shop on its first floor for a time; and in 1800 a partial effort was made at rehabilitation when one Wignell, manager of a troupe of players, received a pressing request to establish a theatre in the new city of Washington. With the request came the offer of the vacant unfinished hotel, a building "every way suitable, situated nearly in the center of the new metropolis." Consisting as it did of a very spacious center building, with two extensive wings, it seemed to Wignell an eligible structure for his purpose. One of the actors of Mr. Wignell's band stated that "its capacious size afforded ample space for such accommodation as would be required in furnishing dramatic entertainment to the citizens of Washington, Georgetown and Alexandria, as well as of the extended neighborhood around."

The theatre seems to have flourished for a time in the embellished central edifice. Thomas Law is recorded as having aided it "not only with his pen and his influence, but with his purse— ably seconded by several other gentlemen of liberality and taste." Yet, while his success in Washington continued to exceed Mr. Wignell's expectations, it fell very far below his expenditures, and he was eventually forced to withdraw. His brief occupancy of the building served historically, however, to mark the future quarters of the Library of Congress also as Washington's first theatre.

After garnering to itself this distinction, however, the building fell gradually into disrepair. Occasional religious services were conducted within its walls. Eventually it served as a refuge for those who could find no other shelter. A number of Scotch and Irish emigrants lived rent free under its dilapidated roof.

It was the growth of the country that saved it from complete decay. The increasing number of government employees in the Capital, and the expansion of executive departments and civil branches, resulted finally in action by Congress. All but one of the five departments were housed in the southwest executive office when Congress stepped in and, in an effort to correct the crowded conditions, appropriated $10,000 to purchase the Blodgett Hotel building, expending $3,628 in 1810 to fit up the interior for the use of the General Post Office, the City Post Office and the Patent Office. Dr. William Thornton, who had designed the Capitol, was serving as Commissioner of Patents when the British invaded Washington. It was owing to his intervention that the building housing these valuable records was spared when all other public buildings were blazing under British torches.

The only contemporary account remaining to us of this invasion is the diary of Dr. Thornton's wife, preserved today in the Manuscript Division of the Library of Congress. Beginning with the first actual movement of troops in defense of the city after the Government had learned that the British fleet with veterans from the Napoleonic War in Europe had entered the Patuxent, the record, kept for this period on sheets of paper, describes what Mrs. Thornton saw and heard daily. On Thursday, the 25th of August, she wrote:

Dr. T went to the City & by his exertions saved the patent office from destruction. They were on the point of setting it on fire & he represented to the officer [Col. Jones] that it was the Museum of the Arts & that it would be a loss to all the world. . . . The war office was not burnt till after breakfast today. The rope walks were burnt. We had a dreadful storm & gust but fortunately accompanied with rain—the weather during all the fires fortunately was very calm, but it appears almost miraculous that the whole place was not consumed.

Thus it was that Blodgett's was left standing when all other public buildings were burned. This circumstance served to add to the picturesque history of the restored derelict which was now called upon to afford shelter to the homeless Congress and protection for what remained of its Library.

Two days before the invading Britishers left Alexandria a beginning was made toward resumption of the normal life of the Capital and the restoration of business. The providential storm that had beaten upon the city had caused damage to the roof of Blodgett's, and workmen were at once engaged to repair it. On the day following withdrawal of the British vessels, and nine days after invasion of the city, directions were given to have the models removed from the quarters of the Patent Office in the building to make way for the hastily-called meeting of Congress—a special session set for the 19th of September, a little more than two weeks later. The Post Office Department was removed to a rented building on the north side of Pennsylvania Avenue, just west of Ninth Street. The City Post Office, however, continued to occupy rooms in Blodgett's after Congress convened. Other executive offices were located in private houses rented for the use of the Government mostly in the vicinity of the White House.

Two days after Congress had assembled in its new quarters the *Intelligencer* reported in its columns: "We hear some indistinct suggestions buzzed abroad of a design to endeavor, in consequence of recent events, to remove the seat of government temporarily or permanently from this place." These "indistinct suggestions" were given definite form a week later when a resolution was introduced in the House providing for the temporary removal of the seat of government to some other place that was safer and more comfortable until such time as the public edifices were rebuilt, when Congress and the public offices were to be established again in Washington.

The citizens of Washington were more than skeptical about the temporary character of the proposed removal, particularly when three days after introduction of the resolution and before a report had been made by the committee to whom it had been referred, offers were received from the common councils of the cities of Philadelphia and of Lancaster, Pennsylvania, placing buildings in those cities at the disposal of Congress. Neighboring Georgetown likewise made a bid for favor, offering Congress the use of Georgetown College, with the additional inducement "that board for the members will be provided in the town at ten dollars per week instead of sixteen dollars as charged by Washington hotels."

The impossibly crowded condition of the quarters in which they were meeting must have furnished a strong argument additional to those being advanced in favor of removal—the defenseless condition of the city and the liability of another attack, for the inconvenience and discomfort to which Members were being subjected was undoubtedly great. It would have been impossible, for example, for every one of the 176 Members to be seated had they attended at one time in the rooms they were then occupying. But, while it looked for a time as if credence would be given to assurances of the temporary nature of the removal, the dignity of the nation and peace of mind of Washingtonians who had invested heavily in the Capital were alike protected by the decision of Congress, three weeks later, to remain on the shores of the Potomac. Rather sit under canvas in their Capital City, one

87

speaker exclaimed, than remove one mile out of it to a palace!

In this frame of mind work was begun with funds raised by thirty-eight public-spirited citizens, on more suitable quarters for the Congress. Using $17,362 raised by the sale of stock to the public at $100 a share, they secured a site on Capitol Hill on A Street, just east of First Street, NE, where the old Tunnicliff Tavern was standing, and some vacant lots to the west. The tavern was torn down and the garden which had bloomed along the First Street front, plowed under. Work was begun on the building which was to house Congress, sitting temporarily in Blodgett's, until the National Capitol could be restored.

While these events were happening, President Madison on the 21st of March, 1815, appointed the gentleman who is sometimes counted the first Librarian of Congress, for the reason that his appointment marked the severance of Librarian's office from that of Clerk of the House. George Watterston was appointed solely to take charge of the Congressional Library. On the 24th of September, 1814, Joseph Milligan had suggested to Thomas Jefferson that such a distinction be made between the offices, and the loss of the old library had eventually brought it about.

Watterston was a man of letters as well as a government official. Despite the fact that the character, the humor, the plots of his novels are of but average quality, the first Librarian's claims to literary recognition are definite and arresting. He was the first novelist to set his scene in the National Capital, the first to make use of the psychological in his writings, while his critical ability and the variety of his interests made their contributions to the literary and social history of his time. The original letters and papers of George Watterston form a valuable part of the manuscript collections in the Library of Congress today and include such interesting correspondents as Thomas Jefferson, John Quincy Adams, Clement Biddle, Daniel Brent, Henry Clay, John M.

The main entrance pavilion

George Watterston, third Librarian of Congress

Clayton, Albert Gallatin, Peter Force, Josiah Meigs, Edgar Allan Poe, Daniel Webster, and William Wirt, as well as the Librarian's important correspondence with Edward Everett, memoranda of Watterston's work in connection with the National Monument and Columbian Horticultural Societies, and historical invoices of shipments of books imported for the Library. In the Rare Book collections of the Library of Congress are first editions of his books on Washington life and his guide-books of the Capital.

Watterston has been described as a man "ardent in temperament, yet modest and unobtrusive in manner." The irrepressible Anne Royall saw him as "a man of good size, neither spare nor robust, a fine figure, and possessed of some personal beauty" with his "fair complexion and his striking countenance" showing "genius and deep penetration, marked with a grave and commanding spirit—a gentleman both in appearance and manners."

A modern analyst refers to him as "a mental hybrid, both shy and bold, conservative and radical, sometimes prudish, sometimes crude," with his writing reflecting "the sober thoughts of the pedagogue and the nice satire of the man of the world." Journalist and author of several books, he knew the power and danger of books as only an author can. "A great book is a great evil," he wrote on one occasion. "Read much, but not many books." Again, he warned, "A man who reads a great deal is like a cormorant—his literary appetite is never satisfied."

Watterston was born in an immigrant family, the son of David Watterston of Jedburgh, Scotland. He was born on October 23, 1783, in the harbor of New York. His father was a master builder who was on his way to settle upon property he had acquired in the neighborhood of the City of New York. The founding of the Federal Capital in Washington offered opportunities, however, that no master builder could resist, and the family moved on to Washington. Watterston considered that the only event of importance in his early boyhood was when he witnessed the laying of the cornerstone of the Capitol by President Washington on September 18, 1793.

When he came of school age he was sent to Charlotte Hall School in St. Mary's County, Maryland, where he received a good literary and classical education.

After leaving Charlotte Hall School, Watterston studied law, subsequently opening a law office in Hagerstown, Maryland, and writing a play, *The Child of Feeling*, in his spare time. In this play he satirized "the prevailing vices and follies of mankind." The philological rhapsodies of Etymology, one of its characters, find expression in such outbursts as "Have I shewn you my voluminous treaty on the nature of adverbs? . . . Deep, profound, incomprehensible, it will cast a blaze of never ending light on the English language." Twenty-six years after its publication Watterston criticized his own first literary venture in an article in *The Southern Literary Messenger*.

Soon after publication of his first play and upon the death of a rich uncle in Jamaica, Watterston closed his law office and started off for the West Indies. He kept a journal of his wanderings during the year 1810 in Cuba and Jamaica. Still preserved, in the Library of Congress, it offers his and his companions' impressions of conditions in the islands, and compares them with conditions in the United States, concluding with the observation, "I prefer the Americans before all other nations." Watterston wrote:

> Nature has indeed done much for this country. She has scattered her bounties in an order wild, but harmonious, irregular, but delightful. She has opened her bosom to the nourishment of man and desired him to live without toil, if he would live without civilization.

The romance and beauty of the West Indies also inspired two poems—*The Indian* and *The Wanderer in Jamaica*, both of which dwell upon the simple, happy life of the Indian before the coming of the Spaniard. *The Indian* appeared anonymously in *The Portfolio* of November, 1810; *The Wanderer in Jamaica* was published in Washington the same year and was dedicated to Mrs. Dolly Madison.

Upon his return from Jamaica Watterston started legal practice in Washington in partnership with Thomas Law. On October 29, 1811, he married Miss Maria Shanley of the Capital, and the following year was candidate for the position of collector of the District of Columbia. When the British threatened the Capital in 1814, he marched with Captain Benjamin Burch's company to meet the enemy at the inglorious "Bladensburg races."

While many of Watterston's writings had been published anonymously he had by 1815 gained sufficient fame as a man of letters to justify President Madison's appointment of him as Librarian of Congress, though gossips of the Capital attributed his nomination more to the dedication of *The Wanderer in Jamaica*, addressed to Dolly Madison:

> Madam, I have presumed to address this poetical effusion to you, from the reputation you have acquired of being desirous to promote the cause of general literature.

Two years before his appointment as Librarian of Congress, Watterston had become editor of the *Washington City Gazette*, established by William Elliot in support of the Republican Party. One chronicler makes the observation that from this time on he ceased to make any notable contributions to literature. The claim is disputed, however, by a subsequent critic who refers to Watterston's *The L—— Family* and *The Wanderer in Washington* as a "very definite contribution to national literature in widening the presentation of American background and manners," while the number and variety of his articles after he became Librarian are pointed out as evidence of his "vital interest in literature and in questions of the day."

Watterston's appointment was brought about by two events—the resignation of Patrick Magruder and the acquisition of the Jefferson library. The latter is perhaps the greatest single event affecting the future destiny and policy of the Library of Congress that was ever debated or voted upon by the national legislators. It was a step considered, and finally agreed to, amidst shameful opposition, in the hot, cramped parlors of Blodgett's Hotel.

VI

JEFFERSON'S LIBRARY

*T*en days after Congress had convened in the old hotel on F Street, organizations and private citizens began to make known their desire to aid members of the Senate and House in securing those facilities for study and research of which they had been at least temporarily deprived by the loss of their library.

On September 29th a letter was read to the Senate from the President of the Washington Library, with a resolution of the directors, offering the use of that library to Members. The next day brought an invitation from the Georgetown booksellers, Richards and Mallory, for Members of the Senate to make free use of their stock of books.

Thomas Jefferson was at this time in retirement at Monticello, where the sad news of the destruction of the Library of Congress had reached him. On September 21, 1814, he dispatched a letter to his friend Samuel Harrison Smith:

> I am imposing a task on your friendship which needs much apology and will be explained in the letter accompanying this. It is to offer my library to the Library Committee of Congress. I would not have trespassed on your time so much but that I hope it will give you little trouble. The delivery of the accompanying letter (which is written separately with that view) and the catalogue will enable them to give you their yea or nay. As the subject, however, can not but be interesting, and I shall feel anxiety until I know their inclinations, you would

greatly oblige me by informing me of them as soon as you can form a probable conjecture what they are likely to decide.

Jefferson had already played an important part in the organization of the Library. He had made generous donations in the past and had drawn up that list which had formed the basis for earlier Library of Congress purchases. Now, in the communication which accompanied his letter to Smith and which later was submitted to Congress, he briefly described his own collections:

DEAR SIR:

I learn from the newspapers that the vandalism of our enemy has triumphed at Washington over science as well as the arts by the destruction of the public library with the noble edifice in which it was deposited. Of this transaction, as of that of Copenhagen, the world will entertain but one sentiment. They will see a nation suddenly withdrawn from a great war, full armed and full handed, taking advantage of another whom they had recently forced into it, unarmed, and unprepared to indulge themselves in acts of barbarism which do not belong to a civilized age. When Van Ghent destroyed their shipping at Chatham, and De Ruyter rode triumphantly up the Thames, he might in like manner, by the acknowledgement of their own historians, have forced all their ships up to London Bridge, and there have burned them, the tower, the city, had these examples been then set. London, when thus menaced, was near a thousand years old; Washington is but in its teens.

I presume it will be among the early objects of Congress to recommence their collection. This will be difficult while the war continues, and intercourse with Europe is attended with so much risk. You know my collection, its condition and extent. I have been fifty years making it, and have spared no pains, opportunity or expense, to make it what it is. While residing in Paris, I devoted every afternoon I was disengaged for a summer or two in examining all the principal bookstores, turning over every book with my own hand and putting by everything which related to America, and indeed whatever was rare and valuable in every science. Besides this, I had standing orders during the whole time I was in Europe on its principal book marts, particularly Amsterdam, Frankfort, Madrid, and London, for such works relating to

94

America as could not be found in Paris. So that, in that department particularly, such a collection was made as probably can never again be effected because it is hardly probable that the same opportunities, the same time, industry, perseverance and expense, with the same knowledge of the bibliography of the subject would again happen to be in concurrence. During the same period, and after my return to America, I was led to procure, also, whatever related to the duties of those in the high concerns of the nation. So that the collection, which I suppose is of between nine and ten thousand volumes, while it includes what is chiefly valuable in science and literature generally, extends more particularly to whatever belongs to the American statesman. In the diplomatic and parliamentary branches, it is particularly full. It is long since I have been sensible it ought not to continue private property, and had provided that at my death, Congress should have the refusal of it at their own price. The loss they have now incurred, makes the present the proper moment for their accommodation, without regard to the small remnant of time and the barren use of my enjoying it. I ask of your friendship, therefore, to make for me the tender of it to the Library Committee of Congress, not knowing myself of whom the Committee consists. I enclose you the catalogue, which will enable them to judge of its contents. Nearly the whole are well bound, abundance of them elegantly, and of the choicest editions existing. They may be valued by persons named by themselves, and the payment made convenient to the public. It may be, for instance, in such annual installments as the law of Congress has left at their disposal, or in stock of any of their late loans, or of any loan they may institute at this session, so as to spare the present calls of our country and await its days of peace and prosperity. They may enter, nevertheless, into immediate use of it, as eighteen or twenty wagons would place it in Washington in a single trip of a fortnight.

I should be willing, indeed, to retain a few of the books, to amuse the time I have yet to pass, which might be valued with the rest, but not included in the sum of valuation until they should be restored at my death, which I would carefully provide for, so that the whole library as it stands in the catalogue at this moment should be theirs without any garbling. Those I should like to retain would be chiefly classical and mathematical. Some few in other branches, and particularly one of

95

the five encyclopedias in the catalogue. But this, if not acceptable, would not be urged. I must add, that I have not revised the library since I came home to live, so that it is probable some of the books may be missing, except in the chapters of law and Divinity, which have been revised and stand exactly as in the catalogue. The return of the catalogue will of course be needed, whether the tender be accepted or not.

I do not know that it contains any branch of science which Congress would wish to exclude from their collection; there is, in fact, no subject to which a member of Congress may not have occasion to refer. But such a wish could not correspond with my views of preventing its dismemberment. My desire is either to place it in their hands entire, or to preserve it so here. I am engaged in making an alphabetical index of the authors' names, to be annexed to the catalogue, which I will forward to you as soon as completed. Any agreement you shall be so good as to take the trouble of entering into with the committee I hereby confirm.

It was not until the first week in October that Jefferson received an answer from Smith, as the ex-President's letter had been delayed in transit. On October 7th Mr. Smith wrote:

It gives me great pleasure to acknowledge the receipt of your favor of the 21st ultimo, which from some casualty did not reach me until the 2nd instant. . . . The Library that is lost was valuable and was the commencement of an institution fitted in its nativity to be the pride and ornament of our country. But valuable as it was, if replaced by your collection, the loss will be more than supplied. Being somewhat of an enthusiast as to the benefits that arise from such institutions, I could only hail the prospect of seeing so broad a foundation laid for a national one on a scale of expanding grandeur.

I submitted, without delay, your letter and catalogue to the Library Committee of the two Houses of Congress. That of the Senate consists of Messrs. Goldsborough, Tait and Fromentin, and that of the Representatives of Messrs. Seybert, Lowndes and Gaston. The tender was respectfully received by both committees, with the assurance that no time should be lost in acting upon it. They each express the opinion that the committee could not go further than to recommend to their

Houses such steps as they should on consultation consider advisable and promised to inform me of the course determined on. I have made several other members acquainted with the offer made by you, and have been happy to find that it is highly appreciated by them and will receive their warm support.

I perceive no obstacle to its acceptance, but the pending proposition to remove the seat of Government. I fear that many of those who are interested in this measure will consider the possession of such a library as depriving them of a strong argument in favor of removal and hence will be apt by delay or evasion to keep back its consideration. Should this prove to be the case, I submit to you the policy of permitting a publication of your letters. . . .

P. S. I am just advised by Mr. Goldsborough that the joint committee have reported a resolution empowering them to contract for the purchase of the library.

Meanwhile, on September 24th, Jefferson had also written to President Madison and to James Monroe, acquainting them with his offer and asking for their support. The President replied on October 10th:

Your favor of the 24th ultimo came duly to hand. I learn that the Library Committee will report favorably on your proposition to supply the loss of books by Congress. It will prove a gain to them if they have the wisdom to replace it by such a collection as yours.

On the same day Monroe wrote Jefferson, assuring him that he would use his influence in effecting the sale of the books. Jefferson could not have foreseen at this point the shameful controversy, politically motivated, that was to ensue—a contest that caused the indignant editor of Walsh's *American Register* at one point to exclaim:

The next generation will, we confidently predict, blush at the objections made in Congress to the purchase of Mr. Jefferson's library. Party spirit, darkling and chafing, spoke the language of an auctioneer or a chapman, and erred egregiously even in its huckstering calculations.

Throughout the whole of the unworthy contest Jefferson's letters reflected the serene dignity, the charm of the great man who was landlord at Monticello.

A week after desultory discussion of a resolution empowering the Committee to contract for the library, debate was resumed in the House, with Joseph Lewis of Virginia in the chair. As one historian relates, the ensuing discussion "betrayed the English prepossessions of some, the narrow parsimony of others, the party prejudices of nearly all." Oakley of New York made a motion that decision in the matter be left to the Library Committee. In the discussion which followed objections were made to the cost, the extent, the nature of the collection, and to the number of works in foreign languages, particularly to the works of Voltaire, Rousseau and other literary apostles of the French Revolution. Language, it developed, was not the sole controversial issue, for English works on progress and speculative freedom, such as Locke's, were also under fire, and even general books considered as probably "too philosophical."

These incredible objections on the part of enlightened legislators moved the *Petersburg Courier* to observe:

> The objections made by the Federal Members of Congress to the purchase of Mr. Jefferson's library are certainly not only extraordinary and illiberal, but they reflect the greatest discredit upon the national character of this country. What can be a greater stigma upon the members of our national legislature than to assert that books of a philosophical description are improper for their perusal? Were Mr. Oakley, Mr. Reed, and Mr. Grosvenor the literary censors of the United States, the works of Newton, Locke, Simpson, Stewart and all others of equal merit, would doubtless be committed to the flames, and their places supplied perhaps by the Tales of Wonder, the Tales of Horror, and the Arabian Nights Entertainment.
>
> Another great objection is that Mr. Jefferson's library contains the works of Voltaire—what a pitiful observation: Will it be said that the

works of an author, which hold the first rank on the shelves of all the libraries of Europe, and which may be found in the libraries of Oxford and Cambridge, and in those of the four Scotch universities, for the express purpose to be perused by students, should be prohibited or forbidden a place in the Library of Congress? Will the force of Federal prejudice and superstition be so powerful as to effect this?

Despite political opposition, there were staunch defenders of the proposal to purchase the library.

"The general library of Mr. Jefferson," wrote a Washington correspondent of the *Boston Gazette* on the 20th, "will undoubtedly be purchased with all its finery and philosophical nonsense." The following day a measure empowering the Committee to contract for the library with the ratification of Congress, passed, and the Joint Library Committee of both Houses of Congress was accordingly authorized.

Needless to say, these discussions had not taken place in Congress without public comment. Jefferson, who had expended a great deal of money on theoretical agricultural business experiments to the point of pecuniary embarrassment, found his creditors enthusiastic in their support of the project. William Short of Philadelphia, to whom he owed $10,500, wrote to congratulate him after the sale had been effected. The Georgetown bookseller, Joseph Milligan, had been the first to express his hearty endorsement, writing Jefferson on September 24th that his "truly magnanimous" offer of the Monticello library to Congress would be very acceptable.

"If Congress should purchase it," Milligan continued, "to literary men it would be a great privilege to be permitted at all times of the year to have free access, not to take away the books, but to read in the Library and make extracts." It was in this letter that Milligan first suggested separation of the office of Librarian of Congress from that of Clerk of the House.

"Therefore the place of Librarian would be well to be a distinct office from the Clerk of the House of Representatives," he wrote. "If they do take it everything that I can do in arranging it shall be done, and I will keep the library for this session free of cost. By this I would have it clearly understood that it is not my wish to fish for it as a permanent thing, for I would not accept a place of profit under any government. . . ." Since Milligan had been collecting books for Jefferson for years, his offer was a logical one.

Quite as enthusiastic as Milligan over Jefferson's offer was the Commissioner of Patents, William Thornton, who had saved old Blodgett's from destruction. Early in December he addressed a letter to the former President:

> What dreadful scenes we have witnessed here! But all may be repaired, and in some respects we shall be benefited, for if the buildings should be repaired we shall never hear any more of the removal of Congress; and I have congratulated the members on the loss of their library since you have offered yours on such generous terms. I advised them to offer you $50,000 at once, for I had seen the books and knew them to be very valuable; that they ought not to value them as books in a common library, for, besides the learning and ability it would require to select the books, they were not to be obtained but at very great trouble, great expense, great risk, and many of them not to be had at all, but I fear they will not give half the value.

It was evaluation of the library that aroused the greatest discussion, the next duty of the Library Committee being, of course, to ascertain the value of the collection they had been empowered to purchase.

Smith wrote to Jefferson on October 21st:

> I was this day invited by the Library Committee to a conference with them. They represented that in consequence of the amendment to their report it became necessary to ascertain the value of the library and to obtain an authority from the two houses to pay it, to enable them to do

which they enquired of me, whether I could specify what would be received for it. I replied that I was unable to state its value, and that I was certain that it would be much more agreeable to you that this should be done either by the committee themselves or by disinterested persons; that I was persuaded that you feel some delicacy, if not repugnance, to setting a value on your own property, and that you might, in forming the estimate, from obvious motives, be driven to the alternative of either depreciating its value, or of laying yourself open to the imputation of extravagance. I, therefore, proposed another course: that the library should be estimated by some one sent for that purpose, or, which I consider most advisable, that it should be brought to this place without delay, valued by the committee, or by persons named by the committee, or by the committee and myself; that this valuation should be submitted to the committee; and if agreed to by them, that a correspondent report and contract should be made to Congress, of whose approbation I did not entertain a doubt; that should, however, a different result ensue, I would take the responsibility on myself.

To this the committee answered that they did not consider themselves authorized to take the proposed steps, and having agreed to receive the library, even provisionally, Congress might be considered as committed in regard to the definitive agreement.

They added that in ascertaining its value they did not wish any estimate *as made by you*, to be submitted to them, that the information I might obtain would be entirely private and confidential, and that *any proposition* that a certain sum would be received for it, which sum they did not mean should be computed with close precision, would be accepted as the basis of a contract.

Our conversation conclusively exhibited their purpose not to proceed without a proposition analogous to that desired. Upon the whole, although not insensible to the delicacy of the step, I would recommend that you authorize me to state that a sum not exceeding a specified amount will be received, and that to guard against any unjust imputation, such sum within that amount will be taken as shall be the result of a valuation to be made after the library is on the spot.

To aid him in complying with Smith's request Jefferson turned to the bookseller, Joseph Milligan, writing him on October 29th:

The Library Committee requires a proposition on my part as to the price of my library, and as a ground of negotiation in making such a proposition I could take no ground but from the number of volumes, their sizes and average value. But having sent them my catalogue, I have no means of coming at the numbers, for the conjecture I had formerly made was on counting a few pages only, taking an average of them, and multiplying the number of pages. In this way I guessed the whole number to be about 9,000. But I ventured to say in a letter to Mr. Smith that I thought you would be so good as to take the trouble of actually counting the numbers of every page of the catalogue, distinguishing separately the folios, quartos, octavos, and duodecimos, so as to inform him how many there are of each format, which would enable him to set a value on the whole, and to propose it to the Committee. And this favor I have still to solicit from you, further, that you will be so good as to call on him and to inform him as to the character of the bindings generally, and state of preservation in which you saw them here. I have tried a rough method of coming at their numbers, by taking the running measure of each format as they stand on their shelves, and counting a few shelves for an average. Then estimating these conjectural numbers at what I thought a moderate price, the average price of the whole volume came out almost exactly what you had conjectured when here, to wit, three dollars a volume. I imagine Mr. Smith will adopt some such method of estimate by the sizes and numbers you will be so good as to furnish him. This mode of guessing at the number of volumes made it less than the former estimate. When this proposition of a sum shall have been made, I have asked the favor of the return of the catalogue, and as soon as I can correct that by an actual review of the library, which will be the work of a week or ten days, I will begin to send you sheets of the catalogue for printing.

About a fortnight later, on November 16th, Milligan answered Jefferson with the report that he had run through the catalogue and had found that the number of the volumes, "if we include *The Edinburgh Review*," would come to "say 6,500, which agreeable to the rule which I have laid down, viz:—for a folio ten dollars, for a quarto six dollars, for an octavo three dollars, for a duodecimo one dollar,—will amount to a trifle over $24,000. . . ."

Mr. Milligan's estimates were duly forwarded to Mr. Smith, and by him presented to the Library Committee. A report, based upon the estimate of Milligan and the consideration of the Committee, was subsequently rendered to the Senate by Mr. Goldsborough, in which the Committee stated that precise terms of sale had been received from Samuel Harrison Smith as agent for Thomas Jefferson. These terms set the number of volumes at 6,487 and the estimated price at $23,950. The report stated that to these terms the Committee had conditionally acceded and had contracted with Smith for the purchase of the library according to the catalogue and number of volumes stated, subject to the ratification of Congress. They thereupon presented the bill authorizing "the purchase of the library of Thomas Jefferson, late President of the United States."

This bill passed the Senate on the 3rd of December, without amendment, and the House was informed the same day of its passage and asked to concur. Two days later, after a second reading, it was committed to a Committee of the Whole and there it rested while more than a month went by. Attempts were subsequently made to postpone consideration, to route it to committees, and to amend it, but, according to the *Intelligencer*, the debate which accompanied these motions—and it lasted to the hour of adjournment—was not of a caliber to influence the judgment of those who listened. The arguments of Cyrus King, referred to by the *Intelligencer* as "a sincere and not uninformed gentleman" were quoted as an example of the eloquence of the opposition:

"It might be inferred," said Mr. King, "from the character of the man who collected it, and France, where the collection was made, that the library contained irreligious and immoral books, works of the French philosophers, who caused and influenced the volcano of the French Revolution which had desolated Europe and extended to this country." He was opposed to a general dissemination of this infidel philosophy, and of the principles of a man [Jefferson] "who had inflicted greater injury on our country than any other, except Madison. The bill would put $23,900 into Jefferson's pocket for about 6,000 books, good, bad and indifferent, old, new, and worthless, in languages which many can not read, and most ought not; which is true Jeffersonian-Madisonian philosophy, to bankrupt the Treasury, beggar the people, and disgrace the nation." Others, continued the *Intelligencer,* among whom were a number of the political and personal friends of Mr. Jefferson, opposed the bill on the ground of the scarcity of money, and the necessity of appropriating it to purposes more indispensable than the purchase of a library; the probable insecurity of such a library placed here; the high price to be given for this collection, its miscellaneous and almost exclusively literary (instead of legal and historical) character, etc. To those arguments, enforced with zeal and vehemence, stated the *Intelligencer,* the friends of the bill replied with "fact, wit and argument" to show that the purchase, to be made on terms of long credit, could not affect the present resources of the United States, that the price was moderate, the library more valuable from the scarcity of many of its books, and altogether a most admirable substratum for a national library.

Gales, the editor of the *Intelligencer,* was taken to task, however, for this piece of reporting by the Washington correspondent of the *New York Evening Post,* who had interpreted the debates otherwise. On January 31st he wrote to the *Post:*

> Should Mr. Gales ever comply with his promise and give a faithful report of the debate upon the bill to purchase Mr. Jefferson's library, we venture to say, it will make but one impression upon the honest por-

tion of his readers. In the place of a fair report of the debate, Gales contents himself with saying, that "the arguments enforced with zeal and vehemence" against the bill, were answered "with fact, wit and argument" by Messrs. Wright, Rhea, Fish, and Hulbert. The latter gentleman was undoubtedly plausible, and reasoned with ingenuity, but where to find the wit, or what are the facts alluded to, we know not, although we were present and heard all that was said. It is true, as Mr. Gales says . . . that the price was moderate, that the library was valuable from the scarcity of the books, and that it could not injure materially the national resources, because it was to be paid for in Treasury bills, the depreciation of which was alluded to as a proof of the soundness of the bargain. This was the amount of the wit, facts, and arguments on the part of the friends of the bill. . . .

The debate was closed with a short, but as eloquent an appeal to the justice, public spirit and patriotism of the house, as we recollect ever to have heard. But the bill passed by a majority of ten votes, and the Pensioner Jefferson wrung from our beggared exchequer its very sweepings.

The report was true that the bill had passed, with 81 for passage and 71 against it; and the act "to authorize the purchase of the library of Thomas Jefferson, late President of the United States" was finally approved on January 30, 1815.

A storm of discussion regarding the value of the collection broke following enactment of this law, and there were many who came forward to point out that the books had been bought at a great bargain. On November 8, 1815, there appeared this comment in the *Essex Register* of Salem, in answer to Republican charges of extravagance:

A writer in the *Richmond Daily Compiler* has attempted to remove the objections to the purchase of Mr. Jefferson's library, upon the consideration of interest.

It is not believed that any objections have been made from pure conviction of error in the purchase, but many will be silent if they know the country has made a good bargain. This writer adduces the London prices, and the prices paid by Congress, and having specified each, that any man might satisfy himself, discovers at the foot of the account that in thirty-seven volumes the Sterling cost would amount to upwards of $1,500, when Congress did not pay $300, gives the country, in these volumes only, the advantage of upwards of $1,200. Surely no man will pronounce that a Government which could purchase at such a rate ought to refuse the purchase.

Two days later a correspondent of the *Intelligencer* replied:

In your paper of yesterday I discovered an attempt to calculate the value of the United States library. I believe no one can form any adequate estimate of this purchase. The library is such as to render all valuation absurd and impossible, if valuation were admitted into literature. It is such a library as cannot be bought in the ordinary mode in which books are purchased, because many of the books that are inestimable are wholly out of print, and many in manuscript that, of course, could not be procured. I have had an opportunity, from the privilege of frequent examination, imperfectly to discover that it is unique—a library which, for its selection, rarity, and intrinsic value, is beyond all price. For the satisfaction of calculators, however, I will barely mention the value marked in English catalogues, of a few books which this library contains:—De Bry's *Collection of Voyages*, 3 volumes £400 sterling, Purchas' *Pilgrims*, 1 volume, £56 sterling, Smith's *History of Virginia*, 1 volume folio, £43 sterling, etc., while the Government paid but $3 per volume. It contains Buffon's *Birds*, 10 volumes, quarto, 5 volumes of colored plates; Catesby's *Natural History of Carolina*, 2 volumes, folio; King James's works; Chaucer's Poems, in black letter; all the Greek and Latin classics extant; Martyr's *History of the West Indies;* the best authors in the French, Spanish and English languages, with a variety of other works it would be difficult to enumerate.

The library subsequently proved to be invaluable for the material illustrative of American history which it contained, and which had been gathered by Jefferson in Europe under conditions which would never present themselves again. The collections made later in America of speeches, books and pamphlets relating to the history of the Revolution, showing the arguments used to bring on the contest, the reasoning which kept alive the revolutionary spirit and induced the people to accept a new form of government and secure their newly-won liberty, were unique and irreplaceable. The books relating to foreign affairs and institutions were of that enhanced value that came of having been personally selected by a statesman of the stature of Jefferson. The deficiencies of the library lay in the mathematical and physical branches, for which Jefferson had had no time, for the past forty years; in the historical and political literature of the preceding ten years; and in the scattered volumes that represented gifts to the ex-President of no particular value.

These deficiencies were minor indeed. Actually the library of Thomas Jefferson was to prove the chief source of information, knowledge, and inspiration for American statesmen down through the years and to serve as the nucleus of collections that were one day to rival and later surpass any in the world. Moreover, proffered as it was at a time when the old library had been practically wiped out of existence, it proved to be the life-stream that restored energy and enterprise to the expiring institution of the Library of Congress. There now remained only the problem of getting it to Washington, where as yet no librarian had been appointed nor any room fitted up to receive it. To correct the first situation, President Madison, on the 21st of March, 1815, appointed George Watterston Librarian of Congress; to correct the second, Watterston, on the 25th of the same month, sent a letter to the President.

VII

A TREASURE IS TRANSPORTED

"*I* have had the happiness to receive the commission of Librarian with which you were so good as to honor me," Watterston wrote Madison. "I accept it with pleasure and tender you my thanks for the favor conferred. Unwilling to intrude upon your moments of leisure and relaxation, I nevertheless deem it my duty to apprize you that, according to an act of last session, you are directed to cause an apartment to be immediately selected and prepared for a library room, etc. In the third story of the present Capitol, a room sufficiently commodious and convenient might, at a small expense, be prepared, and this could immediately be done, by authorizing the Commissioner of the Public Buildings, or the superintendent of the city to have it prepared without delay."

Steps were being taken, meanwhile, for moving the library to Washington. Two weeks after passage of the act authorizing purchase of the Jefferson collection, Samuel Smith received a charming note from the Library Committee in which Mr. Goldsborough of the Senate presented his compliments and begged the favor of seeing him the next day at eleven o'clock in the morning. The purpose of this meeting was to conclude the negotiations for Mr. Jefferson's library.

Jefferson, meanwhile, not having heard from his friend since late October, had written asking to be informed how things stood and requesting return of his catalogue.

After Smith had conferred with the Committee he hastened to write to Jefferson, acquainting him with the fact of the purchase and asking how the Treasury notes in payment should be filled in. He also told him that the Committee would arrange legally for transportation of the library. Jefferson's answer to this letter came promptly. On the 27th of February he wrote from Monticello:

> With respect to the Treasury notes they, of course, should not be made until the library is delivered, or ready to be delivered. When this takes place, I will take the liberty of specifying my wishes as to the notes. As soon as I receive the catalogue, I will set about revising and arranging the books. This can be done only by myself, and admits of no help; in doing it I must be constantly on my legs, and I must ask indulgence, therefore, to proceed only as my strength will admit. I count on its taking me many days, perhaps a fortnight. As soon as all are in their places and numbered, I will give you notice. I am now calling in all which have been lent out as far as noted but there will doubtless be many irrecoverably lost. As these must be struck off the catalogue, and deductions accordingly made from the amount of compensation, it would be not only very desirable to me, but entirely proper to have some agent of the committee here to see what are delivered, and adjust the deductions, as well as superintend the packing, and perhaps the transportation. It would be a great pity to have the finer bindings destroyed for want of this small additional expense. Mr. Milligan in a former letter to me expressed his willingness to come and see to the packing and whatever else might be necessary, and no one could be more competent to the whole business. However, he, or any other person whom the committee shall appoint, will be acceptable to me. I send you on the next leaf some notes which may be useful toward arranging the transportation. The compensation embracing the whole of the catalogue, I shall not retain a single one, the only modification to be made being a deduction from the compensation in proportion to the size and number of the books which on the review shall appear to have been lost.

On the next leaf, with all the care and devotion of a mother sending her children on a journey alone, Thomas Jefferson jotted down instructions for transport of his books. He described minutely the size and shape of the pine cases in which they stood and computed the weight of the volumes, "676 cubic feet at 40 pounds makes 27,046 pounds, or eleven waggon loads of 2,458 pounds each," he wrote.

He suggested that wagons of the neighborhood, rather than those of Washington, be hired since the Washington rate of hire was eight dollars a day and that in his neighborhood half the price.

He drew attention to the fact that bookbinders' paper parings would have to be placed in the interstices between the books and shelves, that elegant bindings would require wrapping in waste paper, with slips of paper between them, and asked if a load of this packing material might not come on from Washington in a wagon which could take back a return load of the books. And the books "should go in their cases, every one in its station, so that the cases on their arrival need only be set up on end, and they will be arranged exactly as they stand in the catalogue."

He pointed out the best road, by far, for wagons at that season of the year. It was from Monticello by Orange Court House, Culpepper Court House, Fauquier Court House, Emil's Mill, Sorgater Lanes, and Georgetown Ferry, "because it is along crossroads nearly the whole way, which are very little traveled by waggons." The road by Fredericksburg was "considerably farther, and deeply cut through the whole. That by Stephensburg is the shortest and levelest of all, but being generally a deep living clay is absolutely unpassable from November to May. The worst circumstance of the road by the Court Houses is that two branches of the Rappahannock and three of the Occoquam are to be forded, and they are liable to sudden swells."

A wagon, he presumed, would "go loaded in seven days, and return empty in six; and, allowing one for loading and accidents, the trip will be of a fortnight and come to $56." He would engage the wagons himself, if it were desired, "to attend on any day which may be named."

A week before Jefferson drew up these suggestions, the Library Committee of the Senate had taken the first steps to provide quarters for the collection. In their report the Committee stated that they had lodged an order with the Secretary of the Treasury "in favor of Thomas Jefferson, Esquire, late President of the United States, for the sum of $23,950 in Treasury notes, as the purchase money for his library, for the use of Congress." They then drew attention of Congress to the fact that their authority did not extend beyond the expenditure of the annual fund of one thousand dollars and "such balances as may have remained on hand for the purpose of making additions to the library," and they therefore submitted to Congress "the propriety of providing a library room, and for transporting the library lately purchased, to the City of Washington."

Three days later a bill authorizing the President of the Senate and Speaker of the House to select a proper apartment for a library room and provide for transportation of the library, was passed in the Senate, and the House so informed. On March 3rd the bill passed the House. It authorized the President of the United States to "cause a proper apartment to be immediately selected and prepared for a library room, and to cause the library, lately purchased from Thomas Jefferson, to be placed therein during the ensuing recess of Congress."

It was this act to which Watterston had called the attention of President Madison in his letter of March 25th. Responding to the Librarian's suggestion, the President authorized that the top floor of Blodgett's old hotel wherein Congress was meeting be fitted up to receive the books.

Including the cost of finishing the staircase which led to the third floor and completing the passageway, and for fitting up and furnishing the library room itself, the sum of $1,520 was expended to house the Library of Congress.

Although Watterston, in his new capacity as Librarian, had suggested in his letter to the President that the books be transported by the safer and less expensive water route, in a previous conference with Smith, President Madison had agreed to the overland journey, although he had suggested to Jefferson's agent that the transfer be postponed until some time in May. Writing to Jefferson of the result of this interview Smith stated that it was "contemplated to employ Joseph Dougherty" to superintend the transfer. Dougherty had served as Jefferson's coachman at the White House and Jefferson had already been in touch with him.

By the 18th of April the books were all ready for delivery. In Washington, George Watterston eagerly awaited their coming. He was now concerned with their proper classification and arrangement. On April 26th he determined to seek the advice of Jefferson and sent off the following letter to Monticello:

You will excuse the liberty I take, as a stranger, in trespassing on your attention. The President has been pleased to appoint me Librarian to Congress, and consequently superintendent of the books now in your possession. I am solicitous to obtain your opinion as a gentleman of literary taste on the subject of arrangement. Your long acquaintance with books and your literary habits have, doubtless, led you to the adoption of some plan of arrangement with respect to libraries, which I should be happy if you would communicate. If you think the plan you have followed in the arrangement of the present library be the most judicious, you would oblige me by having the books packed up in boxes according to that arrangement. I have long thought the arrangement of the old Library was incorrect and injudicious, and must therefore be avoided in the present, which is considerably larger and, I presume, much more select and valuable.

You would oblige me by advising me when you think the books will reach this place. I am preparing a room for their reception, which I think will be completed in the course of a month. You will not neglect to forward a catalogue if you have a spare copy, as I wish to have it printed as early as possible. I fear the room selected is not quite large enough to contain the books. If so, I will have some artificial stands erected to receive them.

Jefferson answered the Librarian of Congress under the date of May 7th. Since this letter established the forty-four chapters or classes subsequently used by the Library of Congress until the end of the century, it is interesting and important:

I have duly received your favor of April 26th in which you are pleased to ask my opinion on the subject of the arrangement of libraries. I shall communicate with pleasure what occurs to me on it. Two methods offer themselves, the one alphabetical, the other according to the subject of the book. The former is very unsatisfactory because of the medley it presents to the mind, the difficulty sometimes of recalling an author's name, and the greater difficulty where the name is not given, of selecting the word in the title which shall determine its alphabetical place. The arrangement according to subject is far preferable, although sometimes presenting difficulty also, for it is often doubtful to what particular subject a book should be ascribed. This is remarkably the case with books of travels, which often blend together the geography, natural history, civil history, agriculture, manufactures, commerce, arts, occupations, manners, etc., of a country, so as to render it difficult to say to which they chiefly relate. Others again, are polygraphical in their nature, as encyclopedias, magazines, etc. Yet on the whole I have preferred arrangement according to subject, because of the peculiar satisfaction, when we wish to consider a particular one, of seeing at a glance the books which have been written on it, and selecting those from which we effect most readily the information we seek. On this principle the arrangement of my library was formed, and I took the basis of its distribution from Lord Bacon's table of science, modifying it to the changes in scientific pursuits which have taken place since his

time, and to the greater or less extent of reading in the science which
I proposed to myself. Thus the law having been my profession, and
politics the occupation to which the circumstances of the times in which
I have lived called my particular attention, my provision of books in
these lines, and in those most nearly connected with them was more
copious and required in particular instances subdivisions into sections and
paragraphs, while other subjects of which general views only were contemplated are thrown into masses. A physician or theologist would have
modified differently, the chapters, sections, and paragraphs of a library
adapted to their particular pursuits.

You will receive my library arranged very perfectly in the order observed in the catalogue, which I have sent with it. In placing the books
on their shelves I have generally, but not always, collocated distinctly
the folios, quarto, octavo, and duodecimo, placing with the last all
smaller sizes. On every book is a label, indicating the chapter of the
catalogue to which it belongs, and the order it holds among those of
the same format. So that, although the numbers seem confused on the
catalogue, they are consecutive on the volumes as they stand on their
shelves, and indicate at once the place they occupy there. Mr. Milligan
in packing them has preserved their arrangement so exactly in their respective presses, that on setting the presses upon end he will be able
readily to replace them in the order corresponding with the catalogue
and thus save you the immense labor which their arrangement would
otherwise require.

To give to my catalogue the convenience of the alphabetical arrangement, I have made at the end an alphabet of authors' names and have
noted the chapter or chapters in which the name will be found; where
it occurs several times in the same chapter, it is indicated by one or more
perpendicular scores, thus 1111, according to the number of times it
will be found in the chapter. Where a book bears no author's name, I
have selected in its title some leading word for denoting it alphabetically.
This member of the catalogue would be more perfect if, instead of the
score, the number on the book were particularly noted. This could not
be done when I made the catalogue because no label of numbers had
been put on the books. That alteration can now be readily made, and
would add greatly to the convenient use of the catalogue.

When the catalogue of 1815 of the Library of Congress was published, under Watterston's direction, forty-four main classes were set down under the chapter headings, with several sub-classes based on these suggestions of Jefferson.

Although Jefferson's library was in Washington a week after it left Monticello, it was not until mid-July that complete unpacking was accomplished—a fact that caused Milligan to delay until July 31st in answering the anxious inquiry of Thomas Jefferson addressed to him the 26th of June. Jefferson, hearing no word of the arrival of the books, wrote on that date wishing to know if they had arrived safely and if they had as yet been unpacked and replaced on the shelves.

As a matter of fact the wagons had rumbled regularly down the ruts and furrows of Pennsylvania Avenue until the last packing box had been placed in the passage of the general post office under the roof of old Blodgett's, now dignified by the name of Congress Hall. Milligan informed Thomas Jefferson that the books had arrived without receiving the slightest injury by transportation and assured the ex-President—no doubt even now lonely for his beloved books—that the room which had been appropriated to receive them was sufficiently large. For three years the Library of Congress was to remain in this crowded, almost inaccessible, room, legislators making their way painfully the long mile from Capitol Hill and climbing three flights of stairs to consult Thomas Jefferson's literary treasures, their own law books and journals under an attic roof. For when the first session of the Fourteenth Congress was called to order on December 4, 1815, Members met no longer in Blodgett's but under the high-pitched roof of the three-story building which now rose, thanks to private enterprise, where Tunnicliff Tavern had once dispensed hospitality and flowers had flourished in the First Street gardens.

Above the wide-arched First Street entrance a large window lighted the new Congressional halls. The Senate Chamber, forty-five feet long and fifteen feet wide, was on the first floor; the House Chamber, seventy-five by forty-five feet with a gallery, was on the second. Built of brick, the structure had cost $25,000, not including $5,000 for special fittings for use of Congress, and the annual rent of $1,650 had been fixed on a basis of six percent on the cost of the building, with an allowance for insurance. Here Congress was to meet until 1819, but no provision had been made on the site to accommodate the Congressional Library, so that neither Watterston nor the books from Monticello went with the legislators under that wide-arched door. The Library of Congress was to remain in the stuffy hotel on F Street until such time as its own room in the National Capitol, already being restored on its old foundations, was made ready to receive it.

This is not to say that no effort had been made to bring their library nearer the legislators. Watterston himself had first brought the question of removal to the attention of President Madison. At about the time that Congress was preparing to move out of Blodgett's and into its new quarters on First Street, what to do with the Library of Congress became an acute question. Should it remain in the old hotel? Should it be removed to quarters in the temporary Capitol on the Hill; should it find shelter in some neighboring house, or should its collections be transferred to the new Capitol, even then being rebuilt?

The Librarian of Congress seemed to be of the opinion that since no existing law provided for another removal it must remain for the present where it was. Madison notified Watterston that he had "referred the case to the members of the Executive."

On December 4, 1814, a new Library Committee was appointed, of which Senators Eligius Fromentin of Louisiana, William Hunter of Rhode Island, Robert H. Goldsborough of Maryland, and Representatives John W. Taylor of New York, Joseph Hopkinson of Pennsylvania, and Henry St. George Tucker of Virginia, were members. More than a year after their appointment they reported on January 26th the results of a survey they had made, to the Senate.

They had investigated, they said, the possibilities of removing the Library of Congress from the old building on F Street to the temporary Capitol on First Street, but did not consider the First Street building a safe enough place for deposit for the Library.

Nor did the room suggested for this purpose seem to them adequate or secure. Their efforts to find a suitable house in the neighborhood of the temporary Capitol for the accommodation of the Library had likewise proved unavailing. The only house which might have served this purpose could not be rented for less than a thousand dollars a year. Taking into consideration not only the expense of the rent, the Committee reported, "but the expense of fitting out, for temporary purposes only, the necessary rooms for the Library; the expenses attending the temporary removal; the portion of the session already elapsed; the length of time which would be consumed in the removal, during which, instead of a rather difficult access, as under present circumstances, no access at all could be had to the Library; considering further that nothing is more injurious to books than these frequent removals; and considering likewise, that the Library is perfectly safe where it is now, and that within a few weeks, at a period probably not much more distant than the period at which the Library could again be opened, if it should now be attempted to be removed on Capitol Hill, the greatest inconveniences now arising from the distance at which the Library is placed, will disappear with the season of the year which had created them,

your Committee are of the opinion that the Library ought not
to be moved this winter, and that their attention should be wholly
directed in securing a permanent place in the Capitol for receiving the Library; which place ought to be ready before the next
session of Congress, and with that view they have inserted a
section which, to them, appears calculated to obtain the object,
in the bill which accompanies this report."

When the bill mentioned came up before the Committee of
the Whole on February 2nd, however, Senator Roberts of Pennsylvania struck out, together with other sections, the provision
for a Library room in the Capitol.

It was Senator Eligius Fromentin, from the Joint Library
Committee, who made what was perhaps the first suggestion for
a separate building for the Library of Congress. While the resolutions he reported on February 18, 1817, providing for a Library of Congress building on Delaware Avenue, were voted
against four days later, the Louisiana Senator had by its introduction set in circulation an idea which was to gain more and
more adherents as time went on and lead eventually to the tenacious and devoted campaign of Ainsworth Rand Spofford for a
suitable permanent home for the nation's books.

The Librarian of Congress himself in a communication signed
"W," published in the *Intelligencer* on March 25th, expressed
his regret at the negative decision of Congress:

> It is extremely to be regretted that the proposition to erect a building
> for the reception of the Library of the United States, presented last ses-
> sion, had not succeeded. A literary establishment of so much importance
> and benefit ought to be accommodated in a style proportionate to its
> dignity and utility—in all other countries, this is an object of national
> pride, and edifices are erected for the accommodation of national libra-
> ries, not only advisable for their convenience, but distinguished for the
> taste, beauty and excellence of their architecture. In the United States,

where reading is so general, one would suppose that the lamentable rage for economy, which now seems to have gained such an ascendency, would not at least extend to their depositories of literature, and that a building would be erected for their library equal in grandeur to the wealth, the taste, and the science of the nation. It is to be apprehended, that if a building be not erected for that purpose, the Library will remain stationary for many years, isolated and inconvenient from its position, for there appears to be no apartment in either wing of the Capitol, though they cover an acre of ground, calculated for its reception, and to wait until the main body be completed, would, to judge from the present economical mania, be rendering the Library almost useless for a long time.

Editorials began to appear approving the idea of a separate Library building, and the possibilities of the eventual realization of the dream were freely discussed on and off Capitol Hill. A new terminology began, too, to creep into the public press; the collections under the roof of Blodgett's Hotel were beginning to be referred to as the *Library of the United States*. Unmistakably the vision of a great national library held by Thomas Jefferson was held now by many others. His own private library had been transformed into a public library for the legislators; and in like manner was the Library of Congress beginning to assume the importance of a national institution.

The idea had first been suggested on the title page of the 1815 catalogue. It appealed especially to the editors of the country as a possibility at the time of acquisition of the Jefferson collection. Said the *National Intelligencer* on July 31, 1815:

This valuable collection of books has, with some difficulty and labor, been at length displayed and arranged in the house now occupied by Congress. From the slight examination we have been enabled to make of this library we are glad to find the selection judicious and the collection rare and valuable.

In all the civilized nations of Europe there are national libraries, the selection and increase of which occupy much of governmental attention. In a country of such general intelligence as this, so laudable an example should by all means be instituted, and the Congressional or National Library of the United States become the great repository of the literature of the world—the medium of information and the source of improvement and gratification to all whom inclination may prompt or whom curiosity may lead to literature. We are happy to say that this is the foundation of such an establishment and that by the fostering patronage of government it may, in a few years, be made the equal to the most extensive and splendid libraries of Europe, the sneers of the British editors to the contrary notwithstanding. . . .

As the foundation of a great national library this is an excellent collection, but it is little more than a foundation. Many works will yet be necessary to complete it and render it worthy of so enlightened a nation. . . .

With a view to rendering this important establishment more valuable the propriety is suggested of increasing the annual appropriation for the purchase of books from one to two thousand dollars. It gives us pleasure to say that the Librarian attends every day, which will render an examination of this fine collection of books easy to the curious and the literati.

Two years later Walsh's *American Register* made the following reference to the collection:

A better nursery or substratum for a great National Library could not be found, and it will surely be admitted that nothing less is to come within the aim of Congress, both on the score of pride and patriotism. If it could be done by no other agency, it was a sort of duty with this body to transfer the literary treasures of Mr. Jefferson to a spot where they would be easily accessible to them and the nation; and stand out as a monument of the national taste and discrimination.

There is absolute obligation on the part of the Federal Government, to provide in the Federal metropolis, in the shape of a library, a great reservoir of instruction in all the departments of human knowledge for the use of the public as well as of its own members, and the library certainly may be so administered as to be open to the one without at all interfering with the studies or researches of the other. In fact, the idea of an establishment of the kind set apart, and peculiar in the character of its materials, for the use of Congress, could only spring from great poverty of invention as to the discipline of such establishments, or of a very imperfect view of the qualifications of an accomplished legislator and statesman. It is not for Congress to presume that there is any branch of human science for which a body so universal in its composition will not hereafter furnish, in some or others of its members, a cultivated or active taste; or that there is any branch which may not fall within its immense scope of constitutional action, so as to make the possession of all the best means of judgment, that is the best treatises on it, highly desirable if not indispensable.

It was easy to see why, when Congress exhibited in the face of public opinion so great an apathy toward the unsuitable environment in which the Library of Congress was operating, the *Washington Gazette* should hail the appointment of a new Library Committee at the opening of the first session of the Fifteenth Congress with sanguine expectation. On December 8, 1817, there appeared this comment in its pages:

> We are disposed to indulge a hope that this committee will be more active than the former, and that as literary men they will not neglect the interests of this establishment. To coop the Library of the United States in a garret almost a mile from the Capitol is degrading both to literature and the nation, and we trust that Congress will see the necessity of erecting a building for its accommodation, nearer the Capitol.

The new Committee was composed of Senators Dickerson, King and Tait, and Representatives Seybert, Whitman, and Middleton. Before any of them could act upon the necessity for removing the Library, Senator Burrill, on the last day of December, submitted a resolution that the Committee on the District of Columbia be instructed "to inquire whether suitable apartments can be had in the Capitol for the reception and accommodation of the Library of Congress, and in case such apartments cannot be had there to inquire into the expediency of commenc-

121

ing the erection of the center building of the Capitol and of making provision for the speedy completion thereof. That said committee be also instructed to inquire whether suitable apartments can be had in the Capitol [when completed] for accommodation of the Library of Congress, and in case such apartments cannot be had there to inquire into the expediency of purchasing or erecting a convenient building for the Library." This resolution was adopted on the 2nd of January, 1818, but it was not until the second session of the Fifteenth Congress that any further step was taken. On the 26th of November the bill introduced by Senator Dickerson two days previously, providing for removal of the Library of Congress to the north wing of the Capitol, was passed. The Act was approved December 3, 1818.

Up on the Hill the National Capitol was fast being restored to its former splendor. Benjamin Henry Latrobe, whom President Jefferson in 1803 had appointed surveyor of public buildings in Washington, had followed Thornton, Hadfield and Hoban as architect of the Capitol. At the time of the burning of the building Latrobe had been in Pittsburgh, engaged in construction of a steamboat for Robert Fulton. He had been immediately recalled to Washington to superintend the work of restoration. After a thorough examination, he had reported that the building could easily be restored, as its foundations and walls remained for the most part unimpaired. To Latrobe is due credit for the old hall of the House of Representatives—now Statuary Hall; the hall of the Supreme Court; the Law Library and the old lobbies. In 1817 Latrobe resigned, and was succeeded by Charles Bulfinch, who was charged with completion of the work according to Latrobe's designs.

When, in accordance with law, the Library of Congress was moved later in December, 1818, into the rooms on the west side of the north wing of the Capitol, it was really transferred from one attic to another, for the new quarters were on the same elevation as the upper gallery of the Senate Chamber, directly under the roof. Scarcely a year passed before they were found to be inadequate for the accommodation of the books, as a Senate report dated December 20, 1819, shows. On December 19, 1820, the Library Committee reported again on the cramped conditions. When they had caused the Library of Congress to be placed in the Capitol they had presumed that "all the duties required of them by the act were performed," they said. They had not thought themselves authorized to provide for the reception of "such books as have since been purchased, or may hereafter be purchased, for the library." They had intended to lay out the greater part of the funds on hand in the purchase of books during the late recess of Congress, but having learned from the Librarian that "no preparations were making, or expected to be made," before the meeting of Congress, for putting up additional shelves in the Library room and that heaps of books purchased during the previous year were still lying upon the tables, "it was not thought expedient to make any considerable purchase of books before the meeting of Congress."

But, crowded or not, the Library of Congress as set up in the Capitol was fast becoming a social and literary center in Washington. Watterston's scholarly attainments and suavity of manner equipped him notably to preside over a combined political, literary and fashionable salon. His nature must have taken delight in the discussions that waxed and waned in the suite of rooms under the Capitol roof. Here legislators gathered between calls to the floor or met by appointment the belles of the day. Here stately gentlemen sat reading beside cheerful fires or launched upon learned discussions as to the comparative poetical merits of Pope, Scott, Southey, Byron and Moore.

Watterston himself, in his faintly satirical worldliness, describes such a scene in his *L—— Family in Washington:*

> It was my misfortune to struggle into one of these [retreats] in endeavoring to find the Representatives' Hall; after groping about for some time, I came to a door, which I opened very unceremoniously, and found myself all at once in a region of learning, where, like the Alps, books on books arose. The room was filled with honorable members and their ladies, more intent, I thought, on gazing at pictures, than on feasting their reason; I confess I felt a little odd in being so suddenly soused, among such honorable company, but knowing that I contributed as much to the public library as anyone else, I thought it was best to stalk about as if it was my own, look big, and take no notice of anybody. Accordingly I planted myself on a settee alongside of a couple of Members of Congress who were engaged in some political discussion, and not wishing to remain mute, I very naturally threw in a word now and then myself, which made them stare confoundedly.
> . . . I walked into an adjoining apartment, for the library consists of a suite of rooms, where I met a man that I thought looked devilish sour at me: This was the librarian, but I passed on, determined not to regard anything or anybody, and to pick up a little diplomatic knowledge, if I could, among such a host of politicians. At the fire in this room I found two gentlemen in conversation, and took my seat by them . . . the merits of the modern British poets were the subject of conversation, and with these they seemed to be well acquainted. . . . My companions were interrupted by the information that a call of the House had been made, and they all hurried out of the room to attend to their Parliamentary duties. . . .

Randolph, who had played so important a part in the original organization of the Library of Congress, was a frequent visitor to the library rooms in these days. Watterston gives this somewhat acid portrait of the Virginia legislator at the time:

> Seeing a tall, meagre, saffron-complexioned man sitting by the fire reading, I took a chair near him and asked him some questions, which he did not seem disposed, I thought, to answer. There was something,

however, devilish cute about the meagre gentleman I was sitting by, that excited my curiosity not a little. His hair was nicely oiled and tied into a queue; his face was like that of a woman, but confoundedly wrinkled, wan and haggard; his eye was black and piercing as a hawk's; he wore a long surtout, yellow buckskin breeches, drab gaiters, and a pair of spurs; he was as straight as a maypole when he stood up, but his knees stuck together a little and spoiled his figure, yet at a short distance he appeared quite young and handsome. . . .

But the attraction of these quarters was as nothing compared to the dignity and elegance, the charm and popularity that were to distinguish the next quarters of the Library of Congress.

VIII

THE BEST LOUNGE IN WASHINGTON

*E*arly in his career as Librarian, Watterston had incurred criticism for what was termed the extravagant cost of the first catalogue of the Library of Congress issued under his hand. In preparation of this catalogue the Librarian had departed from the advice of Jefferson, and some thought with unhappy results. While he had retained Jefferson's chapter divisions, he had thrown the different subdivisions and paragraphs together—a device unsatisfactory to Jefferson and to the Library Committee alike. Jefferson objected to the arrangement on the ground that it was too unscientific and he disliked generally any modification in the system he had suggested. In thanking Watterston for three copies which had been sent him Jefferson courteously commended the "handsome typography, the execution generally pleasing to the eye" and minimized as unavoidable some errors of the press.

"You ask me how I like the arrangement of the chapters," he wrote. "Of course, you know not so well as my own; yet I think it possible the alphabetical arrangement may be more convenient to readers generally than mine, which was something analytical, something chronological, and sometimes a combination of both."

The Library Committee were more direct, and they criticized the catalogue for opposite reasons. It was too scientific, they contended, and Jefferson's system should have been further modified. They thought that such a catalogue might serve well enough the purposes of "a gentleman who, as was the case with the former proprietor of this now the Library of Congress, has classed his books himself, who alone has access to them, and has become from long habit and experience as perfectly familiar with every book in his library as a man who has long lived in a city is familiar with every street, square, lane and alley in it."

But this form was far less useful in the Library of Congress, which consisted chiefly of miscellanies, than a good plain catalogue in the old form. The main point seemed to be that the good plain old catalogue would have cost about a hundred dollars to produce, while the one with which Watterston had presented them—"including three copies of it bound half gilt"—was to cost the country $1,360. This bitter fact was summed up in the statement that this cost represented "one-third more than the annual appropriation made heretofore by Congress for the additional increase of the Library, and more than one-twentieth of the actual cost of our whole Library." In other quarters, however, the form of the catalogue was admired considerably and the same arrangement was observed in later publications. With a touch of sarcasm, Watterston mentioned the attitude of the Committee to Jefferson:

> The Library Committee are dissatisfied with me for having the catalogue printed without having waited to consult their *superior judgment;* but the members generally speak very highly of your arrangement and disposition of the books, and, I suppose, will have no hesitation in allowing for its printing, the report of the Committee to the contrary notwithstanding.

The classification and cataloguing of the newly acquired library had incurred a deficit which required the immediate attention of Congress. The Library Committee was instructed to look into the expediency of increasing the sum appropriated for the salary of the Librarian of Congress and for the contingent expenses of the Library; also of allowing additional compensation to the Librarian "for services performed since the last session of Congress." The deficit amounted to $2,365. Before payment was made, the Committee asked for authorization to investigate the "exorbitant nature of several of the items."

It was in this report that the Library Committee requested an appropriation of $10,000 to correct the lamentable deficiencies revealed by the catalogue in several branches of learning. These deficiencies were not to be wondered at, they said, when one considered "the inconsiderable sums put from time to time at the Committee's disposal, which precluded the possibility of their availing themselves of the many opportunities which, for twenty-five years past, were daily offering in Europe of purchasing large collections of very valuable books on reasonable terms." The Committee reminded Congress that such opportunities had not yet all gone by and that "the convulsions of the eastern might, in a literary view, be made conducive to the interests of the western world. . . . The present Library of Congress is a good foundation; and one half of the sum which it has cost, judiciously employed under the direction of the Joint Library Committee, would place within the reach of every Member of Congress all the most valuable books in every department of arts and sciences, of which there is now such a lamentable deficiency."

The Librarian of Congress at this time, it appears, was not in very good standing with the Committee. At any rate, the language in which they denied his request for additional compensation, was a trifle tart:

By the accounts of the expenditures exhibited, it appears that the mechanical part of the duties required by law to be performed by the Librarian, had been actually performed by people hired by the Librarian, and for whose compensation you are now called upon to make an appropriation. The manner in which the scientific part of the duties, devolving upon the Librarian, had been fulfilled, do not, in the opinion of your Committee, warrant the allowing of an additional compensation which your Committee suppose must be interpreted as conveying on the part of Congress, something like an approbation for past conduct. The only evidence of the literary services of the Librarian, within the knowledge of your Committee, is the publication of the catalogue with which we were presented at the time of the beginning of the session; and the merit of this work is altogether due to Mr. Jefferson, and not to the Library of Congress. . .

At this time George Watterston was receiving a salary of two dollars a day for every day's attendance at the Library. He was required by law to attend three days of every week during the Congressional recess and six days every week while Congress was in session. Up to the time of this report he had been paid $480 for his services—a sum which the Committee stated exceeded "the sum to which he would be entitled by law for his services to this day." They had no hesitancy, however, in recommending an increase in the Librarian's salary. In the bill which accompanied their report, and which was passed on February 8th, the salary of the Librarian of Congress was raised to $1,000 a year, payable quarterly.

It was on this occasion that the Committee complained of the sole power of the President with respect to the office of Librarian of Congress.

"It is difficult to conceive," they said, "why an officer of both Houses of Congress, as much so as the Clerk of the House of Representatives, and the Secretary of the Senate are officers of their respective Houses, should not be appointed by the authority to which he ought to be amenable. The case might happen that a Librarian should neglect his duties. Are the Members of Congress in that case to complain to the President of the United

States? Such a thing need merely be mentioned to demonstrate the impropriety of vesting the President with the sole right of making so inconsiderable an appointment." Yet, while they asked that the power of appointment be vested in future in the Joint Library Committee, this section was not made part of the final act.

When the act was finally approved, on April 16, 1816, in addition to those sections which provided for settlement of the Librarian's accounts and increase of his salary, there was included a provision which extended the privileges of the Library of Congress to the Attorney General of the United States and the members of the diplomatic corps "on the same terms and conditions as it is enjoyed by the Judges of the Supreme Court."

During his first months in office Watterston was, of course, primarily occupied with the proper arrangement of the Jefferson library. Yet early in his administration he gave his attention to possibilities for building up the collections. Dr. Thornton and his Patent Office were still occupying the same building with him, and it is logical to suppose that the extraordinary accumulations made possible under existing patent laws must, wittingly or unwittingly, have had their effect. He was probably influenced, too, by the prevailing system of English copyright laws which provided copies of copyrighted works for all the leading libraries of England. At any rate, when George Watterston inserted a "card" in the *National Intelligencer* on September 15, 1815, he took the initial step in a direction which was to lead to the establishment of an American copyright system that, more than any other single factor, was in time to build up the general collections of the Library of Congress to the extent and scope of a national library. The "card" read:

LIBRARY OF THE UNITED STATES

Congress having supplied the loss occasioned by the rude and conflagrating hand of our late enemy by the purchase of a library perhaps equal in value, as far as it extends, to any in Europe, and intending, as they no doubt do, to make it the great national repository of literature and science, and in some instances of the arts also, it is desirable that American authors, engravers, and painters who are solicitous to preserve their respective productions as mementos of the times, would transmit to the Library a copy of such work as they may design for the public eye. This will serve not only as a literary history of this now interesting country, but will also tend to exhibit the progress and improvement of the arts. The Librarian, so far as his power and means extend, will take due care that such productions, literary or graphic, as may be forwarded to him shall be properly preserved and advantageously exhibited.

GEORGE WATTERSTON,
Librarian of Congress

Six years later another step was to be taken, howbeit an unsuccessful one, for the resolution offered by Mr. Lincoln in the House of Representatives on the 30th of April, 1822, was ordered to lie on the table. Nevertheless, it crystallized and again drew attention to the legislative potentialities of Mr. Watterston's idea. It resolved:

That the President of the United States be requested to cause to be deposited in the Library of Congress the originals or copies of all such reports, memoirs, or documents not heretofore published, as have been made by public officers, Indian agents, private individuals, or exploring parties, to the executive departments of the Government, together with any maps, drawings, or charts, or copies of the same, which in his opinion it may be consistent with the public service to have there deposited.

Prior even to this, other important measures affecting the destiny of the Library of Congress had gone down to at least temporary defeat, for magnificent plans were laid in the years from 1815 to 1817. Plans for a copyright department, a law department, and, embracing all—the plan for a national library had, in these three years, been shaped and come to naught. The Committee's request for ten thousand dollars to be spent in correction of the deficiencies disclosed by Mr. Watterston's expensive catalogue, had been turned down. To Senator Harper's bill, introduced on February 16th, asking for an appropriation of $2,000 for a law library, the legislators had bent a partially deaf ear, it having passed the Senate on March 12th, and met indefinite postponement on April 29th in the House. Despite these setbacks, the Library Committee was active.

The Librarian of Congress, at this time and indeed for some time later, exercised no jurisdiction over the nature of the literary acquisitions. Responsibility for bibliographic direction rested solely upon members of the Joint Committee. Denied their $10,000, they had nevertheless been busy, for there yet remained to the credit of the Library of Congress between three and four thousand dollars which might be spent for books. In a letter from the Chairman, Eligius Fromentin, to the Register of the Treasury, Joseph Nourse, the Senator asked for enlightenment in financial matters connected with the Library. He wrote on April 11, 1816:

> The Library Committee having it in contemplation to authorize one or more of their members to purchase books for the use of the Library of Congress, during the recess, I am desirous to be informed whether it had formerly been the practice and whether you deem yourself authorized to pay any draft from the Chairman of the Committee within the amount of money in your hands for the use of the Library, during the recess of Congress.
>
> The Committee have bought books from Coale and Maxwell, booksellers in Baltimore, to the amount of $311.44. Would it be convenient to you to send those gentlemen a draft for the amount in Baltimore upon the authorization in this letter, or is there any particular form previously used, and to which you deem it more proper to adhere? In that case, please to give me the information, and send me a blank form for the regulation of my future conduct in that respect.
>
> The Committee suppose that the further sum of one thousand dollars

for the year 1816, in addition to the sum of sixteen hundred odd dollars which you informed them was in your hands in December last, is now in your hands at the disposal of the Committee.

In addition to the activity of these members in purchasing new books for the Library, they had given directions for certain periodicals to be sent regularly to the Library room in the Capitol. These included *The Edinburgh Review* and *The Quarterly Review*, republished in New York; *The British Review*, *The Annual Register*, *The Analytical Review*, and *Cobbett's Political Register*, published in Great Britain; *The North American Review*, published in Boston; *The Port Folio*, *The Analetic Magazine*, and *Walsh's American Register*, published in Philadelphia; *The Portico*, and *The Weekly Register*, published in Baltimore; and *The National Register*, *The Daily National Intelligencer*, and *The Historical Register*, published in Washington. They also suggested that at a later date there be added such publications as *The Transactions of the American Philosophical Society*, of the *Royal Society of London*, and of the *Irish Academy*; the *Bath Society Papers*, *Transactions of the Society of Arts*, *Mémoires de l'Institut de France*, *Delaplaine's Repository*, and *Cobbett's State Trials* and *Public Characters*.

Another indication of the bibliographic trend approved by the Committee at this time was their further suggestion that the Library of Congress acquire general catalogues published annually in Great Britain, Leipsic and Paris, and "works of merit to be subscribed for occasionally, and which will require a disposable fund to be used on the emergencies created by the publication of such works, either in this country or in Europe."

It was also the desire of the Committee at this time to extend the usefulness of the Library by increasing its collections of maps or books in those branches of human knowledge which might refer particularly to the business or interests of respective com-

133

mittees. Members were asked to furnish them with suggestions along these lines. A box was also placed in the Library rooms where Members might deposit suggestions for purchases.

The necessity for increasing the law collections was especially stressed. It was counted valuable and "as complete as it is possible to have expected it to be, considering the time at which the books were purchased." But publications which had appeared since its acquisition, both at home and abroad, and the fact that this branch was an indispensable necessity in legislative work, moved the Committee to request $3,000 "for the completion of that particular department of the Library of Congress." They also asked that the $1,000 annual appropriation for the purchase of books for the Library of Congress be continued, as the old law had expired. The Committee at the same time requested that the privileges of the Library be extended to heads of government departments. The Senate, on the 9th of January, passed the bill which increased the annual appropriation for books from $1,000 to $1,500—but on the following day the House, after referring it to the Committee of the Whole, promptly forgot it.

More significant was the second bill passed by the Senate on the 9th of January, which embodied George Watterston's "card" suggestion that the Library of Congress be made a place for the deposit of all American books, maps, and engravings. The bill read:

> That the Joint Library Committee be, and they are hereby authorized to make, from time to time, a selection of such books as they may deem proper to have deposited in the Congressional Library, out of the books which by the existing laws are to be deposited by the authors or publishers in the office of the Secretary of State, and are now lodged in the Patent Office.

But this bill, too, failed to become a law. The fact that the Committee had on hand an unexpended balance of $1,536 for the purchase of books had apparently blinded Congress to the really great importance of these two measures to the future development of the national library.

For ten years, from the day (December 1, 1817) when he had been appointed Chairman of the Library Committee, Senator Mahlon Dickerson of New Jersey made an outstanding contribution to the development of the Library of Congress. Famed for his love of books and literary taste, he was indefatigable in his efforts to build up the collections. The Librarian, in his *L—— Family in Washington* gave this description of him:

> That (tall gentleman) is Mr. D. of N. J., once governor of that State, a gentleman of considerable literary and scientific attainments, of amiable character and excellent disposition. He is unfortunately a batchelor, and descending rapidly into the vale of life. . . . Mr. D. spends a great deal of his time among his books, of which he has become so fond that he may be called a biblical cormorant; and which perhaps are, after all, the best company and the best friends a man can have in this world. Mr. D. is, however, a very diligent and useful member of the body to which he belongs, and the only objection I find in him is, that he is too much smitten with the *radical mania*, which, in my opinion, is a radical defect in the character of a statesman.

Additions made to the Library during Dickerson's chairmanship of the Committee were counted both "valuable and splendid."

The Librarian also paid tribute to the services rendered by Joel Poinsett while that gentleman was a member of the Library Committee:

"His taste and judgment in the selection of books, while acting for the Committee," said Watterston, "were displayed in a manner that pleased all who were concerned." Among other valuable works, Poinsett had secured for the Library of Congress, while in England, a set of the Parliamentary papers.

But appropriations secured by each succeeding committee continued to be small and the combined book knowledge of the members could avail little in the face of this discouraging financial obstacle. In the year that the Library of Congress was moved into the north-wing attic of the Capitol only $2,000 was appropriated to purchase books and the same amount was granted two years later, while $1,000 was voted for in 1821 and 1822, the 1821 appropriation was granted conditionally, and only if the books purchased should include the statutes and reports of the decisions of the courts of law and chancery of the different States, with the latest maps of the several States and Territories. In 1823 the Committee succeeded in securing an increase from $1,000 to $2,000 in the annual appropriation. Only one small publication was issued by the Library in the period from 1817 to 1824, its last year in the cramped Capitol quarters. This was the catalogue of 1820—a quarto of twenty-eight pages. One writer has suitably referred to the years between 1815 and 1824 as "the garret period" in the history of the Library of Congress. With its removal into the reconstructed central portion of the Capitol, however, the Library took a fresh lease on life and began to give evidence of the splendid destiny that lay ahead.

The new library suite, as designed by Charles Bulfinch, based on plans left by Latrobe, consisted of a main room and two reading rooms. With the assistance of three hired men, George Watterston, who had already moved the collections twice, commenced the transfer of the Library of Congress from the north wing to the beautiful and spacious apartment prepared for it in the center. This was on the 17th of August, 1824.

This room must have been a source of the greatest satisfaction to the Librarian of Congress, for as Julia Kennedy said of him, "He was not the vibrant spirit of the frontier but the fastidious one that thrives best in an atmosphere of cultural ease," and he responded best in an easy, settled world. This analyst points out that "had fate so placed him as it did his contemporary Washington Irving, perhaps he too might have become a charming stylist. Nothing would have been more congenial to Watterston's nature or, as he would have said, his sensibility, than a sojourn of several years in Europe absorbing its Old World culture. Nothing would have pleased him more than to have been able 'to loaf and to invite the picturesque.' For he possessed the disposition of the dilettante and a poet's heart."

This poet's heart must have gloried in the softly lighted alcoves, the gleaming, mellowed woods, the lofty columns and the subdued, colorful bindings of old books set row on row along the galleries of the Library's new quarters. The *National Intelligencer* of January 1, 1825, gave this description of the rooms:

The room for the permanent accommodation of the Library of Congress has been completed in a style of great beauty and elegance, which entitles it to particular commendation. It occupies nearly the whole west front of the center building, is 90 feet in length, 30 in width, and about 35 in height. It is divided into 12 arched alcoves, ornamented with fluted pilasters copied from the pillars in the celebrated Octagon Tower at Athens. At the entrance, in the center of the room, which is approached from the great central rotunda, are two columns of stone, with capitals corresponding with those of the pilasters; and immediately opposite, and fronting the window which leads into the western colonnade, stand two similar columns of stone. These pillars, with the alcoves, support two galleries, extending nearly the whole length of the room, from north to south, on both sides, and divided into the same number of shelved recesses as the lower apartment. From these recesses springs the arch which forms the ceiling, elegantly ornamented with rich stucco borders, panel, and wreaths of flowers. On the roof, which is about twelve feet above the ceiling, are three skylights, the wells of which are also beautifully decorated, with stucco ornaments; through these and the five windows on the west the light is admitted into the room, and can be lessened or increased at pleasure, by means

of Venetian blinds. The principal apartment, as well as the reading
room on the north, attached to it, is handsomely furnished with sofas,
mahogany tables, desks, Brussels carpeting, etc. At each corner of this
splendid apartment is a staircase leading to the galleries above, which
are calculated to contain several thousand volumes, and which are so
arranged .as to enable anyone to read or write in them with perfect
convenience. This room opens into a magnificent colonnade, or loggia,
formed by ten pillars of the Corinthian order, between which runs an
iron railing to protect as well as to ornament this fine promenade. The
Library room is admitted by all who see it to be, as a whole, the most
beautiful apartment in the building. Its decorations are remarkably
chaste and elegant, and the architecture of the whole displays a great
deal of taste.

The greatest attention had indeed been paid to detail, with
an eye to beauty. A luxurious carpet had been laid on the floor;
and the two stoves which heated the room had been built in the
form of pillars, to correspond with the architecture. Spermaceti
candles, on the two mantelpieces, the desk, and the tables,
glowed cheerfully after nightfall.

All contemporary accounts and correspondence of the day stress
the social atmosphere that prevailed in the Library of Congress
at this period. This was due in a large part, without doubt, to
the tastes and inclinations of Mr. Watterston himself. *Harper's*
recounts: "In these alcoves the belles of the Capital used, on
pleasant afternoons during the session of Congress, to hold their
receptions and to receive the homage of their admirers."

Harriet Martineau, writing of her American travels, declared:

> We did not go to the library to read, but amused ourselves for many
> pleasant hours with the prints and the fine medals which we found
> there. I was never tired of the cabinet of Napoleon medals; the most
> beautifully composed piece of history that I ever studied. There is a cup
> carved by Benvenuto Cellini, preserved among the curiosities of the
> Capitol, which might be studied for a week before all the mysteries of

its design are apprehended. How it found its way to so remote a resting place I do not remember.

Mrs. Trollope, in her *Domestic Manners of the Americans,* described the resort:

> A very handsome room, opening on a noble stone balcony, is fitted up as a library for the members [of Congress]. The collection, as far as a very cursory view could enable me to judge, was very like that of a private English gentleman, but with less Latin, Greek, and Italian. This room also is elegantly furnished; rich Brussels carpet; library tables, with portfolios of engravings; abundance of sofas, and so on. The view from it is glorious, and it looks like the abode of luxury and taste.

Captain Marryat likewise noted the furnishings, but he did not consider that the books and portfolios were in very good condition:

> The best lounge in Washington is the Library of the Capitol, but the books are certainly not very well treated. I saw a copy of Audubon's *Ornithology,* and many other valuable works, in a very dilapidated state; but this must be the case when the library is open to all, and there are so many juvenile visitors. Still it is much better than locking it up, for only the building to be looked at. It is not a library for show, but for use, and is a great comfort and amusement.

The collection of medals to which Mrs. Martineau referred had been presented to Congress "for use of the national library" by George W. Erving in 1822. This series of medals, cast by order of the French government according to the design of M. Denon, were, at the time, the chief artistic attraction of the room. Commencing with the year 1796 and terminating in 1815, the series embraced all the memorable battles and events which occurred during Napoleon's regime. The same donor had also presented another series in Parisian bronze, this one representing men notably connected with American history. Across the box, which contained the likenesses of George Washington, Columbus, Franklin, Kosciusko, John Paul Jones, William Washington, and J. E. Howard, Erving had had inscribed: "*Post ingentia facta Deorum in templa recepti.*" ["Their illustrious deeds have won them a place in the Pantheon."]

While, strictly, no one was supposed to enter the Library of Congress unless admitted by the Librarian or introduced by a Member of Congress, no visitor seems to have been excluded. The Library became the morning rendezvous of the ladies who were acquainted with Congressmen and of other fashionable loungers who came there to pass the time in conversation, in looking at pictures, or in reading.

The Library also continued to be a favorite resort of Members of Congress—even more sought out than it had been in its previous quarters. They liked to escape in its friendly and cheerful environment the pressure of debates and official preoccupations and there enter upon free literary discussions with chance-met colleagues. In the years of Watterston's administration such remarkable public men as Henry Clay, John C. Calhoun, Thomas Hart Benton, John Randolph, Daniel Webster, Nathaniel Macon, William Henry Harrison, John Holmes, Martin Van Buren, John Tyler, and Edward Everett must have been familiar figures about the crackling fires. Probably here Calhoun found himself able to release those pent-up fires of argument denied him as President of the Senate, doomed silently to listen to the debates of others, bending his tall thin frame and serious countenance, unlighted by a smile, upon his listeners; or William Henry Harrison, tall, spare and gray-haired, may have recounted the adventurous days when he had ridden away from his Virginia home into the Western wilderness as aide-de-camp to General Anthony Wayne.

Here was probably described as it had occurred in the Senate

140

the tilt between John Tyler and John Holmes, when Tyler seeking to annoy his colleague had asked what had become of that political firm once referred to by John Randolph as "James Madison, Felix Grundy, John Holmes and the Devil." How laughter must have shattered the serene quiet of the Library of Congress when Holmes's answer was repeated: "The first member is dead; the second has gone into retirement; the third now addresses you; and the last has gone over to the nullifiers, and is now electioneering among the gentleman's constituents." Perhaps Webster, in simple, sterling words which hit the hardest and made the least show, continued to measure propositions by the Constitutional standard before the Library fires, his heavy frame, his massive head with its wealth of black hair, his heavy eyebrows overhanging cavernous eyes, distinguishing "Black Dan" sharply from his fellows. Jared Sparks led a contingent of literary men who delighted to gather there, and Rufus Choate was an habitué.

"I am sadly at a loss for books here," Choate—then in the office of the Attorney General—wrote to his friend James March on August 11, 1821, "but I sit three days every week in the large Congressional Library and am studying our own extensive ante-Revolutionary history and reading your favorite Gibbon. The only classic I can get is Ovid."

The gift of the Royal Library by George IV to the British people having occurred simultaneously with the completion of the new Library of Congress in Washington, it was inevitable that comparisons should be made between the 70,000 volumes, whose cost had been £130,000 with the few thousand volumes that constituted the American collection. Under the heading "National Library," the *National Intelligencer* on August 28th commented:

We wish we could promise ourselves to see the day when the Library of Congress should be more than half filled with books of acknowledged excellence in every branch of science, and collected from every country. We should like it, also, to be something more national and truly literary in its arrangements and objects than it has hitherto been. . . . We do hope that Congress will make such regulations for the increase and utility of this noble institution as will contribute greatly to the improvement of our country, the satisfaction of literary men of leisure who reside near the seat of Government, and will increase our respectability in this respect in the eyes of foreign nations. It is obvious that a certain frivolous class of books may and ought to be excluded; but there should be no work of high character and unquestionable utility published in any part of the world which ought not, in time, to find its way into the National Library of the United States.

In 1824 Poinsett had been successful in getting $5,000 for the use of the Library of Congress. Another important law passed that same year was that which directed the Secretary of the Treasury to remit all duties upon such "books, maps, and charts, as have been, during the present year, or hereafter may be, imported into the United States, by the authority of the Joint Library Committee of Congress, for the use of the Library of Congress."

From 1819 through 1829 there was expended for books for the Library of Congress only a little over $18,000. A great part of this sum had been contracted for in the bookshop of Pishey Thompson, whose establishment had become a colorful part of Washington life and was a much-frequented place of resort for Congressmen and others of literary taste. Pishey was a rotund little Englishman; his quaint shop was on Pennsylvania Avenue, half-way between the Capitol and the White House. A native of Boston in the Lincolnshire fens, Pishey had published an historical account of his origins before he came to America, which was published in a second handsome edition, after he had secured a competency in Washington and had returned to his picturesque birthplace to prepare the work. Short, stout, with small black eyes, Pishey Thompson was always neatly dressed in black with snow-white shirt ruffles. It was his delight to chat with anyone acquainted with the early history of Boston in New England, and to tell how many of its pioneer settlers, including the Leveretts, the Wheelwrights, the Coddingtons, the Coltons, the Hutchisons, the Bellinghams, the Bradstreets and the Johnsons, were from old Boston or its immediate neighborhood.

That inveterate scold and female journalist, Anne Royall, gives a less prepossessing picture of Pishey—probably influenced by the fact that he sold but few of her books:

> The next day I waited on the best bookseller myself, and inquired for the gentleman. He was not up, it being rather early for gentlemen of dignity to appear. After waiting some time, a man of middling height, in shape resembling a stuffed Paddy, of middling age, red face, with cheeks puffed out as if holding wind in his mouth, two little round pinking black eyes, and an arrogant countenance of ineffable scorn, completed the portrait of the best bookseller in Washington. But his manners are to come yet. Angels and ministers of grace assist us! If you can imagine haughtiness, pride, malignity, scorn and contempt, combined both in look and action—his sleek coat and black silk vest, his pretty ruffle, partly displayed, you may form some idea of this Mr. "Fare and feed." He marched round the counter with all the importance of Gander, whilst I was struck dumb of course with the parade of greatness. Sir Peregrine Maitland (whose countryman he is) was nothing to this monarch of booksellers.

It was in the genial social atmosphere of Pishey's shop that many a sale of books for the Library of Congress was consummated. Other frequent purchases were made in those days from Carey and Company of Philadelphia and from the New York booksellers, J. Eastburn and Company.

The most active member of the Library Committee at that

period was Edward Everett, who had been appointed on December 6, 1825. Everett's taste in books was less scientific, more literary than that of Senator Dickerson. A member of the Massachusetts delegation in the House, Everett had won early fame as a popular preacher of the gospel, as a professor at Harvard College, and as the editor of the *North American Review*. Relieved by a wealthy marriage of financial cares, he became noted for his profound learning and his persuasive eloquence. A contemporary stated that he was "almost electrical in his utterances; his reasoning was logical and luminous, and his remarks always gave evidence of careful study." The same critic observed that as a politician Mr. Everett was not successful—"the personification of self-discipline and dignity, he was too much like an intellectual icicle to find favor with the masses, and he was deficient in courage when any bold step was to be taken." However true this may have been, the Library of Congress owed much of its growth and wise direction at this period to Edward Everett. His interest and exertions were unflagging; and the records give ample evidence of his fitness to assume bibliographical direction of the growing institution. He dreamed of developing a law department second to none and sought the advice of any he considered especially competent to make suggestion. Thus, he wrote to Judge Joseph Story of his plans. From Salem, on November 4, 1826, the Justice replied:

My Dear Sir:

I entirely agree with you respecting the Civil Law books to be placed in the Congress Library. It would be a sad dishonor of a national library not to contain the works of Cujacius, Vinnius, Heineccius, Brissonius, Voet, etc. They are often useful for reference and sometimes indispensable for a common lawyer. How could one be sure of some nice doctrines in the Civil Law of Louisiana without possessing and consulting them? What is to become of the laws of the Floridas without them?

While the relations of Everett and the Librarian of Congress seem to have been satisfactory enough, their letters to one another were not the cordial interchanges of real friends. One is led to believe, indeed, that they did not like each other. The Librarian was haughtily circumspect in his suggestions:

> Perhaps it may not be improper to suggest that it may be leaving too much to the taste and discretions of the Librarian to select such books as he may deem imperfect or defective from any cause, for the purpose of excluding them from the Library.

Everett wrote Watterston frequently about plans or purchases for the Library. On the 16th of October, 1826, he directed him:

> Please inform me (if possible by return mail) whether the Library of Congress possesses the following works: *The Congressional Register*, by Thomas Loyd, 8°, 3 volumes (being a register of the debates in the House of Representatives of the First Congress); the *Collections of the Massachusetts Historical Society*, 8°, 10 volumes, old series; 10 volumes, new series, 1 volume, third series (I see a work in the catalogue, Chapter IV, No. 27, which may be one volume of the preceding). . . .

A few days later Watterston received another letter from Everett:

> I beg leave to trouble you with another list of books, most of which I suppose not to be in the Library of Congress. Being, however, uncertain, from the causes intimated in my last, I will trouble you to make a mark against such as are already in the Library and return me the catalogue.

The last day of the same month he informed the Librarian in a third letter that he had ordered *Silliman's Journal* "up to the present time," and that it was an excellent work. "Besides," he concluded, "I think American works (though not excellent), ought to be in the Library to furnish, I trust, to after times the means of proving the ratio of advancement." He wrote further:

> You will oblige me much if you have any memorandums on hand of works wanted, by furnishing me with them. I intend to propose to the other gentlemen of the Library Committee (provided I shall happen to be of the Library Committee at the next session) that it may be a part of your trust as Librarian to prepare and keep on hand a catalogue of books most wanted in every department, to which new books could be added as they appear. In no other way can the appropriations be expended to the best advantage. It will also be desirable that somewhere there be an authority to sell imperfect or duplicate sets and inferior works, and, in short, any books which may by accident have found their way into the Library and which are not wanted there.

Two years later, on the 23rd of May, 1828, he again brought up the matter of increasing the law collections, writing to Watterston:

> I take this way of reminding you that it is the wish of the Committee of the Library that you should have completed the laws and law reports of each State, also the periodical works of which the numbers heretofore published are in the *Library*, particularly the *Annual Register* and the Parliamentary debates. I enclose you a note from Mr. Wickliffe on the subject of law books from Kentucky, and I would suggest that application by letter to some member of Congress in each State learned in the law, would enable you to effect the object. *P.S.* Would it not be well to make a little interest with the Senators for an appropriation bill?

Everett's report in answer to the instructions of the House to look into the expediency of procuring from the various public offices in England papers and documents relating to the history of America, indicates the temper of his mind and interest:

> . . . the United States of America in general and the several States that compose the Union enjoy an advantage possessed by no people of the ancient world . . . their entire political duration falls within the

146

period of authentic history. Whatever advantageous influence on national character or gratifying effect on national feeling can result from authentic details of the discovery, the first settlement, and early progress of our beloved country may consequently be realized by us in a higher degree than by any other community, excepting those on the American continent similarly situated, in this respect, with ourselves. The only circumstance which diminishes and qualifies this advantage is the fact that the most important sources of our early history are deposited in the archives of foreign governments, over which, of course, the United States have no control. Most of the documents illustrating the early history of nearly all the United States are deposited in the various public offices at London, and it has long been the wish of such of our citizens as have devoted themselves to the study of the early history of the country that measures might be adopted to procure from those officers, by permission of the British Government, copies of such documents so interesting to the American people.

In one or two cases, on special application, this has already been done. Copies of documents relative to the early history of North Carolina and Georgia have been procured from the public offices in London; and permission has lately been given by the principal secretary of State for foreign affairs, in London, to take copies of any documents contained in an ample list of papers relative to the history of Georgia. The subject has excited considerable interest in different parts of the country. The Governor of Georgia has made it the subject of a special message to the legislature of that State. The Governor of New York, in a late message, has alluded to it as matter of interest and importance. The Assembly and Senate of Rhode Island have adopted resolutions requesting that provision be made by Congress to effect the object; and the Massachusetts Historical Society and the American Antiquarian Society have taken measures to bring it under the consideration of Congress. The resolution of the legislature of Rhode Island, the memorial of the Massachusetts Historical Society, and the doings of the American Antiquarian Society have been referred to this committee and have received their respectful consideration.

Regarding the object as one of public interest, and feeling a confidence that the liberal consent given by the British Government in reference to the Georgia documents would not be withheld in regard to the documents illustrating the early history of the other United States, the committee deem it highly desirable that the proper measures be taken to this end, and therefore report the following resolution:

Resolved, That, in the opinion of this House, it is expedient that proper measures be adopted, at the discretion of the President, to procure from the public offices, in England, copies of documents illustrative of the history of America; the expense of the same to be defrayed out of the contingent fund for foreign intercourse.

Everett was perennially awake to possibilities for increasing the collections of the Library by the addition of rare or valuable books that were being offered at private sales at a bargain.

His efforts along this line were not always successful, it is true —the Library did not acquire, for example, the books of Obadiah Rich, United States Consul at Valencia—but often he was able to persuade Congress to make such purchases. It was in this fashion that the Dupontes collection had been acquired. The *New York Evening Post* drew attention to a New York Representative's part in this transaction:

We learn that Professor Everett, acting officially as one of the Library Committee of Congress, has purchased about $500 worth of the rarest and most valuable books in Signor Dupontes' collection.

We are informed that one of our members from New York, whose love of all that's valuable in learning attends him, even in the midst of party dissensions, presented the catalogue and suggested the idea of the purchase. We hardly know which deserves the most praise, the good taste which selected these inestimable books for the Library of the Capitol or the interesting enthusiasm which prompted this venerable savant to risk, with extremely limited means, the importation of a collection which, we reluctantly confess, New York has not been able to appreciate. As a proof that we have not overrated the works we will simply mention to the initiated that it contains a vellum edition of Muratori's *Rerum Italicarum Scriptores* in 39 volumes folio; the Padman edition of Forcellini's *Lexicon Totius Latinitatis;* the entire works of Visconti;

148

the extremely rare *Voyages* of Marco Polo; and other celebrated navigators by Ramusio; and a splendid edition of Dante, in 4 volumes folio, with illustrative designs, which from their majesty and simplicity are sufficiently characterized by being pronounced as worthy as they are explanatory of the author.

The Library of Congress was, as a matter of fact, slowly but steadily achieving increased importance. The largest library in the country at the time was that at Harvard, with an excellent and extensive collection relating to America. Jared Sparks considered that of Göttingen as next best. His journal for the year 1828-29, when he was busy with research in Europe, records:

This morning Mr. Amory called on me, having returned last night. He had accompanied me about the town, and through the library. Professor Benke very obligingly showed me every part of the library, and explained to me the admirable arrangement of the books. It is truly a noble collection, consisting of nearly three hundred thousand volumes, arranged in convenient apartments. . . . The library contains the best and most extensive collection of books relating to America that is anywhere to be found, except at Harvard College.

Earlier, on May 18, 1826, he had noted the deficiency of the Library of Congress collections in this field:

Passed the whole day in the Congress library, examining the Department on American History and Politics. On American history the library is exceedingly meagre, containing nothing but a few of the commonest books; but on American politics it is full, particularly to the year 1808, when Mr. Jefferson left the Government. It was his habit to preserve pamphlets and papers, and they are all deposited in this library. Dined with E. E. [Edward Everett].

As a detailed study of the octavo catalogue of 109 pages issued in 1827 and of the octavo catalogue of 16 pages issued in 1828 shows, however, the Library of Congress was actually entitled to occupy by 1829 fourth place among the libraries of the country, with collections far better-rounded than the foregoing comments would lead one to suppose.

The manuscript collections at this time were least considerable of any of the special collections. Congress had not seen fit to pass Mr. Lincoln's resolution of April 30, 1822, which had sought to have deposited in the Library of Congress all the manuscript records of the Government. Nor had Everett's resolution of the 24th of February, 1827, providing for deposit in the Library of all papers in the archives of Great Britain relating to the history of the American Colonies, met with a better fate. Only one manuscript, secured during this period, had seemed to catch the popular fancy. The *Washington City Chronicle* of August 22, 1829, described it:

> There is among the treasures of the Library of Congress an illuminated manuscript of considerable antiquity and of unquestionable beauty. Its date is 1591; the material is parchment, the characters are German, and the illumination, for its size, splendid. The work is a Catholic missal or breviary in Latin and French, but though admirably executed with the pen it is rather difficult to read, from the peculiarity of the characters. It contains, moreover, some illustrations which are badly drawn and executed, but the specimens of illumination are very rich and beautiful.

More important and valuable to the historian and scholar, however, were the four volumes of the records of the colony of Virginia and two volumes of the records of the Virginia Company acquired early in 1829, at the sale of Jefferson's second library— accumulated after he had sold his first. With the first library had come the manuscript laws of Virginia used by Hening. Jefferson had described these valuable papers in a letter to Hugh P. Taylor on the 4th of October, 1825:

The only manuscripts I now possess relating to the antiquities of our country are some folio volumes; two of these are the *Proceedings of the Virginia Company in England;* the remaining four are of the *Records of the Council of Virginia* from 1622 to 1700. The account of the first two volumes you will see in the preface to Stith's *History of Virginia.* They contain the records of the Virginia Company, copied from the originals under the eye, if I recollect rightly, of the Earl of Southampton, a member of the company; bought at the sale of his library by Dr. Byrd, of Westover, and sold with that library to Isaac Zane. These volumes happened at the time of the sale to have been borrowed by Colonel R. Bland, whose library I purchased, and with this they were sent to me. I gave notice of it to Mr. Zane, but he never reclaimed them. . . . The other four volumes, I am confident, are the original office records of the council. My conjectures are that when Sir John Randolph was about to begin the History of Virginia which he meant to write, he borrowed these volumes from the Council Office to collect from them materials for his work, and they remained in his library, probably unobserved, during the whole life of the late Peyton Randolph, his son. From his executor I purchased his library in a lump, and these volumes were sent to me as a part of it. I found the leaves so rotten as often to crumble into dust on being handled; I bound them, therefore, together, that they might not be unnecessarily opened, and have thus preserved them forty-seven years.

Largest of the Library of Congress collections during this period was the collection of public documents. The entire western gallery was filled with what the *Telegraph* described as "an awful pile of them" 25 feet high and 100 feet long. The eastern gallery was filled with duplicate collections of *United States Statutes,* Pitkin's *Statistics,* and similar books of reference. Speaking of the documents collection the editor of the *Colonial Advocate* remarked: "I perceive they have got British copies of a great many reports of committees of the House of Commons, some of them well thumbed, too."

It was a remark to which Librarian Watterston later took exception, with the comment:

> The reports of the British Parliament are not so well thumbed as he supposes, or as they ought to be by American legislators. These volumes of reports contain an immense mass of political information, and are the result of the wisdom and research of the legislators of Great Britain, which can not be too accurately or frequently examined by those who have been delegated to make laws for their country. On roads, canals, education, currency, the Army, Navy, etc., these reports are full, minute, and able, and deserve the most serious attention of the members of our National Legislature. We are sorry to say, however, that there are but few who have as yet discovered their value. They have been more thumbed by some of the departments of the Government than by those for whose use they were obtained.
>
> Rich as this collection is in rare, valuable, and splendid works, it is a remarkable fact that one-fourth of the members never avail themselves of its literary treasures. The laborers in this vineyard are few compared with the number who have the privilege of drawing from it, and whose parliamentary duties require that they should furnish themselves with at least some of the information it contains.

Certain of the duties of this department of the Library of Congress have since been delegated to the document rooms of the two Houses and to the Superintendent of Documents. The inevitable results of an indiscriminate accumulation of duplicate copies of public papers were foreseen as early as 1828, when, on May 24th, an Act was approved providing for return of certain documents, above twenty-five copies in number, which were to be reserved for the Library of Congress, to Government departments or to Members of Congress.

The Act also distributed such records as *Journals of the Federal Convention,* the *Secret Journals of the Old Congress,* Pitkin's *Statistics,* and Seybert's *Statistical Annals,* "one copy to the public library of the legislature of each State in the Union, and one copy each to each of the universities and colleges as may not already have received them, and one copy to one incorporated athenæum in each State," after all needed for the use of the Library of Congress had been retained. Duplicate copies of other works were also distributed under this act. House and Senate documents were to be sent to the Clerk of the House. Ten sets, only, of documents of Congress, instead of the previous twenty-five, were to be bound and deposited in the Library.

The law collections of the Library of Congress had received especial attention during the years that Edward Everett was active in library affairs. In 1821 the sum of $1,000 had been appropriated for purchase of books, with the expressed provision that statutes and reports of the decisions of courts of law and chancery of the different States, with the latest maps of the several States and Territories, be included. Everett had repeatedly expressed his desire and that of the Committee to build up the law collections. In 1829 Representative Blake had asked Congress to provide more effectual means of obtaining copies of State laws as they were enacted, and the Committee, in a subsequent report, stated that only the statutes of Massachusetts and Delaware had regularly been received at the Library since 1816, despite the fact that Senator Dickerson had addressed letters to the governors of various States asking them to furnish the Library of Congress annually with copies of their laws—a request that had been complied with by but few of the States. The accompanying resolution, which requested the State governors "to recommend to the legislatures thereof the adoption of a standing order," for six copies of their acts annually, was not acted upon. Another resolution affecting the law collections, offered by Representative Wickliffe in 1826 and again in 1828, also failed to pass. It sought to separate the law books from the other books of the Library of Congress and place them under the control of the Supreme Court.

Most of these collections had been threatened, shortly after George Watterston had moved the books into the beautiful central apartment in the Capitol, by the second fire to ravage the Library of Congress. It is Edward Everett who is generally given credit for its discovery. At eleven o'clock on the evening of December 23, 1825, Everett was driving home in his carriage with his wife from the home of Senator Johnston, leisurely encircling Capitol Hill, when he noticed a bright light in some of the windows of the Capitol. The light seemed to come from the Library, which he knew was accustomed to close regularly at seven o'clock. Also it seemed brightest in the center of the room. After driving his wife to their residence near by, Everett returned to the Capitol, determined to investigate the strange brilliance behind the Library windows. A sentry, standing guard on the square, accompanied the Representative as far as the western front, where—convinced that this territory was under the supervision of another sentry—he refused to go farther. Everett proceeded alone until challenged by another sentry who, in turn, called the sergeant of the guard. Assured by this gentleman that there was nothing unusual about this and that it might well be no more than a glowing brand in the fireplace, Everett, after asking the man to go at least to the Library door for safety's sake, continued on his way home.

The guard's first trip seemed to offer no cause for alarm. The heavy, closely fitted mahogany doors, enforced by baize doors within, gave no clue to anything unusual, so the man returned to the guard-room. That glowing light, however, troubled him, and after a few minutes he went to the bottom of the western steps of the Capitol to reconnoiter. The light was stronger than ever, but still he did not feel it within his authority to force the doors of the Library. Instead, he made hurried inquiries in the neighborhood in an effort to discover where the Librarian of Congress, Mr. Watterston, might be found.

The Library of Congress, west front

The Annex of the Library of Congress, with the Folger Shakespeare Memorial Library at the left

Mr. Watterston's home being at considerable distance from the Capitol, it was some time before the troubled Librarian and his companion returned. When the doors of the Library of Congress were opened, a fire was discovered burning brightly in one of the galleries of the hall. As Everett stated later, a bucket or two of water if then at hand, would have extinguished it. But no buckets were near by. Moreover, the distance from the pump on the eastern front to the hall of the Library was so great that more than the few hands available were needed to cover it. A small bell in the Capitol yard, used for calling workmen together, was frantically dangled, and the sergeant and guard ran breathlessly around the neighborhood awakening inhabitants.

Edward Everett had just retired when he heard the faint ringing of the Capitol bell. He hurried into his clothes and was off again to the Capitol, stopping with others on the way, to wrench open the locked door of an engine-house and seize all the buckets and hose in sight. Although only a few buckets were available, someone had managed to secure an admirable hose, several hundred feet in length, which had been drawn through the entire building into the hall. While Members of Congress began to push through the great crowd of citizens that had collected, the hose was effectively played upon the fire, which was just reaching the timber of the arched vault of the hall.

After two hours of fighting the flames the Library of Congress, lately so beautiful and luxurious, was reduced to a sad spectacle. The loss of books, had not, however, upon the whole been heavy, as most of those burned in the gallery were duplicate sets of public documents. None of the books which could not be replaced was destroyed.

An absent-minded gentleman, reading in the gallery by the light of a spermaceti candle until a late hour, had neglected to extinguish the light, when he finally slipped away.

155

While the damage was fortunately not considerable, the experience served to emphasize the need for better protection of the nation's books. Despite a series of resolutions growing out of the disaster and of determination to render the Library of Congress fireproof, Congress, it seems, had to have the need brought even more sharply to their attention. For nothing was done to guard against this danger until a third fire swept with devastating and appalling completeness through the unprotected halls of the Library of Congress.

In 1818, Congress had raised the salary of the Congressional Librarian to $1,500, so that he might devote all of his time to the increased duties of his office, both bibliographical and clerical. Out of the contingent fund Mr. Watterston hired a servant at a dollar a day to act as messenger during the days the Library was kept open. The Librarian and his messenger, and a certain E. B. Stelle, who had been serving without pay, constituted the entire staff of the Library of Congress until 1827, when, on February 16, Representative Cook of the Committee on Ways and Means, reported a bill recommending an allowance for an assistant librarian.

The bill passed, and the office of Assistant Librarian of Congress was made permanent by the Act of May 24, 1828, when the Librarian was authorized to employ such a helper at a salary of $800. Stelle's previous free services were recognized and rewarded when he was designated to receive first $400, and then was appointed to the permanent post of Assistant Librarian of Congress.

Watterston kept a book recording "books received since the arrival of Mr. Jefferson's library," and "books, maps, etc., presented to the Library of Congress." This latter record was apparently discontinued after September, 1816, and was replaced by catalogues of additions to the Library. There had been four supplements issued to the general catalogue of 1815—one in 1820, another in 1825, a third in 1827, and a fourth in 1828—184 pages in all.

In addition to his duties in connection with classifying the library and labeling the books, the Librarian had rendered direct and genial service to the many readers who frequented the Library rooms. A modern analyst describes him as "an enlightened librarian . . . willing and able to help any reader in his research." Certainly there is evidence that George Watterston thoroughly enjoyed the role he was called upon to play, presiding over his salon with the tact and graciousness of a man of the world, furnishing facts and dates, official and poetic quotations for deferential inquirers, communicating his knowledge of the rare and precious items of literature with such distinction that they seemed to be products of his own creation.

Into this haven of culture and refinement was dropped a bombshell on the morning of May 28, 1829. On that day Watterston was apprised of his immediate dismissal. President Jackson, with dramatic suddenness had removed the Librarian of Congress from office, and a few hours later an indignant Watterston quit the Capitol with the records of the Congressional Library under his arm. To understand what lay back of this peremptory move on the part of the President, one must remember the place Watterston had shaped for himself in the life of Washington, his closeness to the political scene, and the temper of the times.

IX

THE SPOILS OF POLITICS

*I*n the fourteen years that George Watterston had served as Librarian of Congress, many changes had taken place in the Capital, both material and political. Watterston had played some part on both the domestic and the political scene. He had, during his tenure of office, published six books —*A Memoir of the history, culture, manufacture, uses, etc., of the Tobacco Plant*, in 1817; *An easy method of learning Roman History*, in 1820; *the L—— Family in Washington* or *A Winter in the Metropolis*, 1822; *A course of study preparatory to the Bar or Senate*, 1823; *The Wanderer in Washington*, 1827; and *Tabular statistical views of population, commerce, navigation, public lands, post office establishments, revenue, mint, military and naval establishments, expenditures, and public debt of the United States*, 1828.

The most important of these had undoubtedly been the two which picture Washington customs and manners. In addition to their literary importance they reflected the Librarian's own intimate knowledge of life in the Capital, for he had come to take an active part in the affairs of the growing city. Even aside from his journalistic work and his duties as Librarian, his interests were diverse and variable. Among other things he had served as the first secretary of the Washington Botanical Society, when it was formed in 1817, and had been devoted to horticultural pursuits. He had intended, during his Librarianship, to write histories of the Madison, and other administrations, but had not been able to obtain the necessary encouragement. Politically, he had supported Clay's cause at every available opportunity, first in his *Letters from Washington* in 1818, and frequently thereafter "as the conductor of a press or a contributor." It was his support of Clay that brought about his eventual removal from his post by President Jackson. To understand how this state of affairs might be, one must consider the Capital of that day and the politics with which even the drawing-rooms were teeming, particularly in those later years of Watterston's librarianship, when the administration of John Quincy Adams was giving way before personal intrigues for the succession. While Congress remained, so far as legislation was concerned, in a state of masterly inactivity, this absence of immediate political questions and the evident Congressional indisposition to enact any of the measures proposed by the President gave wide scope to the labors of Clay's and of Jackson's supporters. As Webster's biographer indicated, it would be impossible to unfold the griefs, the interests, the projects, the jealousies and the mutual struggles of the leaders and the factions who "with no community of political principle entered into this warfare," which was so adroitly managed by Senator Van Buren and Representative Livingston in the interests of Andrew Jackson.

The unpopularity of Adams had led to his early estrangement from his cabinet, of which Henry Clay, as Secretary of State, was the most important member. It was Clay who, not wishing to be regarded as a restorer of the old Federal Party, created the Whigs, of whom he became the leader. Other members of Adams' cabinet either aligned themselves with Clay or became partizans of General Jackson. Watterston had made no secret of where his interests lay.

The nature of Washington society at this time contributed in a curiously effective manner to the circulation of political gossip,

159

for the group was limited in extent. Few Senators or Representatives brought their families to the Capital during the sessions, and it was said that a parlor of ordinary size would contain all of those who were accustomed to attend social gatherings. A few diplomats, with the officers of the Army and Navy stationed at headquarters, were accompanied by their wives, and there were generally a few visitors of social distinction. Those who met at dinner parties and at evening entertainments were as well acquainted with one another's views as if they had been members of a single family.

Even at the fashionable balls when belles, in costumes classically scant, whirled through the dances in ankle-length skirts of white India crêpe, showing the clocks on their cotton stockings, politics was on every tongue. And the conversation of those gentlemen who gathered about the punchbowl in their gay claret or green Bolívar frock-coats, with ruffled linen, and voluminous Cossack trousers tucked into high gold-tasseled boots, inevitably turned upon such topics of general interest as the hauteur of Mr. Adams, Henry Clay's American plan, or the bluff democracy of Andrew Jackson. The President and his chief advisers stood, in their minds, for the old aristocracy of brains and wealth that had for so long governed the country; Jackson represented a new conception of democracy—the right of the people to choose their rulers from among themselves. The defeat of Adams and election of Jackson in 1828 had long been foreseen and Jackson's inauguration brought to Washington a "noisy and disorderly rabble" bent on celebrating the rescue of the Government from the hands of the aristocrats. Huge crowds of celebrants overflowed the boarding-houses of the Capital and surged later, like the Paris mob at the Tuileries, through the Executive Mansion, upsetting the Presidential punch and grinding muddy feet into Mr. Adams' expensive carpets.

The people were encouraged in this belief that they had at last taken over their government, by President Jackson's subsequent appointments. His decision to remove from office a large number of the men whom his predecessors had appointed, was quite in keeping with the revolt against aristocracy in government that had brought him to power. Jackson stated his belief plainly—that the duties of all public officers were "so plain and simple that men of intelligence may readily qualify themselves for their performance"; and again, "More is lost by the long continuance of men in office than is generally to be gained by their experience." Giving expression to this philosophy, he began to weed out of the service hundreds of office-holders who had come to look upon their appointments as secure, lifetime positions. Thus Watterston, who had freely expressed his views and sympathy for Clay in the columns of the public press and in the drawing-rooms of the Capital, was called upon to relinquish the Librarianship of Congress to a Washington printer who, it was said, had performed efficient service in the political campaign which resulted in the election of the military hero. John Silva Meehan was appointed Librarian of Congress in his stead and Mr. Steele—"the sole support of an aged mother and her family"—was superseded as assistant librarian by E. J. Hume.

The fact that the long arm of politics had reached at length into the cultural cloisters of the Library of Congress did not escape comment in the public press. The *Petersburg Intelligencer* drew attention to the fact that the new Librarian of Congress was the third person attached to the *Telegraph* who had been appointed to public office. "We are far from wishing to disturb the tender nerves of our brethren of the Administration presses," the paper observed in mentioning this fact, "by urging it as evidence of dictation exercised over the Chief Magistrate. Perhaps it may be more agreeable to their sensibility to style it a curious coincidence."

George Watterston was the object of sympathetic attention in many quarters after his dismissal. The *New England Palladium* said:

> The removal of Mr. Watterston will be the subject of great regret with all Members of Congress and others who have been in the habit of frequenting the Library for the purpose of availing themselves of its literary and scientific stores. He is himself a sort of compendium of all that the Library contains, for he is a man of sense and learning, a good linguist, an accomplished bibliographer, and has been assiduously devoted to the Library for fourteen years. Withal he was always prompt in aiding the inquiries of every visitor. He is formed by habits and education for the place which he had filled, and would fill with reputation the same place in the first libraries of Europe. Mr. Watterston, we believe, was not dependent on his salary, he can do better without the office than the office without him. . . .

But, despite such friendly comments as these, Watterston was bitterly indignant over his removal, and never resigned himself to its accomplishment. He felt that his devotion to the development of the Library of Congress had deserved something better than summary dismissal. In his opinion a capable scholar and a gentleman had been replaced by a political panderer. It was a belief he expressed freely in the journalistic war that followed. Though he was forced for a time to drop the battle of words that had gone on between Jackson's administration organ, the *Telegraph*, and the *National Journal*, whose editorial staff he had himself joined on the 9th of June, 1829, he never entirely ceased his attempts to be reinstated. It is evident from his correspondence that he used all the political influence he possessed to obtain what he considered justice and a vindication of his honor. But he did not succeed in getting back into the Library. A year after he had joined the editorial staff of the *National Journal* he became its editor and made it a definite Whig organ. Great in his determination to have the Librarianship of Congress restored to him, and seeing his only hope in the return of the Whigs to power, it was toward this end he bent all his energies. But even after a twelve years' wait for the passing of the Democratic régime, his hopes were not fulfilled, although he had served as one of the city managers of the Inaugural Ball of 1841 and no doubt felt certain recognition would soon be forthcoming. When one after another of his political associates turned a deaf ear to his pleas, Watterston became thoroughly disgusted with the Whigs. On October 27, 1850, his daughter Sarah wrote to her sister Eliza: "Father has seen Mr. Filmore and he says he does not like to remove the present librarian. . . . The result is that father is disgusted and very much hurt, and has left the Whig party." The staunch Federalist, the supporter of Clay, the enemy of Jackson, had joined the Democratic Party.

In the years following his dismissal, Watterston founded the Columbian Horticultural Society, continued his literary pursuits and journalistic career, and presided over that household of sons and daughters that, despite his modest income, was always a center of hospitality in the Capital and drew such frequent visitors as John Howard Payne and other literary figures. But bitter in his heart until the last was the fact of his dismissal. He died unobtrusively on February 4, 1854. Two days later the notice of his passing appeared in the *National Intelligencer*. Ironically enough, it did not stress his career as Librarian of Congress. Instead it paid tribute to his "early and untiring labors" in aiding the project which had resulted in erection of the Washington Monument.

Yet George Watterston had made a real contribution to the development of the Library of Congress. He had been responsible for its reorganization after the British invasion in 1814. He had made the Library the cultural and intellectual center of Washington life, establishing a tradition which persists in a measure to this day; and under his direction the Library had grown in extent and usefulness; it has not ceased since to be the haven of those engaged in scholarly pursuits.

The Library of Congress suffered from the effects of the partizan attacks that centered upon it after the removal of Watterston. Many measures that would have advanced its interests or prestige were tabled or ignored for purely political considerations. There can be no question, for instance, that the Librarian's removal was the reason for Henry Clay's tabling of Preston's motion for the purchase of the Boutourlin library, and there were other later examples of failures in legislation and administration that might be laid to the same cause. It was not until after the brief and unfortunate career of J. G. Stephenson—Meehan's successor—that politicians were to learn their lesson and realize that the Librarian of Congress must be a librarian and not a political beneficiary if the Library of Congress was to survive.

The *New England Palladium* had concluded its eulogy to George Watterston with these words:

> The new Librarian, Mr. Meehan, does not possess the peculiar qualifications of his predecessor. But as he is an amiable and respectable man, we are better pleased with his appointment than we should have been with that of any other on whom, he being out of the question, it would probably have fallen.

This was probably a pretty fair estimate of Watterston's successor and represented, rather shrewdly, the general attitude of the public and Congress with regard to the new Librarian. Meehan's chief contact with books, prior to his appointment, had come through his association with the printing and publishing trades.

His contemporaries described him as a man of amiable and unobtrusive manners, and assiduous in his duties. Peter Force pictures him as "eminently qualified for the position to which President Jackson had appointed him." It was mentioned in some quarters that Mr. Meehan had accepted the appointment after it had been turned down by Charles Pendleton Tutt, who had preferred the office of Navy agent at Pensacola.

John Silva Meehan was born in New York City, February 6, 1790. All his boyhood and early manhood had been spent in the metropolis. When he was twenty-two years old he went to Burlington, New Jersey, to superintend the printing of Walker's Dictionary. Although the War of 1812 was under way, it was not until his printing enterprise was completed that Meehan saw service. Then he was appointed midshipman in the Navy and served aboard the *Firefly* until the close of the war, when, through the influence of a former assistant secretary of the Treasury, Tench Coxe of New York, he was offered an appointment as lieutenant in the Marine Corps.

Meehan seems, however, to have preferred civil life, for he declined the appointment, returned to his trade as a Burlington printer and, in 1814, married Miss Margaret Jones Mornington, of that city. Shortly after his marriage he moved to Philadelphia and became a partner of Robert Anderson in a printing and publishing business which undertook publication of the religious monthly, *Latter Day Luminary*, under the auspices of a committee of the Baptist board of foreign missions.

When this firm moved to Washington in 1822, it became the center of Baptist interests because of the location of Columbian College in the Capital. The firm commenced publication, in this connection, of the weekly religious and educational review, *Columbian Star*. Columbian College did not stand very high in the esteem of the acid-tongued Anne Royall, who thus referred to it in her *Black Book:*

> Columbian College exists only in name, and with the exception of two New England professors, may be said to be destitute of instructors. As for the president, Dr. S., he is no more than an old woman. With such a head, Columbian College must soon come to naught.

And later:

> Since this was written, Columbian College has died a natural death, and is no more; and Dr. S. must now go preaching, and ogling the women, with whom, I am told, he is a great favorite. Shame on my sex; if they had no more prudence, they might have more taste, as he is both old and homely.

On July 9, 1825, Meehan resigned his interest in the *Columbian Star* and early in the following year purchased the *Washington Gazette*. The memoirs of John Quincy Adams reveal the fact that Meehan had been only the nominal purchaser of the *Gazette,* that John H. Eaton had made himself responsible for the purchase and John P. Ness—who was later sued for payment— had indorsed the notes.

Meehan remained publisher of the *Gazette*—whose name he had changed to *United States Telegraph*—from February 6 until October 17, 1826, when Duff Green became sole editor and publisher. Meehan the following year was made secretary of the board of Trustees of Columbian College. Here he remained until President Jackson, rewarding him for the support he had enjoyed at the hands of the *Telegraph,* made him, on May 28, 1829, the fourth Librarian of Congress.

Up to the time that Meehan took office, the principal function of the Library Committee had been the selection of books. This duty had fallen pleasantly into the hands of Mahlon Dickerson and was as equally enthusiastically undertaken later by Edward

Everett. Since the members of this committee consisted, as a rule, of men of high literary or scientific reputation, the Library had not fared badly in the selections that had been added in this way to its collections, though they had been somewhat biased by personal tastes. During a later period, when James Alfred Pearce served as Chairman, from December 2, 1844 to March 4, 1863, there was excluded from the collections all works calculated, in Mr. Pearce's opinion, to engender sectional differences. This chairman even went so far as to refuse, on this ground, to order *The Atlantic Monthly* when that periodical appeared. From December 6, 1825, to March 3, 1835, Edward Everett had played an important part in building up the Library, and from December 3, 1821 to March 3, 1825, Joel Poinsett had made worthwhile contributions. Other Committee members who had added to the value of the collections were G. C. Verplank and Levi Woodbury. Members of the Committee other than the Chairman took part in directing the policy of the Library of Congress in these years. As is apparent from the minutes, the executive duties were usually delegated to the chairman or to subcommittees and, later, to the agents of the Committee and to officers of the Library.

The very diversity of taste among Committee members precluded the wisest direction, so far as bibliographical suggestions went. Samuel Knapp recognized this when he said that under proper direction the annual appropriation of $5,000 might be so utilized as to make the Library one of the finest libraries of the world in twenty years. But some members, like Dickerson, were interested in developing a scientific library; others, like Everett, wanted to build a library of literature, while still others wished to consider the tastes or needs of Members of Congress, of the diplomatic corps, and of heads of government departments, when adding to the collections. Not a few members of the Committee were not at all interested in the Library; some cared only about those sections which were of direct or immediate use to themselves. Very few, in or out of Congress, had visualized a great national library and scarcely any could have defined the functions of such an institution. True, bibliographical plans were drawn up, from time to time, that might have achieved this end, if carried out. But they were not realized.

Voices outside of Congress were heard upon this point. A citizen asked why Congress did not appropriate more than $5,000 annually for its library and further stated, in the *National Intelligencer* early in 1834:

> . . . Contrast for a moment the advantages enjoyed by the European literati for scientific research with those of our own country. It is calculated that in 31 libraries of Germany there are at least 4,000,000 volumes, while probably the 31 largest of our country do not contain more than 350,000. The University of Göttingen, which is of more recent establishment than some of our colleges, contains 300,000; the library at Leipzig has 100,000; Dresden 260,000; and 4 at Vienna present an aggregate of 590,000 volumes. When will the United States, the boasted land of civilization and knowledge, afford to its students such facilities for the advancement of science and learning as these?

The Hon. Lewis Cass, when Secretary of War, had drawn the attention of the American Historical Society to this need in an address delivered in the Hall of Representatives on January 30, 1836:

> An extensive library has already been collected, at the national expense, which contains many rare and valuable works, illustrating our general and local history. This collection is annually augmented, but not in proportion to the great means of the nation. There should be one place in our country, where every work may be found which has any relation, however remote, to the discovery, settlement, and history of America. . . . And why should not such additions be made to this collection, in *all* the departments of human learning, as will render it worthy of the age and country, and elevate it to an equality with those

great repositories of knowledge which are among the proudest ornaments of modern Europe.

Thus the trend, while not clearly defined, was certainly toward a national library when John Silva Meehan took over his post as Librarian of Congress. Well-meaning and industrious as he no doubt was, Meehan was scarcely fitted for the stupendous task of shaping the collections to this end. He seems to have devoted all his energies, however, to the duties at hand. In 1830, Meehan was accused of being "acquainted with no language but English, and not very well acquainted with the books written in that language." By the time the Civil War had broken upon the country this could scarcely be said with truth. For he was destined to serve until 1861, and—despite his deficiencies—see the Library of Congress through a period of real development. In the thirty years between his appointment and the conclusion of his services, he was to grow intimately familiar with the books in his custody; moreover, he had enjoyed opportunities for acquainting himself with the collections and administration of other great libraries. On June 23, 1832, the Library Committee authorized him to visit the public libraries at Baltimore, Philadelphia, New York, West Point, and Boston. His expenses were paid out of the Library fund. In 1856 he was one of the incorporators, among other distinguished men, of "Columbia's Library for Young Men."

Meehan's outlook was, however, admittedly limited. The popular books of the Library meant more to him than its scholarly items, and he was not equipped to anticipate the research needs of legislators or scholars, giving his attention rather to such books as were immediately in demand. Up until 1851 this weak bibliographical policy did not very materially affect the Library of Congress, but, after a third fire had swept devastatingly through the alcoves in the Capitol and it fell upon him to build up new collections on the ashes of the old, his limited background and lack of scholarly training were revealed as a real handicap to the restoration of the Library.

On the day of this third fire the Library rooms were in appearance much as they had been when Meehan took office. There had been additions of furniture, the titles of the chapters in the alcoves had been regilded, shelves and closets had been fitted up in the law and committee rooms and doors of mahogany woven with brass wire had been hung before the bookshelves in the main room. In 1841 an additional room had been provided in an adjoining passage, and, in 1843, had been given over to the law books. The room near the Supreme Court, occupied by the law department, had also been fitted up to receive additional law books. The committee room and an adjoining chamber ordered to be used as a library room had been carpeted. The growing collections were even then overflowing all available space and the need for enlargement had become every day more evident. Although a documents room had been provided and the law library enlarged, the Library of Congress had reached the limit of its physical expansion. Further expansion would have to depend upon enlargement of the Capitol building itself.

Before the fire of 1851, however, the general appearance of the Library room was essentially the same as it had been in 1847. Robert Mills gave a description of its arrangement in 1847:

> The first thing that attracts the attention when entering is the admirable order of arrangement of the different subjects embraced in the room. The several works are classed according to Mr. Jefferson's arrangement, corresponding to the faculties of the mind employed on them—1st, Memory (result, history); 2nd, Reason (philosophy); 3rd, Imagination (fine arts). Labels in large characters point out the position of the several classes of books in the order named above—for instance,

alcoves Nos. 1 to 4 contain works connected with history, ancient, modern, and ecclesiastical; natural philosophy, agriculture, zoology, botany, mineralogy, technical arts; alcoves Nos. 4 to 8, works connected with philosophy, namely, moral philosophy, law of nature and nations, religion, common law, equity, ecclesiastical, merchant and maritime codes, statutes, politics, commerce, arithmetic, geometry, mechanics, statics, dynamics, pneumatics, phonics, optics, astronomy, geography; alcoves Nos. 9 to 12, works connected with the fine arts, architecture, gardening, painting, sculpture, music, epic, tales, fables, pastoral odes, elegies, didactics, tragedy, comedy, dialogue, epistles, logic, rhetoric, orations, criticism, bibliography, languages, and polygraphical, or authors who have written on various branches.

Over the mantelpiece at the south end of the room was hung—rather too high for artistic effect—an original likeness of Columbus which had been presented by George Banell, American consul at Malaga. Between the alcoves all about the room and in intervening panels were spaced Stuart's paintings of the first five Presidents, and portraits of Hancock, Peyton Randolph, Bolívar, Baron Steuben, Tyler, Baron de Kalb, and of Amerigo Vespucci. Marble busts of Thomas Jefferson and of the Marquis de Lafayette flanked the door leading into the balcony. Over the cornice alcoves were marble busts of Washington, John Quincy Adams, Marshall, Van Buren, and Taylor, and plaster busts of Jackson and Moultrie, and a medallion of Madison. Cases on either side of the mantelpiece contained the famous Erving collection of medals and others struck at the Philadelphia mint in honor of General Gates and of Captain Hull, as well as an American collection ordered by Congress. Tables lined the center of the main room, the drawers of which were filled with engravings. Each of the alcoves also contained a table and chair for reading, and the books in the shelves along the walls were protected by wire screens. On cold winter days, or those mornings and evenings when spring or fall chills were in the air, ruddy fires blazed in the open grates, sending warm tongues of light across the Brussels carpet.

The beauty of the room still made it one of the attractions of Washington, and its location between the two Houses of Congress assured a pleasant lounge for Members wearied with continuous debate and for the numerous strangers who visited the Capitol. James Silk Buckingham, the English traveler, looking upon the throng which frequented it, concluded it was a public library:

> As access to the Library is just as free from all restraint as access to the halls of Congress, in the galleries set apart for strangers, or to the President's levees and drawing-rooms, so this Library is a very valuable resource both to the residents and visitors in the city.

It was, as a matter of fact, a privilege that was not regarded highly enough by those who enjoyed it. Many of the visitors misused the Library deplorably. Books were mutilated and lost; a constant buzz of conversation worried the readers; students were crowded out of the room by curious visitors. An attempt had been made to enforce an earlier rule that visitors must be introduced by Members of Congress, and, after January, 1834, the Librarian kept locked, and unlocked only upon request, the gratings which protected the books. Senator Cass, who persistently ordered large collections of novels and books on travel sent to his room, and Senator Benton, who consulted all available encyclopedias before preparing his exhaustive speeches, were habitués of the pleasant retreat.

The facetious "Ebenezer Lovermuch" and "Captain Marcius Mucklewrath" in their impudent and amusing chronicle, *The Champagne Club,* satirically described the Library room during John Meehan's administration:

> Crowds of pretty fair ones with their pretty beaux filled the area and chatted and flirted and carolled their merry lays of laughter as they

thumbed irreverently the hallowed and illumined pages of *Paradise Lost* to look at the pictures, or, disdaining the society of the master spirits of time, occupied themselves with the self-styled Byrons and living Tom Thumbs of the day. One old gentleman alone, almost hidden in a corner, seemed to be aware of the place in which he was, and to have come with the wedding garment to the feast. I approached him upon pretense of looking for a book, and had an opportunity of observing him. His countenance was calm, and yet enthusiastic; benignant yet stern. His forehead was lofty and full, and overhung his quiet, dark eyes. He wore his few surviving hairs tied into a queue, and I remarked that he was lame. The book in his hand, like its reader, must have relied upon its subject rather than its body for distinction, as it was bound in pale and unpretending sheepskin and had an ancient look. It was one of the rare Latin authors, and it had the good fortune just then to fall into the hands of one who seemed devoted to its attraction.

"Percy," said the Baron, "why don't somebody give that gentleman a hint of the usages of this place? Bless me! I should not have dreamed of such rudeness. To sit down in the very heart of the dominions of fashion and the ladies, turn his back upon them, hold his tongue, and read a book! Abominable! Is he mad? Really, this is a beneficent and generous government of yours! To give the fair sex a chatting-room in the very Capitol itself! A lounge! A sort of public boudoir for belles and their favorites! Bon diable! This is the climax of liberty! the apex of civilization!"

The Baron was startled, when he learned that the old gentleman was a Senator, one of the few who have the true and simple dignity of nature, and that he was actually putting the apartment to its legitimate use.

The cry was taken up by "Petrus Penwaggler, Esquire" in a subsequent issue of *The Champagne Club:*

Almost thrown into asphyxia a few days ago, by the upas eloquence of a member from the far West, I instinctively sought the Library of Congress as a means of relief. A group of laughing, chatting ladies were nonchalantly turning over the elephant sheets of Audubon's *Ornithology;* a sort of obbligato amusement, like a flute accompaniment in a concerto, for all the fashionable idlers, who put to the test the urbanity of the Librarian. Here and there a bon ton saunterer cast a listless, unmeaning eye on the glorious array of the shelves such as would say, I care not to cultivate acquaintance with unknown persons. . . .

These conditions seem to have been corrected by Meehan to the best of his ability as years went by, for in 1844 Caleb Atwater wrote pleasantly of the refined taste, the polite manners and the agreeable conversation of those he encountered in the library room: "I have always found reading people more placid and agreeable in their manners than others, and were any whole nation wholly composed of such materials it would be the happiest and the best nation in the world."

The throngs were to be turned from this room in an unexpected manner. The rarities and treasures within its walls, the room itself, and 35,000 of the choicest and most valuable volumes of the Library of Congress, were—without warning—to be effaced from the halls of the Capitol by the tragic fire of 1851.

At a quarter to eight o'clock on the morning of the 24th of December in this year, smoke and flame were observed in the windows of the Library. When guards forced open the Library room, the large table at the north end of the apartment was found to be ablaze, as well as portions of shelving and the books in the northeast alcoves. Between the table and the door leading to the law library, flames were mounting. Despite the lesson learned in 1825, no buckets of water were handy. When they returned it was to find the interior a raging furnace, with flames leaping and darting through the upper galleries. The whole vaulted hall was filled with smoke and flames.

The first fire company to arrive, the Columbia, was delayed by a frozen hose which had to be taken off to the new gas factory on the canal for thawing. A few minutes later the Anacostia engine arrived and it was not long before seven engines were on the scene, playing streams of water upon the blaze. A body of United States Marines from the Navy Yard helped to bear water, keep order and protect Capitol property generally. One engine was drawn up the steps of the east portico and another was run into the Rotunda itself.

Despite the height of the Library walls, the fire had reached the main roof of the Capitol, where it was stopped by chopping away portions of the roof and the stairway to the dome. The heat of the fire was so intense in front of the Library that pillars not reached by the flames scaled off to a depth of a quarter of an inch.

Only about 20,000 of the 55,000 volumes which comprised the Library of Congress at this time, were saved. Most of these were in the north room and the law library which, due to their thick walls, had not been reached by the flames. The paintings, the statuary and many of the medals, were completely destroyed. The *Intelligencer* reported that only three books were spared from the principal library room. These were the Librarian's record, an account book, and an odd volume of Lord Kingsborough's work on the antiquities of Mexico. Despite freezing weather, citizens and firemen worked without stopping until noon the next day, when the fire was at length subdued. Even as late as three o'clock on Christmas afternoon, the engines were playing upon immense masses of charred, smoking, steaming rubbish to make sure that the last spark had been extinguished, and city police joined the marines in a night vigil around the Capitol.

Sadly the Librarian of Congress reported the loss to Congress in a letter written Christmas Day, stressing the unaccountable origin of the blaze "as no fires have been used in it for a long time, and no candles, lamps, or other lights have ever been used in it during the whole time that it has been under my charge." He estimated the loss of books at 35,000, adding that among the 20,000 saved were many belonging to Jefferson's library. These books remain today, a valued reminder of its origins, in the Rare Book Room of the Library of Congress, where they are available to the public.

An inquiry was ordered into the origin of this fire, which resulted in the report of the architect of the Capitol, Thomas U. Walter, that it had been caused by the timbers which formed the alcoves of the Library having been inserted in the chimney flues. The architect called attention to the fact that it was customary to make large wood fires in the committee rooms very early in the morning and that these rooms were then closed until occupied by the committees.

On January 15th a bill was passed which provided $1,200 to fit up the document room and a portion of the adjoining passage temporarily to receive the books of the Library of Congress. While workmen were busy removing the rubbish, sorting out of the mass of books those which might with trimmed margins and new bindings be made suitable for placing in the new collections, the Library of Congress made its third start in life operating as best it could in one little room and a portion of an ill-lighted passage. With the determination that their library should survive, Congress had appropriated, meanwhile, $10,000 to purchase replacements for its sadly depleted collections.

A movement was at once started to provide a permanent, fireproof home for the Library of Congress within the Capitol. As the result of a resolution submitted to the Senate on January 27th by Senator Pearce that the Committee on Public Buildings be at once instructed to report on the expediency of "enlarging, repairing, and refitting the principal apartment heretofore occupied by the Library of Congress, so that it may be entirely fireproof and capable of further extension in harmony with the general plan of the Capitol," Thomas Walter sent detailed plans for such an apartment, stating that it would cost $72,500 to construct. Before it was completed, the new apartment was to cost around $100,000. Delay after delay was occasioned by the need for additional appropriations as the work progressed, by lapses due to the late arrival of choice materials, by the scarcity of skilled workmen and —not of least consideration in Washington—by the weather. On the 18th of May the Washington correspondent of the *New York Tribune* sent this dispatch to his paper:

> The workmen are rapidly pushing the finishing off of the chamber of the Library of Congress, though they have an awful time of it. They are compelled to keep all the doors and windows closed while putting on the gold leaf, creating a heat so intense as to compel them actually to labor shirtless, the atmosphere being next in intensity to a Turkish bath. Faith, they should indeed be well paid.

The Librarian of Congress, John Meehan, took possession of the sumptuous new quarters on the 6th of July, 1853. Meehan closed the old library on July 21st and did not reopen the new until August 23rd. In the meanwhile Meehan, with the aid of Assistant Librarian Hume and a handful of helpers, had transferred the books and maps and manuscripts to their new quarters.

The opening of the new Library of Congress was the occasion for the most enthusiastic praise on the part of the public and of the press. On the opening day Mr. Meehan, "with his well-known cordiality and bonhomie," played host to the distinguished visitors who thronged the rooms. President Pierce visited the Library, accompanied by Sir Charles Lyell, who pronounced it the most beautiful room in the world.

It was indeed a beautiful room, equipped in every way possible for the purpose it was to serve and remarkable for the rich detail of its architecture and appointments. The main room was 91 feet long, 34 feet wide and 38 feet high—considerably larger than the old apartment. Openings between the main room and the adjoining rooms were crowned by elliptical arches, magnificently embellished. Even the galleries encircling the room were of generous proportions, with 9½-foot ceilings and as richly decorated as the twelve alcoves, with paneled pilasters, ornamented with medallions. The architraves which crossed the alcoves were furnished with shields, crowned bands and corner ornaments, and the shields were designed as tablets to receive the names of the general subjects to which the books in the respective alcoves related.

The ceiling was said to be the only iron ceiling in the world and was made up of massive iron plates with the appearance of blocks of brown marble panels. Twenty-four magnificent consoles, each weighing nearly two tons, and decorated with carvings of fruit, foliage, and scrolls, supported the ceiling, whose deeply-sunken panels were embellished with ornate mouldings and foliated pendants. Across the upper skylight, as if flung there by some careless hand, glowed a cluster of stars. The soft tones of the panels and pilasters were tinged with palest green and burnished with gold leaf. The tiled floor was laid in black and white marble.

In these splendid surroundings John Silva Meehan, business man rather than scholar, faced the task of suitably restoring the collections of the Library of Congress. It was a task far more difficult than restoration of the Library room. Everyone agreed that this new Library should surpass the old, that careful selection in its purchases would be necessary. But it was not at once apparent how that selection was to be made, nor if the Library were to be administered by experts or not.

No one was quite sure what direction it would take, nor if its ultimate destiny were to be that of a national library.

Certainly no single member of the Committee was equipped to take full charge of the purchasing at this time. And there were other difficulties in the way of acquiring desirable books. There were few good books on the market, for one thing. Joseph Cogs-well, the famous collector of the Astor library, declared that Paris and London booksellers said all the good books had gone to America—and by America they meant New York and Providence.

The need was certainly urgent, for there was no public library in Washington which could to any degree supply the place of the Library of Congress. The largest single collection, including those of the War and State Departments, the Patent Office, and the Smithsonian Institution, did not exceed 10,000 volumes, nor did they contain the class of books needed. Moreover, the best months of the year for European purchases had already passed; few sales of importance were made later than May. An anonymous writer in the *Intelligencer* deplored the small grant that had been made for purchases:

> The appropriation which has been made of $10,000 for the purchase of books was understood to be merely for the purchase of such books of reference as are most immediately important. Everybody anticipates a much larger grant before this session closes, one more worthy of an intelligent, rich and liberal nation.

Time, it was pointed out, was also an important element in the purchase of books, even when funds were unlimited. The old Library had not, on the whole, been so well selected as if more system, science and unity of plan had been taken into account in its composition. Though it was one of the four largest in the country it had cost proportionately very much more than any of the others. The new Library of Congress should be a systematic collection of books chosen with competent bibliographical learning for a specified and well-defined purpose; and in order to be judicious the selection should have primary reference to this purpose, to the design of the Library, if it were not to be procured merely as an ornamental appendage to the Capitol.

Meehan's task, considered from all these angles, was certainly a stupendous one. Moreover there had been little in his education and experience to equip him to make the wisest selections. How was he to know, for example, what books among contemporary publications might be esteemed most valuable a century hence? How was he to discern the potential importance of seemingly insignificant works? The first diagram of iron suspension bridges, for instance, is buried in a volume of neglected and forgotten plates published in Venice by Fausto Verantio toward the end of the sixteenth century, and even a book which contains no new fact or fresh thought may serve incidentally to illustrate some custom of the age or the state of language at the time it was written. "Who would have imagined," asked Libri, "that the obscure author of a small pamphlet, *Le Souper de Beaucaire*, would subsequently become the Emperor Napoleon, and that to write fully the life of the execrable Marat one ought to have the very insignificant essays on physics that he published before the Revolution?"

It is little wonder that Meehan did not meet the problem with distinction. A great many books were bought, and cheaply. A letter from a Washington observer to the *New York Tribune* indicated the lack of discrimination that was apparently shown in the selections:

> What has already been done toward replenishing the empty shelves of the Congressional Library has been directed rather by booksellers, eager for lucre, than by a bibliograph or a bibliophile, or any systematic intellect whatever. It shows clearly before one's eyes that these booksellers wished to get rid of costly works and editions which for years had found no purchasers and thus formed a dead capital in their shops. They have succeeded thus far. . . .

In a resolution offered at the next meeting of the Library Committee on August 18, 1852, an effort was made to correct these conditions when the chairman was instructed "to address scientific and literary gentlemen on the subject" of procuring complete lists of books in the various chapters included in the catalogue of the Library. Nothing came of this plan, however, and at the meeting of the Committee on March 3, 1853, another resolution requested the Librarian to prepare catalogues of books "according to chapters or departments, including all geological works under the head of geology, all ancient and modern histories, with American, English, and French, etc., all works in the departments of ancient classics, and modern belles-lettres, etc. (so far as the same are not in the Library), under their respective heads and according to the languages in which they are written."

This resolution is an important one in the history of the Library of Congress for it delegated the bibliographical direction of the Library, formerly the work of the Library Committee, to the Librarian. While it was perhaps unfortunate that so great a power had been given at this time into the hands of a man of very limited bibliographical experience, it proved ultimately to be a very wise provision. The lists which Meehan drew up in consequence of this resolution embraced, for the most part, merely such works as had been lost in the fire, compiled from the last printed catalogue of the library. A wonderful opportunity was thereby lost for laying the foundation for a library second to none in the world.

This was especially true as Congress was in a very generous mood at the moment with respect to its Library. Although many doubted if Congress could be brought to vote more than $30,000 for the purchase of books, the resolution of Mr. Chandler of the Library Committee, proposing $75,000, was readily granted. *Norton's Literary Gazette* quoted Professor Jewett as saying that $200,000 would have been given as readily, had Congress thought that sum necessary and believed it would be honestly and judiciously devoted to gathering a good library.

Most of the purchases from this generous appropriation were made through the London agent of the Library of Congress—Rich Brothers. Their activity along the book-buying line seems to have made itself felt in the bookshops of London, where native shoppers complained that "all the good editions of old books are rising in value."

A chronicler in the *London Athenæum* of September 10, 1853, remarked that "within these dozen years memoirs and collections of the contemporary literature of the sixteenth and seventeenth centuries in this country have advanced in price from 30 to 100 percent," and attributed the rise partly to the fact "of greater attention being paid to historical matters, and that day being past when a minister of the Crown might confess, as in the anecdote told by Mr. Macaulay, that he had never heard of 'Empson and Dudley' "; but chiefly "by the growth of a large demand for such books in America. Congress has two agents in London—one literary, one political, and we fancy the former is the more active and important functionary of the two. One of these agents has his headquarters in Piccadilly, and his papers accredit him to the Court of St. James; the other has his quarters at Charing Cross, and his commission is to the bookstalls of London streets. We could tell the story of many a literary treasure which has found its way—sometimes at the price of an old song—into this officer's hands, and thence into the archives and libraries of the United States. He is always on the spot, he has a liberal discretion in his purchases, and he never throws away a good thing for lack of power or appreciation. With such agencies at its service we need not feel surprised that accidental losses of literary treasures, whether by fire or by flood, are speedily repaired in the United States."

When the new room opened on August 23, 1853, the Librarian of Congress had already arranged close to 30,000 volumes on the shelves; the collections then numbered about 35,000 volumes, about 4,000 of which had been secured and added by May 22nd of the previous year. The replacements had been made at an average cost of $1.95 for each volume; the Astor library had been collected at an average cost of $1.25 a volume; the cost of the Library of Congress before the fire had averaged considerably higher—$3.50 for each volume. As it stood in 1853 the Library was no more than a good reference library for the average legislator, with some rarities—such as De Bry's *Voyages,* the rescued work of Lord Kingsborough on Mexican antiquities, Napoleon's work on Egypt, and Champollion's works.

Its store of Americana was very meager. Selections generally had been influenced by events of the times. Thus, when excitement over Cuba raged in 1832 the Committee had authorized the purchase of books and periodicals in Havana to the amount of fifty dollars annually; at the time of the Mexican War the Librarian was authorized to purchase all the constitutions and laws of Mexico and also to subscribe for newspapers published in Vera Cruz and in Mexico City. When the unsuccessful revolution of 1848 broke out in Europe, the Librarian of Congress was asked to purchase at once all works of any reputation relating to the modern history, existing conditions, and prospects of Hungary and Germany.

Many opportunities to acquire famous collections or outstanding literary and historical items had been overlooked or bungled by Congress. Notable examples had been the loss of the magnificent collection of the Count de Boutourlin, comprising 25,000 printed volumes of the earliest and richest specimens of the Greek and Latin classics and 240 unique and curious manuscripts all of which might have been purchased for around

$50,000; and the offer of the library of the Durazzo family at
$30,000, consisting of about 10,500 volumes in handsome uni-
form bindings and esteemed for its subject matter as one of the
choicest private libraries in Europe. Congress had likewise refused Henry Stevens' offer of the *Laws of Vermont* and *Journals of the General Assembly of Vermont* from 1779, together
with about 500 volumes of Vermont newspapers from 1783 on;
to say nothing of their having neglected to acquire the library
of George Washington. Fortunately the patriotic efforts of a few
citizens of Boston prevented Washington's library from finding
a home in a foreign land when, purchasing it by subscription,
they presented it to the Boston Athenæum.

The law library and documents division of the Library of Congress saw the greatest growth in the years before the Civil War.
Marcy, of the Senate Judiciary Committee, had been responsible
for the act approved July 14, 1832, "to increase and improve
the law department of the Library of Congress." As a result of
this legislation the room north of the main Library had been
fitted up for the use of the Law Library, and here it remained
until 1843, when it was removed to an apartment in the basement of the north wing of the Capitol, near the Supreme Court.
Here the Justices had free access to the books and were empowered to make their own rules and regulations during the sittings
of the court. Provision was also made at this time to purchase
the reports of cases determined in the superior courts of the several States and the laws of every State in the Union. For the
first time, too, the Supreme Court was consulted on the subject
of law books for the Law Library. The department remained,
however, and remains to this day, a branch of the Library of
Congress, under the jurisdiction of the Librarian. In 1837 an
additional grant of $5,000 was provided for the Law Library,
as well as an annual appropriation of $1,000—increased to $2,000

in 1850. In 1832, including 639 volumes of the Jefferson library, the Law Library contained 2,011 volumes; at the period of the Civil War it was considered the best and largest collection of law books in America. Catalogues of its collection were printed in 1839 in 98 pages, in 1849 in 139 pages, and in 1860 in 225 pages.

One of the tasks undertaken by Meehan had been to complete the collection of documents in the Library. Senator Allen, early in 1839, had expressed surprise that while all the proceedings in the English Parliament could be had in the Library, the complete journals and public documents of the various States were not available. This had led Meehan to prepare a catalogue of all the laws and of all the legislative and executive journals and documents of the States and Territories, in the possession of the Library. Soon afterwards he addressed the executives of the various States requesting regular receipt of these items. Out of this activity grew a renewed interest in Federal documents, and the collections began to increase. The acts of 1848 and 1857, providing for the exchange and distribution of public documents, gave added impetus to the collections.

Meanwhile a system of international exchanges had been established through the interest of Alexander Vattemare of Paris, who had, in 1815, begun an investigation into the conditions of European libraries which had resulted in his discovering large collections of duplicates. This discovery had led him to establish a system of exchange among the different nations of Europe designed to bring into circulation these valuable but useless treasures. Vattemare had arrived in the United States in 1839 and laid the plan before Congress. It resulted in establishment of a system of exchange which, due to the fact that a proper medium was not set up, was not at first very successful. To correct this, Congress later empowered the Joint Committee on the Library to appoint the necessary agents for the purpose. Accordingly, on July 25, 1848, Alexander Vattemare himself was named to carry into effect the donation and exchange of certain duplicate books and other publications. So far as the Library of Congress was concerned, the system worked so satisfactorily that by 1850 a member of Congress had better opportunities for information regarding France than he had for almost any State in the Union. With other countries it did not work out well enough to suggest its continuance, and on July 26, 1848, the act was repealed, and Vattemare paid $1,000 for his services. For the remainder of the period—up to 1865—only $1,200 was appropriated for the purpose of effecting international exchanges. In 1857 Congress transferred the distribution of public documents to the Department of the Interior and the exchange of public documents with foreign countries to the Department of State. The move was an unfortunate one. In the first place it degraded the Library of Congress from its proper position as custodian of the public documents, in drawing from it its most important source for the supply of a class of literature of greatest importance in a national library; in the second place it represented an unwise separation of the functions of distribution and exchange.

On the 10th of August, 1846, an important step had been taken in the interests of accumulations of copyright deposits. On this date Congress provided that the Library of Congress should receive one copy of every work copyrighted under the laws of the United States. Up until that time provision had been made for copyright registration and deposit, since 1790, with Clerk of the District Court and the Secretary of State. The law of 1846 was so generally disregarded that on February 5, 1859, it was repealed. At the same time the copyright business was transferred from the Department of State to the Department of the Interior. It was not until after the Civil War that that system was to be

firmly established which was to prove one of the most voluminous sources of materials, good, bad and indifferent, for the Library shelves at no cost to the Federal Government.

There were few manuscripts among the collections of the Library of Congress before the Civil War. The few items in its
possession, can, indeed, be listed without difficulty. There was a
copy of *Instructions of the Count Revillagigedo, Viceroy of Mexico, to his successor in 1794*, which had been presented by José
María Tornel, minister from Mexico, on April 10, 1830; there
was a journal kept on board the British ship *Zealous* in the year
1792, presented by Colonel Joseph Watson, on March 13, 1830;
there were the Jefferson MSS. which had been acquired in 1815
and in 1829, twenty-eight volumes, including laws and orders
of the General Assembly of Virginia, 1622-1712, eight volumes;
there were the minutes of the Assembly and other Colonial records, 1606-1700, seven volumes; there were the records and
papers of the London Company of Virginia, 1619-1624, two volumes; and notes on Virginia, law notes, historical notes, and
copies of treatises upon religious and philosophical subjects.
These comprised the collections.

Just as Congress had allowed many priceless collections of
books to escape them, so did they lose many opportunities for
acquiring rare and valuable manuscripts that were offered for
sale in the period before the Civil War. Although the Library
Committee authorized its Chairman, Senator Pearce, to purchase
the De Brahme manuscripts relating to Florida which were then
owned by Harvard University, nothing came of it. The remarkable manuscript collection of William Upcott of Islington, England, was refused by Congress on December 27, 1856; Obadiah
Rich's offer of January 29, 1845, to sell the Committee for £240
Sterling 24 volumes of unpublished manuscripts relating to early
American history, was referred to Mr. Pearce for examination,

where it appears to have rested. Charles B. Norton's memorial asking Congress to purchase for $4,000 original manuscripts which included the famous "Hartley correspondence" and Benjamin Franklin's original sketch of a map of the United States— referred to in the Treaty with Great Britain in 1783—was considered and laid on the table.

Chief loss to the country, however, was probably that sustained when the proposition of W. Noël Sainsbury of the British State Paper office, for copying and calendaring the manuscripts in the English archives relating to the American colonies, was rejected. Thus work which might have been done by one authority once for all was left to be done by different persons having different objects in view, and so has never been completed.

At various times, it is true, Congress had appropriated $25,000 for the Washington papers, $30,000 for the Madison papers, $20,000 for the Jefferson papers, and $20,000 for the Hamilton papers. But these documents were not at the time transferred to the Library of Congress. The purchase of the manuscript of Washington's Farewell Address was so long delayed by debate, petty bickering, and sometimes pointless argument, that it was snatched from the very hands of Congress; for on February 12, 1850—the same day that Clay's resolution for its purchase was finally approved, the precious manuscript was sold at auction, as had been advertised. James Lenox of New York had purchased it for $2,300.

Up until the Civil War period no extensive collection of maps had accumulated in the Library of Congress. In 1830, Librarian Meehan, on instructions of the Committee, had purchased Burr's *County Atlas of the State of New York* and other State maps not already in the Library, but there were not even the beginnings of a map collection suitable to the needs of Congress and the growing nation. The need was even greater because of the fact that nowhere in the United States—nor on the continent for that matter—was there even a tolerably complete single collection of geographical materials. The collections of the State Department, of the Hydrographic Office, of the Topographical and engineer bureaus of the Coast Survey, even the Harvard and Smithsonian collections, had been formed for some special and limited purpose. Nowhere was there a true geographical library for investigating geographical questions of sea and land, at home and abroad.

Thus the suggestion of Lieut. Edward B. Hunt of the United States Army, that such a department be established in the Library of Congress, aroused the immediate attention and interest of the public and of scientific men all over the country. Lieutenant Hunt's suggestion had been offered and discussed at the annual meeting of the American Association for the Advancement of Science at Cleveland, in July and early August of 1853. After citing the general lack of such resources, Hunt said:

> At this stage of affairs it occurred to me that a complete and special geographical library, not only of materials on the United States seacoast, but of those relating to the whole country—to America at large, and to the whole world—would be a highly valuable aid to all researches, whether undertaken for the Coast Survey or for any other purpose— either of history, of commerce, of home policy, or of foreign relations. This idea at once connected itself with the Library of Congress as the place of all others where it could be executed and where it would prove of most value and convenience. Congress is reinstating the Library, after its burning, and now is the time when this plan can best be undertaken. These geographical aids are greatly needed in Congress for the clear understanding and discussion of many important questions, both domestic and foreign, and in no place could such a collection better serve all interest. . . .

Hunt laid down plans for a distinct map department for the Library of Congress, and these were later presented in a memorial by the Association to the Joint Library Committee. The materials to be embraced in such a collection were listed—"first, all maps and charts, whether published or unpublished, which relate to the United States and its waters or to any portion thereof, however minute; second, a complete collection of maps and atlases which have been published abroad, and which relate to other countries; third, geographical society publications, the results of the various exploring expeditions sent out by the various governments, and such other books and periodicals as are especially devoted to such intelligence; fourth, works on geographical bibliography; and, lastly, a pair of first-class terrestrial and celestial globes."

The memorial was referred to the Committee on the Library. Congress did not act further upon it and the maps, like the manuscript collections, remained for many years longer in an inchoate state.

The beginnings of a periodical division for the Library of Congress can probably be traced to the decision of the Committee on January 16, 1836, to subscribe to all newspapers of Washington City that were not being received. These files were destroyed in the fire of 1851, and later, with complete files of the *National Intelligencer* and of the *Richmond Enquirer*, had to be replaced. Files of the *Philadelphia Aurora*, the *National Intelligencer*, the *Boston Centinel* and the *Paris Moniteur* were added in the years between 1852 and 1854. Although issues of the *London Gazette* from 1665 to 1846, and of the *London Times* were available, there were no New York newspapers. The *London Court Journal*, received regularly, was bound at the end of each year. The only American magazine subscribed to was *De Bow's Review*.

It was an expensive matter to secure periodicals published in Europe, as Meehan's letter to Obadiah Rich in 1844 illustrated.

In it the Librarian of Congress complained that the Harnden Express had charged him $1.50 to carry one number of the *Edinburgh Review* to Washington, and 12½ cents for its delivery at the Library.

With the increased activity and interest in the Library of Congress it soon became apparent that John Meehan would not be able to take care of the manifold duties himself. In 1829, when he came to office, he had one assistant librarian—E. J. Hume. A second assistant librarian was appointed in 1841, and a third assistant librarian in 1855. In 1831 a messenger had been added to the staff.

Hume had held office for only a year after Meehan's appointment, and in 1830, E. B. Stelle, who had previously assisted George Watterston, was reinstated. Stelle held this position until the political revolution of 1861 swept him out of power and Ainsworth Rand Spofford in. In 1833 the salary of the first assistant librarian had been increased to $1,150. In 1855 the salary was increased to $1,500, and in 1856, to $1,800.

When Meehan was appointed, the salary of the Librarian of Congress was $1,500. In 1854, Congress had voted an increase to $1,800, and in 1855 the salary of the head of the Library of Congress was fixed at $2,160. Meehan's son, C. H. W. Meehan, had entered the Library's service in February of 1833, before the office of second assistant librarian had been created, and was paid $1.50 a day during Congressional sessions. From December 2, 1833, to March 4, 1835, the younger Meehan received $398 for his services at this rate, Sundays excepted.

In a similar manner, before the creation of the office of third assistant librarian, Charles W. Hinman had been employed, at a salary of $1,150, which was paid from the contingent fund. The messenger received $500 a year, to which was added $150 extra in 1832 for that and the previous year. In 1834 the messenger's salary was raised to $700 annually, increased to $1,200 in 1854 and to $1,440 in 1855. In 1842 the Committee had taken into account the additional burden placed upon the messenger by the necessity of building fires and suggested that he receive "about $25 per month, or whatever it may be shown to be" for the expense he was thus put to. Later a boy was engaged who, for ten dollars a month, made the fires and did "the chars of the law room." Laborers were later hired for similar work.

Book agents for the Library of Congress were appointed by a resolution of the Committee in 1830. Obadiah Rich—that relentless pursuer of bargains in the London book marts—was appointed in England, and Pishey Thompson of the immaculate shirt ruffles, for America. When Pishey returned to the Lincolnshire fens to complete his literary labors he was succeeded by Frank Taylor of Washington. Taylor served as the Library's agent from 1843 until 1863.

After a line of steam packets had been established to Le Havre in 1847, the position of agent on the Continent was created. Arrangements were made in 1854 with M. Hector Bossange, who had wanted the job since 1842, for the purchase of French books. Consignments of imported books from the Library's European agents were sent in care of the collector at New York. A special agent in the New York Custom House was assigned by the Committee to look after these importations. He was given formal power of attorney in 1847. There was a similar agent in the Boston Custom House to care for Library business, especially to forward periodicals and books wanted without the delay attendant on transmission by the New York liners that the Cunard Line was sending to that point.

With the succession of each new President there were murmurs of a possible change in the Library's administration. It is possible that a man whom a political gesture had placed in office

192

would be more or less resigned to such a probability. Meehan, however, saw two such rumors come to naught and his own position as Librarian of Congress survive the administrations of both President Pierce and President Buchanan. At Pierce's accession, in 1853, the *Portsmouth Chronicle* speculated upon the possibility of Meehan's displacement in favor of Samuel E. Cones. It was a rumor deplored by the *Washington News,* which declared the following day that while it had no knowledge of Mr. Cones, personal or otherwise, it regretted "that so excellent a citizen as Mr. Meehan, of whom we have never heard an evil word spoken for more than twenty years by members of Congress, or citizens of any party, should be deprived of a valuable office, the duties of which he had so acceptably discharged." It is apparent, from the letter he wrote, with little show of taste, it would seem, to Eliza Watterston, daughter of the former Librarian, on March 19, 1857, that Donald Macleod hoped to profit upon accession of President Buchanan:

> . . . Entre nous, my application for the office of Librarian of Congress has been placed before the President. I also took occasion, as I could not see him again before leaving Washington, to leave a note alluding to days of "auld lang syne" and very delicately to yourself, our common friend. I mention this in case he should mention the circumstance in your first interview. . . .

John Meehan did, however, eventually fall victim to a political move. He was removed from office, like his predecessor, by a Presidential hand. Abraham Lincoln, succeeding to power, regarded the Librarian of Congress as a Southern sympathizer. On May 24, 1861, he requested his dismissal, and in his stead appointed Dr. John G. Stephenson as fifth Librarian of Congress.

Meehan had worked hard and he was well liked by Members of all parties. Caleb Atwater expressed the opinion of many when he said that the Meehans, father and son, and their assistants were "among the most polite and agreeable gentlemen" in Washington. And there were many to agree with his estimate of Meehan's administration:

> They are always ready to attend to the wishes of all who call on them. Personally acquainted with nearly all who call at their room, they are always ready to introduce a stranger to any gentleman who is in the room. Fatigued as they sometimes are with the constant labor of a long day, yet they never complain of their toil, but cheerfully attend to all the wants of the visitors. This room is opened very early in the morning, and not closed until a late hour. If any officers of the Government deserve all their salaries and more too, they are the Meehans, father and son, Stelle and Kearon. Their salaries are small ones, and their labors are great and fatiguing all day long, during the whole session of Congress. Having known these gentlemen fourteen years and upward in their present stations, I take a real pleasure in bearing this testimony in their favor.

X

SCHOLAR AND VISIONARY

*D*uring the years of the Civil War the Library of Congress was little used by the legislators or by the public. Congress was no longer the settled, unified body of happier times, concerned solely with national interests. As the secession movement got under way and the cotton States, one after another, voted in favor of secession, their representatives in Congress were saying their farewells to fellow members, just as in other branches of the Federal Government officers of the Army and Navy and those holding civil appointments were rapidly resigning, their decisions hastened by the Union sentiment which prevailed in the Capital. How general this exodus of Southern sympathizers from the Government service had been was evident a few months later when only a scattered number resigned rather than take an oath of allegiance—so worded as to meet the Union view of the great issue of the day—required under the law enacted by the first Republican Congress. At the President's reception in January it was noted that "with few exceptions, the party that elected Buchanan to office was absent. The party that opposed him was represented by its best men in Washington."

What the fate of Washington itself would be if the Government were broken up, was not even certain. Some reasoned that even a division of the country would not necessarily mean that the city along the Potomac would cease to be a capital city. For if Maryland and Virginia went with the South, then Washington would become the seat of the Southern republic. It was a time of great uncertainty everywhere, but selfish interests were submerged in a rising tide of patriotism when the nation's existence was threatened. This impulse of devotion to country was typically represented by a statement in the *Washington Star*—a paper that had advocated the election of Breckinridge, the Southern candidate, and had then the largest circulation in the District—to the effect that "the doctrine of secession on the part of the South because of the election of Lincoln is obnoxious to the democracy of this section of the country." While business men and property holders in the District had expressed themselves as being in favor of observing the will of the majority, some residents had defiantly donned the blue cockade. Even at the President's reception on New Year's Day both Union and Secession cockades were seen. The truth was that Washington, while a slaveholding community in a slave territory, was neither a Southern nor a Northern town; nor did it take its political hue from the national administration, as self-interest would seem to dictate. The campaign of 1860 had illustrated the current variety of political expression, and Lincoln's election had been marked by disorders.

At the beginning of the war, Congress was largely occupied with maintaining order in the District, protecting the Capital from possible invasion, investigating charges of hostility to the Government, and passing emergency legislation—immediate measures whose urgency did not permit of the leisurely research enjoyed in their Library in earlier and less troubled times.

The disturbed condition of the Union, where two flags floated instead of one, had not, however, affected the scramble for offices customary on every change of administration. To Lincoln in the White House considering the flood of applications, it seemed as if he were "sitting in a palace assigning apartments to importunate applicants, while the structure is on fire and likely soon to perish in ashes." The Librarian of Congress, John Meehan, as an alleged Southern sympathizer, had come in for the President's scrutiny, and John G. Stephenson, who had accompanied Senator Henry S. Lane of Indiana to Washington in February, 1861, had succeeded in securing the appointment as Librarian of Congress. That Lincoln was persuaded to make it was due largely to the influence of the Secretary of the Interior, Caleb B. Smith, who came from the same State as Senator Lane. Undoubtedly Stephenson's greatest contribution to the development of the Library of Congress was his choice of Ainsworth Spofford as his first assistant. There was nothing in his own background, in his training, or in his predilections to fit him especially for the Librarian's post. Born in Lancaster, New Hampshire—the son of Reuben Stephenson—he had attended Lancaster Academy where in the 1840's he had been occupied very pleasantly for the most part in amateur theatricals. When his studies there were completed he prepared for a medical career and after graduation practiced medicine for a time in Terre Haute, Indiana.

It was from this city that he started out with Senator Lane, accompanying his friend to Washington, where neither lost any time in pulling the necessary political strings for his appointment. That fact was scarcely accomplished before Stephenson, leaving the Library in charge of the Assistant Librarian, Ainsworth Spofford, the third assistant, L. L. Tilden, and L. G. Duckworth, the messenger, was off to the wars, acting as volunteer aide to General Meredith. In this capacity he seems to have conducted himself with some distinction, for on December 14, 1863, Major General Abner Doubleday reported that John G. Stephenson, Librarian of Congress, had "exposed himself freely on all occasions and rendered many valuable services." It is to Ainsworth Rand Spofford, chief assistant librarian during these years, that credit must be given for holding the Library together, for Dr. Stephenson's later interest in war speculation left him little time for his library duties and as 1864 drew to a close he resigned as Librarian of Congress. He died almost twenty years later—in November, 1883. When Stephenson resigned in December, 1864, President Lincoln rewarded the faithful service of Spofford by appointing him Librarian.

Very unostentatiously Ainsworth Rand Spofford began that administration which Herbert Putnam was later to refer to as the influence most potent in the development of the Library of Congress and in the determination of its scope and character. In the *New York Times* of January 5, 1865, there appeared five lines of small type buried in a column headed, "News from Washington":

> The President has appointed Mr. Ainsworth R. Spofford, Librarian of Congress, to succeed Dr. J. G. Stephenson, resigned. Mr. Spofford today entered upon the duties of his office.

Up to the time of his appointment as first assistant in the Library of Congress, Spofford had spent practically all of his adult life in close association with books, or in literary pursuits, as bookseller, publisher, editor and writer in turn. Born at Gilmanton, New Hampshire, on September 12, 1825, he was prepared under private tutors and later at Williston Seminary for the course at Amherst College. A threatened weakness of eyes and lungs, however, prevented his entering Amherst as planned, and at nineteen he left for Cincinnati in search of some activity that would suit his natural inclinations. Beginning his literary career at the bottom of the ladder, as clerk in a Cincinnati bookshop, he was to remain for fifteen years, from 1845 to 1860, in the Ohio city, stepping from bookselling to bookpublishing and from bookpublishing to associate editorship of the *Cincinnati Commercial*. It was this journal which dispatched him to report the Battle of Bull Run. The assignment turned the whole course of his career and shaped his entire future destiny. For it was while he was returning to Cincinnati from the battlefield by way of Washington that he was offered, and accepted, the position as first assistant in the Library of Congress. Herbert Putnam has given an excellent word picture of Ainsworth Spofford during the early days of his librarianship:

To those who visited the old library of Congress at the Capitol (and during the latter half of the 19th Century they numbered thousands) he will always be associated with it—a long lean figure, in scrupulous frock, erect at a standing desk, and intent upon its littered burden, while the masses of material surged incoherently about him. From time to time—an inquiry interrupting—a swift, decisive turn, an agile stride, a nervous burrow in some apparently futile heap, and a return triumphant, yet staidly triumphant, with the required volume. Then again absorption in other volumes already subjugated, in auction catalogs, in copyright certificates, in correspondence (invariably autograph), in notes for editorial use, in the countless minutiæ of insistent, direct, undelegated labor. A figure of absorption and of labor, consonant with the collections as they then existed; quaint indeed in mode and expression, yet efficient; immersed in the trivial, yet himself by no means trivial, imparting to it the dignity that comes of intense seriousness and complete sincerity. Grave in the task of infinite detail upon a mass of infinite dimension; grave but never dour. Cheerful rather, even buoyant. Disdaining the frivolous as a waste of time; yet appreciating humor, and even responsive to accredited jest, although the response might concede no more than an "it pleases you to be facetious!" A lover of nature, too, as booklovers often are, and pursuing her on occasions with deep breath and long stride. Granting himself, nevertheless, few vacations, and generally ignoring even the "annual leave" so scrupulously observed by most Government employees. Glorying, rather, in the assiduity which his hardy, if attenuated, frame permitted; for the weakness of the lungs survived only in a mechanical cough, and the weakness of the eyes was remedied so completely that in his eighty-second year he resisted a prescription for glasses as premature and derogatory. A circulation free and abundant; the palate of a child, and a digestion unafraid.

This was the man who superintended the growth of the Library of Congress through a period of rich development, saw it expand from a collection of some 63,000 items in the early '60s to 1,006,055 items in 1897, and was to see it number, before his death on August 11, 1908, 1,534,346 books and pamphlets, and about 900,000 miscellaneous items, with 1,200,000 copyright entries from the year 1870 until 1897, when they were moved into the new building. He was to usher in an era when revised copyright laws added with almost appalling immediacy to Library collections; when private collectors, visualizing development of a great national library, were, like Peter Force, to turn over magnificent private libraries to the Library of Congress. He was to witness tremendous physical expansion in the Library's quarters—beginning with the addition of two wings in the Capitol, and culminating, in his lifetime, in the palatial structure of which he had dreamed and for which he had labored every year since he had first tentatively set down the daring vision in his report of 1871, and, a year later, outlined his plans for housing a great national institution.

On March 3, 1865, Congress had enacted a law which, as much as any other single factor, was to lead to the building up of a great general collection, representative, in time, of American literary trends and the development of American thought. This was that act which provided that copies of all books published in the United States, and other creative works, should be deposited in the Library of Congress.

Prior to this act the provisions observed for copyright had been very defective. The first law of 1790 had required a book to be deposited, within three months after its publication, in the office of the clerk of the district in which the author resided. It also directed the clerk to transmit the copy to the State Department in Washington. No provision was made for the transmission and no supervision was established, so that not more than one half of the number of books for which copyrights were secured ever reached the State Department and no records were kept when books were not sent. The books received were stacked in a room by themselves, not properly stamped, recorded, or catalogued, and inaccessible for general use. Although the Supreme Court had decided that deposit of the copy in the State Department was essential to a valid title, in case of loss of certificate the author was left with no means of establishing his claims, and though he might have fulfilled all the conditions of the law, the benefits were still lost to him.

In 1846 in the tenth section of an act which established the Smithsonian Institution, deposit of one copy each of every published work was required to be made to the Library of the Smithsonian Institution and to the Library of Congress.

Since no penalty was attached to neglect of this requirement, it was generally considered no more than directory and was only half-heartedly complied with. As a result the whole value of books received during the year 1851 had amounted, in the Smithsonian deposit, to no more than $450, exclusive of maps, music and other articles, while the expenditure for postage and transportation of these and the time and labor spent in issuing certificates was about $225.

The Library of Congress had fared no better under the clause than had the Smithsonian Institution. *Norton's Literary Gazette*, on July 15, 1862, commented upon this failure of the public to comply with the requirements:

> We are surprised at the apathy shown by some of our leading publishers in complying with the law in relation to copyright, which directs

that a copy of every book copyrighted shall be placed in the Library of Congress, and also in that of the Smithsonian Institution. If publishers would look merely to their own advantage they would see that there could be no better advertisement to their publications than a position where they can be seen and judged upon by the first men of the nation. Books intended for these libraries, if sent to the office of this paper, properly directed, will be always promptly forwarded.

Professor C. C. Jewett, Librarian of the Smithsonian collections, outlined the deficiencies of the existing law in the early reports of that Institution, and general dissatisfaction led to a later transfer in 1859 of the copyright business from the Department of State to the Department of the Interior, when the Library of Congress ceased to receive deposits. The privilege was revived in 1865, however, and five years later was enlarged by the law which transferred to the Library the entire copyright business and incidentally required both copies of the articles copyrighted to be deposited there.

The accumulations that resulted from this legal provision, valuable though they were, were to prove a source of continuous embarrassment to Mr. Spofford, and, in time, to develop an almost desperate necessity for adequate housing space.

But it was a situation met, on the part of Spofford, with the greatest optimism—jubilance, almost, in the midst of the clutter and chaos of his inadequate quarters—as he realized that the Library of Congress, now expanding by leaps and bounds, was rapidly outgrowing its rooms in the Capitol, and must inevitably secure a home of its own in the not too distant future.

Meanwhile another event had brought the fact home with additional poignancy. Space had to be found without delay to receive the deposit whose transfer Congress had authorized in 1866 from the Library of the Smithsonian Institution to the Library of Congress, with the stipulation that future acquisitions should follow. More than 40,000 volumes thus were to become, at a stroke, an integral part of the Library of Congress, although the books were to remain as a deposit, capable of being withdrawn on reimbursement of the expense of binding and care.

Aware of these needs for additional space, Congress had authorized the construction of two new halls to be added to the Library's quarters in the Capitol, extending eastward from the north and south ends of the main hall, forming three sides of a square. These additional halls were built, like the main room, entirely of iron, and each was 95 feet long, 29½ feet wide and 38 feet high—practically the same dimensions as the central Library room, although each contained an additional tier of galleries. By early December, in 1866, one of these wings was completed and fully occupied with books, and the second wing was finished soon after.

Spofford himself considered that the light and ventilation of these enlarged quarters were superior to those of the main library, while he now had more than 21,000 feet of iron shelving —enough to provide space for about 170,000 volumes. Taking into account the shelf accommodation of the law library room and the long attic room which communicated with the upper gallery of the main library, nearly five miles of shelves were available to the hard-pressed Librarian. These, he computed, should offer harbor to more than 200,000 volumes.

But even so great an addition to available space proved hardly adequate to meet the demands of the growing collections. With the Smithsonian deposit alone had come more than 40,000 volumes that, because of their great value as reference sources, had to be made easily accessible. Spofford described the deposit as "especially valuable in the range of scientific books, comprising by far the largest collections of the journals and transactions of learned societies, foreign and domestic, which exist in America.

It would also be found to be, he said, "an important supplement to the present library in the departments of linguistics, bibliography, statistics, voyages and travels, and works relating to the fine arts, in each of which departments it embraces works of great cost and value, while its collection of books in all branches of national history is invaluable."

By the beginning of 1867 about half of this collection had already been removed and partially catalogued and the remainder only awaited completion of the south wing to be transferred and arranged upon the shelves. It was in this same year that Congress purchased by special grant for $100,000 the magnificent collection of Peter Force, and Spofford was confronted with the additional necessity of classifying, cataloguing and finding room for the valuable items thus acquired. This was no inconsiderable task, for the Force collection contained nearly 1,000 volumes of American newspapers, including 245 volumes printed prior to 1800; a large collection of the journals and laws of the Colonial assemblies, showing the legislative policy which culminated in their independence; the highly prized publications of the presses of the Bradfords, of Benjamin Franklin, and Isaiah Thomas; forty-one different works of Increase and Cotton Mather, printed at Cambridge and Boston, from 1671 to 1735; a perfect copy of that rarest of American books, Eliot's Indian Bible; and a large and valuable collection of incunabula, the "cradle books" of the history of printing. Even more valuable than the books were the manuscripts of the Force collections, which included two autograph journals of George Washington, one dated 1775, during Braddock's expedition, and one 1787, written at Mount Vernon. Besides these priceless manuscripts there were two volumes of an original military journal of Major General Greene, from 1781 to 1782; twelve folio volumes of the papers of John Paul Jones while he commanded American cruisers, 1776-78; a private journal left by Arthur Lee while he was minister to France, 1776-77; thirty or forty orderly books of the Revolution; forty-eight volumes of historical autographs of great rarity and interest; and an immense mass of manuscript materials for the "American Archives"—a documentary history of America, publication of which was ordered by Congress. All these treasures may be freely consulted or studied by the American public or by citizens of any other country in the Rare Book wing of the Library of Congress today.

Exclusive of the Smithsonian and the Peter Force acquisitions, by the end of 1866, there were in the Library of Congress 99,650 volumes. The pamphlet collection was small, as it did not exceed more than 6,000 items, exclusive of duplicates. Early in his career Spofford expressed his intention of enlarging the collection of these materials, "often so valuable for political history."

The Librarian of Congress was insistent, in these early years, on the need for a good catalogue for the Library. He recognized the importance of an index by subjects that would embrace not only the supplementary catalogues of the past three years but would include the entire contents of the Smithsonian collection and other acquisitions as well. Spofford abandoned, with this labor, the old Jeffersonian system of classification as unsuited to the necessities of readers consulting a large library, and in the next catalogue he issued, the books were arranged alphabetically under the head of authors; a subsequent publication arranged the books according to subjects. The Library's collection became of more practical use thereafter to Members of Congress, who were showing ever greater liberality in their appropriations for its increase and maintenance. More newspapers and other periodicals were added to the subscription lists and, encouraged by the Librarian, the Committee kept a sharp look-out for literary bargains to be discovered in auction lists, trade catalogues and the stalls of second-hand book dealers. By the end of 1866 the copyright law had added 836 volumes, 386 pieces of music, and 202 maps, engravings and photographs to the collections. Spofford suggested a modification of this statute in his first annual report to Congress in 1866:

> The undersigned is of the opinion, founded upon experience, that the benefits of the law to the Congressional Library will depend greatly upon the means provided for its enforcement, and the vigilance with which it is administered. Comparatively few owners of copyrights, outside of the leading publishing houses, comply with the requisition of the law without notice. These notices, to the number of several hundreds, have been regularly served upon delinquents whenever the undersigned could obtain authentic evidence of a copyright having been issued. In most cases, the requirements of the law have been complied with after notice, although there are many exceptions. The provisions of the English law of copyrights, which are much more exacting than our own (requiring the deposit of five copies of each work instead of one) prescribe a penalty of five pounds sterling, and the value of the books withheld, recoverable at the suit of the proper officer of the institution in which the work is required to be deposited. This provision is found to be amply sufficient to secure a general compliance with the law. A similar modification of the present statute is respectfully suggested to the consideration of the committee, as also a provision by which books and other publications may be transmitted through the mails, free of charge, to the Library of Congress. These amendments would remove the chief obstacles which exist to a full compliance with the law.

Before Spofford had issued his second annual report in 1867, the law had been amended in accordance with his suggestions. Four years later, in 1870, Congress transferred the entire copyright business from the Department of the Interior to the Library of Congress. Ainsworth Spofford was now confronted with the problem not only of providing space for the volumes accumulating under the law, but also for quarters in which to conduct a business exacting enough, in itself, to occupy the full time and attention of one or more individuals.

In the midst of the multifarious duties that were piling up about him, the Librarian of Congress gave his attention to correcting some of those conditions that had, for so long, made the Library an unsuitable place for study, and which "Petrus Penwagler" and his colleagues of an earlier day had so deservedly satirized. Seeking to restore that "still air of quiet and delightful studies" of which Milton wrote, to the legislator's library, he was successful in bringing about a revision of the by-laws regulating use of the Library rooms. Those flocks of children who had hitherto delighted noisily to turn the pages of folios and picture books, interrupting Congressional reflection by their animated chatter, were henceforth excluded by a provision that closed the Library of Congress to readers under sixteen years of age. Likewise there was enforced, not without public dissatisfaction, the regulation which barred access to the alcoves and galleries to all but Members of Congress or those who were accompanied by some officer of the Library.

There still remained to readers, however, the unrestricted use of any number of volumes called for at the tables, and unhampered access to the catalogues. Members of Congress gained additional seclusion when a private reading room, lying between the central library and the rotunda, was cleared and fitted up in 1867, with current periodicals for their sole use.

As Spofford said, this was "an improvement long needed," and greatly facilitated "the use of the numerous and valuable files of newspapers, magazines and reviews, foreign and American, now received at the Library." The room also contained bound sets of leading American journals, arranged for easy reference, and was furnished with comfortable chairs and long tables at which the Members might read at ease and in seclusion. This little room in the Capitol was the forerunner of the luxurious "Senators' Reading Room" and the "Representatives' Reading Room" later built into the separate building of the Library of Congress and now merged into that one beautiful chamber known as the "Congressional Reading Room."

Spofford yet found time, in these early years of his administration, to give attention to the needs for additional legislation "to render effective the exchanges of public documents for the publications of foreign governments"—a system set in motion by a Congressional joint resolution approved on the 2nd of March, 1867. Spofford was receiving enthusiastic response from Great Britain, Russia, Denmark, Belgium, The Netherlands, Greece, Switzerland, Chile, and Costa Rica, and was delighting in the prospect of supplying those deficiencies in the works published at the expense of foreign governments that he felt were hampering research into the history, legislation, statistics, and condition of the countries they represented.

By 1869 Spofford had completed the appalling job of cataloguing the collections of the Library of Congress. He announced the work—one "of great magnitude"—as "necessarily very imperfect in some particulars." The catalogue filled two large volumes, more than seventeen hundred pages printed in double column type. Of the arrangement he said:

On the score of scientific or logical arrangement this method may be open to grave objections; on the score of utility and convenience, its superiority scarcely admits of a doubt. From the nature of the cases, all classification of knowledge, save an alphabetical one, must be purely arbitrary. Every man can produce a system which admirably suits himself, but unhappily it is found that his system is clear to nobody else. To save the time and patience of readers, there is no method that will avail but one which is its own interpreter; and the alphabetical arrangement of topics, with a copious system of cross-references, solves every difficulty as it arises, instead of keeping the reader on a baffled search for knowledge.

Spofford, first to suggest that catalogues of the Library of Congress be made available to the general public by the Congressional Printer supplying them at cost, took an important step forward in expanding the boundaries of service hitherto maintained by the Library of Congress and laid the foundation for such later enterprises as the Union catalogue and other co-operative functions of a national institution.

Owing to his generous interpretation of his duties and his conviction that the treasures of the Library should not be restricted to legislators alone but should be made available to the American public, as early as 1869 he was asking that some provision be made to open the Library to the public during evening as well as daylight hours. He wrote:

> A great library, much the largest in the United States, has been built up at the seat of government, primarily for the use of the national legislature, but secondarily, and by usage as a library of reading and reference, for all who desire to resort to it. The withdrawal of books for use outside its walls is properly restricted by statute to members of Congress and the higher officers of the government; nor would any wide extension of the privilege of taking books from the library be compatible with its highest utility as a library of reference, its safety, or its careful preservation.
>
> Nevertheless it remains true that the public intelligence and welfare are promoted by every extension of the means of acquiring knowledge. The very numerous class of persons in the employ of the Government at the Capital are at present without the ability to avail themselves of any privilege which this library presents.

By 1874 nothing had been done by Congress to make evening openings possible and again Ainsworth Spofford called the attention of Congress to the rights of the public in the growing institution. "It might prove of incalculable benefit to the public intelligence and even tend to the improvement of the Government service," he suggested, "were these rich stores of information thrown freely open every night for the use and reference of all." Nothing was done along this line, however, until the new building was opened.

This desire to make the great Library under his care accessible to all became an obsession with him. He realized the illimitable wealth of the collections, the invaluable store of knowledge and information imprisoned along the cluttered shelves of his library. Again and again he besought Congress to open it to every seeker after learning. Through the years his reports contained an almost impassioned plea for extension of service and usefulness. In the most trivial things this motive predominated. Thus, in 1869, he told Congress: "No provision had ever been made for lighting the library at night, and even when Congress holds evening sessions it must be closed at dusk, from mere inability to find books after the going down of the sun. The occasional inconvenience thus caused to Senators and Representatives, who may need authorities or references, would go far to justify the expense of introducing gas, which, in a library constructed wholly of iron, would be attended with no risk from fire."

As 1874 drew to a close, with no provision made toward making the collections more accessible, he lamented, "That we should continue to see this great Library, as a means of education and enlightenment, so confined and limited in its uses, cannot fail to be viewed with regret by every liberal mind. . . . It is true that, in a Republic which rests upon the popular intelligence, and one of whose chiefest glories is its literature, a great national collection of books, while formed primarily for the uses of the legislative and judicial branches of the Government, ought to be utilized by a far wider circle of readers."

Again and again the theme recurs: Thus, in 1875, "The American people should rely with confidence upon finding in one great and monumental library, and that belonging to the Government, every book which their country has produced." . . . "The Library of Congress," he declared a year later, "has become, by liberal legislation and extensive growth, the library of the Nation."

Meanwhile the Librarian of Congress was pressing his almost solitary campaign for adequate quarters. A thin, tentative note it was at first, bidding modestly in 1870 for additional shelf room and exulting in acquisition of a small ante-room and a storage room under the north wing of the Library which the Architect of the Capitol Extension had "courteously and efficiently" connected with the alcoves for his use; requesting "the construction of about thirty cases of shelves, of light material, to be placed in the upper alcoves." But the note swelled as the months passed, and Ainsworth Spofford's busy figure was almost hidden at times behind accumulating stacks of unshelved books.

"The constant and rapid growth of the Library under my charge renders it necessary to call the attention of the Committee to the emergency which will soon compel the provision of more rooms for books," Spofford wrote in 1871. Despite the addition of seven thousand linear feet of shelves and the opening of a room beneath the Library for the storage of duplicates— "kept within the appropriation of $1,000 made for the purpose" —available space was totally inadequate to accommodate even two years' growth of the Library.

"Where are we to look for more room?" Spofford inquired of Congress. The old hall of the House of Representatives had been suggested and the Librarian thought it might be feasible to line the walls of that considerable space with alcoves, "without encroaching upon the use of the hall as a thoroughfare, and a gallery for statuary." Spofford's objection to this plan was that it would, at best, only provide accommodation for five years' growth, at the end of which time Congress would be confronted by the same problem, besides the disadvantage of breaking up the library into supplementary divisions more or less remote from the central hall.

The copyright business transferred to the Library of Congress in 1870, was creating its own problems. "There is now no suitable space for the transacting of the heavy copyright business of the Library," Spofford wrote the Committee in 1871, "and the records of copyright of the whole United States, numbering several hundred volumes in folio, are stored in a remote room in the basement of the Capitol, at much inconvenience and loss of time for reference. The large and often complicated business involved in the receipt of masses of books from all quarters, the heavy receipts of copyright books, periodicals, and other articles by the daily mails, and the preparation for the binding and receipt from it in return of thousands of volumes; all these operations, constantly going on, are, from necessity, huddled into a narrow space in that part of the Library which should be kept clear for the public."

This entire labor, in addition to his duties as Librarian of Congress, Spofford was, at the time he wrote this, at the close of 1871, undertaking with a Library staff of twelve, including himself.

The previous year he had requested two additional assistants, at salaries, respectively, of $1,800 and $1,200, to help him with the increased responsibilities he had inherited with the changed copyright law. After less than six months' operation of the new law, he and his staff had already recorded more than 5,000 copyrights, and prepared and dispatched the necessary certificates in connection. "To continue this with the present force at my disposal, and still keep up the efficient administration of the rapidly growing Library, with its catalogues and accessions, is quite impossible," the Librarian reminded the Committee. When one considers that a year's operation of the copyright law had brought 11,512 articles into the Library of Congress, including more than 2,000 books and more than 3,000 pamphlets and periodicals, and had, during 1871, added nearly 20,000 items to Library collections, some idea may be gained of the problems that harassed the Librarian in his cramped quarters, and with his very limited staff. The Library itself at this time was closely approaching a quarter of a million volumes and, it was predicted, would exceed half a million in twenty years. Spofford himself foresaw that it "must in time become one of the largest collections of books in the world."

At the same time he suggested to Congress the expediency of erecting a separate building, designed expressly for the Library's accommodation and for the copyright business of the country. "Should this be determined upon," he wrote at the close of 1871, "it would still be expedient to retain in the central hall of the existing Library a sufficiently complete collection of books for a library of reference, to include copies of all the leading writers in science and literature, as well as a full library of jurisprudence. The halls of the two wings might be appropriated as reading rooms for periodicals for the use of Congress, and the alcoves and galleries, with their spacious fire-proof and numbered shelving, would serve admirably for the orderly arrangement of the archives of the Senate and House of Representatives, now so inadequately provided for. That the entire Capitol building will, at no distant day, be required for legislative purposes, is apparent." If, however, a separate building were not expedient, there was, the Librarian suggested, an alternative that would retain the whole collection in the Capitol and, at the same time, make provision for its increase "for at least a quarter of a century to come." This could be accomplished by extending the west front of the Capitol building, the entire projection of which was then occupied by the Library of Congress, from sixty to one hundred feet, and by constructing underneath the extensions rooms for the rapidly accumulating copyright archives and material.

"A spacious reading room for periodicals might also be secured," Spofford suggested, "while the western front of the Capitol, so conspicuous from the most thickly settled portion of the city, might be made to assume for the first time an architectural appearance worthy of so noble a structure."

The Library of Congress continued relentlessly to grow. One by one the wooden cases reluctantly introduced into the alcoves to accommodate the overflow, were filled up. Newspapers remained unbound, stacked in indiscriminate heaps for want of the space to file bound volumes; the Library had no packing room and, as Spofford pointed out, "the heavy receipt of books from all quarters, by daily mails and otherwise, the bindery business, the cataloguing of the books, the correspondence of the Library, the direction of assistants, and the extensive daily labors of the copyright department, are all constantly going on in those public parts of the Library which should be kept free for readers."

Visitors to the Library of Congress in these days commented freely on "the disarrangement always visible." Masses of books, pamphlets, newspapers and engravings, in the course of collation, cataloguing, labeling and stamping, were under the eye, and often under the feet, of Congress. With some spirit the Librarian answered criticism with the remark, "A moment's reflection would convince the most critical observer that where no place but a public one is provided for labors so multifarious and full of detail as those of a great library constantly receiving extensive additions to its stores, there must be apparent disorder in the very process of reducing it to order. Until Congress shall provide adequate space for performing these varied labors, they must of necessity go on directly under the public eye; and if the marble floors are littered with books in various stages of preparation for use, it is because that body has not yet provided quarters where processes can be separated from results, but has left the Librarian no chance to exhibit his results without at the same time exhibiting all the processes by which those results are attained."

It was not to be wondered at that under these conditions the Library of Congress became—as the Librarian himself put it—an unfit place for students. With regret Spofford was compelled to admit that, with the exception of one narrow reading room in the north wing, seating twenty-five readers, the entire Library of Congress at this time afforded no place for the quiet pursuit of study. Spofford described it as "subject to the constant annoyance of compulsory violations of its rule of silence by its own officers, and by the invasion of frequent processions of talking visitors," and again importuned Congress to make suitable provision for the great institution which was developing with appalling swiftness under the dome of the Capitol.

If further extensions of the Capitol building were not feasible, he reiterated, the alternative must be a wholly distinct building for the Library and copyright department; and he sketched a brief outline of his plan for such an edifice. The wants of the future, he contended, must constantly be kept in mind, and, considering these, space should be provided for no less than three millions of volumes. He drew attention to the largest existing library, the *Bibliothèque Nationale* of France, then numbering 1,400,000 volumes, and the Library of the British Museum, then closely approximating 1,000,000 with an annual growth of nearly 30,000 volumes a year.

"Whatever may be the present rate of growth of American libraries," he stated, "it cannot be doubted that their prospective

increase, with the growing development and intellectual enterprise of the country, will be in an accelerated ratio as compared
with the past. The Library of Congress has twice doubled within
twelve years. In 1860 there were 63,000 volumes in the Library;
in 1866 there were 100,000 volumes; and in 1872 there are
246,000. Without calculating upon specially large accessions, it
is reasonable to assume that by ordinary additions to its stores
from copyright and from all other sources, it will reach 700,000
volumes by the year 1900; one million and a quarter by 1925;
1,750,000 by 1950." How conservatively he had judged is apparent today, when—including six million volumes—almost ten
million products of the mind of man are sheltered under the Library's green-gold dome or are accessible in its white marble
annex just across the square. Spofford would scarcely have ventured to predict so phenomenal a growth as this. His imagination
only dared to fix the number of the collections at 2,500,000 in
1975—a century later.

In every country, he insisted, where civilization had attained
a high rank, there should be at least one great library, not only
universal in its range, but whose plan it should be to reverse the
rule of the smaller and more select libraries, which is exclusiveness, for one of inclusiveness. Unless this were done, he contended, unless the minor literature and the failures of our authors
were preserved, as well as the successes, American writers would
be without the means of surveying the whole field trodden by
their predecessors in any department. This comprehensive library
Spofford believed should be the library of the Government,
"which enjoys the benefit of the copy tax, and has thus supplied
without cost a complete representation of the intellectual product
of the country in every field of science and literature." To supplement this national collection the best books of ancient and
modern date, in all languages, should be acquired each year.

216

In offering his design for a suitable building to house such a collection, Spofford believed there was but one way in which room could be reserved for a library to grow in all directions, preserving a constant unity of plan and avoiding those obstructions which split up most great collections into several libraries. That was to construct the walls, at least of the interior, in circular form. "By this plan," he said, "the books can be arranged in alcoves rising tier above tier around the whole circumference of the circle, while the desks and catalogues for the use of readers occupy the center of the Library, and the time occupied in producing the books to this common center, through all the radii of the circle, is reduced to a minimum." This circular apartment, he suggested, should be surmounted by a dome of iron and glass, "thus yielding adequate light at all seasons, and in every part of the Library." Such a building should contain a copyright record room, a map room, a department for fine arts, a periodical room, and a packing room where all the mechanical operations of the Library could be performed.

If anyone were painfully aware of the necessity of this latter provision it was Ainsworth Spofford. The Library in which he labored daily with such devotion and concentration, was by now a veritable Tower of Babel, so cluttered and confusing that it was with difficulty that Members of Congress picked their way about among the piles. As for the public, it almost gave up hope of finding anything it required in the tumultuous masses of books, manuscripts and periodicals by which it found itself surrounded. Long since, the "grievous necessity" of piling books on the floor had been reached. Spofford assured the Committee in 1875 that if the Library were left much longer in its crowded, disorderly condition, the neglect of Congress would soon place its Librarian in the unhappy predicament of presiding over "the greatest chaos in America." A year later, nothing having been done, he an-

217

nounced, with unexpected humor, that the dilemma plainly would be, "that the legislature will crowd out the Library, with the alternative that the Library will crowd out the legislative body," and that "which of these migrations shall first take place is a matter which addresses itself to the sound discretion of Congress."

In the midst of these chaotic and disheartening conditions, the work of the Library of Congress went steadily forward. An index to the documents and debates of Congress was prepared and published; annual purchases of books, amounting to $11,500 at this time, were carefully made; beginnings were laid in 1876 for later rare book collections when rare and expensive books, early American imprints and other valuable items, not usually available, were purchased at special auction sales in American cities and on the Continent; the first volume of original historical documents on French discoveries and explorations in the United States, was published; new general catalogues were made ready; the growing copyright business was conducted; books were found and charged out; fines were received, money orders entered, questions answered, demands met.

The influx of money added to the worries of the harassed and overworked Mr. Spofford, to whom bookkeeping always remained one of the mysteries of life—and one of its unnecessary mysteries at that. Absorbed as he always was in the task at hand, moving about with the inevitable book in his left hand, snatching what time he could for his omnivorous reading, absentmindedly giving attention to those minor interruptions of what he considered more important occupations, the Librarian received and tucked away in whatever book or corner was immediately available money orders, checks, even coins received in the course of the day, and promptly forgot them. This indifference to the commercial side of his mounting duties, and his natural distaste for such mundane preoccupations, to say nothing of lack of clerical assistance, which made efficient records impossible, was to lead later to an embarrassing situation, when uncashed checks and money orders, distributed in out-of-the-way corners of the cluttered Library, mounted to the distressing amount of $30,000 in funds unaccounted for. This shortage was not made evident until after a Treasury Department investigation in 1896, though all who knew the gentle and scholarly Librarian recognized it for the clerical negligence it was, and nothing more. Unable to account for the missing money, and with complete forgetfulness of the uncashed money orders stored away in hundreds of handy books, Spofford paid the entire amount out of his own pocket without a murmur. It was not until his successor, John Russell Young, prepared to move the nation's collections to the new building across the Capitol lawns, that these old mementos of dues long since paid, came to light, and the Librarian of Congress was reimbursed for the entire amount. Commenting on the discovery and Mr. Spofford's "vindication" in its issue of December 10, 1897, the *New York Daily Tribune* reported:

"Hundreds of old money orders which the former Librarian had forgotten to cash discovered—the amount will be repaid to him"; and under a Washington dateline of December 9th, continued:

An investigation now being made by the officials of the Congressional Library and the Post Office Department, promises to throw a great deal of light on the recently widely discussed shortage of Ainsworth R. Spofford, the former Librarian. An examination by the Treasury Department about a year ago showed Mr. Spofford to be about $30,000 short in his accounts. Few people who knew him looked upon this at the time as anything more than an evidence of clerical negligence in his department. Now it appears that a large part, if not all, of this deficiency, which Mr. Spofford promptly made good out of his own pocket, will be accounted for by a great batch of old money orders which the absent-minded Librarian forgot to cash.

The Post Office Department gets a great many records of money orders from postmasters which are never presented for payment by the persons receiving them. The number of these uncashed orders addressed to the Librarian of Congress is perhaps greater than all others combined. While Mr. Spofford was in office, Mr. Metcalfe, chief of the Money Order Division of the Post Office Department, would inform the Librarian that there were orders on hand which he should cash. Sometimes he would get a few in response to these notifications, and sometimes not. Since John Russell Young has been placed in charge of the Library, however, he and Perry S. Heath, the First Assistant Postmaster General, have made a systematic search of the old Library records, and tucked away in one place or another they have unearthed hundreds of old orders, which the former Librarian had put aside, and apparently forgotten, and more are coming to light every day. Just what the total sum will amount to has not yet been estimated, but it probably will come near wiping out the discrepancies in Mr. Spofford's account. Some of the orders date back twenty-two years, and one of the largest was for $36. Many of the orders have expired by limitation, but they will all be paid by cash or warrant on the Treasury, and the money will be turned over to Mr. Spofford up to the amount he has paid out in rectifying his own accounts.

When one considers the Library of Congress of the late 1870s, one wonders how Ainsworth Spofford operated at all. For they were, indeed, years of administrative anguish. When he had taken office in 1864, the Library contained 99,000 volumes. Within a decade these had grown to 293,000 and space for further increase was wanting.

Year after year had gone by, as he fought for proper quarters, in appeal, reference, discussion, report, while books accumulated in heaps on the floor, in closets, in attics, in vaults. As Herbert Putnam later pointed out, it was not to be expected that larger appropriations should be granted for purchases, in this embarrassment, and that a normal accumulation was continued at all was due to the indefatigable optimism of Spofford himself. That

220

any practical use was made of a collection in such dire confusion was due solely to that marvelous locative memory which in him perhaps excelled that of any librarian of any generation. It was Putnam's belief that in the marvels of his memory Spofford, of all librarians, most nearly resembled Magliabecchi, except that he would not have been willing to claim the learning that tradition ascribes to the famous Italian. For it was the books that Spofford knew; not, except in certain fields, the subject matters. He was not, for instance, a classical scholar or a thorough linguist. He had no special knowledge of, or interest, in any branch of science or the arts, for he was a reader rather than a scholar. When he read, which he did constantly, he gave to reading his absolute attention, and, with him, the memory of the thing read followed as a matter of course. The extent and precision of his memory was impressive. Combining with what Putnam has called "the wonderful progressive agility" of Spofford's mind, they enabled him to render an indispensable service, during a half-century when the Library of Congress was a veritable chaos, in giving life to the collections and ensuring their future. Certainly only his extraordinary memory could have enabled Spofford, without complete catalogues, without proper bibliographic apparatus, with an inadequate staff and a trivial purchasing fund which averaged $11,000 a year, to gather into the collections the mass of invaluable material which they represented when they were moved from the Capitol.

With the meager funds at his disposal Spofford had pursued what seemed the only method possible in adding to the collections. He had bought here and there, chiefly from auction catalogues, individual items as such. He had not followed any method of systematic selection, which, while it would have built up a more nearly organic collection, would have lost to him many an item of extraordinary interest. In his choice of books Spofford was an antiquarian, interested, not in their future, but in their past. His dominant ambition for the Library of Congress was to see it rich in Americana. Years after Spofford had ceased to serve as Librarian of Congress, Herbert Putnam remarked this: "He could not bear the thought that precious original imprints should be lacking in it, though found in the Lenox or the Carter Brown. It was no consolation to him that we had the text itself in some other form, even in the facsimile, and he was obviously anguished when we decided against the expenditure for some such imprint, because we had to decide in favor of some text in itself, indispensable to research. Yet his enthusiasm would seem just as keen for some item of an interest purely particular and in no sense bibliographic, but (as his ardent blue pencil would proclaim against it) 'long sought.' "

The fruit of Spofford's report of 1872, in which he had described a design for a new library building, had been to bring forth several schemes for additional room for the Library of Congress, all of which contemplated enlargement of the Capitol. In the last month of 1872 Congress had recommended an appropriation—made the next year—of $5,000 for a committee made up of the chairman of the Joint Committee on the Library, the chairman of the Joint Committee on Public Buildings and Grounds, and the Librarian of Congress, to obtain plans for a new building and also to consider a proper site. In August, 1873, Spofford had prepared a list of specifications, brief and general in character, for the guidance "of those who may submit designs for a new building for the Library of Congress." This list itemized the circular reading room he considered indispensable, exterior walls "to be within a space 270 by 340 feet, with an elevation not to exceed 60 to 65 feet"; no dome or towers more than 70 feet high were to be admitted "on account of the proximity of the projected Library building to the Capitol"; the building was to be stone for the exterior and iron for the interior and all parts fireproof; there were to be five stories of well-lighted alcoves; provision was to be made for eight rooms "of large dimensions, not less than 40 to 60 feet in diameter, and 20 to 25 feet high, for map rooms, newspaper files, copyright records, works of art, cataloguing rooms and packing room"; the building was to be calculated to contain 2,000,000 volumes, eight volumes allowed to each linear foot of shelf; it was to front on two streets, probably on three, depending on the site selected, and the lot was to be either 300 by 520 feet or 400 by 475 feet with suitable approaches and decorative shrubbery; the building was to front on a park "the dimensions of which are 500 by 800 feet, lying directly east of the Capitol. . . ."

Out of the $5,000 appropriation the Committee offered a first prize of $1,500, a second of $1,000, and a third of $500, for suitable designs, to be judged by the Committee. In response twenty-eight specifications and estimates were received from American architects and one from an architect in Europe. The firm of Smithmeyer and Pelz received first prize immediately; the second prize was awarded to A. E. Melander of Boston, and the third to an architect named Adolph Cluss.

There followed a series of bills introduced in both Senate and House, covering a plan for a new building but without making definite propositions for immediate construction. Elaborate debates took place in the Senate, but none of the suggested propositions was acted upon.

From the time of passage of the Act of June 23, 1874, which appropriated $2,000 for procuring plans, until 1886 Congress wrestled with considerations growing out of suggestions for sites and designs for a new building or with propositions for extension of the Capitol. A special commission created in 1878 reported unanimously in favor of erection of a separate building. A Joint

Select Congressional Committee in 1880 selected three architects to secure suitable plans and estimates. Accordingly, Edward Clark of Washington, Alexander Esty of Boston, and J. L. Smithmeyer of Washington submitted separate designs for the structure.

It was not until April 15, 1886, that definite action was finally taken which fixed the plans and determined the site of the new Library of Congress, despite the fact that in 1884 a bill had passed the Senate almost unanimously, providing for a separate fireproof building on grounds "immediately east of the Capitol, and separated therefrom by the eastern park and by the line of First Street."

In the Act of 1886 reference was made to the winning plans of John L. Smithmeyer. The new building was to be constructed substantially in accordance with Smithmeyer's design, in the Italian Renaissance style, "with such modifications as may be found necessary or advantageous." These plans had previously been exhibited in both Houses of Congress. The Act of 1886 also appropriated $500,000—the first substantial appropriation—for construction of the building. It created a commission of three to take over complete charge of the business of construction. The officers of this Commission were the Secretary of the Interior, L. Q. C. Lamar; the Architect of the Capitol Extension, Edward Clark; and the Librarian of Congress, Ainsworth Spofford.

Many difficulties lay ahead of the Commission, which at once took steps to clear the ground of houses and other buildings. The matter of the value of the various properties was referred to a commission of real estate men and merchants, after which offers were made to the propertyholders on what had been judged fair terms. But not all the dwellers on the desired ten and a half acres were satisfied. The owners of some of the forty-odd houses which occupied the squares between First and Second Streets East, and East Capitol and B Street South, on Capitol Hill, took the matter into the courts, after condemnation proceedings started, but the action of the Commission was confirmed by the district court of the District of Columbia and the entire site was eventually purchased in 1887 for $585,000.

With acquisition of the land the trials connected with completion of the new building had only begun. After a delay of several months in perfecting the Government's title to the site, draughtsmen were set to work, under the direction of the victorious architect Smithmeyer, upon working drawings and specifications, while the ground was cleared and the soil of the site tested to make sure it was fit to contain the foundations of a large building. Two or three wells of water were discovered in one corner; in another section there was uncovered the bed of an old stream. But the bulk of the soil, found to be clay and loam, was declared suitable for a good foundation, and excavations were begun during the summer of 1887. The ground, which rose above the street on the side facing the Capitol, had to be cut down to the level of the surface of the site. Delay after delay occurred in getting the proper foundation materials. These delays were due, Spofford said, to the architect's insistence at every step upon the very finest quality of cement and other materials and his frequent rejection of constituent elements of the foundation. The delays led to a great deal of controversy, appeals to the Commission, and finally an investigation, when hearings of the complaining contractors were held and the decision of the architect to reject unsuitable materials was finally sustained by the Commission. After two years of this dissension, Congress, on October 2, 1888, appointed the Chief of Engineers of the United States Army, General Thomas Lincoln Casey, to superintend the construction of the building. The same bill contained an appropriation of $500,000 for continuing the work. The ultimate cost of the building was limited to $4,000,000. The following year this limitation was lifted and fixed at $5,500,000. The building was to provide ultimate accommodations for four and one half million volumes. Under the new law all contracts were to be made by General Casey. The Act appointing the Commission, which had repeatedly asked to be relieved of direct supervision of the work, was repealed. Spofford viewed the change with gratification, for he had felt from the beginning that supervision of actual construction should be in the hands of a competent engineer of the Army.

Meanwhile the new Secretary of the Interior, William F. Vilas, who had succeeded Lamar on January 17, 1888, was having difficulties in settling claims that various contractors had presented for adjustment. Brigadier General Casey had brought with him to the job a civil engineer, Bernard R. Green, who was appointed Superintendent and Engineer in charge of construction, on March 22, 1888. Smithmeyer had been employed by the Commission as an architect at $5,000 a year and his partner, Pelz, at $3,000, and Smithmeyer had traveled considerably in Europe, investigating library buildings at the expense of the Commission. When General Casey took charge he employed architect Edward Pearce Casey at $4,000 a year for three years and a half. Smithmeyer and Pelz later went before the Court of Claims and obtained a judgment of $48,000 for compensation of their plans, which, while materially adhered to, were altered considerably during the course of construction; the altered design was counted much more "expressive than the original." An appeal to the Supreme Court affirmed the judgment of the Court of Claims.

Despite these unpleasant interruptions to progress, the work went steadily ahead under General Casey, so that Spofford was able to report in 1890: "The new library building has made gratifying progress during the year, and promises to advance still more rapidly in the work of construction the present season. There is every reason for the belief that the long-deferred public necessity has at last been provided for with a liberality and energy worthy of the great end in view."

The first stone of the cellar walls had been laid in the north-west corner on May 15, 1889; the first stone of the superstructure was set in the northwest corner on November 25th, of the same year, when the entire building had been brought up to the exterior ground level. By the end of August, 1890 the court walls were built fourteen feet above the exterior ground level and the exterior walls at various heights from two to thirteen feet above the same level. As early as May workmen had been ready to lay the chief cornerstone of the superstructure of the building, but had been deferred by a joint resolution introduced on May 17th, providing that the stone should be laid with suitable Masonic ceremonies under the management of the Joint Committee on the Library in co-operation with the Chief of Engineers of the United States Army. So workmen waited upon the result of the resolution.

Two months went by, spring had gone and summer was drawing to a close, and Congress had not acted. The resolution, with similar bills in the hands of the Library Committee of the House, making appropriations of money, was laid informally aside. Workmen could no longer wait upon Congress without serious delay to construction.

Thus it came about that the cornerstone of the Library of Congress—destined to become the greatest storehouse of knowledge in the world—was laid entirely without ceremony, in the presence of a handful of overalled workmen, on August 28, 1890, at three o'clock in the afternoon.

Those charged with construction of the building had placed in a cavity in the middle of the bottom bed of the stone an hermetically sealed copper box, $9\frac{1}{2}$ inches by $3\frac{1}{2}$ inches in size. In this box were placed the annual report of the Librarian of Congress for the year 1872; the annual report of the Librarian of Congress for 1888; the first annual report of the Chief of Engineers of the United States Army for 1888; the annual report of the Chief of Engineers of the United States Army for 1889; a photograph of a drawing of the perspective southwest view of the building, and a photograph of the work itself in progress on the 15th day of August, 1890, both enclosed in a sealed glass tube within the copper box; a synopsis of Legislative and official acts and proceedings for the erection of a building for the Library of Congress, signed by Thomas Lincoln Casey; the last edition, May 10, 1890, of the *Congressional Directory*; an issue of the *American Almanac* for 1889; two daily newspapers of Washington, D. C.—the *Evening Star* of August 27, 1890, and the *Post* of August 28, 1890; and two daily newspapers of New York City—the *Tribune* and the *World*, both of August 28, 1890.

Thus passed, almost unremarked, the founding of an institution that might shape a world.

By the time the building was ready to receive the nation's library it had cost $7,000,000. But as Herbert Putnam wrote later, a workable building, honestly built, it carried "no remorse to either legislator or citizen."

It had been provided for by ample appropriations, and kept within them; it was deliberately planned, erected under able supervision, and it stood, when completed, as the largest, most imposing, most sumptuous, and most costly library building in the world, covering three and a half acres of ground, containing eight and a half acres of floor space, and providing, when opened, accommodations in its stacks alone for 2,000,000 volumes. Ainsworth Rand Spofford might well regard with satisfaction this materialization of his tenaciously held dream. With completion of the new building he had every right to look back upon his long and arduous administration as a continuous series of accomplishments. As 1896 drew to a close the Library of Congress numbered 748,115 volumes, and 245,000 pamphlets. The Librarian had entered 72,470 copyrights during that year and in the same twelve months had paid into the Treasury $54,870 in copyright fees. In the midst of incalculable difficulties, with books overflowing from the very dome to the very crypts of the Capitol, he had managed to continue his service to Congress and to the public—his mind and energies unflaggingly bent on enlargement of service. He had added by purchase with very limited available funds rare, old, and otherwise valuable items to the Library's collections. He had received, classified, catalogued and stored such libraries as the Smithsonian deposit, the Peter Force collection, the manuscript collection of the Marquis de Rochambeau, and—in 1882—the Toner collection of scientific and literary treasures, newspaper clippings, maps, periodicals, manuscripts and exhibits.

He had done away with what he termed the Procrustean system of classification. "The best system in classifying a library" he declared with customary directness, "is that which produces a book in the shortest time to one who wants it"—and he rode over all rules that interfered with that promptitude of service.

He had seen 100,000 volumes accumulate in the Smithsonian deposit; thousands of documents pile up under the system of foreign exchange. He had guided the Law Library through to individual expansion and partial independence from its parent library. He had developed a library of periodicals that included 18,000 bound volumes of newspapers dating from 1655, American and foreign, and a great mass of reviews and magazines devoted to science, literature, art, agriculture, religion, medicine, law, music and every human achievement.

A great collection of music had taken shape under his busy hand and discerning eye, numbering some 200,000 pieces, while musical compositions were flooding in at the rate of 15,000 a year by 1897. He had assembled works of graphic art—engravings, etchings, photographs, chromos, lithographs—a pictorial record numbering a quarter of a million, of the progress of the art of design in America. More than 40,000 maps had been gathered during his administration, unique records, some of them, of the Revolutionary campaigns, and all of them valuable historical material. He had acquired manuscripts of enough significance to supply a separate department and items of incunabula of black letter-works in English such as editions of the Bible, the first folio Shakespeare, original editions of Burton's *Anatomy of Melancholy* and similar works that later were to form a nucleus for the Library's rare book collection. His keen interest in Americana had enriched the collections of books illustrative of the discovery, settlement, history, biography and natural history of America.

But Ainsworth Spofford's contribution was something even more than the result of his energy and discernment. His courage, his zeal and his enthusiasm had been the mainstay of the Library of Congress during a period when, in other and less persistent hands, it might have been permitted to flounder into a restricted reference collection for the sole use of the legislators. His vision was for a great national center of learning, available to all; and his thirty-six years in the old library had been an incessant and arduous struggle of lofty aims against adverse conditions. This long lean figure in its frock coat will always be a part of the Washington picture. So, too, will that memory of him retained by Herbert Putnam when in that one hour of recreation that he allowed himself out of the twenty-four the Librarian of Congress cantered about the streets of Washington on horseback, "the tails of the still tenacious frock flapping behind him, untethered trousers riding toward the knee, an umbrella, if the sun beat hot, in his rein hand, and possibly an auction catalogue in the other—

unless, indeed, history (in his friend Bancroft) supplied him livelier companionship and converse." Or when, during the heated spells "he substituted a carryall for the saddle—urging the horse with whip and slapping rein in the one hand, the invariable catalogue still in the other." No mere jog for Spofford then, "but a smart trot, always verging on a canter, and without abatement for a curve or corner. Then indeed would the passerby marvel, and the passenger," wrote Putnam from experience, "grip the seat and thank his stars that there is a special Providence for the confiding and reckless."

From 1882, when Amherst conferred upon him an honorary LL.D., the Librarian of Congress had been "Dr. Spofford" to his contemporaries. Despite the demands of his office, he had found time to make his own contributions to literature. Apart from reviews and the *Book for All Readers*, these were chiefly compilations: *The American Almanac* from 1878 through 1889; *A Manual of Parliamentary Rules* in 1884; ten volumes of the *Library of Choice Literature*, from 1881 through 1888; five volumes of the *Library of Wit and Humor*, in 1884; and ten volumes of the *Library of Historic Characters and Famous Events*, from 1894 to 1905.

As a member of three Washington societies—the Literary, the Historical and the Anthropological—Dr. Spofford had also contributed historical, descriptive, or critical papers which "were always notable for their fullness of detail, if somewhat formal style." Herbert Putnam recalls one of Dr. Spofford's latest such contributions to the Literary Society when, "with eloquent indignation and a wealth of resource, he delivered Shakespeare from the depreciations of Tolstoi."

It was little wonder that, when the prospect loomed of transferring the Library of Congress from the Capitol of the United States to the magnificent new building across the park, Ainsworth

231

Spofford and those nearest to him felt that another and younger man should undertake the gigantic work, supervise the installation of the material in the new building, and reorganize the staff for the larger service ahead. There were to be 108 assistants now to manage, instead of the 42 to which the old staff had swelled. So, at that moment when the institution he had fostered was emerging from a pinched and narrow to a spacious and glorious life, Dr. Spofford surrendered the prestige and privilege of his office. When President McKinley named John Russell Young Librarian of Congress to succeed him, on July 1, 1897, Ainsworth Spofford became Young's chief assistant. He was destined to outlive his successor by several years. In the time between, the venerable Librarian whom Abraham Lincoln had appointed endeared himself not only to Young but to Young's successor in turn as he entered upon the last decade of his life—a period of cheerful contentment and still active and useful service—perhaps the happiest time of all. The reckless rides continued until long after his eightieth year, and only impaired ability—not failing zest—brought them to an end. Standing as usual one day at the center desk in the great rotunda of the new building, intent upon the mass of material before him, the sustaining muscles of Dr. Spofford's left side gave way and he crumpled to the floor. He "would be back in a day or two" he insisted. When he returned six weeks later his left arm was fastened inert across his chest and his left leg faltered. All his nervous vigor was now concentrated in his right hand, with which he continued to manage even folios with dexterity and uncomplaining patience. Putnam described him as "an old man now for the first time; but resisting doughtily the inabilities as he resisted the insignia of old age; and ever, and until the last inability of all, the simple, arduous servant of his office and his duty."

To Spofford only the thoughts and the facts garnered up in

books were endowed with perennial life. "Men may die, and legislators may perish, and librarians are mortal," he said at Concord, "but libraries and literature are immortal. Even though the ever-gnawing tooth of time should one day undermine this beautiful structure, and its granite walls should crumble to decay —yet through the ever living power of the magic art of printing, books will survive, and the thoughts of the mind will far outlast towers of granite, and monuments of marble."

"A book," said Benjamin Disraeli, "may be as great a thing as battle"; and it was no more than a whisper in the mind of Gutenberg, looking on the woodcuts of Laurentius Coster, that rang later like a trumpet through the land, awaking Europe to the startling intelligence of the birth of printing. So cataclysmic can the accidental thought of one man be, in any age, that it may shatter without warning or preparation the whole astonished darkness of the world.

XI

THE NATIONAL LIBRARY

*W*ith the completion of the new Library building and while Spofford was still serving as Librarian, Congress had become acutely aware of its increased responsibility as custodian of a nation's books. The Joint Committee on the Library decided to call upon the most distinguished librarians of the United States for advice and counsel in reorganizing the institution that had grown to such proportions. In addition to Superintendent Bernard Green, and the Librarian, they summoned to Washington Melvil Dewey, Secretary of the University of the State of New York and Director of the State Library for the State of New York; Herbert Putnam, Librarian of the Boston Public Library; George H. Baker, Librarian of Columbia University; William I. Fletcher, Librarian of Amherst College; Rutherford P. Hayes, Secretary of the American Library Association; W. H. Brett, President of the American Library Association; Dr. W. T. Harris, Commissioner of Education; S. P. Langley, Secretary of the Smithsonian Institution; and other distinguished men.

These experts, under the terms of a Senate resolution of May 5, 1896, were to meet during the recess of Congress to assist members of the Committee in their plans for organization, custody and management of the new Library building and the Library collections. The management of the building had already been placed in the hands of the Superintendent, Green, appointed by the President and confirmed by the Senate. The same House bill had also provided that the Librarian of Congress should have "complete and entire control of the Library proper, including the copyright business" and that he should "prescribe rules and regulations under which his assistants are to be employed and have the custody and management of the Library." This provision repealed in effect the previous law which had given authority to the Joint Committee to approve rules and regulations made by the Librarian of Congress. It gave the Librarian complete, unquestioned, power in his own domain. The records show that all the witnesses remained for two days in Washington, with the exception of Charles Soule of Boston, who attended one day of the hearings. Each was paid $2.00 a day for attendance and mileage at five cents a mile. The value of their testimony was immeasurable; for they placed freely at the disposition of Congress the wealth of their combined experience and talents. There can be no question that members left those hearings of 1896 with an enlarged vision and appreciation of their trust.

Dewey gave them a fresh picture of the changed responsibilities of the public library. It was a totally different institution, or should be, from that of the past, he said. Only a fraction of the work of the Library of Congress was to acquire with skill from all sources every book, pamphlet, serial, or other article pertaining to its collections and keep them safely housed in the new building. These last years of the nineteenth century would surely be known in history as "distinctively the library age." A generation or more preceding, the schools had passed through such an experience as libraries were then going through. It was difficult to understand that it had once been necessary to urge upon the public recognition of the function of the public school in our American civilization, yet they were then repeating exactly that experience with the public libraries. The most the schools could do "is to give the tools with which to acquire an education and teach the masses to read intelligently, to take the author's meaning from the printed page." It was generally known that the ideas and ideals of most people were shaped not so much by what they were taught in school, nor by what they had heard from the rostrum or the pulpit, as by what they had read. So that if we were to educate most of our people, it must be done by guiding the reading after the school age. There was no practical way of doing this, Dewey contended, except by the free public library, and the time was coming when it would be taken as an insult for a man to ask in any community, Have you a public library?

Any great work, Dewey reminded the committee, could only be accomplished by competent organization. "We shall never accomplish our best results in librarianship till we can have at the National Library in Washington a center to which libraries of the whole country can turn for inspiration, guidance, and practical help." The building and the books were less important than the other work which should properly be done by the National Library, and it would be a great disappointment "to those who know this subject best if in the administration of the new National Library it does not do a work for the people of this country as much superior to that done by any other national library as this wonderful building excels other homes for books."

Dewey held hopes that "with the new order will come a new name." He believed the name *Library of Congress* conveyed a false impression—"as much as it would to call the British Museum the parliamentary library." Dewey also believed that provision should be made in the government of the new Library for a board of the most eminent citizens of the country who could give an amount of time and attention to it that it was quite impossible for hard-pressed Members of Congress to give. The first great requisite of the new Library would be, he thought, a well made cata-

236

logue. There were three catalogues essential to any good library
—the accession book or business record giving the essential facts
of source, cost, rebinding, loss or other items, for each book; the
shelf list, or inventory book showing the resources of the library
as they stand on the shelves; and the catalogue proper, which
includes all books under their authors and also the resources of
the Library on each subject.

The preparation of these inevitably costs infinite pains and
much money; all over the world it was the thing that "frightens
trustees and brings out the criticism of the public, because it takes
so long," yet the ablest administrators, studying for years, had
found it impossible beyond a certain point "to reduce either the
time or the cost that must be given, for a library without such
catalogues is of little use. It differs from the well organized
library exactly as a well trained army differs from a mob. Whatever it costs, it is essential, and the fact that the cost is so great
only emphasizes the necessity of doing as much of this work as
possible in the national collection, where the work, which is for
the benefit of the entire country, can be done at the common
expense of all."

There were, Dewey said, "perhaps 4,000 public libraries in
the country of 1,000 volumes or more. If a book is published that
500 of these libraries will buy, where can you think of greater
waste than that every one of the 500 should have to undertake,
each for itself, with, in most cases, limited bibliographic machinery and insufficient force, to catalogue that book when it has been
already catalogued in the National Library by the most expert
staff in the country, having at their disposal every known resource? Printing is very cheap. Any library willing to pay the cost
of paper and postage could have a copy of these cards furnished
without extra expense to the Government, which had already paid
for making its own cards. This distribution of printed catalogue

cards had long been the dream of librarians. . . . It would mark an era when the National Library was ready to do this incalculable service to the libraries and students of the country."

Dewey outlined further extension of the scope of service for the Library of Congress:

> Any person in the United States should be at liberty to send to the Library, provided he is willing to pay the actual extra labor thrown upon the assistant, for extracts from any book carefully typewritten and verified before a notary; for translations; for any bit of literary work which a skillful assistant could do in the Library. Often a scholar must have access, for an hour or two before he can go on with his work, to something to be found only here. If he had to ride 1,000 or 2,000 miles away, the time and cost of the journey may be prohibitive, but at an extra expense to your Library of a single hour of an assistant's time, costing perhaps a single dollar, the whole purpose of the journey could be served. . . . In many cases this service can be rendered by telephone or telegraph without even the short delay of the mails. . . . I would venture to defend the thesis that such a department could be made more useful than any single university in America.

The appropriation of $11,000 for buying books Dewey referred to as a "beggarly item." "This is a great, rich nation," he said, "of which we are very proud, and yet in its snug little island England feels that she is not doing enough when she gives ten times this amount for books to the British Museum, some $45,000 if you limit it strictly to the book account, or over $100,000 if you count in the allied expenses as in making up the meager $11,000 at present granted to our National Library."

A great work could be done in the distribution of duplicates of public documents, Dewey thought, and in the promotion of bibliography—functions which properly belonged to a national institution and which Ainsworth Spofford, without "men, money or rooms," had not been able to perform. Yet he would not confuse the function of the university with that of the library. The library expert would make his investigation not about the facts or the thing, but about the books concerning them. The national library ought, under certain circumstances, to lend books all over the country, although rare books of great value should never be permitted to leave the fireproof building.

Melvil Dewey thus briefly sketched in divisions of service that have since developed into the Union Catalogue, servicing libraries all over the world; the Reference Department, answering hundreds of thousands of inquiries a year; the Documents Division, with its system of domestic and international exchange; and the Interlibrary Loan Service, which makes books available all over the United States, to accredited students.

Herbert Putnam made a valuable contribution by outlining the systems and expenditures of his own organization—the Boston Public Library—an institution then numbering some 675,000 volumes, including 200,000 volumes in its branch depositories. He explained his method of making appointments, his catalogue system, the organization of the library and its bibliographical policy.

A national library, Putnam stated, "should properly stand nationally for what the State libraries are to the State, with regard to all documentary material, because the National Library is the final depository of national archives." It could set an example, by uniformity of system, in methods of lending books, of passing on duplicate documentary material. One thing was certain, the new Library of Congress should be staffed by experts and adequately staffed. In these hearings Herbert Putnam gave expression to that policy which was to play a large part in the later development of the Library of Congress. When asked what he thought of a system of appointments for the Congressional Library which empowered the Joint Committee on the Library to make appointments upon recommendation of the Librarian, he replied: "I believe in centering responsibility. I should say that if the Librarian of Congress is absolutely free from political control in the selection of his men, if he will not have to recommend persons who are forced upon him, then it is safe to leave it to him. I believe that librarians in general, if they have the responsibility vested in them, that, as a class—I speak, of course, of the Library of Congress as belonging to that class—they will not misuse their authority."

It was on this occasion, too, that Herbert Putnam outlined what he considered should be the qualifications of the chief administrator of the Library of Congress:

This should be a library, the foremost library in the United States— a national library—that is to say, the largest library in the United States and a library which stands foremost as a model and example of assisting forward the work of scholarship in the United States. And you will be spending for it a sum that must be nearly $500,000 a year to make it what your committee seem to purpose that it should be made. I should suppose you would have to have for the administration of that library a force exceeding numerically 200 employees, perhaps 250. I should suppose that the man who is to have the final administration of that library must have above all things else administrative ability—the same kind of a man who is to manage the property or interest of any large corporation, is to handle large funds, is to manage a large force of employees; such a one should have administrative capacity. It is as much required in a library as anywhere else. . . . I do not believe that your chief administrative officer, attending properly to the business problems of the library, need be a profound bibliographer or need to know the most of all the persons in the library, as to what the library contains. I should regard him as bearing a relation to the library something similar to that corresponding to, or borne by, the president of a university to the several departments of that university. . . . I presume that the modern college president considers that his chief function is to secure the best men for each department, and to administer on a large scale this business, and see that the business is conducted properly, and to secure great efficiency, and more especially at the beginning, to consider and determine the scope of the work to be undertaken, to form plans on a large scale which might serve as recommendations to the committee . . . with reference to the larger service to be rendered. I don't say a knowledge of specialties, in addition to these capacities, would be inconsistent with them, but it seems to me that those capacities are undoubtedly necessary, and that the chief executive must have them preeminently.

Later, after reviewing testimony he had given on this point, Putnam wrote from Boston to the Committee to correct "inadvertences which were certain to occur in such testimony given offhand."

He felt that his description of the capacities requisite to the chief executive of the Library had been "ill balanced," that he had laid stress upon "the requisite that he should be predominantly the man of affairs . . . rather than the man of books." In so doing he had slighted that other, equally indispensable requisite "that he should know enough of the literary side of the Library, of bibliography, etc., to appreciate intelligently the needs of the several departments of specialized work."

Putnam rejected the idea that Congress should maintain in connection with the Library a museum of fine arts. "While a library universal in scope is pleasing in idea," he said, "I am quite clear that a library universal in scope is not practicable, unless you are sure of unlimited funds. . . . I should say that there was danger in too large a scope, with reference to this library, as to others, because . . . there is danger that undertakings will be begun that can never be carried out and which, if abandoned, will mean a waste of funds."

The librarian from Boston believed, with others, that the time had come to introduce into the Library the mechanical aids that would render it more independent of the physical limitations of any one man or set of men. "In other words," he said, "the time had come when Mr. Spofford's amazing knowledge of the Library shall be embodied in some form which shall be capable of rendering a service which Mr. Spofford as one man and mortal can not be expected to render."

Before the Committee had opportunity to formulate a report on this testimony or even to print its proceedings, the appropriation bill of 1897 was reported to the House. It contained a provision which incidentally carried with it a scheme for the organization of the Library of Congress in the new building. The scheme was partially modified in discussion, but was substantially adopted, and, in a general way and exclusive of changes wrought naturally by expansion, represents the organization today.

The man charged with the tremendous responsibility of carrying out these enlarged plans for the development of the Library of Congress had little experience along the highly-specialized lines laid down for him to follow, for John Russell Young was, first and last, a journalist, with a colorful career behind him when McKinley appointed him Librarian of Congress.

He had been born on a farm near Dowington, Pennsylvania, in 1841, but his family had moved two years later to Philadelphia, where their son was placed in the Harrison grammar school, at a suitable age. When the boy's mother died in 1852, he was sent to New Orleans to reside with an uncle.

Young was graduated from the New Orleans high school in 1856—a good student and a favorite with his teachers. He showed an early interest in the journalistic career he was to follow, editing the school paper during these years.

After graduation from high school, Young returned to Philadelphia bent upon learning the printing and publishing trades and entered the firm of William S. Young and Company. A year later, when only sixteen years of age, he joined the staff of John

W. Forney's newspaper, the *Press*, of Philadelphia, as copy-holder. It was not long before he was receiving assignments and covering stories for the city desk and was recognized in time as a full-fledged reporter. Before he was twenty-one he had advanced to the status of editorial contributor.

When Colonel Forney was elected Secretary of the United States Senate, he took John Russell Young along with him as his private secretary. In Washington, Young continued to write for the press, and when the Civil War broke out he was, upon his own request, assigned to duty at the front as a war correspondent. Just previous to the Battle of Bull Run he joined the Army of the Potomac, and his first letter from the front was a graphic account of that engagement. Later he was an interested observer in the Red River campaign of General Banks and of other important military operations.

Returning to Philadelphia, Young became managing editor of the *Press*. At the close of the war he and several others, including his brother, founded the *Philadelphia Evening Star*, of which he later became the principal owner. In 1865 he had left the *Press* to accept a position with the house of Jay Cooke and Company in New York, where he used his journalistic gifts to arouse popular interest in the loan for the aid of the Government. Subsequently he became a member of the editorial staff of the *New York Tribune* and remained with that paper from 1865 to 1869. Horace Greeley had appointed him managing editor in 1866, to succeed Sidney Howard Gay. Only twenty-five years old at the time of this important appointment, Young was nevertheless ambitious to study law, and as a result of his studies while on the *Tribune* he was, in 1867, admitted to the bar.

The Secretary of the Treasury sent him abroad in 1870 in the interest of government financial measures. He was to spend many years of his life from that time forward in foreign countries, for the *New York Herald* dispatched him in 1872 to take charge of their foreign news service in Great Britain, France, Germany and Spain.

While he was residing in London, in 1877, John Russell Young was invited by General Grant to accompany him on his tour around the world. In 1877 Young published a description of this trip in two volumes of articles, *Around the World with General Grant*.

Between the years 1879 and 1882 Young resumed his editorial contributions to the *New York Herald* and to other periodicals. While on his world voyage he had met in China and had become a good friend of Li Hung Chang, who had later visited him in his Philadelphia home. He was interested, therefore, in 1882 to accept a diplomatic portfolio when he was sent as minister to China. He remained in this post until 1885 when President Arthur's administration came to a close. At the termination of his mission Young returned to London, editing the English edition of the *New York Herald* until 1890, when he went back to New York.

John Russell Young's journalistic contributions upon current politics and events of the day were notable for the accuracy of the facts they contained and for his estimates of the trends and purposes of political movements. This was due largely to his intimacy with public men and the confidence in which he was held by party leaders, which gave him special knowledge and privileges.

In the midst of these journalistic activities Young's appointment as Librarian of Congress was announced. The new Library building was completed, but there yet remained the stupendous task of transfer of the collections, their orderly installation on the shelves, and the complete reorganization of the staff for the larger service that had been outlined as a result of the hearings of 1896. These were the duties which faced him upon taking office.

With a due regard for the convenience of Congress, Spofford had not attempted a complete removal of the collections while that body was still in session. He had, however, transferred a large portion of the duplicates and of the copyright collections by the end of 1896 across the lawns. Young's duty was to write finis to that chapter in the history of the Library of Congress where masses of books, pamphlets, newspapers and engravings had hemmed in the reading public, and books stored in obscure nooks and crannies had gathered dust in the Capitol crypt. Out of the chaos he had to bring some sort of order and round up, sort and segregate the collections preparatory to their removal. Copyright and other material that had lain for indefinite periods in indiscriminate heaps upon the floors of the old Library rooms had now to be evaluated, its character determined.

The new building was completed in February, 1896, and the act providing for the removal of the Library from the Capitol had been passed under the assumption that Congress, according to custom, would adjourn on March 4th. The transfer of books, it was thought, would thus be over by July.

But Congress did not adjourn on March 4th. Instead, they went into an extra session that made it necessary for the main Library to be kept intact in the Capitol until adjournment. While large amounts of miscellaneous matter, chiefly duplicates, were taken out of the Capitol and deposited in the new building meanwhile, plans for transferring and housing the important collections had to wait upon consideration by the Library authorities.

The problem was truly a stupendous one. Each of the 787,715 volumes had to be carried from its place in the Capitol to a corresponding place in the new building. Moreover the transfer had to be effected with such care that the volumes in question would

245

be at once accessible to readers. Adding to this difficulty were such necessary considerations as the care of valuable properties, the renovation of books, the vagaries of weather, and the combating of all those accretions of time that had affected the multiple and disorderly accumulations in the Capitol.

On July 31, 1897, the old Library was closed, the copyright division alone remaining open to serve the public. On August 2nd preparations for the historic transit were begun. Library work, except that necessary for the transfer of books, was suspended. Only in emergency cases were any leaves of absence granted the personnel. As evidence of the industry, the care and foresight of the limited staff, the various and manifold treasures of the entire library were removed within the incredibly short space of time of ten weeks. Moreover, this vast mass was transferred without loss or apparent misplacement of a single volume, so skilfully and tactfully was the undertaking carried out. Convenience of access and speed of service were the considerations governing the arrangement of the books in the new library. Those books which experience had shown to be most sought after, such as Americana, genealogy, biography, local history, reference books and fiction, were ranged on shelves in alcoves near the reading room. Other subjects, such as geology and chemistry, were grouped together, with only one half of each shelf occupied, to allow for growth in every section. United States documents were placed in the reading-room gallery.

The Library had closed on July 31st; on November 1st it was opened to the public, in the new library building. More than 400,000 books had been adjusted in the interim and made available. Some idea of the efficiency and order that had evolved in those few weeks may be gained from the results of the first experimental operation of the device for transmitting books from the Library to the Capitol. This ingenious contribution to efficient administration consisted of a pneumatic tube, a tunnel, and the necessary electric machinery for operation.

On October 27th, under imperfect conditions and before the telephone system was in operation, Library officials tested the efficiency of this system. Without prearrangement or forewarning, a request for books was conveyed through the pneumatic tube from the Capitol to the reading desk in the new Library. In ten minutes and five seconds the volume asked for reached the Capitol. The second request was for four books—one in English, the other three in Italian, German and French, respectively. Within eight minutes and eleven seconds the Italian, German and English books arrived. Two minutes later the French volume, *Les Châtiments*, was delivered.

The third request was for that issue of the *London Times* which contained an account of the Battle of Waterloo. The *Times*, the volume of 1815, was promptly located on its appropriate shelf in the upper part of the Library building. Despite some delay at the reading desk, it arrived at the Capitol twelve minutes after the request had come in.

This was a far cry from the old days when the location of a book depended upon the dispensation of Providence or the phenomenal memory of Ainsworth Spofford. Then it had been an uncertain and time-consuming matter to poke blindly among the books heaped in the crevices and corners, hidden in the crypt or under the ceiling of the Capitol. Unfortunate indeed that Member of Congress whose speech had waited upon delivery of the volume. Now delivery was almost automatic; a Senator at his desk, a Supreme Court Justice in the conference room might with confidence expect whatever he required from the Library within twelve or fifteen minutes after summoning a page. "This," exclaimed John Russell Young in happy wonder, "is not a theory or an anticipation, but a practical demonstration!" The national literary treasures and records were now practically at the finger-tips of those privileged under law to make free use of them.

The Library of Congress as transferred, contained 787,715 volumes and 218,340 pamphlets. Young estimated that the percentage of books lost in thirty years had been about five in a thousand, and that from 33 to 40 percent of the Library's collections were duplicates.

The magnificent Library of Congress building was by any standard worthy to receive the wealth of empires. A vast pile of white granite set in the midst of its landscaped park, it fronted on four streets, two thousand windows reflecting the light on one side or another throughout the day, its golden dome glinting opulently above the trees, yet scaled to its proper importance with relation to the rambling white Capitol across the square.

Its dimensions were 470 by 340 feet, and it contained, on the day it opened, four large inner courts, almost 100 by 150 feet in area. The quarries of Concord, New Hampshire, had provided the white granite of its exterior walls; the inner courts were built of slightly darker Maryland stone, from the quarries of Balti-more County. Two of these courts were to give way in time before the relentless march of the collections and fill with stacks, but for many years they served as pleasant grass-grown retreats, reflect-ing in quiet pools gray stone walls and a blue arch of sky.

The building contains three floors—a basement level with the ground, a first story, or library floor, nineteen feet high; and a second story which rises to the height of twenty-nine feet. The walls are sixty-nine feet high to the roof, and the apex of the dome is 195 feet from the ground. In the style of the Italian Renaissance, its central front and four corner pavilions are mod-erately projected, so that there is no monotony in the long façade. The casings of the many windows are treated in high relief and

248

foliated carvings decorate the cornices and pediments. In the central front stand sixteen ornate pillars and capitals, and twelve additional columns add dignity to the corner pavilions. Upon the keystones of thirty-three of the window arches on the four sides of the building are carved thirty-three human heads, types of so many races of men, modeled from drawings from the National Museum. Sculptured in the solid granite, they are decoratively strong and effective, pleasantly replacing the hideous gargoyles of old European architecture and serving as an object lesson in ethnology.

The central pavilion on the west front is further enriched, just below the roof, by four colossal figures, each representing Atlas, and surmounted by a pediment with two sculptured American eagles as the center of an emblematic group in granite.

A massive front stairway, its wide balustrade cut from granite, mounts from the street to the main floor, forming an impressive approach to the building. Underneath, an arched porte-cochère provides an entrance now for the constant stream of taxicabs and private vehicles that deposit the hopeful at its lower door; in Spofford's day the shining carriages of the legislators and the visiting public rolled up there on thin rubber-tired wheels.

The building is topped by a carved balustrade running all around the four sides. Over the arches of the three entrance doors at the head of the main approach are carved three spandrels in relief, each representing two female figures—one group emblematic of Art, another of Science, and the third of Literature. The base or lower story of the building is in rusticated or rock-faced stone; the walls of all the upper stories are of smooth, bush-hammered granite, relieved at the corners of the pavilion with vermiculated work. Sheet copper roofs the building; and its modest dome, of beautiful proportions, is gilded by a thick coating of gold leaf, twenty-three carats fine—flecked now with a mellow brush of green. The dome, above the lantern, is crested with a gilded finial—the torch of Science, ever burning.

Within this noble building, the main Reading Room is the central feature, its marble pilasters rising, tier on tier, to its beautifully decorated and lofty dome, through the softly colored glass panes of which shafts of light stream downward upon absorbed figures bent above mahogany desks for reading or study.

When James Truslow Adams declared in the Epilogue to his *Epic of America* that the Library of Congress has come "straight from the heart of democracy" he probably had these desks in mind:

> As one looks down on the general reading room one sees the seats filled with silent readers, old and young, rich and poor, black and white, the executive and the laborer, the general and the private, the noted scholar and the schoolboy, all reading at their own library provided by their own democracy.

Octagonal, nearly circular in shape, this impressive hall is 100 feet in diameter and 125 feet high and is lighted by eight semicircular windows, each thirty-two feet wide. It was designed originally to seat 250 readers, furnishing each with four feet of desk room. Originally, but since largely discarded, there were lightly curtained desk screens between the stalls.

In the center of the hall rises the distributing desk, headquarters in the early days for the Superintendent and his assistants. Centralized within a railing and set well above the floor level, it commands a view of every part of the Reading Room. Here slips for books are returned to attendants and sent on their several ways to the proper decks, where the items called for are located by other attendants. Here, too, continuously moving belts carry required books to the Capitol, return them to the Library shelves, or shunt them today to the white marble annex of the Library.

Overlooking this core of silent and intent activity are the corridors of the galleries, where visitors may admire the rich marbles of the interior or the ornate, delicately painted dome without disturbing the readers below. The interior walls of this central Reading Room are lined with light-colored variegated marbles, harmonious in tone. The eight massive pillars which rise forty feet to the concave ceiling are of a rich, dusky, red Tennessee marble at their base, surmounted by Numidian marble of a lighter shade, and crowned by heroic statues.

These eight statues set upon the entablatures over the columns represent eight characteristic features of civilized life and thought. Beginning with the figure directly to the right as one enters the west gallery of the rotunda, the order is: *Religion,* modeled by Theodore Baur; *Commerce* by John Flanagan; *History* by Daniel C. French; *Art* by M. Dozzi, after sketches by Augustus St. Gaudens; *Philosophy* by Bela L. Pratt, who also modeled the granite spandrels of the main entrance; *Poetry* by J. Q. A. Ward; *Law* by Paul W. Bartlett; and *Science* by John Donoghue. Each is ten and a half feet high, made of plaster toned on ivory white and bears in its hands some distinguishing object. President Eliot of Harvard University selected the inscriptions carved above each statue. Above *Religion* there are the words: "What doth the Lord require of thee, but to do justly, and to love mercy, and to walk humbly with God?" Above *Commerce:* "We taste the spices of Arabia yet never feel the scorching sun which brings them forth." Above *History:* "One God, one law, one element, and one far-off divine event, to which the whole creation moves." Above *Art:* "As one lamp lights another, nor grows less, so nobleness enkindleth nobleness." Above *Philosophy:* "The inquiry, knowledge, and belief of Truth is the sovereign good of human nature." Above *Poetry:* "Hither, as to their fountain, other stars Repairing, in their golden urns draw light." Above *Law:* "Of law there can be no less acknowledged than that her voice is the harmony of the world." And above *Science:* "The heavens declare the glory of God; and the firmament sheweth his handiwork."

The great clock over the entrance to the rotunda was a point of great interest in the early days of the Library, and as a sculptural group represented one of its most sumptuous pieces of decoration. The work of the sculptor of *Commerce,* John Flanagan, the clock is constructed of various brilliantly colored marbles, and is set against a background of mosaic, on which are displayed encircling it the signs of the Zodiac in bronze. Above is a life-sized figure, executed in bronze in high relief, of Father Time, striding forward with scythe in hand. To the left and right are maidens with children, representing the Seasons. The dial of the clock is about four feet in diameter, with a gilt sunburst in the center and gilt hands jeweled with semi-precious stones. No less than nineteen American sculptors contributed to the decoration of the rotunda.

The walls of this central hall are divided into eight bays or alcoves, which are on the radii from the distributing desk to the stacks. These alcoves are arched and enclose the stained-glass, semicircular windows. The arches, springing from the piers, support the great dome. The dome, with a framework of iron and steel filled in with terra cotta, is ornamented with elaborate arabesques of figures in relief. At its top, where it prepares to join the lantern, is a broad circular collar, painted decoratively by Edwin Howland Blashfield, whose work was designed to be the crowning glory of the decorative scheme, occupying not only the highest, but the exact central point of the Library, to which all other decorations are relative. The painting occupying this important position pictures the Evolution of Civilization, the records of which it is the function of a great library to gather and

252

The Main Reading Room

The Grand Staircase, with Martiny sculpture, main entrance hall

preserve. In the blue field of the lantern, surmounting all, floats the female figure of *Human Understanding*.

On all sides of this central Reading Room open the stacks for shelving the books. Before the growth of the collections dictated a more utilitarian purpose, the green quiet courts afforded pleasant outlooks to the deck attendants and admitted light to every corridor.

At the time that John Russell Young took over administration of the new Library of Congress building, the remaining first-floor space was devoted to Copyright Record rooms, the Librarian's office, a newspaper and periodical room, committee rooms, a lecture hall, and private reading rooms for Congress and special students.

Almost as impressive as the Main Reading Room is the entrance hall of the main floor of the Library, with its grand staircase of gleaming marble, its high, richly ornamented arches, its decorated columns and marble floors set with brass inlays of the signs of the Zodiac. With the exception of a portion of the attic story and two or three small rooms in the southeast and northeast corners of the first floor, this entire central pavilion serves as a single lofty and imposing entrance hall. In the center is a great well, seventy-five feet high, enclosed in an arcade of two stories, the arches of the first supported on heavy piers and of the second on paired columns. The center of the well is left clear and on either side, north and south, winds the massive marble staircase, ornamented with sculpture by Philip Martiny. The heavily paneled ceiling is finished in white and gold; the whole effect is opulent.

The north, south and east corridors on the first floor of the entrance hall, are paneled in Italian marble to a height of eleven feet. Their floors are of white Italian marble, blue Vermont marble, and brown Tennessee marble, and their beautiful vaulted ceilings are of marble mosaic. In all these corridors tablets bearing the names of distinguished men are introduced as part of the ornament. In the east corridor are decorative trophies or discs emblematic of the various arts and sciences. Series of paintings occupy the large semi-elliptical tympanums at the ends of the corridors. Charles Sprague Pearce was the artist for these spaces in the north corridor; H. O. Walker in the south. The broad, arched border at the west end contains two female figures floating in the air and holding between them a large scroll on which is inscribed this admonition of that practical idealist, Confucius: "Give instruction unto those who cannot procure it for themselves." The Pearce series as a whole illustrates the main phases of a pleasant and well ordered life. The Walker decorations take *Lyric Poetry* for their general subject and picture single youthful male figures suggested by various poets—the spirit of each scene being invariably lyrical. Tennyson, Keats, Wordsworth, and Emerson are represented on the south side of the corridor and Milton and Shakespeare on the north.

The six tympanums on the east corridor, by John W. Alexander, illustrate *The Evolution of the Book*, with such individual subjects as *The Cairn, Oral Tradition, Egyptian Hieroglyphics, Picture Writing, The Manuscript Book,* and *The Printing Press.*

The Librarian's room, also on this main floor, at the left as one enters the building, looks out upon the northwest court. Its paneled walls, its shallow softly painted dome, and the muted tones of its mural decorations, create an atmosphere of quiet and secluded beauty. As if in anticipation of that great American poet who was one day to occupy it as Librarian of Congress, there is in one panel a charming arabesque unfolding the story of the evolution of the poet. The lobby outside contains paintings by

Elihu Vedder in a series which, taken together, illustrate *Government*.

Similarly, the corridors of the second-story arcade, most impressively entered by ascending the main staircase, are vaulted and decorated with that rich ornamentation of detail characteristic of the Italian Renaissance. Here again mosaic floors and mural paintings add color and brilliance to the general effect. On this floor Walter Shirlaw was artist of the west corridor, Robert Reid of the north corridor, George R. Barse, Jr., the east corridor, and Frank W. Benson of the south corridor. In the side corridors the arch of the vault at the west end is spanned by an ornamental band containing a series of octagonal coffers, executed in relief by Hinton Perry, and illustrating *Prophetic Inspiration*.

While the vaults of the corridors throughout the building are distinctly Renaissance in decoration, the walls are colored and decorated in the Pompeiian manner—as if the artists had sought to emphasize in thus joining two styles so remote from one another in period of time, the rebirth, in the Renaissance, of Greek and Roman forms. Thus panels of a rich Pompeiian red and of a deep olive were ornamented by George Willoughby Maynard with female figures of *The Virtues* in floating, classic drapery: Fortitude and Justice; Patriotism and Courage; Temperance and Prudence; Industry and Concord are here along the corridors of the entrance hall.

Under the circular windows of the hall, below the wall paintings of Benson and of Reid, twenty-nine inscriptions occupy gilt tablets. "Too low they build who build beneath the stars," says Young; Carlyle's "The true university of these days is a collection of books"; Ovid's "It is the mind that makes the man, and our vigor is in our immortal soul"; Milton's "Beholding the bright countenance of Truth in the quiet and still air of delightful studies"; Bacon's "Books will speak plain when counsellors blanch"; Dr. Johnson's "The chief glory of every people arises from its authors"; and similar electric truths.

The pavilions of the Library are connected by long galleries, two on the west and east sides, and one each on the north and south sides. The corner pavilions of both floors contain octagon-shaped rooms which have domed ceilings and mosaic floors in the second story and are embellished with paintings, relief decoration and sculpture. The rooms on the second story were intended for the most part as exhibition halls, for the display of rare books and curious manuscripts. The north gallery was originally used for a map room; the south gallery for what was then known as the print room, for display and protection of engravings, lithographs, etchings and other examples of the pictorial arts. Decorations varied from room to room, but were united in a single harmony of color. In the southwest gallery was the artistic work of Kenyon Cox, painted panels depicting the arts and sciences. The pavilion opening from this gallery was known as the Pavilion of the Discoverers, from the paintings of George W. Maynard—*Adventure, Discovery, Conquest,* and *Civilization.*

Again, there is the Pavilion of the Elements—the southeast pavilion, where the paintings were done by Robert L. Dodge—*Earth, Air, Fire,* and *Water.* The third of the second-story pavilions was known as the Pavilion of the Seals, located at the northeast corner of the building. Here the wall surfaces were gilded and ornamented with painted laurel bands arranged in regular patterns. W. V. Van Ingen painted the seals of the various Executive Departments of the United States and the domed ceiling disc after a design by Elmer Garnsey showing the great seal of the United States surrounded by allegorical emblems.

The fourth, or northwest, pavilion on this floor was known as the Pavilion of Art and Science, with the paintings in tympanums and ceiling disc by William de Leftwich Dodge—the subjects

256

being *Literature, Music, Science, Art,* and in the ceiling disc, *Ambition.*

The northwest gallery contains two paintings by Gari Melchers—*War* and *Peace.* Above the doors and windows are inscribed the names of Cyrus, Alexander, Hannibal, Cæsar, Charles Martel, William the Conqueror, Frederick the Great, Charlemagne, and other of the world's most famous military figures.

Above the corridors leading from the main entrance hall are other series of paintings, such as those of Walter McEwen relating to incidents in Greek mythology. From one of these corridors opens the beautiful "Congressional Reading Room," known when the building was opened as the "House Reading Room." Farther along is the richly carved chamber first used as a Senators' reading room and now given over to the bustle and stir of the business connected with the Legislative Reference Service.

These rooms were two of the most beautiful in the Library of Congress in the days when John Russell Young served as Librarian. The "House Reading Room" of that time was dedicated to the private and exclusive use of Members of the House. No apartment in the Library is more lavishly ornamented. The floor is dark quartered oak; heavy oak paneling about eleven feet high runs in a dado about the walls, which were hung, above it, in olive-green silk, since faded to a pale gold. The deep window arches are finished in the same rich dark paneling; the ceiling is beamed and paneled, finished in gold and decorated with softly colored panels encrusted along the beams. Over the three doors are carved oak tympanums, the work of Charles H. Niehaus. At either end of the room is a magnificent mantel of Sienna marble, crowned with mosaic panels by Frederick Dielman—*Law* at one end of the room, *History* at the other. Along the center of the ceiling are seven panels containing decorations by Carl Gutherz—*The Spectrum of Light.* Each panel is a different color of the spectrum, and represents a "light" of the world: yellow, *The Light of Creation*; orange, *The Light of Excellence*; red, *The Light of Poetry*; violet, *The Light of State*; green, *The Light of Research*; blue, *The Light of Truth*; and indigo, *The Light of Science.*

The Senate Reading Room at the end of the corridor was reserved for many years after the building opened for the use of members of the Senate. It is an example of pure architectural design, with walls of Vermont marble, paneled with Sienna marble, and a moulded ceiling finished entirely in gold. Below a low gallery enclosed by a delicately carved balustrade of Sienna marble, runs an oak dado inlaid with arabesques of white mahogany. Above this dado the walls are covered in red silk brocade. In the southwest corner of the room is a fireplace of Sienna marble, with a sculptured panel above it—the work of Herbert Adams. The oaken doorhead tympanum also contains a carved panel by Adams, with a heraldic shield bearing the monogram *U.S.A.*, supported by mermaids. In each of the six square panels of the gold ceiling William A. Mackey has painted a graceful female figure with a garland in her hands.

Along the windows on the other side of the main entrance hall, leading north, is a series of paintings by Edward Simmons, representing the nine Muses. The northwest gallery, leading from this corridor, is decorated in a cheerful, springlike green, ornamented with garlands; the neighboring northwest pavilion is finished in a deep Pompeiian red, with medallions containing the figures of dancing girls, by R. L. Dodge. In the six window bays is a series of signs of the Zodiac.

With the exception of the Congressional reading rooms, the galleries and pavilions of this floor were designed originally to accommodate the clerical and cataloguing work of the Library of Congress and the Copyright Department, or to furnish quarters for special collections of books. In the northwest pavilion John Russell Young, as the first Librarian to occupy the building, had placed the separate collection given to the Library by Dr. J. M. Toner; which he hoped would be followed by similar donations from others.

Under the lofty entrance hall, in the basement of the building, corridors extend on four sides, the walls sheathed in a dado of white Italian marble, ten feet high, above which the vaulted ceiling is ornamented in green, blue and yellow arabesques in a cream-colored ground.

This was the Library of Congress as it was first opened to an admiring public. There have been many changes in the main building since then. Today the basement floor contains the Whittall pavilion, the Coolidge auditorium, the extensive music division, and the modern broadcasting studios of the radio project. Above stairs are the rooms of the Hispanic Foundation and the Federal wing of the east front that now houses the priceless Rare Book Collection. Stacks rise today where green courts once lay open to the sky, and many of the Library's luxurious chambers have lost their air of secluded elegance before the increasing pressure of a nation's business. But what may have been lost to luxury has been gained to progress, for the Library of Congress is today a living, vital institution contributing in a thousand ways undreamed of when it occupied the Capitol, to the expanding interests and preoccupations of the American people—almost the last citadel of that tenet of democracy which not only assures to man the right to think as he pleases, but develops his powers to do so.

John Russell Young foresaw such a possibility when he wrote in his annual report of 1898:

In the highest sense the Library is the home of research. The Capital can never be other than the center of library work. Here on Capitol Hill must be found the national treasure house of knowledge . . . it should be our aim to broaden the Library, safeguard its integrity as a library of reference, and bring it home to the people as belonging to them—a part of their heritage—to make it American in the highest sense, seeking whatever illustrates American history—the varied forms of American growth, theology, superstition, commonwealth building, jurisprudence, peace, and war. And, while accepting this as the chief end of the Library, it is no less incumbent to seek out and gather in the learning and piety of every age. With the considerate care of Congress, and a due appreciation of what has been done and what may so readily be done by the American people, there is no reason why the Library of Congress should not rival those noble establishments of the Old World, whose treasures are a people's pride and whose growth is the highest achievement of modern civilization.

This was the last report that John Russell Young was destined to make as Librarian of Congress, for, quite suddenly, his brief administration was brought to a close by his death on January 17, 1899. He had been responsible for the safe transfer of the collections, and had made all subsequent appointments to the Library staff. Into this later obligation he had introduced an innovation, breaking down the barriers hitherto erected against the admission of women to library service. Twenty-five percent of the appointments made by him were of women. "With few exceptions," he said, "women have not had service in the Library, and therefore the nominations were an experiment. It was believed that as there were various features of the Library work apparently suitable for women, they were entitled to recognition. In the administration of other libraries the experiment had been successful, but so far as our Library is concerned, the appointment of women is still open to debate." He was wise enough to see that this might well be the result of the exceptional conditions that prevailed. "The Library," he wrote, "is in a state of change—its new departments created by the new law, involving the handling and organization of the vast material, outside of books, now first brought to view. The classification and removal of this material is manual labor, with little opportunity for rest—as a rule hard and exacting. In a year or two, when these new departments are arranged and in good working order, there may be gentle and useful offices suitable for women. . . ."

This represented a broad view at this time, for at the turn of the century women were only just beginning to receive recognition in national economic life. In 1900, in an introduction to *The 19th Century, A Review of Progress,* a writer had reminded his generation, "We must make record of the opening doors of opportunity through which whole races and entire classes are pressing—women, for instance, with their beginnings of enlargement and enfranchisement certain to result in immense social and political changes before the 20th Century shall close."

The *New York Daily Tribune* believed Young's policy of making appointments had been a successful one. Three days after his death, an editorial stated:

That the late John Russell Young made a success as Librarian of Congress is admitted by nearly everyone, including the professional librarians and other educators who so strongly opposed his appointment, but the satisfaction he gave was not due to his previous training as a journalist, but rather to his fine executive ability and the good judgment he exercised in choosing many of his assistants. It was a perilous thing to place the foremost library of the country in charge of a newspaper man absolutely without experience in executive library management; but in this one case it seems to have been without detriment to the literary public, and even to its advantage.

Under Young's administration the copyright, map, manuscript, music, and print collection—designated by him as "the graphic

261

arts"—were set off in distinct departments, and an entirely new department, the reading room for the blind, in which he was warmly interested, was established. He had begun to plan also for a reading room for children before the gift of Andrew Carnegie, insuring an adequate library building for the District of Columbia, with especial responsibility for popular educational service, had intervened to make such a special department unnecessary in the Library of Congress.

Young also reorganized the Copyright Department during his brief administration. He had inherited it in a state of great disorder, with crediting and indexing considerably in arrears, deficient bookkeeping methods, and with correspondence largely a matter of printed forms. He had arranged at once a fiscal system that would adequately account, to the satisfaction of the Treasury, for all money passing through the bureau from day to day. Rules were revised so that every person sending a remittance would receive a prompt answer and every person sending a fee covering the cost of the copyright certificate would receive that certificate as soon as possible after the entries were made. Deposits of copies were noted, assignments or other valuable instruments returned by registered mail, remittances of money were at once acknowledged and money was refunded where necessary as soon as possible, accompanied by a letter of explanation. Correspondence was kept in copying books, and index cards were made for titles on the day of their receipt. Young had also suggested to Congress the advantage of more rigidly enforcing the copyright statute which made two deposits of any article copyrighted essential to the validity of a copyright, pointing out that the Librarian of the British Museum had testified before a royal commission that the poems of Wordsworth were not on the Museum shelves for the reason that the publisher declined to furnish certain volumes which he claimed to be reprints, and therefore free from copyright, and had held that to acquire Wordsworth by purchase would have been an invitation to every publisher to evade the law. Young wished to fix a limit of time within which deposits could be made to complete the entry of copyright, making obligatory a new entry of title when the time fixed had been passed. He had hoped to build up a great catalogue, quoting Carlyle's observation that a library without a catalogue is "a Polyphemus without an eye in its head." And he had looked forward to developing a reference library dedicated to Congressional research, where—taking the cue from Napoleon, who had declared that there should be no book in any public library in France that was not on the shelves of the Imperial Library of Paris—there should be no book under Government subvention that was not already in duplicate in the Library of Congress. He had planned, too, to transfer the crowded Law Library which had remained in the Capitol, into one of the sections of the new Library building, where the volumes would be "superbly and safely housed" and afford students special rooms for study with every comfort and advantage.

John Russell Young did not live long enough to see these suggestions bear fruit. In his two brief years, however, as administrator of a great institution, he had adequately justified the criticized appointment of a journalist to a place of power and of some literary prestige.

XII

THE CRITICAL APPOINTMENT

*O*n the very day that John Russell Young unexpectedly departed this life in the large second-story front room of his residence on Q Street, there was speculation as to his possible successor in the pages of the evening press. Everybody seemed to agree that Ainsworth Spofford would not again be a candidate for the Librarianship. Mr. Spofford was, indeed, finding his minor position very congenial after the years of official turmoil and confusion through which he had passed, and his name was not brought up in connection with the vacant office.

Others were, however, in great number. Bernard Green, who was in charge of the Library building and served as its disbursing officer at the time, was named as a possible candidate, though his chief qualification seemed to be his connection with the construction of the new building before and after the death of General Casey. The Library's chief clerk, Thomas G. Alvord, who was then serving double duty in charge of the art department, was commended as "thoroughly familiar with all details in the administration of the great institution, while he understands its needs." Even the private secretary of President McKinley was "understood" to be under consideration.

All these possible candidates were mentioned in the public press the day of Young's death. It was but the beginning of a flow of suggestions from all quarters interested in playing a part in naming the new Librarian.

264

Shortly before Young's funeral the *Evening Star* of Washington offered the opinion that the journalist's successor would be "a man of standing in the literary world" and possessed of "executive ability of high order." President McKinley's deep, personal interest in the welfare of the Library, the *Star* reported, would probably preclude the appointment of a successor "at least until after the funeral of the late Librarian." At the same time it mentioned its own Cuban correspondent, Charles M. Pepper, as a likely candidate, ingenuously adding that Mr. Pepper's letters to the *Star* from Cuba had been widely read and highly praised.

Meanwhile the names of George Alfred Townsend, whose chief claim to fame seemed to be that he wrote under the nom de plume of "Gath," and that of Cortelyou, the President's assistant secretary, were added to the list of aspirants to the post.

Three days after Young's death, Representative S. J. Barrows of Massachusetts began the arduous and persistent campaign that actually was to end with publication of the gentleman's picture, erroneously announcing him as "New Librarian of Congress" in the *New York Daily Tribune* on February 11th some three weeks later.

Barrows had to compete in the press with such names as W. W. Rockhill, then United States Minister to Greece, and James H. Canfield, then President of Ohio State University, J. M. Greenwood, Superintendent of the Kansas City Public Schools, to say nothing of the Washington correspondent of the *Boston Herald* and *Philadelphia Record*, Henry B. F. MacFarland, and, within the Library itself, in addition to Alvord, the Chief Clerk, with P. Lee Phillipps, head of the maps department and a "recognized American authority on catalogy—familiar with all the details of library work."

As January drew to a close the *Washington Star* announced

that the White House expected the coming week "to be a lively one in the fight for librarian of the Congressional Library." Nearly every Senator had his own candidate—a state of affairs that led the *Star* to believe that the President would "quickly settle the matter if he can find time, as he will thus escape the importunities which will continue until a man is nominated." Meanwhile Henry Garfield, son of the ex-President, and John Addison Porter, the President's secretary, dropped out, declaring, artlessly enough, that they intended, however, to "continue in politics." Political and journalistic ranks were soon filled in again with the announcement of a new candidate—Murat Halstead—referred to as one of "the best-known newspaper men in the country," and one who had "filled every position from reporter up to editor-in-chief." Halstead was also one of the four Republican editors who had supported Greeley for the Presidency in 1872 and formed what was then known as the great quadrilateral, a situation arising—his supporters hastened to point out—not because they liked Greeley but because they hated Grant.

Orville Victor, another candidate, was designated as "a prominent litterateur, who had contributed some important works to the world of letters," the owner of a fine library in Americana and a "life-long student of American history, public men and policies and international affairs."

As one after another the names of outstanding journalists or politicians came up for the consideration of the public, librarians of the country began to ask for consideration. President of the American Library Association the previous year had been Herbert Putnam, the Boston Librarian. His name was advanced as candidate for the Librarianship by that organization. Educators, too, took a lively interest in the campaign and the possible future of the Library.

266

On January 25th, Nicholas Murray Butler sent the following letter to the editor of the *Tribune:*

> SIR: The present public interest in the appointment by the President of a successor to Mr. John Russell Young as Librarian of Congress makes appropriate renewed efforts to secure the adoption of a well matured plan for the permanent administration of this library. The suggestion has been cordially received by a number of leading Senators and Representatives that the Library should be governed as the Smithsonian Institution is governed, namely, by a board of regents composed in part of public officials and in part of citizens designated to serve upon such a board; and that this board of regents should choose the Librarian and also, upon his nomination, his chief assistants and principal subordinates. It would then be possible to disregard entirely political considerations in the selection of this conspicuous and responsible representative of the Nation, and to develop an administrative policy for this great and rapidly growing collection of books, just as a university's policy is developed. On either side of the Capitol there would then be found the scientific and literary collections of the Government, cared for, developed and used in a way that would be a source of pride and gratification to the people.
>
> The Library of Congress has outgrown the provisions that now exist for its control. At present the Librarian has no official advisers, excepting the Committees on Appropriations and on the Library, the membership of which changes more or less completely every second year, and who are by no means always in agreement.
>
> NICHOLAS MURRAY BUTLER
>
> Columbia University,
> January 25, 1899.

Other voices were being raised against the intrusion of politics. A "daily user of libraries" wrote from Boston: "The institution itself, in government and appointments, ought to be as distinctly out of politics as is the Smithsonian, which furnishes an admirable model for the board of regents to direct all the affairs of what should soon be the finest library in the world. To make its positions in the slightest degree a matter of spoils to be distributed among the clamorous horde that always infests Washington is educationally a crime. With the new building, larger appropriations and a proper organization wholly outside of practical politics, opportunities offer to increase many fold the Library's field of practical usefulness."

Librarians, meanwhile, were becoming more vocal in their clamor for consideration. They pointed out that in the fall of 1896, when a joint committee of Congress had taken voluminous testimony on the question of proper organization of the Library of Congress and had heard the opinions of outstanding men in the library field, these specialists had been insistent that if a director were to be put at the head of the institution, outranking Mr. Spofford, only a man of wide and unusually successful library experience should be trusted with what were clearly by far the most important library problems that had yet fallen to any American.

One writer complained bitterly in the columns of the *New York Daily Tribune* of the discouraging results. "Many Members of Congress," he charged, "evidently were determined not to lose any of the loaves and fishes for which they had hoped in the way of appointments." One of the leaders of the majority, warmly interested in putting the Library on a proper basis, finally declined to make further effort on the ground that it was hopeless when, as he phrased it, the chief recommendation for a prominent candidate for the Librarianship was that the climate of a foreign country in which he had held an appointment did not agree with the health of his wife.

Men from whom better things were expected seemed to have no conception of what the modern library has become, and to be dominated still with the idea that the Librarianship was a desirable berth for men of a literary turn who liked the atmosphere of books and who ought

to be provided with something at public expense to show public appreciation of their tastes and literary service. . . . The less people know
about the modern library and the less they are fitted for its duties the
more thoroughly are their minds imbued with the notion that it is the
long-sought haven for those who must live somehow and who enjoy
being in a dignified association with books, pictures and other tangible
evidences of culture.

When, in the fall of 1896, preparation was being made to
reorganize the Library of Congress, and the Joint Congressional
Committee on the Library had called on several leading members of the American Library Association to give their views on
the changes necessary to meet the new conditions, it was generally understood that the scope of the Library of Congress was
to be so expanded as to make it a National Library. Dewey had,
as we have seen, even suggested that its name should be changed
to "The National Library."

As the voices of the librarians of the land swelled louder and
they grew more persistent that one of their number be appointed
to the coveted post, reference was made again to the findings of
this committee, and editorials sanctioning their claims began to
appear in the leading newspapers of the country.

"At this juncture," asserted the *New York Daily Tribune* on
January 20th, "it seems entirely feasible to secure the services
of one of these eminent men, or another equally prominent in
the library world, not simply to give a few suggestions, but to
administer permanently the library along the lines of the latest
library methods and in keeping with the requirements of a truly
National institution."

Commenting upon the newspaper's stand, a contributor designated as a "prominent librarian" wrote: "I am deeply interested
in the appointment, and anxious that, if possible, a competent
librarian should receive it, one who has already shown conspicu-

ous success in the management of a large library, such a man as Herbert Putnam of Boston, Dr. John S. Billings of New York, Melvil Dewey of Albany, or F. M. Crunden of St. Louis." Whereupon this correspondent drew up a scholarly seven-point plan for reorganization and administration of the institution.

The Library of Congress, he stressed, ought to be the national library of the United States. It had a duty to this country comparable to that of the British Museum in England and the Bibliothèque Nationale in France. That duty was to seek out, gather up and preserve all material, documentary, pictorial or purely literary, which might prove the origins and record and illustrate the progress of the national life, "not merely the political but the literary, scientific, industrial, artistic and social life of the United States."

With reference to the United States, its collections should represent pre-eminently original documents and sources.

The national library, moreover, should accumulate and preserve documents and records, undertaking for the country as a whole a duty for which state libraries were unfitted, being "unequal in equipment, heterogeneous in organization and method and isolated in endeavor." Thus the national library, this librarian pointed out, would be the agency through which state libraries would become "associated in co-operative service . . . a medium of exchange" that would utilize them in turn as a central bureau for a vast co-operative undertaking in cataloguing, indexing, bibliography and reciprocal service in the exchange of books and of information. "As the Smithsonian Institution is for scientific bodies the medium in international transactions, so in communications between the libraries of this country and those abroad the National Library should be the national medium."

The writer moved on to a discussion of the need for a staff of expert specialists, "a great collection of books is not made useful simply by being brought together," he wrote, "it is not made fully useful by catalogues, however elaborate. Above the catalogues there must be men, not men of merely routine capacity who can hand out a particular book in response to a particular demand, not mere bibliographers, but in each department of knowledge specialists—men who have had particular training in that department, and if possible who are experienced therein. The majority of the demands in any library of reference, and certainly its most important demands, is not for particular books, but for the best material on a particular subject. These demands can rarely be answered directly by the catalogues. They must be translated; but they can only be translated adequately by an authority who knows both languages, by one who has had experience as a practical worker in the same field as the inquirer, and is also a library expert."

Much was said of the shortcomings of the Library. Only numerically, it was pointed out, was its collection the greatest in the United States, and even numerically it was nearly equaled by other American libraries. Its increase it owed chiefly to accessions by copyright and to gifts; it was strong in but a few directions and weak in most; and as a general collection for scholarly research it could not compare with certain other libraries in the United States. There was not even an indication that a definite policy had yet been formulated for the development of its collection. It was not a leader in schemes of co-operation among American libraries, nor was it representative in international undertakings.

The critical lament was taken up:

It does not offer them models of administrative methods, nor does it seek to reach out its own benefits through them, nor attempt to organize them into any general service of which it shall be the exponent and chief medium.

271

When it was removed to the new building its only catalogue was an author catalogue on slips, and it lacked accession and shelf lists. It has yet to construct a proper subject catalogue and to equip itself with other apparatus such as other libraries have perfected only after years of patient skill. The classification in use (the Baconian) is on a system obsolete and generally discarded, and it must either be discarded there or carefully manipulated, or it will prove a serious impediment to future growth. The library lacks a bindery, a printing office and various other departments regarded by some libraries of lesser scope as necessary adjuncts. The library has not yet developed highly specialized service in many directions within its own walls, and it has not sought to extend its service beyond them. This institution is not merely undeveloped; it is not yet even organic.

The natural outgrowth of publication of such detailed lists of shortcomings as this was the emphasis placed publicly upon the need for a librarian qualified to overcome them.

The responsibility for the organization and development of the Library of Congress, the librarians contended, rested "with its librarian-in-chief," who was chief executive to an extent hardly paralleled in any other library. Appropriations once granted by Congress, the Librarian was supreme. The Congressional Committee on the Library exercised almost none of the control exercised by an ordinary board of directors. It did not even pass on the Librarian's choice of assistants, still less did it interfere with his choice of books. It rarely and only on the most special occasions interposed itself between the Library and other institutions. With the Librarian the character, the conduct and the future of the Library rested. It lay with him to determine a policy, to organize and in the larger sense to administer.

In this crisis, remarked the librarians, the office is suddenly left vacant. Clearly the capacities required of the man who is to fill it are personal probity, tact, firmness, proved success in conciliating various interests; capacity for immediate and vigorous initiative; enthusiasm, "without intemperance, credulity or superficiality"; breadth of view; a knowledge of communities and of affairs not merely provincial; administrative ability, and actual successful experience in administration. A specially important test, said they, should be judgment and independence in the selection of his subordinates, general education, a certain familiarity with libraries and systems of library administration "and such professonal experience as may feasibly be secured."

Librarians, writing in to the press, asserted that a national library should be entitled to the best professional experience obtainable—experience not confined to the librarian's subordinate officials. Granted, said they, that the chief executive must leave detail to his subordinates, and that he is not himself called upon to exercise minute technical knowledge in any one branch of library science, it is at least certain that he must have "sufficient knowledge of the scope, mechanism and methods in each department of library science to enable him to choose fitly the subordinate who is to administer that department under him, to determine a proper policy and to appreciate intelligently and sympathetically the problems with which the subordinate has to deal and the recommendations which he lays before him."

An analogy was drawn between the duties of the chief executive of a national library and those of a business executive. Each, declared the librarians, had to administer a great undertaking and to care for and direct a large plant, in some respects highly technical. Each had to direct the expenditure of large sums of money, to select a large force of employees, organize and direct their work.

"These employees are themselves professionally trained," they declared, "and the work which they do is professional work. Can he select them judiciously, can he direct them intelligently, without some measure of professional experience of his own?" Moreover, they asked if it were safe or economical that he should gain his experience at the expense of the Library, or if it were just that the advance of the Library should be delayed while he was gaining it "and overcoming the timidity inevitable when the problem to be dealt with is unfamiliar?"

Out of the hue and cry came, it is true, certain admissions upon the part of the nation's librarians. There had been instances, in the administration of libraries, they granted, where men imported into the work without particular experience had, by reason of their special intelligence, insight and vigor, made a success. But, they asked, what are the presumptions? Why is it that other great libraries select their chief executives with preference predominantly for professional experience, and should the National Library be the one exception?

One interested observer wrote:

At this juncture the Library requires in its chief executive the highest capacity that may be secured in any one person. If they can be found united in the person of a librarian, that man should be preferred. . . . Impartially it is conceivable, however, that such a librarian cannot be secured. The head of the Library of Congress has a larger responsibility and opportunity for a wider service than any other librarian in the United States; but Congress has not as yet recognized this in the compensation that it pays to him, nor in the resources that it places at his disposal. Until it does so it cannot expect to draw to its service the highest expert capacity now serving other institutions. If the list of available librarians of the requisite capacity be exhausted, and choice must be made of a man without professional experience, this at least should be insisted upon: that he be a man of proved administrative capacity, and finally that he be sufficiently young to acquire his professional training easily and naturally in the conduct of his office. A man beyond middle life cannot be expected to be facile in the acquisition of a new art. Nor can a man beyond middle life be expected to bring to such an office the fresh vigor of initiative, the interest in planning new undertakings, the zeal for labor at unaccustomed service, the long look ahead, indispensable to the library at this present stage.

On January 30, 1899, the *New York Daily Tribune* added its own editorial comment to the contest:

> The librarians of largest experience and greatest reputation look at the matter from the point of view of a desire for the greatest good of the whole nation, and are not governed by a spirit of self-seeking. This is evinced by the suggestion that it would be far better that a man of force and independence, who has had large administrative experience in some other employment, should be chosen for Librarian rather than an inefficient or narrow-minded professional librarian. But unless it be because of the smallness of the salary which the position carries it is not at all necessary to go outside of the library profession to get a man who combines in himself the qualities desirable in the Librarian of Congress. It is to be hoped by all friends of education that the President will search out the best man for the position instead of weighing the claims of candidates who are pressed upon him.

Editorially this paper referred briefly to Mr. Young's record as Librarian. "Much may be said in praise of his administration," it stated, "another equally good appointment outside of the ranks of professional librarians can hardly be expected. But Mr. Young's lack of experience showed itself after he had made a number of capital appointments for his heads of departments. He did not grasp the problems with which he had to deal well enough to co-ordinate their work and make it efficient. Influenced perhaps a little by the common opinion that 'anyone is good enough for library work,' and, not realizing that long training and a combination of many special qualities are essential for success in a library, he appointed at times incompetent persons who were urged upon him, thus bringing the library staff as a whole down to an undisciplined if not also incompetent standard."

275

While nearly everyone is ready to admit that the Library of Congress has passed the stage of confining its usefulness to the legislators at Washington, and has been broadened so as to become a National Library, yet some may doubt if the very enlarged functions for which some librarians argue are feasible.

The *Tribune,* however, agreed with this concept for national usefulness:

Our National Library in point of size, and still more in point of usefulness to the whole country, is far behind other national libraries in the Old World, and less efficient than many libraries in this country. Many of the duties proper to be taken on by the central library are now performed by other American libraries, but less efficiently than they could be done by the Library of Congress, with the prestige of its name and its character as a National institution, if it is only given the funds and has the proper administration. International exchanges; economical cataloguing, once for all; the encouragement and supervision of small libraries; the training of librarians; interlibrary loans, and many other schemes for co-operation and the extension of the mission of books could be accomplished through the library if administered on a broad and liberal basis. The scheme involves the making of the Library a central bureau of national library activity of such a character as to render the libraries of our land collectively one of the most potent forces in the educational field. It is not a visionary idea, but one entirely practicable.

An examination of the proceedings of the American Library Association and statements of its most prominent members, the *Tribune* asserted, had caused it to feel justified in assuming that they considered this to be the proper field for the Library of Congress. The plan, national in scope, had then, they contended, the sanction of the national organization of American libraries, "a body which since its founding in 1876 has succeeded in transforming the dead-and-live institutions that went by the name of libraries before that time into efficient educational institutions of the highest order."

So far comparatively little had been heard, outside of scattered references to his earlier appearance before the Library Committee, of the man who was the choice of the American Library Association for the Librarianship of Congress. Indeed, an announcement in a New York newspaper seemed to put an end, once and for all, to the hopes and expectations of this organization that the post would go to one of their number.

When the *Tribune* published a linecut of Barrows, the column in which this illustration appeared was boldly headed, "New Librarian of Congress." Under a Washington dateline it was stated that "indirect but apparently authentic information had been received by the Massachusetts Members of Congress to the effect that the post of Librarian of Congress has been offered to and accepted by Representative Barrows. Senator Lodge, accompanied by Mr. Barrows, called at the White House today and spent some time with the President. On departing, Mr. Barrows strongly intimated that he would be the successor of the late John Russell Young." The *Tribune* then recounted the romantic story of Mr. Barrows' career which, like those of Mr. Alger's heroes, was said to have begun at the age of nine as an errand boy in an office, where he labored for the next nine years. Mr. Barrows then in turn enlisted in the Navy, where, "on account of ill health he was not mustered in," became a reporter on metropolitan dailies, a "shorthand secretary" to the Secretary of State, a student at Harvard Divinity School, and correspondent with battling expeditions into Yellowstone and the Black Hills, after which he served as editor, pastor, and Representative in Congress.

Unhappily enough for Mr. Barrows, however, he was not destined, despite the announcement, to add Librarianship of the Congressional Library to his list of diverse achievements.

Visitors to the White House before Mr. Barrows had come

away with sanguine expectations. On the morning of February
9th, Thomas G. Alvord was ushered into the presence of President McKinley, who was recovering from an indisposition of
some days' standing. He was accompanied by Senator Platt of
Connecticut, who was sponsoring him for the Librarianship. They
entered the President's ante-room together and the President
conversed with Alvord on the general subject of the Library.
Alvord stated later that McKinley had shown an intimate knowledge of the institution. The *Washington Star* later reported,
however, "While nothing was said of his intentions regarding the
selection of a librarian, it is regarded by Mr. Alvord's friends that
his chances are better than formerly." An amusing sidelight upon
the strong political cast of considerations for the appointment by
journals of the day—which no doubt represented the general impression—is furnished by the *Star's* concluding comment:

> It is understood that several protests have been made against the ap-
> pointment of Representative Barrows, the Western sentiment being
> declared to be very strong against him on account of his alleged sec-
> tionalism. Then again it is asserted that Mr. Barrows voted for Cleve-
> land, Russell and Quincy, for President, Governor of Massachusetts,
> and Mayor of Boston respectively. Owing to these developments it is
> believed that the President will further consider the librarian question
> and it may be that the appointee will be a dark horse who has not yet
> been prominently classed among possibilities.

As the closing days of the Congressional session drew near, it
became apparent that the Senate, at least, had no intention of
confirming the appointment of Mr. Barrows. Almost the entire
time of the executive session of the Senate on the closing day of
Congress was given to consideration of the nominee for National
Librarian, and in withholding confirmation of the Massachusetts
contender, statesmen asserted that, in their opinion, expert knowledge was an indispensable prerequisite for the position in ques-

tion. The stand taken by the Senate Committee on the Library, in its adverse report, and its avowed intention of defeating such a nomination should it be forced to vote, was considered by some as an indication that this committee meant to reject all future nominees not fitted by training and experience for the post.

While Washington was busy digging itself out of the worst blizzard the East had known since '88, and the gas lamps went unlighted in the streets of the Capital because the gas men were unable to make their way through the snow, trips between the Hill and the White House in the interest of the Librarianship were noticeably fewer; Senatorial pressure in behalf of favorite candidates seems to have eased in the interim. However, it was on the 13th of February, a day described as "one of the wildest, most terrifying days in the record of the Capital" because of the raging snowstorm that imperiled the lives of those who went abroad, that word was made public to the effect that President McKinley had offered the post of Librarian of Congress to Herbert Putnam.

Quietly as the offer was made, the offer was considered. The *New York Tribune* commented upon the fact that it would be "a matter of chagrin to every intelligent American" if the President should be unable to secure the man he wanted to manage the National Library. The paper stated:

He has offered the place of Librarian to Mr. Herbert Putnam, now the head of the Boston Public Library. It is universally recognized as an ideal appointment. But Mr. Putnam hesitates to accept the position at Washington. He is now librarian of one of the greatest and most liberally managed libraries in the country, and is in receipt of a salary $1,000 greater than that authorized by law for the Librarian of Congress. His hesitation in making the change can readily be understood. But we hope that he will consider something beyond the immediate circumstances. He will have a greater opportunity as the head of the National Library than has ever before been offered to a man of his standing and attainments. As to the salary, we hope and believe that Congress will not hesitate to make it such as a man at the head of his profession can afford to accept. If Mr. Putnam should decide to accede to the President's wishes it would be cause for congratulation to all who have the highest interests of literature and literary culture at heart.

The offer made by President McKinley to Herbert Putnam was highly pleasing to American librarians and the organization he represented. They began to express satisfaction in the pages of the press and to urge upon Mr. Putnam the wisdom of accepting. They stressed this unexampled opportunity for national service in so important a post and appealed to his patriotism.

Under the heading of "A great opportunity" one librarian commended the *Tribune* for its recommendation of Putnam and expressed himself thus in a New York paper:

> For twenty-five years the Library of Congress, which the librarians of the country have always wished to have as their recognized leader, has been practically a cipher in the wonderful development which has made America recognized as the first country in the world in modern librarianship. There is the most magnificent building yet erected, a great heterogeneous collection of books and an opportunity such as the world has never before seen for just the right man to build a great library and to make its influence felt throughout the entire nation.
>
> To appoint to such a position any man who has not fully proved his ability in charge of a great library is as dangerous a mistake as it would have been to appoint as Commander-in-Chief of the Army a man who had had neither the training of West Point nor the experience of a volunteer officer. Possibly such a man might overcome the obstacles and make a marked success, but the chances are very large that any man who could secure the appointment would be a little too good to be removed from office and not good enough to do the work, and so would prevent any proper development of the library for a generation.
>
> There has never been in the history of libraries a more critical moment. The appointment of Mr. Putnam will inspire with new courage every man who understands modern library needs and opportunities.

The appointment of a man whose qualifications consist chiefly in the persistence with which he seeks the office and the political or personal influence which he marshals in support of his desire to draw public salary would be a disheartening rebuff to the great number of Americans who feel that their National Library should be such in name and in fact, and that its official head should be a man who has deservedly won general recognition as a master in what is now regarded as a distinct profession.

Herbert Putnam, who had rejected the offer at first, reconsidered. Under a dateline of March 13th word came finally from Washington: "The President has appointed Herbert Putnam, of Boston, to be Librarian of Congress." The contest for the coveted post was at an end, and the man who had never actively contested had come off victor.

XIII

A CENTURY OF AMERICAN LIBRARIES

*P*rofessor Eliot of Harvard had referred to Herbert Putnam, early in Putnam's career, as "one of the best three librarians of the country." Though he was only thirty-eight years of age when appointed Librarian of Congress, Putnam had already distinguished himself in the library field.

His earliest background had been a literary one, for he was born the youngest son of George P. Putnam, New York publisher and founder of the house of G. P. Putnam's Sons. Born in New York City in 1861, Putnam's early education was gained in New York's public and private schools. Later he went to Harvard and after his graduation in 1883 continued his studies at the Columbia Law School.

In 1884 he moved to Minneapolis and there was admitted to the Minnesota bar. He had not lived long in this Western city when he became librarian of a proprietary library—the Minneapolis Athenæum. It was largely through his efforts that the Minneapolis Public Library was subsequently founded and the Athenæum merged with it. This combined library, under Putnam's intelligent direction, grew to be in a few years one of the best equipped and most progressive libraries in the United States.

But the young Harvard law student could not completely give up the idea of practising before the bar. In December, 1891, he resigned as librarian at Minneapolis and went to Boston, determined again to take up law. But for the second time his legal career was interrupted—this time fatefully by an offer of the post of librarian of the Boston Public Library. At the time his name was under discussion in this connection, Dr. Cyrus Northrop, then President of the University of Minnesota, described him as "courteous and affable. He understands his business. He is familiar with books. He knows how to help people who want to study a subject and do not know what books they want. He knows how to organize a library. He is pleasantly master and yet guide and helper to his assistants. He is catholic in his spirit and tastes. He is, in brief, a model librarian."

Four years of administrative experience in an American library generally conceded to be foremost in point of efficiency, had certainly proved Herbert Putnam's talents and industry in the library field. During the time he was in charge of the Boston Public Library that institution far excelled the national library in Washington in the scope and completeness of its collections and in its influence as an educational institution; although in number of volumes the national library was somewhat more extensive.

The Boston Public Library and its branches at the time of Putnam's appointment consisted of 716,000 volumes and was spending between $35,000 and $40,000 annually for books and periodicals. More than 72,000 people were making use annually of its collections and almost one and a half million volumes were circulating yearly. Due to the great impetus given to library construction, it had just republished an index to illustrations of library buildings in this connection. It was being increasingly used for reference purposes and had just established a special department of documents and statistics to which the American Statistical Association had turned over its library of some 5,000 volumes, works on vital, economic, political and social statistics, and work was in progress under Worthington Ford—a former chief of the U. S. Treasury Bureau of Statistics—on cataloguing British Parliamentary papers and United States Congressional documents. It was, in all respects, a forward-looking, active institution and universally considered one of the finest American libraries. Much of this progressive spirit was undoubtedly due to Herbert Putnam's initiative, industry and vision.

Putnam was destined to bridge two eras of tremendous import in American library development, carrying the Library of Congress from a primarily Congressional service center into an institution national in scope and character, seeing out the era of proprietary, private, and mercantile libraries with their restricted field for service and limited public appeal, and seeing in the new era of free libraries, special libraries adequately equipped for study and research, and expansion everywhere of opportunities for public service.

In the first year of the nineteenth century the United States, with a population of five and a third millions, had sixty-four libraries intended for popular use. Counting as public the parochial libraries founded by Dr. Bray, and assuming that most of them survived the Revolution, the number might be expanded to one hundred, which contained in all perhaps fifty thousand volumes. In the last year of the century there were more than ten thousand libraries, containing forty million volumes in all, and half of the number of libraries each had more than a thousand volumes. Our territory at the close of the century was less than four times as large as it had been when the century opened; our population was about fifteen times as large. Yet the number of libraries increased a hundredfold and there were eight hundred times as many books.

The beginning of the nineteenth century was a time of solid books and slow readers, and it is unlikely that the output of those years exceeded the stock. There were fifty million volumes issued in 1900, so the circulation may be assumed to have grown a thou-sandfold.

The history of libraries in America is an old one. It goes back to the Puritans, who founded a college, and with it a library, shortly after landing on these shores. Harvard College Library, founded in 1638, was followed in 1700 by libraries at Yale and at William and Mary, and—within the next hundred years—by twelve others; so that the nineteenth century began with fifteen college libraries. It ended with more than forty times as many.

Later, with the growth of cities and the accumulation of wealth, joint-stock libraries originated—the first being estab-lished in 1731, twenty-seven years before the first proprietary library sprang up in Liverpool, England. By 1800 there were thirty-two such libraries and they continued to spread through-out the country—the "Athenæums" of the cities and the "Social Libraries" of the country—until the free libraries gradually dis-placed them. Many proprietary libraries were founded in the decades before and after the Civil War, but only fifty-seven such institutions had more than a thousand volumes apiece in 1896.

In 1790 Harvard College Library had only 12,000 volumes; and in 1807 the largest of the proprietary group, the Philadel-phia Company, after absorbing three similar libraries, had only 18,400 volumes. In 1793 the New York Society Library had 5,000 volumes; in 1791 Yale College had only 2,700 volumes. The Charlestown Society Library had 7,000 volumes in 1811; and the Boston Athenæum, founded two years earlier, had 5,750. These represented the outstanding collections among li-braries of the country.

In the college libraries, theology held leading place, which was natural enough when one considers that the colleges had been founded mainly to educate ministers. In fact, 150 pages of every 350 in the Harvard College Library catalogue of 1790 were concerned with works of theology, ten with Greek and Latin classics, four with books of travel, and only three-fourths of a page with periodicals. On the other hand, Shakespeare, Milton, Chaucer, Pope, Dryden, Spenser, Rabelais, Gay, La Fontaine, the *Gentleman's Magazine,* Boccaccio and Voltaire were represented in literature. Yale College, in 1765, had a goodly showing of ancient authors "such as the Fathers, historians, classics, many and valuable works of divinity, history, philosophy, and mathematics, but not many authors who have wrote within these thirty years."

The social libraries, on the other hand, were patterned after the Library Company of Philadelphia, where selection had been largely determined by Franklin's taste. In these there were few, if any, theological books or controversial, or political tracts; and science, travel, natural history and the mechanic arts formed the bulk of the collection. Art was not to be found in the early libraries. It was the Boston Athenæum which became the pioneer of bibliothecal art development when it received a contribution of a large number of art works from a proprietor in 1838. Fiction, which accounts for probably 75 percent of the circulation of the modern city library, was not furnished by college or association libraries. For that, readers went to that "evergreen tree of diabolical knowledge," the circulating library.

The mercantile library, together with the mechanic's institutions and apprentice's libraries, were next to spring up in connection with the marked educational movement of the second and third quarter of the century. They usually had classes for evening instruction and courses of lectures, and were designed mainly for young men who could not afford shares in the proprietary libraries.

While small annual fees were paid, the mercantile libraries were definitely a step forward in bringing knowledge within the

286

reach of all. They were, like all libraries, continually in need of money, so that membership was extended in time to anyone who would pay the annual fee. Thus brought into competition with the circulating libraries, the mercantile libraries adopted their methods, a program which resulted in mitigated austerity in book selection and lessened cost to readers, thereby paving the way for the free public library. Out of the inadequacy of such libraries for research and investigation, special libraries—historical, legal, medical, theological, scientific and oriental, came into existence. Compared to five or six of these when the century began, there were some five hundred at its close. As yet there were no libraries for all the people, and none was free.

The era of free libraries may be said to have started with the second third of the century, in the little town of Peterborough in New Hampshire. There, in 1833, a Unitarian minister was responsible for the founding of the first free library under an appropriation raised by people who were willing to tax themselves in order to read. It was thirteen years before a second town —this time Orange, Massachusetts—took a similar step, and four years later Wayland followed. The illegality of such expenditures of community funds perhaps only served to contribute to the passage of the act of 1849 in New Hampshire and of 1851 in Massachusetts, which authorized any town to tax itself for a free public library.

Boston, despite its cultural traditions, did not consider the matter of free libraries until it was more than two hundred years old, and eleven years expired between the first suggestion in this direction and decisive action in 1862. The idea once adopted, it was carried out with characteristic thoroughness and Boston ended by collecting the largest stock, erecting the costliest building and having the largest circulation of any city in America for the first forty years. A contemporary critic, commenting upon this, states,

"In other places some parts of a library's function may have been better developed, but nowhere yet had the happy combination of private and public liberality made it possible at once so thoroughly to suffice for learned research even of the specialist, gratify cultivated curiosity, please the bibliomaniac and the dilettante, foster idle meditation, or stimulate vigorous thinking, while yet not neglecting to meet every want of the general reader, even the want of amusement and illusion, and, even more than this, to attract to itself and to train adults who have never been in the habit of reading at all, and children who have not yet learned to read with profit."

Another library system—but this one destined for complete failure—grew up shortly after the inauguration of town libraries. A law of New York State, passed in 1835, permitted each school district to tax itself thirty dollars a year, twenty of which sum was to found, and ten to maintain, a free public library. Three years later, when it was discovered that the people would not tax themselves for this purpose, the Legislature was persuaded to appropriate $55,000 a year for the purchase of books. Within fifteen years the libraries had more than 1,600,000 volumes, very little used except in the cities. After another eleven years and the expenditure of half a million more dollars, there were half a million volumes less. School boards had to learn the lesson that reading will not take root among a people not eager for it, except by wise management, and that wise management in the library field never results from administration in the hands of men not interested in libraries. They had to learn that libraries always suffer at the hands of a school board which, if not chosen for political reasons, is selected for ability to administer in fields where aims, material, methods, and personnel differ from those in libraries. Moreover, school trustees were frequently incompetent to select books and were at the mercy of commercial booksellers. Libraries under these conditions did not, of course, attract readers; and in 1892 New York wisely separated school libraries confined to school use under direction of school authorities from town libraries for public use under direction of trustees.

In library history the first three quarters of the nineteenth century was a period characterized by poverty, few books, slow increase, conservatism, slow development of purposes and methods, limitation and restriction. The latter quarter showed an amazing increase in number and size of collections and in money donations, library buildings under construction all over the country, with improved suitability to their purpose. It was, too, a period of experimentation in administrative methods, with channels of library influence constantly opening. Moreover, a change in aims and purposes was apparent, with the use, rather than the collecting, of books the supreme consideration.

This astounding awakening may be traced in part to increased population and wealth and to a spread of education and culture. But it was largely due also to the efforts of the librarians themselves, their enlarged ideas of the library's mission and their discovery of more effective ways of working, so that the reach and power of libraries was doubled and their hold upon popular favor so strengthened that appeals for philanthropic support were reinforced.

A main factor in stimulating interest in libraries and regard for the librarian's profession was certainly established when a hundred librarians met at Philadelphia during the Centennial Exhibition to exchange views. Up until 1876 the librarian, busy in his own library, had seldom heard of his colleagues' activities in the same field; so that there was little spread of professional ideas and no co-operation.

Out of that Philadelphia meeting grew the American Library Association and the *Library Journal*, bringing improvement in all branches of library economy. True, the time was ripe for such a concentrated effort as it had not been when a previous convention met in 1853. By 1876 the question of slavery had been eliminated, there was time for interest in cultural things. Essays written by librarians of that day, their papers and conference discussions show that greatest progress was apparent in library establishment, in the profession, in the building, and in the management and methods of reaching the public.

At the time that Herbert Putnam was actively engaged in managing the Minneapolis Library, the trend was toward libraries established by legislation, supported by taxation, helped as far as possible by private generosity, managed by their own authorities and free to all—true libraries of the people. Such libraries were then fast coming into existence, their establishment assisted by State library commissions, the first of which was organized in Massachusetts in 1890. These commissions had as a common purpose stimulation of the use of libraries, arousing of public interest, distribution of library aid in the poorer towns, and encouragement of private giving.

There had also grown up in the nation a changed conception of what a librarian should be. Hit-and-miss methods of the first half of the century had given way before the realization that the best work could be done by specially educated persons; that time was constantly being lost and progress checked in training new assistants. Apprenticeship was first suggested as a solution and the next step was, logically enough, establishment of the library school.

While library practice advanced, architecture lagged behind. Library needs were expanding rapidly; many library buildings had been designed primarily for show and not for practical use; bad ventilation was common, bad lighting universal. No characteristic style of architecture, taking into consideration continuously enlarged stocks and expanding fields of public service, had been hit upon. The library building of 1801 was in most cases a single room, with shelves around the walls. During the century this single cell evolved into various divisions for special purposes. In their early efforts at uniformity librarians paid a prodigious amount of attention to details; they spent a great deal of time distinguishing tweedledum from tweedledee and showed a pedantic tendency to forget the things of the spirit in absorption with mechanical details.

But in the last quarter of the century these tendencies gave way, as they were bound to do, before American inventiveness and the missionary spirit. Great strides were made in that period in reaching the public, and making available to them all library resources; imaginative and interpretative talents were brought more and more to bear upon the office of librarianship, until gradually the libraries, with the nation, found themselves committed to the experiment of universal education. By 1899 the idea had advanced to a point that the secretary of the New England Education League could read a paper before the session of the American Library Association in Atlanta on May 11th, advocating that the Federal postal system carry library books at cost, so that every postoffice might serve as a library delivery station, and every carrier a library helper to bring reading to every part of the country, to enable any citizen to get a book as readily as a magazine, a paper or a letter through the mail.

In the year that Herbert Putnam was appointed to head the national library, the entire United States was becoming increasingly library-conscious. In the upper West Side of New York City alone, in some ten or eleven public libraries scattered between 57th Street and Harlem, west of Eighth Avenue, more than 350,000 books were being used by the public, free of charge. In West 91st Street there was a library devoted to the needs of the blind; some 530 volumes in raised type acquainted these readers with Shakespeare, Longfellow, Macaulay, Goldsmith, Gray, Milton, Whittier, Moore, Scott, Bryant, Coleridge, Tennyson, Holmes, Huxley, Lamb, Cooper, Conan Doyle, Irving, Emerson, Addison, Swift, Vergil, Homer, Cicero, Byron, and Pope, as well as with authorities on religion, history, physiology, geography, biography, political economy, tales for children, and music.

More than 9,000 volumes were being circulated by the Bloomingdale Branch of the New York Free Circulating Library on West 100th Street, to persons over ten years of age with a reference. About 16,000 readers a month were taking advantage of this privilege. At the St. Agnes Free Library at Amsterdam Avenue and 85th Street, 10,000 readers were making use of the 6,500-volume collection and the stock was increasing at the rate of a hundred new books every month.

In West 57th Street the library of the Young Men's Christian Association offered aid educationally and in practical training to any reader who wished to enter and consult its 42,000 volumes. In one month of that year (1899) more than 16,000 readers were accommodated in this way. The collections here were exceptionally strong in the fine arts, and patrons were encouraged to pursue systematic courses of reading. Bound volumes of newspapers, from the first days of their publication, were accessible for reference and a careful index system was maintained.

At about this same period, the library at Columbia University, with more than 270,000 books, was making an especial appeal to the historian, the man of letters, and the scholar generally, outside of its own student body. The 35,000 volumes of the American Museum of Natural History and the 5,000 volumes of the Genealogical and Biographical Society were also available to students. This brief review of library facilities in only one section of one city may serve to show what was taking place all over the country during the period.

In his annual report for the year ending June 30, 1899, Dr. J. S. Billings, Director of the New York Public Library, had stated that 459,248 volumes were on the shelves, available to the public, and about 117,000 pamphlets, while 55,593 volumes had been received and catalogued during the year. With more than 111,000 visitors during the year, about 360,000 volumes were called for by the public at the Astor Branch alone.

The movement was, as a matter of fact, so widespread that libraries were being trundled from town to town to take care of the needs of the smallest rural communities which were demanding to be served. State library commissions were planting libraries in hundreds of villages and hamlets. The Federation of Women's Clubs of Herbert Putnam's own previous sphere of activity— Minnesota—had just succeeded in getting through the Legislature a Traveling Library bill, for which they had fought through three sessions, and were planning to bring libraries to the frontier towns. In the seaboard States of Virginia, North and South Carolina, Georgia and Florida, publishers, railway and express companies were co-operating with the efforts of Mrs. Eugene B. Heard to circulate her Free Traveling Library in boxes of thirty volumes each, distributed within ten-mile radii of small centers.

Newspapers were publishing suggestions to women's groups urging their co-operation in establishing free libraries in towns and villages of their States. Only $100 was needed as capital, they stated, and a little free service from the people. The State would do the rest. If twenty-five taxpayers petitioned for a library, under law a popular vote was taken. This might be taken at any village, town or school-district election, or it might be done by village trustees or school authorities. It was suggested that five trustees should be elected, one of whom should go out of office each year, and that a tax of $100 should be levied for the maintenance of the library.

One paper advised its readers that should the raising of the $100 by tax prove impracticable an association might be formed, trustees elected, and the money raised by private subscription, with a like sum pledged to continue the work for the second year so that the regents would grant a charter. These formalities concluded, the State would provide, up to $200, as much as the local authorities would pay for approved books, serials and binding or library supplies. Such State aid was a yearly gift and the library could call again upon the State, in its second year of existence, for as much, up to $200, as it could raise from local sources. To encourage establishment of such local groups some State libraries distributed circulars and blanks on the subject free of charge to all interested communities.

Women were taking an interest in the library movement in other ways. A real campaign for women librarians was under way when Herbert Putnam was on his way to Washington. There were three large training schools for librarians in the United States at this time, all of which were open to women on equal terms with men. Women's pages of the press and periodicals were bringing the field to the attention of women everywhere. They were apprised of the great number of public libraries in the United States, besides private, reference, and college and school libraries, and of the resulting demand for trained librarians. The *Tribune* warned of special "mental qualifications," and, frightening all but the intrepid, surely, *Harper's Bazaar* fearlessly listed them:

> For the thorough mastering of the profession the generalizing and the analytic faculties must be well developed and nicely balanced: the mind must be capable of taking in without confusion large groups of subjects, and at the same time of entering clearly into the minute details

of all the subjects of each group. Its power of concentration must be equal to, but must not exceed its versatility. It must be able to detach itself from and give itself up entirely to a subject with equal readiness. And, like the mind of the teacher it must be eminently altruistic, for the interests which will constantly engage it will have for their purpose the satisfaction of other needs than its own, and in these interests it must find its stimulus to even higher effort.

As the journals of the day pointed out, preference in these training schools was given to college graduates, while "a thorough high-school education and a wide knowledge of books is essential for all candidates."

Regarded as one of the best such schools in the country, the New York State Library School at Albany—a continuation of the Columbia Library School—was then headed by Melvil Dewey, its founder and director. Dewey's system of cataloguing was then being generally adopted throughout the country. This school was offering a two years' course, of forty weeks each, with forty hours' work a week. The cost of the entire two years' course was $100, to which was added $25 a year for an annual visit to the New York or Boston libraries, and $20 for text books or supplies.

Colleges were also beginning to offer courses in library science, including Illinois State University, and Pratt Institute in Brooklyn. In short, the library field was opening up in all directions at the time Herbert Putnam left Boston for Washington. He stepped prominently into the picture at a time when a unique opportunity offered. His service might have taken the way of limitation—such as primary concentration on Congressional needs, or have followed the broader concept of national usefulness. Putnam's vision was for national service and he was to witness materialization of that vision in very large part during the years that lay ahead.

XIV

A JOB IS LAID OUT

"*T*he new librarian," wrote a Washington reporter on April 5, 1899, with unexpected foresight, "has come to Washington to stay." The *Star* had sent a member of the staff up to the Hill to interview the small, modest man just arrived from Boston.

Herbert Putnam's first action, once he had arrived in Washington, was to call upon the President. The *Star* assures us that they had a pleasant conversation, concluding with the safe statement that Mr. Putnam evidenced his appreciation of the responsibilities of his new position and expressed his determination to meet them to the best of his ability.

The following morning Putnam made his way to the magnificent new building over which Ainsworth Spofford had been presiding in the capacity of Acting Librarian since the death of John Russell Young about three months before. Spofford escorted the new Librarian about the building, introducing him to the heads of the various departments. Later Putnam left for the Capitol, just across the way, to take his oath of office.

The *Star* reporter was much impressed with the youth of the appointee. He described him as "a young-looking man, when one considers the work he has done and the results he has accomplished." He commented, too, upon that quality which was always noted by those who had dealings with Putnam—his reserve. "His most striking characteristic," wrote his interviewer, "is reserve of manner, not reserve which suggests coldness or haughtiness, however, for, on the contrary, he is very genial. His personality is attractive and he would impress one as a man who makes friends easily and without much effort upon his own part."

In answer to questions about his general policy in the new post that first day of office, Herbert Putnam gave characteristic answer: "I am not insensible to the consideration of a policy, but if I were asked the direct question as to what it shall be I would have to reply that I have administered a library in Minneapolis, I have administered a library in Boston, but I have never administered the Library of Congress. The policy, I imagine, will be a question of the future."

He then went on to say that such a large undertaking could not be grasped as a whole, that necessarily it must be taken in detail, and a detail which could only be worked out day by day. He must come to know his subordinates thoroughly, to know the demands of their positions and to have his own work unfolded to his understanding by daily experience. He stated that ideas and theories about the Library he certainly had, but that now he would have to consider facts, weigh his theories carefully and consider them in the light of the conditions surrounding him.

"The impression which one gets from Mr. Putnam at this stage of the proceedings," wrote his interviewer, "is that he is a conservative and cautious man, going slowly about his business, understanding it thoroughly. He will apply the knowledge that he has gained in other fields to the work before him, but with a regard for the conditions existing here, which may differ from those surrounding his labors heretofore. He says that in a great library the results of a mistake made at the outset become more embarrassing as time passes on and the library grows, and he has found it advisable to be absolutely certain before going ahead."

There was plenty of hard work ahead of the Librarian of

Congress. To realize its exacting nature one must consider the extent of the collections he had taken over, the limitations and prerogatives of office, the status of national affairs, the trend of national thought, the tastes, interests and inclination of the American public at that time.

A century was on the way out—another was on the way in. What was the setting of the times? Little more than a month before, Queen Victoria, cabling via Lord Salisbury, had assured the country that she would be glad to receive Joseph H. Choate as Ambassador to Great Britain. There was another "grave crisis" in Samoa and the flagship *Philadelphia* had recently sailed off to protect American interests. The restless bones of Christopher Columbus had been transported from Havana via the cruiser *Conde de Venadito* and the Spanish auxiliary *Giralda* to be interred amidst extraordinary pomp and ceremony in the Cathedral of Seville. In Bolivia the Federalists had recently won a victory. Russia had just placed an order for a 6,250-ton cruiser with Prussian yards and was building for herself three steamers of 12,800 tons apiece.

In the world of the theatre Blanche Bates was enjoying a great triumph as the wicked countess in *The Three Musketeers,* and Mrs. Fiske was making a tremendous hit on Fifth Avenue in the double bill, *Love Finds a Way* and *A Bit of Old Chelsea.* The Lyceum was putting on a new play—*Americans at Home,* and Miss Della Fox was pleasing audiences at the Grand Opera House in *The Little Host.*

Editors were lamenting foreign seizures on the Chinese coast and Russia's partitioning of the Chinese Empire. Comparisons were being made between London's system for consolidation of its boroughs and New York's. There was grave speculation as to possible reasons for the six-million-dollar decrease in the nation's export trade. In New York the street railway companies were being denounced as impudent, and Robert Hill of the United States Geological Survey, lecturing in Chickering Hall, was affectionately referring to the Cubans as the highest product of the Tropics and congratulating the President for so firmly ending the war. Madame Schumann-Heink was canceling her engagement to sing in *The Ring of the Nibelungs* because of illness; Madame Emma Eames and Jean and Edouard de Reszke were appearing together in the season's final performance of *Faust*. New York art galleries were exhibiting the works of Maurice Boutet de Monvel, of Fernand Lungren and of Carolus Duran. The President had just accepted an invitation to attend the unveiling of a monument to General Grant in Fairmount Park in Philadelphia. Congress was momentarily occupied with matters not much more serious than the question of selling beer to the boys in the Army camps. So much for the immediate setting.

There was a general movement abroad in the land for education and the development of cultural interests, and this, as we have seen, was finding expression through the increased number of libraries, the extension of library services. The Library of Congress stood in a different relation to this movement than other libraries of the country. It had first of all been founded for a unique purpose and its problems and potentialities were correspondingly unique. Putnam had made a fine distinction when he remarked that he had administered two public libraries but had never administered the Library of Congress.

The last report submitted by John Russell Young in 1898 shows clearly that even during an administration as brief as his the journalist-librarian had realized the gradual, inevitable transition of the Library of Congress into an institution of national importance.

Herbert Putnam had served but a few months as Librarian of Congress before he undertook to acknowledge this problem of

299

the scope and purpose of the Library of Congress. Writing in the *Atlantic Monthly* in February, 1900, he asked these direct questions of his readers: What is the Library of Congress? What is it to be? If a national library, how far has it advanced toward such a title? What have been its opportunities? He admitted that, begun as a legislative library for the use of Congress, it had only gradually struggled into the notion of a larger career. As custodian and distributor of legislative documents, it was a document room in addition to being a library. Under its constitution it ranked, not as an executive department, but as a branch of the legislative, although, since 1802, its librarian had been appointed by the head of the executive division of the Government—the President of the United States. On the other hand, the reports submitted by this appointee were addressed, not to the President, but direct to Congress, while general supervision of the Library was in a joint committee composed of three Senators and three Representatives. Its general organization, Putnam pointed out, its proper scope, its functions, had not, down to 1896, been the subject of detailed discussion or deliberate investigation on the part of Congress or of any commission created by Congress.

He recalled that in May of 1896, on the eve of completion of the new building, the joint committee on the Library had been instructed to inquire into the condition of the Library and report, with recommendations. They had also been asked to report a plan for the organization, custody and management of the new building and of the Library itself.

Putnam referred to the session held in the following November and December when testimony was taken and outside librarians served as witnesses. The testimony of particular value, on this occasion, said Putnam, had been that of Dr. Spofford, and this had been chiefly historical.

John Russell Young, during his brief administration, from July 1897 to January 17, 1899, had been primarily concerned with the installation of the collections in the new building and reorganization of an enlarged staff. Dr. Spofford, marking time until the appointment of Young's successor, continued this work. When Putnam took over the tremendous burden of administration he had first to acquaint himself with the Library itself. What is the Library of Congress today? he asked early in 1900, and suggested that it could be considered most simply by applying to it the tests applicable to any library, of whatever type. That is to say, what are its collections, and what is the provision for their increase? What is its organization for the business of getting and caring for the books, what for making them available to the public? What is, what may be, its "public"?

Reviewing the situation, Putnam had his own answers ready. A very good picture of the Library of Congress when he took over may be gained by his own first analysis.

The collections, he noted, exceeded in mere mass that of any library in the Western Hemisphere and, "through historical causes special to it," comprised elements not found in any other single library. It consisted nominally of 850,000 printed books and 250,000 pamphlets, 26,000 pieces of manuscript, 50,000 maps, 277,000 pieces of music, and more than 70,000 prints —including photographs, lithographs, engravings and etchings. These figures included 103,000 volumes of the Law Library, then in the Capitol, and about 90,000 volumes of the Smithsonian deposit. They included duplicates, which were, in 1897, estimated at one third of the entire collection. In the case of printed books and pamphlets they included not merely copyright deposits which had been transferred to the general collection, "but those others which still as record copies remain in the copyright department and do not form part of the library proper—a number estimated at 140,000 volumes and pamphlets."

At the time that Herbert Putnam became Librarian of Congress the major part of the general material in the Library was the result of the operation of the copyright law. While nominally this law should seem to have secured to the Library all issues of the American Press published during its operation, this actually was not the case. Many important publications then as now failed to be entered for copyright, either from negligence, indifference, or because in some cases their production cost defied piracy. Also, many applicants, having received their certificate of entry, did not perfect them subsequently by the requisite deposits.

As may be guessed, the material coming into the Library through copyright was bound to be miscellaneous in character— some of it of great value, and a considerable amount of small literary worth. Up to 1900 the entire collection of music, the entire collection of prints (with the exception of about 1,300 from the Smithsonian) were the fruit of the copyright law; and more than 80,000 volumes were derived from the Smithsonian collection.

While the Library's last twenty years in the Capitol with a limited staff and amidst congested conditions had made impossible any methodic arrangement or systematic receipt of this material, it represented, in the aggregate, by 1900, the most important collection of scientific serials in the United States, with Smithsonian correspondents numbering more than 30,000 co-operating in exchange of transactions and proceedings of learned societies with other serial publications and monographs. However, excellent as this collection was, it was yet incomplete. Applied science was very meagerly represented, the technical arts were hardly represented at all.

Out of a gross total of 850,000 printed books, there was left a miscellaneous collection of about 500,000 volumes, after the collections of the Law Library, the copyright record copies, and the Smithsonian deposit were deducted. There were, in addition, about 250,000 pamphlets—so that, numerically, the Library of Congress was not greatly in excess in 1900 of such collections as the Boston Public Library, the Harvard College Library, or the New York Public Library.

Putnam expressed the opinion, during his first year as Librarian, that the Library of Congress was first of all a legislative library, with a primary duty to Congress, and that its other duties were "only opportunities that, with the assent of Congress, may be put to use without neglect of this." He expressed the belief that the material, therefore, which the Library should amass, should be primarily such as would serve a legislator in Congress —in other words, any material which recorded the origins and development of the United States, legislation in every country and, so far as might be practicable, the discussions attendant on legislation. Such material should also include all history, constitutions, statute laws, administration, statistics, the literature of comparative institutions, political science and political economy, sociology in its largest sense, finance, transportation, public improvements, education, international law, and diplomacy.

Despite the resources at its command, the Library of Congress had not built up, by 1900, a pre-eminent collection of Federal documents, and in State and municipal documents was still more defective; its system of international exchange was operating only irregularly.

Similarly, its Law Library collection, numerically one of the largest in the United States, was excelled in efficiency by that of the New York City Bar Association, by the Social Law Library of Boston and other law libraries of the United States; and jurisprudence was not broadly represented.

In 1900 practically the entire manuscript collection of the Library of Congress consisted of 26,000 items covering a limited area and that thinly; only two items went beyond America; the material relating to the Colonies related to but few of them, with the major portion touching the Revolutionary period. Some of the more valuable items at that time were the only extant copy of the *Records of the Virginia Company* from 1619 to 1624; documents relating to early Delaware and New Hampshire; early laws of Virginia; the Vernon-Wagner, Chalmers, Johnson, Dickinson, Trumbull, Washington, John Paul Jones, De Rochambeau, Du Simitière, and Vergennes papers; the orderly books and letters of Greene, Blaine, Sullivan, and other military heroes; military journals of British officers, and other autograph material of the Revolutionary period; minutes of certain committees of safety; 365 folio volumes of transcripts of the entire material used by Force as the basis of his Archives; the letter books of Monroe while minister at St. James; and an unpublished manuscript of Las Casas. Through the Smithsonian it was also in possession of thirty-five volumes containing the proceedings of the commissioners sitting at St. John's, Halifax and Montreal for inquiring into the services, losses, and claims of American royalists who were later indemnified by act of Parliament; and fifty-four volumes of bills, accounts, and inventories covering the years 1650 to 1754 —this latter Halliwell-Phillips' collection given to the Smithsonian in 1852.

Of manuscript material later than the eighteenth century the Library possessed at this time only one important item—the correspondence of Schoolcraft, 1815-1860. There was, in effect, nothing of original manuscript sources of the history of foreign countries. Such material as it possessed was incidental to the purchase of the Force and De Rochambeau collections and the gift of the Toner collection—about 900 volumes in all. Putnam compared this number with the 110,000 volumes of manuscripts in the British Museum. "Last year," he said, in 1900, "the Museum spent £5,000 for manuscripts; the Library of Congress $300."

The year that Herbert Putnam took charge it was in Americana that the Library of Congress possessed its most distinctive strength. It had at that time a collection of 18,000 volumes of newspapers, of which 350 volumes were published prior to 1800. It had likewise nearly complete files of nineteenth-century dailies dating back to the Civil War, representing at least partial files of two of the leading papers of opposite political philosophies in every State and Territory for the past quarter of a century.

The map department contained a larger number of maps relating to America than any other single collection in the world, including the Force collection of more than 1,000 military maps and plans covering the French War and the Revolution—300 of which were in manuscript. There were few specimens of early cartography and a scant representation of areas beyond the United States.

These were the areas in which the Library was strong in 1900. In other divisions of history and, in fact, in all other departments of knowledge, it was necessarily weak. Putnam lamented particularly the inadequacy of available bibliographic aids. "The Library of Congress cannot obtain every book in existence," he remarked, "it can secure and furnish the best information procurable as to what the book is and where it may be found."

In technology and the useful arts there was little beyond that which had come in through copyright, and the same was true of the literature of natural science and of mathematics beyond what was represented by the Smithsonian serials.

The new Librarian believed that specialization in medicine would be extravagant, with the "admirably catalogued and liberally administered" library of the Surgeon General's office which was within easy reach. He was not clear, however, he admitted, that the duty of the Library was fulfilled with the proper care of the Smithsonian serials and the completion of the broken files. He said:

> The Federal Government is annually expending large sums of money at Washington, in the formation and maintenance of scientific collections and in the support of scientific research. The books which are the essential tools for the men engaged in this work can be secured only in part out of the department appropriations. Space for them and administrative facilities are difficult to provide in the department buildings. Moreover, the files of scientific serials in the Library not possibly to be duplicated elsewhere have their effective use only with the monographs at hand, which are the great reference books in each department of science. The Library of Congress, therefore, appears committed to some expenditure in the domain of scientific literature; to some in the natural sciences, in archæology, in ethnology, and, to a certain extent, in the sciences which are called "applied." To the philosophic sciences (in the narrower sense, including theology) the obligation would not appear so direct, nor to the literature merely "polite."

He expressed, that first year, a desire to broaden the field of the Library. Among the Federal institutions at Washington of which students are invited to avail themselves, Congress had deliberately placed the Library first, so that if it were to do as a library what the various scientific departments of the Government were expected to do in their various branches of science, it would have to expand its collections to include material illustrating the origins and general progress of arts and letters.

As it was, the Library possessed, in 1900, almost no specimens of early printing, outside of incunabula acquired through the Force collection, which consisted of 161 books printed in the fifteenth century, 250 printed from 1500 to 1600, and other items. Wilson, it is true, had just presented the Library with eleven Flemish manuscripts on vellum, ranging from 1450 to 1700, but it possessed practically no literary memorials prior to the invention of printing and had only recently acquired a few works on the subject of paleography. There was a fair representation in belles-lettres, of the works of the most notable English authors, and these often not the best editions. Of modern Continental literature it had little or nothing.

By 1900 the collection of Orientalia, which was later to become world famous, numbered no more than 237 books and 2,547 pamphlets in the Chinese language, from the library of Caleb Cushing, and a few works in Turkish—the gift of Abram S. Hewitt. There was only a scattered volume here and there of other Oriental literatures, or of Slavonic. There had been no funds available up to that time for development of collections in the literature of music, the fine arts or architecture.

These were the contents and proportions of the Library's collections when Herbert Putnam took charge. Resources for their increase consisted of future accessions from copyright, from the Smithsonian and from international exchanges. But, as the Librarian pointed out, these special resources could not be fully utilized without an expenditure for investigation and solicitation, for which provisions had not been made. Only once in its history had the Library of Congress sent a representative abroad in its behalf and on that occasion the Smithsonian had shared the expenses of an agent sent to collect European documents and to stimulate international exchanges. The agent had acquired more than 4,000 volumes for the Library as a result of that trip. But, though maintenance of regular agencies in the chief book marts of the world and the occasional dispatch of special emissaries to investigate opportunities for acquisition by purchase were necessary to the accumulation of a great collection of books, there subsequently had not been funds for repetition of the experiment. The 1899 appropriation for the Library had been $25,000, in addition to

$2,500 for the Law Library—a sum, the Librarian declared, which could not cover even the area of current publications and could apply but feebly to existing deficiencies.

It was important, he stressed, that those deficiencies be supplied at the earliest possible date, "not merely in the interest of the scholars of the generation, but as an economy, prior to the reclassification and cataloguing of the Library."

There were, indeed, economic considerations. A large proportion of the material needed by the Library had at that time an artificial market value; little of it was in demand by the Library of Congress alone and in attempting to secure it the Library of Congress would have to come into competition with other great libraries. These other libraries were fast increasing in number and resources. Many of them enjoyed regular incomes for books in excess of the appropriation granted the Library of Congress and were in possession of reserve funds for emergencies. Moreover, they were able to count upon special gifts from individuals interested in furthering special purchases.

The Library of Congress, on the other hand, had no individual benefactors to whom it might apply when opportunity offered for the purchase of special collections or unusual items at auction sales, and public sales of special collections were seldom announced long enough in advance for the operation of an ordinary appropriation bill, which, moreover, would only serve to herald in advance the buyer's limit of price. Putnam suggested that a special fund of $100,000 would be none too great for such emergencies, in addition to regular appropriations for the purchase of books.

Problems of classification, as well as of finance, confronted Herbert Putnam. The Library was still classified under the Baconian system adopted by Thomas Jefferson for his collection of 6,700 volumes. Its weakness was, of course, that it had been devised as a classification of knowledge, and not as a classification of books. Its original three main divisions—history, philosophy, and fine arts—had been expanded into forty-four groups or "chapters," but the system did not admit of further indefinite subdivisions. "The inability of forty-four groups to meet the requirements of a modern library of nearly a million volumes," the Librarian remarked, "may be guessed from the fact that a single system now popular in libraries of but a tenth of the size provides a thousand principal classes, with possibility of continued subdivision."

A reclassification had been begun in 1898; by 1900 it had been applied to but one of the forty-four chapters, and, for lack of staff facilities, the work was at a standstill, with accessions continuing to be classified under the old system. Putnam suggested that under a new classification a system of notation assigning each volume a number should be inaugurated. Books were then being called for and recorded by author and title only. He believed that the minimum catalogue for the Library of Congress was a card catalogue on the "dictionary" system, that is, one in which a single alphabet would indicate what books the Library contained by a given author and on a given subject. At least three copies of such a catalogue, he said, would be necessary; one for official use in the catalogue room, one for the main reading room, and one for the Congressional Reference Library in the Capitol. A complete printed catalogue in book form, which could not be undertaken until after completion of the card catalogue, he estimated, would involve in its preparation and publication perhaps fifteen years and the cost of publication alone would be more than a quarter of a million dollars. Such an enterprise, therefore, he refrained from discussing.

That the general catalogue of the Library needed revision there could be no question. It consisted of a single alphabet list under authors, on large slips, kept loosely in drawers behind the delivery counter, and was for official use only. It was certainly in no form that could be made accessible to the public. It was, as a matter of fact, mostly in manuscript in various handwritings—the result of gradual compilation in the old building, a relic of the days when bibliographic tools were scanty, the force was meager and confusion reigned to an extent that made reference and comparison difficult.

Moreover, it covered only the books and 50,000 of the 250,000 pamphlets and had not been verified since removal of the stock to the new building. The only subject catalogue in existence was that issued in book form in 1869 and partial subject entries of the accessions of 1899 and part of 1898. There were, too, the lists of annual accessions from 1867 to 1875 and the author catalogue of 1878 to 1880. In addition, the weekly bulletin of the copyright office provided a list of publications entered for catalogue, but, since this represented in the course of the year fifty-two distinct alphabets it could not conveniently be of service as a catalogue. There was therefore no subject catalogue of the collection as it then existed, and there was no catalogue of any description accessible to the public.

One of Putnam's first considerations, in the light of these facts, was to catalogue new accessions as they came in, under authors and in part under subjects, on cards of standard size and form; titles representing copyright accessions were printed and fifty copies of each struck off, so that they began at once to serve as catalogues within the Library, and in part for exchange. The rigorous official records known as "accession book" and "shelf list" were begun under his supervision, for the Library possessed neither, the only check list for inventory purposes being the same loose slips that had served until then as catalogue.

The task of bringing order out of this chaos was certainly one of great proportion, particularly when one considers that Putnam was from the start hampered by inadequate funds. He himself computed the cost of reclassifying, shelf-listing and cataloguing the collection of some 800,000 books and pamphlets on the dictionary system within a year's time, at more than $350,000; moreover, it would require about 450 persons; and the staff of classifiers and cataloguers then provided by law numbered seventeen.

Arrearages existed everywhere in the Library. He was confronted with the problem of handling some 40,000 newly acquired books and pamphlets each year, of supervising arrangement in sequence and shelving more than 200,000 articles in the copyright office alone, and there were constant problems of organization.

Exclusive of the twenty-four individuals engaged in copyright work in the old Library, there had been eighteen persons on the staff. When Putnam became Librarian the force proper numbered 105 persons, of whom 56 were assigned by law to the direct service of the reading room. By law the organization consisted of the reading-room service, the catalogue, manuscript, music, map, print and periodical divisions, and the administrative officials. The staff of the Law Library operated in the Capitol. Putnam was disconcerted by the fact that this organization took no account of an order department or a shelf department. In the library he had just left these two departments comprised a force of eighteen persons. In the Library of Congress no provision was made for them at all by law.

Another cause of regret to the new Librarian was the lack of a distinct department of documents. Here again the Boston Public Library had found it worthwhile to establish such a department, with a distinguished statistician at its head. Certainly, Putnam agreed, it was still more obviously to the advantage of the Library of Congress, with its certain duty toward legislation and probable duty toward research. He also believed a well-equipped department of bibliography to be an immediate necessity.

He was impressed, too, with the lack of a printing department in the Library, the lack of a bindery, and absence of a department of Oriental literature.

"The Library of Congress," he wrote, in 1900, "is not now, as a collection, an organic collection, even for the most particular service that it has to render; it is not yet classified, nor equipped with the mechanism necessary to its effective use; the present organization is but partial, and the resources have yet to be provided not merely for proper development of the collection, but for the work of bringing the existing material into condition for effective service."

It was up to the frail little man from Boston to bring about these things. He took heart in the conviction that Congress, providing the most magnificent habitation at the service of any library, could not but have intended that the Library itself should take corresponding rank.

XV

THE TREASURE HOUSE, 1897-1940

*T*he Act of February 19, 1897, reorganizing and increasing the Library service, had created the office of Register of Copyright, divided the service of the Library into its several departments, and provided for a force of 104 in the work of the Library proper. By 1899 the staff had been increased by 20 for the night service in the Reading Room. The rapid development of the various divisions, the need for divisions not provided for in the original reorganization and the necessity for reclassification and recataloguing, made a larger appropriation important. Granted in 1900, this further increased the force— mainly in the Catalogue Division; the next year this number had grown to 256.

At first the new building had been opened only from nine o'clock in the morning until four o'clock in the afternoon. On October 1, 1898, the Reading Room hours were extended to ten o'clock at night; and after June 4, 1900, the Periodical Room, which was first opened to the public on January 22, 1900, did not close until ten.

The Division of Music, established early in 1898, opened for evening service on October 23, 1900. The Law Library, still in the Capitol, served the public from nine in the morning until ten at night. The remaining divisions of the Library closed at four o'clock in the afternoon. In 1900 a branch of the Government Printing Office (and bindery) was installed in the Library.

As we have seen, the salary of the Librarian of Congress had been fixed on April 16, 1816, at $1,000 annually, and raised to $1,500 two years later. In 1870, Congress had set his compensation at $4,000 annually, at which sum it remained until the reorganization of the force in 1897, when it was raised to $5,000. Herbert Putnam, under another increase, was receiving an annual salary of $6,000 in 1900.

Larger appropriations during the next four years made it possible for Putnam to remedy to some extent imperfections in the collection. He had introduced a division of Bibliography almost at once and completed those standard sets "which are the tools of the classifier and cataloguer, his guides in selection." He had also acquired miscellaneous material important to serious research.

The Library began the new century, therefore, in a condition far advanced over that in which it had started its career in the new building. Putnam felt, after four years of service, that it was "now in a position to consider and determine what the service shall be:—to Congress, to the Executive Departments and scientific bureaus of the Federal Government, to other libraries, and to scholarship at large." Nor did he believe that what the Library might do for these should be measured by the nature, still less by the extent, of what it had done in the past. "Its future opportunities," he told Congress, "appear in its constitutional relations, its present and developing equipment, its organization, the character of the material which it now has, and its resources for increase." At this time not a single gift of money had come to the Library of Congress, although gifts of documents or ordinary publications had been numerous. Early in his career Putnam expressed the hope that the American people would make valuable donations of money or material to their national library. Such gifts, he contended, could be attracted only by three means:—"First, by a building which will house them safely and commodiously—this

One of the public reading rooms in the Annex, with the mural, by Winters, depicting *The Canterbury Tales. Below:* The public catalogue in the Annex

Dr. Herbert Putnam, eighth Librarian of Congress

it has. Second, by administration which will safeguard them and render them useful—this it is developing. Third, by considerable expenditures of its own in the acquisition of material which will bring the material given into honorable company and will attract notice to it by increasing the reputation of the general collection." He was to prove eminently successful in bringing about these conditions. Years later Gertrude Clarke Whittall, the donor of the priceless Stradivari instruments and Tourte bows, now in the Library of Congress, the annual concerts during which they are used, and the Whittall Pavilion which houses them, was to say that Dr. Putnam had been her "whole inspiration, the motivating spirit" of her decision with regard to the endowment—that his were the vision and understanding completely responsible for her gift.

Herbert Putnam had been astonished from the first by the lack of a division of Orientalia in the national institution. He set about its development. By 1901 there were more than 9,500 volumes of Oriental literature, and in certain directions the collection was said to be the most important in the United States. "With proper attention," he said early in the century, "it is thus capable of conferring great distinction upon the Library. It justifies a separate division for its custody and administration, and expenditure for its suitable development." The collection had been almost wholly the result of gifts, its basis being the books brought from China by Caleb Cushing, first United States Minister to China, under President Tyler—works rich in history, medicine, the classics, poetry, ritualism, ethics, astronomy, essays and dictionaries. Cushing's collection had been added to by a number of volumes presented by the Emperor and further developed by William Woodville Rockhill's collection of Oriental books. Rockhill's great learning in the languages and literature,

315

as well as in the history, habit, and usage of the East, had enabled him to supplement the Caleb Cushing collection in a distinguished manner.

In the whole Orientalia collection at this time the Library of Congress possessed five sets of the *Vinaya* or Discipline, of the *Sutra* or Precepts, and the *Abhidarma* or Metaphysics; various historical works; the writings of Confucius; a catalogue, in 200 volumes, of the Imperial Library; and many works in Buddhist literature which did not appear in the Chinese catalogue of the British Museum, the Wade collection of Cambridge University, or in Wylie's *Chinese Literature*. There were also highly curious books from Tibet—loose narrow leaves set between boards richly inlaid and wrapped in silk. In 1909 the treasures of this Division were augmented by the gift of the Chinese Government of the great Chinese encyclopedia—the *Tu Shu Tsi Cheng*—comprising over 4,000 volumes. The collections, rich as they were growing to be, remained unclassified and only inadequately catalogued until 1912.

The fortunate circumstance of the presence in Washington that year of Dr. Hing Kwai Fung, gave an unforeseen impetus to organization of the division. Hing Kwai Fung had first approached the Library in behalf of the Department of Agriculture, seeking early descriptions at first hand by the Chinese themselves of certain rare plants which the Department was endeavoring to domesticate. The Chinese scholar became so interested in the collection as a whole and the project of its development and utilization that he consented to undertake the initial task of classifying and of cataloguing it. When Dr. Fung returned to China the following year, Herbert Putnam took advantage of the opportunity for judicious expansion in the field of Orientalia. He instructed Dr. Fung to seek fundamental source material to strengthen the Library of Congress collection, but not to duplicate lesser materials already accessible in other American libraries. As a result almost 7,000 volumes were added to the Library in that year and nearly 11,000 the next.

The Librarian of Congress lost no opportunity for utilizing the services of experts in building up collections in this field. In 1914 he made a singularly fortunate arrangement with a scientist whose discriminating knowledge and interest were continuously to benefit the Library until the present time. In 1914, when Dr. Walter T. Swingle of the Bureau of Plant Industry was sent to China and Japan to investigate certain plants, he carried with him an assignment from Dr. Putnam. Dr. Swingle's first purchase for the Library of Congress contained 1,409 volumes, including 116 volumes issued during the Ming Dynasty or earlier, 260 volumes of geographical works, and 147 miscellaneous volumes. Since that time important additions have been made by Dr. Swingle to the extent of more than 175,000 volumes, particularly in the field of old Chinese herbals. Through his special knowledge and Putnam's foresight there has been built up a valuable source of information on present-day agricultural problems, based upon these ancient works. In 1928, Congress gave recognition to the importance of these expanding collections by providing for a permanent chief for the division and an assistant. The collection exceeded 100,000 Chinese volumes at the time of the appointment of A. W. Hummel, and under his care they have grown to occupy a pre-eminent position here and abroad.

The Librarian of Congress welcomed this expression of Congressional appreciation with the prediction that the Division of Orientalia was "certain to be the center on this hemisphere for the pursuit of Oriental studies, with possible consequences of great import, not merely to culture but to international understanding and good-will"—a prediction amply justified.

While Herbert Putnam was thus giving attention to building

up the collections, he was not overlooking the importance of making those collections of value and use to the American student or reader. In 1905, speaking before the American Library Association in Portland, he had said: "The expert service of a research library must extend beyond its classifiers and cataloguers. It must include interpreters. The expert service of the Library of Congress does include some interpreters—men of special training in the subject matter of knowledge, in addition to classifiers and cataloguers, as well as accomplished bibliographers who are, to some extent, specialists trained in the subject matter of literature. Our faculty for these is small, and but partially covers the various departments of knowledge. . . ." The year before in his report to Congress he had mentioned the possibility of a personal service in interpretation with the suggestion that a library with the collections, the equipment, the organization, and the relations of service of the Library of Congress, offered opportunity for a valuable experience which a national library might furnish as a school of experience for the higher grades of library work. And, on more than one occasion he had quoted the words of Edward Everett, whom he referred to as a "sensitive soul":—"Who can see without shame that the Federal Government of America is the only government in the civilized world that has never founded a literary institution of any description or sort?" This philosophy was to lead to Putnam's gentle and persuasive campaign for endowments of various "chairs" in the Library of Congress and to establishment of the system providing consultants, without administrative responsibility, to interpret the collections or assist systematically to develop them in fields not reached by governmental appropriation. Today there are in the Library "chairs" in Music, the Fine Arts, Manuscripts, Aeronautics, and Maps, each held by the chief of the corresponding Library division, and consultants in such subjects as Economics, Hispanic Literature, Islamic Art and Archæology, Poetry, Political Science and Public Administration, Classical Literature, International Law, Military History, Musicology, Paleography, Sociology, Roman Law, Japanese Law, and many other subjects, sustained by private endowments and a direct outgrowth of Herbert Putnam's effort to "interpret" the Library's collections.

By 1924 the Librarian's first objective had been won as spaces in the building had been duly differentiated and equipped for specialized, as well as general, uses; the specialized material had been installed in appropriate cases; there had been developed a scheme of classification, systematic and adaptable, with an appropriate nomenclature; processes of cataloguing, including forms of entry, now standardized for American libraries, had been adopted; and such classification and cataloguing had actually been applied to a large portion of the collection of printed books. The Library had become increasingly the resort of scholars.

The service to Congress had been intensified by the creation of a Legislative Reference division. Foundation for this had been laid by Putnam as early as 1902, when the Librarian of Congress had incorporated in his estimates for the fiscal year of 1903-1904, an item of $28,000 "for the preparation of an index to Comparative Legislation," with an explanation of the project embodied in an accompanying letter. While this item had not been granted in the form proposed, a small appropriation had been made available—$5,840 for each of the years of 1906, 1907, 1908; $10,000 for 1909, and $5,840 again for 1910—to prepare indexes to the statutes and "to prepare such other law indexes, digests, and compilations of law as may be required by Congress for official use." The work was necessarily limited to the Statutes at Large and, the appropriation coming to an end at the close of 1910, had been suspended and the corps of indexers dispersed. When, during the second session of the Sixty-first Congress several bills had been

319

introduced looking to the establishment of a legislative reference and bill-drafting bureau at Washington, Putnam had sent a letter to the President of the Senate (on April 6, 1911) with accompanying documents outlining the functions of such a bureau and the experiences of New York State and Wisconsin. In it he emphasized that an organization suitably equipped to meet the research needs of Congress must be "elaborate beyond that provided by any State, since the subjects to be dealt with are far wider in scope, the material more remote, more complex, and more difficult, and the precedents less available"; that the organization needs could only be ascertained by experience, as the field was unique, and therefore the first appropriation should be a lump sum; and that the work of such a bureau being scientific—that is, having only truth as its object—it should be strictly nonpartizan.

By 1914 Putnam felt that while the Library of Congress had achieved for the general public a status and prospect reasonably befitting its position as the national library of the United States, it had not been able sufficiently to meet the appeals of Members of Congress for services that often reached beyond the functions of a library to those of a reference bureau. Increased demands for statements, rather than books, either of the facts, the law or the merits of any given subject, were being made, and the Library's organization for utilizing its excellent collections for the benefit of Congress, was imperfect. The existing force had found itself unable to do little beyond accumulating, classifying and listing usual materials and producing documents specifically asked for. The Library which had begun as a private research library for Members of Congress had developed so unpredictably that now its attention to the general public was taking all of its time and resources, reducing Congress to a minor consideration. Putnam saw the need of restoring a more proper relationship, although it is doubtful if he ever admitted Congressional service to be the primary function of the Library of Congress, and certainly not to the extent which Archibald MacLeish, while not losing sight of the national, even international scope of the institution, has stressed that original function.

To Putnam the Library of Congress was, first and last, the national library, with all other service incidental or complementary to its prime objective of serving the people.

The actual establishment of the Legislative Reference Service in the Library of Congress was due primarily to the persistent interest of Senator Robert La Follette, whose enthusiasm had been kindled by the success of a similar enterprise in his own Wisconsin, where Dr. Charles McCarthy had, with singular efficiency, attended to the research needs of Wisconsin legislators. Basing the requirements upon those outlined at various times by Dr. McCarthy, Senator La Follette had introduced a bill asking for $25,000 to establish a reference service within the Library that would be peculiarly the Members' own. Dr. McCarthy had broken down the functions of such a service into:—the "comparative," charged with gathering laws and cases from all over the world upon legislative subjects; the "critical," charged with gathering critical data upon the working laws; and the "constructive," for the purpose of assisting in the work of drafting legislation with evidence already mentioned at hand for reference. With the passage of La Follette's bill and the subsequent appropriation, the Library of Congress entered upon a period of increased usefulness to Congress within the Congressional authorization "to gather, classify and make available, in translations, indexes, digests, compilations, and bulletins, and otherwise, data for or bearing upon legislation, and to render such data serviceable to Congress and committees and members thereof. . . ."

As early as 1901 the Librarian had inaugurated a system for the distribution and sale of printed catalogue cards that, before the close of his active administration, was to account for a sum of three million dollars covered into the Treasury of the United States, and was to effect economies and improve efficiency in thousands of libraries all over the country.

As the nation became increasingly aware of the great cultural center that was rising under Herbert Putnam's busy hand and discerning eye on Capitol Hill in Washington, and as the modest Librarian himself worked quietly but assiduously to interest individuals in the collections, more and more gifts and of increasing value were offered for the inheritance of the American people. Private collectors, conscious of their debt to posterity, began to look upon the Library of Congress as the one logical and suitable permanent depository for their treasures. Out of this development and the immediate Coolidge Endowment, grew the Library of Congress Trust Fund Board, created by an Act of Congress on March 3, 1925. Five members were appointed under this act, three *ex officio*—the Secretary of the Treasury, the Chairman of the Joint Committee on the Library, and the Librarian of Congress—and two others, appointed for five-year terms by the President of the United States. This legislation not only foresaw authority to accept endowments but also to receive gifts of money for immediate disbursement. The Trust Fund Board thus made possible an extension and diversification of the forms of outlay feasible from the public treasury. As a result of it Putnam was able to write some time later: "The collections have been enhanced by a huge importation of source material of concern to the investigator, and the personnel by the accession to our staff (in the incumbents of our four 'chairs' and in our corps of 'consultants') of numerous specialists in various fields of learning, who with the equipment of teachers or investigators are here not to teach or pursue research but to aid in the serious use of the collections by assisting in the interpretation of them." When Herbert Putnam closed the years of his active Librarianship endowment funds exceeded $2,000,000 and gifts of money received for immediate disbursement had amounted to about $1,415,000. A notable provision of the 1925 Act had permitted endowment funds, up to a total limit of $5,000,000 to be treated as a perpetual loan to the United States Treasury, at an assured interest annually of four percent—a provision so advantageous that the bulk of the funds are now held in this form.

One of the most important of the early collections acquired by Herbert Putnam was the Yudin collection of 80,000 volumes, all but 12,000 in the Russian language, accumulated by Gennadius Vasilievich Yudin over a period of thirty years. Since every volume relates to Russia and Siberia, it is doubtful if there exists, outside of Russia, so well balanced a library in this particular field. No important work of the Russian historians and critics, from Tatishchev and Karamzin to Pogodin, Soloviev, Kostomarov and Kluchevskii, is omitted, and source materials include complete sets of the Russian annals, and of the publications of historical and archæological societies and of the provincial commissions whose object was to collect and publish documents relating to the national history. In pure literature the collection of texts includes the best edition of every important Russian writer. Since Mr. Yudin had been for most of his life a resident of Siberia, living at a central point upon the Trans-Siberian Railroad, and also had traveled much in Asia and throughout Europe, his opportunities to secure Siberica, including Siberian imprints—a difficult field beyond reach of the ordinary collector—had been unusual. A curious and sentimental interest was also attached to an acquisition which contained certain manuscript records of the early Russian settlements in Alaska. This collection is the foundation of the Division of Slavic Literature in the Library of Congress today, now administered by Nicholas R. Rodionoff.

There gradually accumulated under Putnam's watchful eye a Japanese collection of 45,000 volumes; the Huitfeld Kaas collection of 5,000 books representing Scandinavian literature; 4,000 volumes known as the Weber Collection of Sanskrit Literature; the Hoes pamphlets relating to the Spanish-American war; the collections of Whistleriana and Pennelliana and other branches of the fine arts, established by Joseph and Elizabeth Robins Pennell; 13,000 items that constituted the collection of Justice Oliver Wendell Holmes, and many other extraordinarily interesting additions to the Library's treasures.

Noteworthy among such acquisitions during Putnam's Librarianship was that bequeathed to the Library of Congress in 1927 by Mrs. Thacher—the collections of John Boyd Thacher, consisting of 840 titles of European incunabula; 2,400 printed volumes relating to the French Revolution; outlines of the French Revolution told in autographs—a collection of 1,460 letters and other manuscripts; and autographs and other documents, numbering 1,365 items, of the crowned heads of Europe and other notables. These valuable items had been entrusted to the Library of Congress by Mrs. Thacher shortly after the death of her husband in 1909 and by her will were permanently transferred to the national institution at her own death.

That same year brought to the Library the collection gathered for years by the noted magician Harry Houdini. The entire Houdini library, with the exception of his dramatic collection, became the property of the American people, in custody of their Library, at Houdini's death on October 31, 1926. The bequest, including notable works on magic, spiritism, occultism, and psychical research, represents one of the most provocative assemblages in the Rare Book Room of the Library of Congress today. Some idea may be gained of its interest and value by the fact that the famous magician who collected it had seized every opportunity to study in libraries, to interview retired magicians and collectors, and to browse in old bookstores and antique shops and had assiduously searched catalogues or advertised his wants. Professor Alfred Becks, in charge of the "theatrical collection" at Harvard University for some ten years, had helped Houdini purchase and arrange the items. In his book, *A Magician Among the Spirits,* Houdini thus referred to his library:

> I have spent a goodly part of my life in study and research. During the last thirty years I have read every single piece of literature on the subject of spiritualism that I could. I have accumulated one of the largest libraries in the world on psychic phenomena, spiritualism, magic, witchcraft, demonology, evil spirits, etc. . . .

The year 1930 of Herbert Putnam's administration proved to be a red-letter year in the history of the Library. In that year Congress passed legislation carrying, in the words of the Librarian, "a remarkable assurance for the future, not merely in the specific resources which it provides, but in the evident disposition of Congress toward it, an acceptance by Congress of its appropriate destiny as not merely a collector of material for purposes purely utilitarian, but an embodiment, so far as may now be possible, of influences for the promotion of culture."

The year had, for one thing, seen a strikingly useful service inaugurated in a new division—the Aeronautics Division under the direction of the specialist, Professor Albert F. Zahn. This division had been made possible by a generous donation known as "the Guggenheim fund for the promotion of aeronautics." The grant, comprising in all the sum of $140,000, was in part an endowment, in part a gift "for immediate application." The endowment consisted of a fund of $75,000 for the establishment and maintenance of a chair of aeronautics; the gift of $51,000 directly applicable to the acquisition of material, and of $14,000 to cover personal services pending suitable provision through appropriations, which it was understood would be asked after a period had demonstrated the utility of the undertaking. An experience of a year had been assumed to be requisite, but no such delay proved necessary. As soon as the grant became available an expert in the field—Professor Zahn—was promptly secured; four collections of material, including the distinguished Tissandier, were acquired by purchase, and one—the Langley collection—transferred to the Library of Congress from the Smithsonian. By the middle of the session, the division was fully functioning and, instead of delaying his request for Governmental provision, Putnam immediately asked Congress for funds. These were granted in the Act of July 1, 1930, and the Aeronautics Division was made thereby a permanent division of the Library of Congress.

Adding to the extraordinary richness of the Library's good fortune in the same year of 1930 an Act of June 13th authorized the actual construction of an Annex to the Library of Congress at a total cost of $6,500,000 on a site known then as "Grant Row," which had already been authorized and appropriated for, just across the way, between 2nd and 3rd Streets. This beautiful building was to cost more than $10,000,000 before its completion in 1939, but it provided for future growth of the Library to the extent of accommodating some 10,000,000 volumes. Making still more memorable this year of 1930 was the acquisition of the famed St. Blasius-St. Paul copy of the Gutenberg Bible—one of three extant perfect vellum copies of the forty-two-line Bible printed behind closed shutters in the little town of Mainz by Johannes Gutenberg and his helper Peter Schoeffer, in defiance of that ominous murmur that was to attribute the art of printing, as it has attributed other arts, to the devil. That the Library harbors and the American people possess this treasure today is largely due to that Member of the House of Representatives from Mississippi whose name has been actively and agreeably associated with a great many projects for the extension of education and culture in the United States—Ross Collins of Mississippi. It was "the Collins Bill" which authorized the appropriation for the fifteenth-century books. The collection was about to be taken to Europe and auctioned off when this bill assured American possession. A decade later this same gentleman, as a member of the Appropriations Committee of the House, appealing then for suitable headquarters for the library of the Army Medical College, was to coin a provocative phrase for Capitol Hill—crowned by the Library of Congress and its white marble Annex, and by the Folger Shakespeare Library—referring to this intellectual center as "the Acropolis of America." On that occasion Ross Collins had closed his appeal for the best facilities for study and research for the American people—such as would "enable them to express themselves in works of literature, science, and art," and "help us understand one another, for literature had ever spoken a common language for the children of men"—with the effective words of Archibald MacLeish:

> *How shall we have speech?*
> *The water cries all night upon the beach—*
> *How understand?*
> *The wind calls all day across the sand—*
> *How hear*
> *With listening of the earth so near?*
> *Must we be deaf, be dumb*
> *Till the silence come?*

In a case especially constructed to receive it, the Gutenberg Bible has been on constant view in the exhibit halls of the Library. With the entrance of the United States into the Second World War, however, it was immediately removed to a place of safety for the duration. In the Rare Book wing anyone who asks may turn the leaves of the priceless books that issued from the first printing presses of man.

So notable a year cannot be reviewed without mention of the far-seeing Chairman of the Joint Library Committee at the time —Senator Simeon D. Fess of Ohio, chairman from 1925 through 1933.

Senator Fess had served on the Committee on the Library many years before, while a Member of the House, and in that connection had never lost an opportunity to spread word of the extraordinary library that had grown up in Washington and had come to occupy the position, numerically, of third largest in the world. Fifteen years later, as a Member of the Senate, he was to say of its collection of books and other material, that it stood first of all the libraries of the earth. "I am constrained to believe," he told the Senate on that occasion, "that the workings of the Library are not generally appreciated. I know they are not by the public, and I think they are not fully appreciated even by those who are intimate with the Library—Members of Congress." This was in 1933. Senator Fess quoted Albert Jay Nock's words in the preface of his *Life of Jefferson:* "If ten percent of the patriotic pride now frittered away on silly and vicious objects were engaged upon our first national possession, the Library of Congress, we should have a new civilization. What an incomparable instrument it is!" He quoted James Truslow Adams' epilogue to the *Epic of America* wherein that writer had reiterated his belief in the American dream: ". . . I often think that the one which best exemplifies the dream is the greatest library in this land of libraries, the Library of Congress. . . . It has come straight from the heart of democracy, as it has been taken to it, and I here use it as a symbol of what democracy can accomplish on its own behalf . . . a perfect working out, in a concrete example, of the American dream."

Thus was Herbert Putnam helped along the way to realization of his great and selfless ambition for the Library of Congress, by Members of Congress, by writers and educators, by collectors, by the people of America themselves—all of whom played some part in its glorious development.

Many projects got under way in the Library of Congress during Putnam's régime that were of direct benefit to the public and to libraries generally. The project for reproduction of source material for American history; the Union Catalogue of Classical and Medieval Manuscripts; the general Union Catalogue; the project for distribution of Braille books to the blind; reproduction from foreign archives under a grant contributed by John D. Rockefeller, Jr.; development of the system for inter-library loans; publication of selected topical lists and of special catalogues and calendars in book form and of actual texts of manuscript sources; expansion of the system of foreign exchange and many similar extensions or intensifications of service.

The Law Library, observing its centennial in 1932, under the direction of Law Librarian John T. Vance, was able to announce, as evidence of its own development: "The Law Library contains more than 275,000 volumes, exclusive of large collections on Constitutional law, public and private international law, and on many special subjects such as banking, commercial law, criminology, education, marriage and divorce, military law and other subjects which are classified with the main collections. It includes 70 percent of the English yearbooks, 450 incunabula—including approximately 300 in the Vollbehr and Thacher collections, extensive collections of trials, session laws of the Colonies both in manuscript and in printed form, practically complete collections of all American court reports, session laws, statutes and codes, and a set of the printed Records and Briefs of the United States Supreme Court. In the field of foreign law the collection representing the British Empire takes precedence, but practically every other country is represented by an approximately complete collection of its session laws, codes, statutes, judicial decisions, and a selective group of commentaries. In addition to extensive collections on Roman and Canon law there are special collections on the history and philosophy of law and jurisprudence."

Most of the collections of the Law Library had been moved to the new building in 1902. From 1908 to 1911 the Law Librarian, acting under special authorization from Congress, had directed the compilation and publication of an index to the Federal Statutes covering the period from 1789 to 1907. This was later brought up to date, after the creation of the Legislative Reference Service, by the American Law Section of the Service. Rich in collections on the history and philosophy of law; foreign, civil, and ecclesiastical law; legal biography and miscellany; and already outstanding as a bar library, the Law Library offered opportunities of incalculable value to the legal scholar using its special resources in relation to the great reference collections of the main library on economics, logic, sociology, ethics, history and statecraft.

Serving primarily Members of Congress and Justices of the Supreme Court, at first, the legal library expanded its field of service under Putnam's administration to make its wealth of material freely available to the bar, the bench, and the layman alike. There still remains in the old quarters of the Capitol today a branch library of about 50,000 volumes for the use of Congress, the Supreme Court and members of the Supreme Court Bar.

But if Herbert Putnam were expanding the scholarly resources and activities of the Library of Congress he was concurrently increasing opportunities for education and cultural development along other and very material lines. The field of music and the advantages to be derived from enjoyment of music received his earnest attention. He wished to make more available to the public those valuable resources which were accumulating under the copyright law, by ever more extensive purchasing and by donations, and he wished to go further in developing appreciation for them. For five years after the Division of Music was organized in 1897 it had mainly the unrelated accretions of copyright law as the basis for its musical store. By 1922 there were more than 950,000 items in the custody of the Music Division, with accessions mounting at the rate of 30,000 a year. Many rare editions of the classics, from Bach to Debussy and a representative assemblage of original manuscripts of master composers had gradually been acquired.

The Music Division had been enriched in 1910 by purchase of the famed collection of the Marquise Martorell, a collection which had been honored by the jury of the Paris Exposition in 1900. It contains nearly thirty full scores in manuscript of old operas, among them Meyerbeer's *Semiramide riconosciuta* and a dedication copy to the Prince of Asturias of Haydn's *Isola disabitata,* in addition to manuscript scores by Haydn, Durante, Zingarelli, Jommelli, Pergolesi, Palesi, Brunetti, Schmidl, Dittersdorf, Bruni, and many others. Of more permanent significance is the fact that the Martorell collection contains about 1,300 full scores of favorite arias from eighteenth-century operas, in neat, contemporary manuscripts, uniformly bound.

The Library was causing to be transcribed in 1910 the scores of old operas unprocurable in the original or in print and in that year more than 100 scores had been added by this means alone. This was the year, too, when the classes "dramatic music" and "chamber music" were added to the subject catalogues, and cat-

331

alogues in book form were being considered for orchestral music and dramatic music—including vocal scores and libretti.

One day in 1924, the librarian from Boston, seated at his desk in the Library of Congress, received a letter from Mrs. Frederic Shurtleff Coolidge that was to mark a milestone in the Library's development. That letter contained an offer of $60,000 for the construction in connection with the Library of an auditorium suitable for chamber music but available for other uses. Here was a gift unique in its particular purpose and almost unique in its nature as from an individual to provide physical resources for the Federal Government. Herbert Putnam communicated the offer to Congress on December 4, 1924. Upon the unanimous recommendation of the Committee on the Library, it was accepted in a joint resolution approved on January 23, 1925, which also provided for the construction of the auditorium under direction of the architect of the Capitol. Mrs. Coolidge increased her gift to $90,000 to meet subsequent estimates of cost, and made additional contributions later. The general scheme of the structure and its location were determined in consultation with the architect of the Capitol and members of the Fine Arts Commission and with the approval of the Joint Committee on the Library. Charles A. Platt of New York, who designed the Freer Gallery, was consulting architect. Arthur L. Smith and Company of Washington so hastened the work of construction that the Coolidge Auditorium was opened for its first festival of chamber music under the Elizabeth Sprague Coolidge Foundation on October 28, 1925.

At the time of making an additional endowment Mrs. Coolidge had expressed her purposes to the Library of Congress:

> . . . I have wished to make possible through the Library of Congress, the composition and performance of music in ways which might otherwise be considered too unique or too expensive to be ordinarily

undertaken. Not this alone, of course, nor with a view to extravagance for its own sake; but as an occasional possibility of giving precedence to considerations of quality over those of quantity; to artistic rather than to economic values; and to opportunity rather than expediency. For this reason I believe that advice should be sought from broadminded and disinterested musicians, whether or not official, whether or not professional. And for the same reason, I hope that the audience may be chosen very largely from those whose musical taste and experience qualify them to listen sincerely and appreciatively.

This endowment with the exception of Mrs. Gardiner Greene Hubbard's $20,000 bequest, the income of which had been made to apply to the purchase of prints, marked the beginning of an era when funds were to be received by the Library for discretionary use. It opened the way for subsequent acquisitions beyond the ordinary in scope and form.

The Librarian had long since realized that for material of distinction the Library of Congress must look to private gifts, and that for the development of a staff of specialists "who will apply the highest discretion to the selection of material and authority in its interpretation," it must look to private endowment. Putnam stated at the time that the Library of Congress needed an endowment similar to that made by Mrs. Coolidge in the field of music, for the fine arts, for history, for law, for economics, for political science, for cartography, for Semitic, Slavic and Oriental literatures. It was not long before a $75,000 endowment from William Evarts Benjamin of New York, the income to serve as an honorarium to the Chief of the Division of Manuscripts, assured the Library a Chair in American History, while a similar amount endowed by the Carnegie Corporation to provide an honorarium for the Chief of the Division of Fine Prints, added a Chair of the Fine Arts to the Library's resources.

Just as Elizabeth Sprague Coolidge's endowment had been

333

preceded by her gift to the Library of Congress of her collection of holograph music and her extensive correspondence with important musicians of the day, so was the establishment of the Gertrude Clarke Whittall foundation preceded by Mrs. Matthew John Whittall's magnificent gift to the Library of her five Stradivari instruments and five Tourte bows.

Mrs. Whittall had frequently attended the chamber music concerts sponsored by Mrs. Coolidge and the pleasure she had enjoyed because of them made her determine to present her own collection of Stradivari instruments to the people of the United States—a gift of perpetual music. These, consisting of three violins, a viola, and a violoncello—as well as five matchless bows made by the greatest bow-maker of all time—François Tourte, of Paris, about 1800, had been collected over many years, at a period in Mrs. Whittall's life when, in her own words, she "had to have something precious to look after."

The outstanding instrument in the collection is the famous Betts violin, which bears the date of 1704—the so-called "grand pattern" period of the great violin maker. It is acknowledged to be one of the most perfect and valuable violins in existence; the Ward violin in the collection, is dated 1700 and is also an instrument of great beauty and perfection; the Castelbarco violin, dated 1699, foreshadowed "the end of the period during which the 'long Stradivari' was the instrument of the Master's predilection," as Alfred Hill has said. The fourth instrument in the group—the Casavetti viola—is dated 1727; it was once part of the Wanamaker collection. The fifth instrument, the Castelbarco violoncello, dated 1697, is one of the three cellos of its period which have not been reduced in size; it is indeed, practically free from restoration. Among the bows, two of the collection are among Tourte's most famous and perfect productions

334

—the Baillot, which takes its name from an early owner, and the Russian, once owned by a Russian gentleman.

Mrs. Whittall once said of the instruments:

> The three violins are as different as human beings. They have strong personality; the Betts is of royalty; it is outstanding in beauty and perfection, and, as Walt Whitman once said of Mt. Shasta, "Alone as God." The Castelbarco is feminine. The Ward is sophisticated—it lived long in London and knows so many things. The Casavetti is marvelous. A viola, when played by a great artist, can wring your heart. It can express secret thoughts that you have felt and never could put into words. It can say unsayable things. As for the Castelbarco cello, any artist who had once drawn his bow across its strings will be haunted forever by its unforgettable tone. When all the strings are playing together the ensemble is like a heavenly choir, for they all speak the same language.

The instruments were placed temporarily in a glass case in the Rare Book Room of the Library. A short time later Mrs. Whittall increased her gift to include construction of the beautiful Whittall Pavilion. In this lovely room, its walls painted a soft green and its windows looking out upon the Court of the Musicians, where Pan pipes beside a lily-pool and the immortals of music are commemorated in a series of tablets along ivy-covered walls, the priceless instruments made by the master of Cremona are enshrined forever. The Whittall Pavilion is connected to the Coolidge Auditorium by this charming court, across which the musicians may pass into the auditorium or in which they may find a pleasant retreat before or after concerts.

For Mrs. Whittall—determined that the instruments of Stradivari should not suffer the same fate as the Guarneri violin which Paganini had bequeathed to the museum in Genoa, and which, kept in idleness, had deteriorated until today it is unfit for concert purposes—provided, under a magnanimous endowment, for perpetual concerts free to all music-lovers, in which the Stradivari quintet would be used.

> *No kind of instrument? Ah, yes, there is;*
> *And after time and place are overthrown,*
> *God's touch will keep its one chord quivering.*

Under the terms of the gift the instruments must remain forever in the Library of Congress, removed only for necessary restoration or repair, thus eliminating the tragedy of possible injury or destruction. Yet the American people are by no means deprived of the joy of hearing them by this wise provision, for frequent broadcasts are made under the Whittall Foundation and an increasing number of concerts are being opened to the public in the Library of Congress auditorium, occasions when the most distinguished artists and outstanding ensembles are engaged for performances of chamber music. In addition, on December 18th each year, a special program in commemoration of the anniversary of the death of Stradivari is given. "This collection of instruments," Mrs. Whittall said on this anniversary in 1937, "I held in trust for a short time. Now they belong to every one of you, for they are given to our Government to hold and protect forever. In presenting these instruments to the Library of Congress, it is my aim to give to the people of this country an opportunity to see and hear these rare Stradivari. They may be viewed at the Library of Congress by anyone who wishes to view them. They may be heard in concerts held in the Library, and through the medium of the radio by an even larger audience. If the appreciation and enjoyment of music in America will be advanced thereby, the purpose of my gift will have been fulfilled."

Dr. Harold Spivacke is in charge of the Library's Music Division today.

Many rare treasures, literary as well as musical, found their way into the Library of Congress during Herbert Putnam's administration. In 1933 an extension of the east front of the Library had provided on its second floor a permanent repository for all those books and periodicals which had been accumulating in the various stacks and which for early imprint, beautiful or unusual binding, exclusiveness of edition, or other special value were designated as rare. Here had been constructed a beautiful foyer and Georgian reading room behind heavy bronze doors decorated with the colophons of early printers. Opening from the white-pillared chamber with its rich hangings of blue velvet, tier on tier of air-conditioned stacks had been built into veritable vaults where the rare items that constituted these collections might be preserved in a uniform temperature of 70 degrees and a humidity of 50 percent designed to restore flexibility to paper and bindings and reduce disintegration.

This beautiful wing, opened in 1934, contains the literary treasures of the Library of Congress. When it first opened, under Putnam's régime, there had been segregated for the convenience of students many special collections. Among these were early editions and rare issues of the Bible in all languages; a collection of British almanacs from the sixteenth century and American almanacs from 1660, including all the issues of *Poor Richard* after 1738; the Benjamin Franklin collection of books written, printed and edited by Franklin; Susan B. Anthony's personal library, including scrapbooks and manuscript notes of biographical importance; the Henry Harisse bequest of profusely annotated copies of his writings on the Columbus period and his correspondence with European scholars; the Hawaiian collection of publications of the dynastic and provisional governments and a notable array of Hawaiian language books and periodicals, dating from the establishment of the printing press at Oahu in 1827;

337

a collection of popular and sensational publications which preceded the era of the dime novel; and a collection of juvenilia comprising children's literature, mainly American, covering the period from the late seventeenth century to 1900.

Later, with the use of a grant from an anonymous donor, this collection was to be developed, and an extensive bibliography prepared containing descriptions of the more important "juveniles" of the nineteenth century.

The Library's fine collection of incunabula was housed in the vaults of the Rare Book Room, including those which had been acquired with the Gutenberg Bible. In the first report given of the collections in this wing almost a thousand Greek and Latin classics in incunabula were noted. Of the twenty-nine titles listed by Goldsmith as printed by Aldus before 1501, the Library of Congress possessed twenty, including the Grenville copy of the Aristotle. Rare assemblages, the gifts of private citizens, were turned over to this Division of the Library as time passed. Such was the Voragine collection of Dr. Ernest C. Richardson, which included a manuscript on vellum of the *Legenda Sanctorum* from the Library of the Earl of Ashburnham; and the colorful and valuable collection of Dr. John Davis Batchelder of books, broadsides, manuscripts and fine bindings—all "firsts" in many fields of human endeavor.

First issues of the McGuffey readers, primers and spellers were the gift of Miss Maude Blair. Rear Admiral Lloyd Chandler presented his interesting collection of Kipling items for safekeeping and reference in this Division of the Library of Congress, making thereby three hundred volumes of Kipling's works, with cross-indexes available to students. A priceless collection of American eighteenth-century newspapers, early broadsides, the Luther Reformation Tracts, and diverse medieval manuscripts on ecclesiastical, legal and scientific subjects were all accumulated

338

during the administration of Dr. Putnam. In fact, within the short space of a decade there was evident as great a contrast in the nature and extent of the collections as there was in the quarters of the Rare Book Room. For it was from temporary, inadequate cells, sandwiched between steel decks in a filled-in court, that the Rare Book collection had expanded to occupy one of the most charming and restful wings of the Library of Congress.

Out of similarly small seeds sown while Putnam was Librarian has grown another special reading room of great distinction —that of the Hispanic Foundation. This foundation owes its origin to the establishment in 1927 of a generous fund of $100,000 by Archer M. Huntington, the founder of the Hispanic Society of America in New York City. The fund, in the words of Mr. Huntington, was for the purchase of books relating to "Spanish, Portuguese, and South American arts, crafts, literature and history only"; and the terms provided "that the said books shall have been published not more than ten years previously; that a list of such books shall at once be forwarded upon receipt by the Library of Congress to the Hispanic Society of America; and that the latter shall be permitted to select those needed by the members of the staff and competent scholars for use at the Hispanic Society for the period of three months; that the entire income of the fund be expended annually."

The following year, the Librarian was able to report an additional endowment from Archer Huntington of $50,000 to provide an honorarium for a consultant in the field of Hispanic literature. The first recipient was Señor Don Juan Riaño y Gayangos, who had continued to reside in this country since his retirement from the diplomatic service of Spain. Concluding his diplomatic career as Spanish Ambassador at Washington from 1914 to 1926, this gentleman by his willingness to serve American

339

scholarship had revived interesting remembrance of the friendly scholarly relations which his distinguished father, Don Juan Riaño y Montero, and his maternal grandfather, Don Pascual de Gayangos, had maintained with Irving, Prescott, and Ticknor. Since the creation of this fund the Library of Congress has acquired each year about 2,000 books published in the Hispanic world within the ten years preceding the date of purchase. The limitation of the fund, stipulated by the donor, has served to encourage new and youthful authors, these purchases of their first works making their names known in this country early in their careers. Dr. David Rubio of the Catholic University of America succeeded the original consultant in October, 1931; and through his guidance and the operation of the Huntington fund, the Library of Congress for the last ten years has been performing an important cultural work.

It was natural that some generous and patriotic citizen should see the need for suitably housing the Hispanic collections that were thus accumulating, and it was not long before an anonymous friend came forward with generous funds for establishment within the Library of one of its most artistic reading rooms—the Hispanic—destined to be dedicated by Archibald MacLeish.

In 1912, Herbert Putnam had recorded as "the most notable event of the year" the foundation of a department of Judaica, through the gift, by Jacob H. Schiff, of the Deinard collection. The collection, the Librarian reported, would ensure the Library of Congress "a fundamental beginning in a field in which it had as yet done practically nothing." He predicted that its presence would "invite additions which will not merely reinforce it in Jewish literature, but expand it into a significant department embracing all Semitica."

Such a department could be fully of service only if vitalized

340

by the interpretations of a scholar. When the Act of July 1, 1914, provided for organization of a Division of Semitica and Oriental Literature, Dr. Israel Schapiro, scholar and bibliographer, was placed in charge of the Semitic section and remains today, after organization of his section into a separate division, as Chief of the Semitic Division.

Mr. Schiff's gift in 1912, which had laid the foundation for this division, consisted of about ten thousand books and pamphlets that had been brought together over a period of years by Ephraim Deinard of Arlington, New Jersey. It covered a period of nearly three and a half millenniums, from the beginning of Jewish national life to modern times. Dr. I. M. Casanowicz of the United States National Museum thus described it, after an examination of the manuscript catalogues of the collection:

> As might be expected in the literature of the "People of the Book," the books relating to the Bible fill a large and important space in it. There is a long series of editions of the Bible and of parts of it, many of them accompanied by translations in ancient and modern languages— Greek, Latin, Syriac, Arabic, Persian, English, French, German, Italian, Spanish, Polish, Hungarian. Among the more notable editions may be mentioned the great Rabbinical Bible, with the commentaries of Rashi, Kamchi, Ibn Ezra, Ralabag, and others; the Polygot and Hexaglot Bibles, and a "parallel" Bible, giving variants of the Samaritan, Septuagint, and Vulgate versions. There is also the philological apparatus for the study of the Bible—grammars, dictionaries and concordances.

Next in volume and importance in this collection is the "Rabbinical" literature, which emanated or evolved from the Bible, the Talmud, and Midrashim—"those grand repositories of the meditation of Israel's scholars and sages through nearly a thousand years." And alongside this literature, a voluminous collection of books bearing on liturgy, ritual, religious ceremonies and practises, apologetics and polemics, on Jewish sects, such as the

Samaritans and the Karaites. The literary products of the "golden renaissance" of Jewish letters under the Arab rule in the Middle Ages are fully represented.

More modern in spirit is the large division of the *Haskalah* or liberal literature, written in elegant, classical Hebrew, and dating from the time when European nations began to admit the Jews to share in their life and culture. Its subjects are varied, comprising science, poetry, history, philosophy, romance—even periodical publications.

A second notable gift from Mr. Schiff, consisting of more than 4,200 volumes to reinforce this collection and, like it, brought together by Dr. Ephraim Deinard, was made to the Library in 1914. Except for a few hundred items of Judaica, this collection, like the earlier one, consists chiefly of Hebraica, in all branches of literature from earliest antiquity to modern times. These acquisitions were so noteworthy that Dr. Cyrus Adler, President of the Dropsie College for Hebrew and cognate learning, referred to them enthusiastically at the Menorah convention dinner in New York on December 30, 1913:

> Any Jewish student in America who today has the desire to pursue Jewish learning has opportunities which he would not find surpassed in many places in Europe. This growth of libraries in our Jewish institutions is supplemented by the growth of libraries on Jewish subjects in our general institutions. You doubtless all know that there is being brought together in the National Library at Washington a very distinguished collection of Jewish literature, which is being housed and cared for in a way that I do not think has ever been equaled. I have never seen a collection of Hebrew books in such a beautiful dress.

Two additional collections of about 6,000 volumes were purchased by the Library of Congress from this same collector in 1917 and 1921, and yearly accessions by purchase, copyright and gift had increased the number of Hebrew books to more than 40,000 volumes as Herbert Putnam's administration drew to a close.

The Manuscripts Division was one of the divisions that had been created under the reorganization plans of 1897; it knew, under Herbert Putnam, an almost phenomenal expansion. Four persons originally made up the staff as it operated in the new building. In 1901 the pieces in its custody numbered about 36,000, which could, it was said, "be compacted into perhaps 1,500 volumes." Previous to removal to the new building the manuscript collections had been built up from the major portion of the library of Thomas Jefferson, purchased in 1815, and the additional Jefferson manuscripts purchased in 1829; from the papers of Dolly Madison, purchased by Congress in 1848; from items in the Smithsonian collection obtained by virtue of the legislation of 1866; from items in the Peter Force collection purchased in 1867; by the De Rochambeau papers purchased by Congress in 1882; and from items in the Toner library, presented to the Library of Congress in 1882. An important additional acquisition made before transfer of the Library from the Capitol was that of the papers of Henry R. Schoolcraft relating to his researches among the Indians and the history of the Northwest. Since purchases of individual manuscripts had been meager, these represented practically the only sources of the manuscript collection as it was originally set up. Herbert Putnam's administration was marked throughout by the outstanding items added to these collections and the general development of the division. As early as 1902 the Librarian had secured the services of Worthington Chauncey Ford as chief of the new department. Ford was to develop and organize particularly the collections relating to American history, a field in which he was an authority. The items had increased, during the year, by 65,036 pieces, which, grouped and bound, added some 3,000 volumes to the shelves, and gifts were beginning to come in—a Chinese manuscript, a portion of the original manuscript of President Lincoln's last annual message to Congress, letters, memorials, account books, proclamations and state papers, the papers of Salmon P. Chase, and the letter book of David Porter.

Collection by collection there began to accumulate in this Division the papers of the Presidents and other valuable manuscripts. First of these were the personal papers of Thomas Jefferson, about three hundred autographed letters, dating from 1774 to 1826; there has followed acquisition of papers of practically every President of the United States—a rich store being added to constantly, either in original or duplicate copies, by patriotic citizens everywhere who, possessing fugitive items in their own libraries, have wished to see them a part of the national deposit.

There was also built up during the Librarianship of Herbert Putnam a varied and significant holding of literary manuscripts. In 1918 one such collection especially notable was deposited by Thomas B. Harned of Germantown, Pennsylvania, who turned over a large portion of the literary remains of Walt Whitman— scrapbooks, pamphlets, periodicals, various editions of Whitman's works, and a mass of manuscript and newspaper clippings. In that same year Miss Emily Wilde of New Orleans added the papers of another American poet—Richard Henry Wilde—to the Library's store. Nearly two hundred box portfolios were prepared in this year to receive the manuscript volumes of the Continental Congress and the papers of George Washington that were still in the original bindings. Today St. George L. Sioussat is chief of the Manuscripts Division.

In 1924 the Librarian of Congress had had occasion to write:

344

An investigator who, to personal enthusiasm for the history of New England, adds enlightened and magnanimous ideas of the claims of American history as a whole, and of the duty and the opportunity of the National Library in providing for it—Mr. James B. Wilbur, of Manchester, Vt.—has initiated a gift to the Library which will widen very rapidly the area covered in reproduction. He is himself meeting the cost of reproducing, by photostat, groups of source material outside of our regular scheme, the resultant copies being added to our collection. Begun with a group of Washington papers in the New Hampshire Society, these reproductions will extend to groups of national importance in other institutions and—where permission may be had—in private collections. Nor will it be limited to this country.

Originally intending a bequest of a fund whose interest would be applicable to the acquisition of such source material chiefly in photostat or other reproductions, Mr. Wilbur, in 1925, had proposed to the then newly created Trust Fund Board that his bequest be changed into an immediate gift of the principal, with a stipulation that a portion of the income derived from it should be turned over to him, perhaps until his death. The principal consisted of 1,000 shares of seven percent preferred stock of the Public Service Company of Northern Illinois, par $100 a share, quoted at the time at 107. Thus was founded the Wilbur endowment which has added richly to the manuscript collections ever since, providing photoduplications of priceless historic materials available in no other form.

Stimulated by the Wilbur fund for reproduction of historic materials, and the Richard Rogers Bowker fund for bibliographic service, John D. Rockefeller about three years later placed additional resources at the disposal of the Library in these two fields, as being of great utility to learning. He gave the Library leave to draw upon him during a five-year period to the amount of $450,000 for the reproduction project and to the amount of $250,000 for bibliographic expansion. Work was commenced

345

soon after in photoduplication, chiefly abroad, in the libraries and archives of England, France and Spain. Photostat plants belonging to the Library of Congress were set up—Mr. Wilbur meeting a portion of the cost—in the British Museum and the Public Record Office, and elsewhere the use of such apparatus was secured, so that a great mass of source material, in transcript or facsimile, since accumulated, has saved thousands of historians the time and expense of a trip abroad—or—as Dr. Putnam had suggested—induced them to take it.

The second project, bibliographic in nature, under this Rockefeller fund, described as "the enlargement of our bibliographic apparatus," meant particularly the Union Catalogue of books in other American libraries that might be useful to research. Beginning in September of the year of Mr. Rockefeller's gift, more than thirty people, under competent direction, were set to work revising the 3,000,000 cards that had been accumulating over a period of many years, down to a compact basis of 2,000,000, and augmenting it by new titles as acquired. Its components at first chiefly the printed or otherwise manifolded cards received on exchange from a small group of libraries, the Union Catalogue was destined to embrace, in time, more than 10,500,000 entries, representing about 7,000,000 different books of value for scholarly purposes, and indicating the libraries in which they might be found. In 1927 and 1932 the original Rockefeller grant was augmented by additional funds from the same source, and since 1932 the Union Catalogue has been maintained by Congressional appropriation. Today it maintains supplementary catalogues containing entries in specialized fields and card catalogues of the contents of the Vatican Library as well as of accessions of the British Museum and other foreign libraries.

These catalogues in combination constitute the most extensive bibliographical repertory in the world, and are kept up to date

346

through co-operative arrangements with other American libraries. A decade after establishment of this invaluable extended service, the Library of Congress, with the aid of another grant from the Rockefeller Foundation, inaugurated the Photoduplication Service. This latter was organized to supply distant investigators with microfilms and other photoduplicates of material not otherwise available for use outside of Washington. The most modern equipment for these purposes, as well as for purposes of photostat and photography, were acquired under the grant and have been operating continuously since in the interests of Congress, of the American public and of American institutions, under the present direction of George A. Schwegmann, Jr., who also serves as Director of the Union Catalogue.

The maps, the documents, the fine arts, the Periodical Divisions all knew great expansion of collections and service under Herbert Putnam's Librarianship. The Maps Division, like that of manuscripts, had been organized under the original reorganization plan of 1897. The Documents Division, while formally organized July 1, 1900, was without a chief until October 1st, and can hardly be said to have acquired individuality before January 1, 1901; the Division of Fine Arts grew out of the Division of Prints, which had been established under the original reorganization plan, and was expanded to deserve the designation *Division of Fine Arts* in 1929; and the Periodical Division may be said to have originated, as an entity, with the opening of its public reading room on January 22, 1900.

Five years before Herbert Putnam became Librarian of Congress, the maps collection had been no more than a confused mass in the various corners, corridors, and cellars of the Capitol. Brought to the new building it was gradually separated from other material and spread out on packing cases in one of the Library's halls. Storage cases were prepared to receive the sheet maps; special cases for atlases and other bound materials were installed; catalogues made ready; and reading rooms, equipped with special racks and drafting tables, were furnished. Classified and arranged by geographical divisions, the maps for the first time became of practical use to Congress and the public. General atlases were arranged according to authors and valuable collections and manuscript maps were placed under lock and key. Age-worn and mutilated specimens were restored to good condition, repaired and mounted and made ready for reference use. P. Lee Phillips, who served as Chief of Maps Division in these early days, had been largely responsible for organizing this inchoate mass into an integral collection, and later compiled the analytical lists which, as publications of the Library of Congress, proved useful tools for the cartographer. Lieutenant Colonel Lawrence Martin, a former cartographer of the Department of State, succeeded Phillips at the latter's death on January 4, 1924, and presides as Chief today.

By the time Herbert Putnam's active administration drew to a close, the Maps Division of the Library of Congress, with its special reading room, was famed among scholars, representing as it did the richest cartographic representations of the United States and other portions of the American continents. Many special collections had accrued to it meanwhile—the Rochambeau, the Faden, and the Howe maps; about six hundred maps of the Harisse collection, the Lowery maps; the Kohl maps; Chinese, Korean, and Japanese maps and atlases, and almost all the editions of Ptolemy's geography, and editions of the atlases of Ortelius, of Blaeu, of Mercator; charts and plans and manuscripts.

At the time of organization of the Division of Documents in 1901, Herbert Putnam said: "This division of the Library must not be confounded with the Bureau of Documents, which under the 'Superintendent of Documents' is a division of the Government Printing Office. . . . The function of the Division of Documents in the Library is to acquire, arrange and make available for use, the publications of governments, national, local, and municipal, and of quasi-public bodies, such as commercial organizations and the like." To the Division has been assigned also general supervision over the works on economics, politics, and sociology.

Before its establishment as a separate division, part of the work outlined had been carried on by the Reading Room, by the Catalogue Division, and by the Periodical Division of the Library. But since it is only by "systematic and continued solicitation" that this class of publication can be obtained, and also because there were serious omissions in a collection which had received no attention whatever in the cramped quarters of the Capitol, Dr. Putnam set up the separate division.

It was charged not only with care of the documents collections but, like every reference division of the Library of Congress today, with furnishing information in person or by mail involving the material in its custody or as to which it had special knowledge.

Under the copyright law important additions in economic, political and sociological works were continuously received by this division, which built up concurrently extensive collections in United States documents, State documents, municipal documents, and—under the system of international exchange inaugurated in 1867—foreign documents.

As early as 1901 Herbert Putnam had entered into communication with several foreign governments in an effort to secure books lacking in the Library collections, and through these efforts had made very considerable additions to the collections of

Austrian, French and Italian documents. The Library already possessed a complete set of journals of the Senate and House of Deputies of Spain, dating from 1800, by an arrangement with the United States Minister in Madrid, and had acquired from the Palace of the Governor-General of Puerto Rico a valuable collection of printed documents relating to the Spanish administration there and in the islands of the West Indies generally. Putnam had also secured, through direct application to the commissioners of the several countries to the Paris Exposition of 1900, much of the official literature that had grown out of the Exposition. By direct correspondence, the Librarian had likewise succeeded in completing the sets of Norwegian statistics, publications of the Chamber of Commerce in Hamburg, and the "Annales des Travaux Publics" of Belgium. He had largely supplemented official collections of historical documents published by the British Record Commissions through transfer from the library of the Department of State.

These early efforts of Herbert Putnam to round out the collections of the Library's Documents Division were but the beginning. As time went on and collections grew, the division issued, beginning with January, 1910, a *Monthly Check List of State Publications;* in 1930 it published *An Account of Government Document Bibliography;* in 1932 *A Guide to the Memoria of the Republics of Central America and of the Antilles,* and a short time later *A Guide to the Publications of the Government of Mexico.* Before the close of his active administration Herbert Putnam was also to inaugurate a program of bilateral agreements to regulate the international exchange of all official publications concluded by the Department of State, which brought forth commendatory resolutions in 1938 at the sixth conference of teachers of International Law and related subjects, and has evoked the gratitude of students generally ever since. The Documents Division is now in charge of James B. Childs, a scholarly and able chief.

The original reorganization plan of 1899 for the Library of Congress had provided for a separate Division of Prints to care for the engravings, etchings, photographs and other products of the graphic arts which were appropriate to its custody. It was also charged with the special selection and care of certain exhibits.

The collection of prints that had accumulated over a period of many years in the Capitol had arrived at the new building in much the same embarrassing condition as the maps and the collections of music, and analogous work was required to restore to some semblance of order more than 55,000 items. In the first year of Putnam's tenure of office about 5,000 pieces had been added and this great mass of material was in the process of being stamped, accessioned, classified, catalogued, and made available for public inspection or ready for selected exhibits.

One of the earliest valuable donations to this Division had been the gift of Mrs. Gertrude M. Hubbard, accepted by Congress on July 7, 1898, of the large collection of engravings formed by her husband, Gardiner Greene Hubbard of Washington. The result of many years of careful collecting, it is rich in examples of the work of engravers of all schools, many of great rarity, and contains an extensive series of portraits of Napoleon and Frederick the Great. In presenting the collection Mrs. Hubbard had expressed the intention of adding to it from time to time and in her will to make provision for increasing it by creating a fund of $20,000, the interest of which was to be used in the purchase of additional engravings. The collection has now grown to notable proportions and constitutes a valuable accession.

When Dr. Leicester B. Holland, the present head, became chief of the Division of Prints on September 1, 1929, the name of the department was changed to Division of Fine Arts. Dr. Holland became incumbent simultaneously of the Chair of Fine Arts, taking active charge on September 13th. By that time many rare and varied collections had enriched the holdings, such as the eighty-eight etched copperplates of E. K. K. Wetherill, a former pupil of Whistler, the Johnston collection of some 6,000 photographic negatives of gardens and architectural subjects, and the Chadburne collection of Japanese woodblock prints and other material illustrating Americans and Europeans as they appeared to the Japanese after the opening of the country to foreign trade by Commodore Perry in 1853. These had been purchased by Mrs. E. Crane Chadbourne in Paris and presented by her to the Library of Congress. Famous Japanese prints, etchings and dry points of famous artists, and outstanding photographs, had been acquired by purchase; and books acquired by copyright and purchase had brought the number of volumes in the collections to more than 45,000 by 1930. Fine old lithographs by Currier and Ives had been salvaged in that year from the indiscriminate stored mass of copyright material, many in full color and almost all in perfect condition, and these were added to the art stores.

One of the most important gifts in the history of the Division of Fine Arts of the Library of Congress was that which originated in London in 1917, when Mr. and Mrs. Joseph Pennell, the authorized biographers of James McNeill Whistler, on May 24th, in the office of the American Consul General, legally transferred fourteen heavily insured cases of Whistleriana to the United States Government, awaiting a safer time for its shipment to Washington.

These cases contained not only a complete representation of books in which Whistler is mentioned or his art discussed, but several hundred unpublished letters of Whistler and many letters and tributes from the most distinguished people who knew him in Europe and America. The collection of Whistler prints, etchings, lithographs, photographs of his paintings and other reproductions then acquired is the most complete in existence, including an original pen drawing of Whistler's portrait of himself and many of his choicest etchings represented in several states. Press cuttings and magazine clippings alone filled some sixty folio volumes. These gifts were later considerably augmented by Mr. and Mrs. Pennell; and when Joseph Pennell died on the 23rd of April, 1926, in Brooklyn, New York, his will—with the exception of a single bequest of $10,000 and subject to a life interest in Mrs. Pennell—left his entire estate for the benefit of the Library of Congress, in promotion of the collections and service of the Division of Fine Arts. The Whistleriana now in the custody of the Library of Congress, with that at the Freer Gallery in Washington, forms a record of the artist and the man such as probably does not exist of any other personage in history. Pennell himself had given as a reason for his general bequest to the United States, "The United States is spending money on prints and encouraging arts and artists, and has encouraged me."

A fine collection of the work of Pennell himself was also presented in this connection, a move that proved highly gratifying to the Librarian of Congress: "Mr. Pennell was not merely an amiable idealist, swayed by emotional or sentimental impulse," Putnam commented, "he was a thinker, unsparingly analytical, critical, and independent in his judgments. His conviction that the United States Government, through the Library of Congress, will prove a competent agency for the promotion of the arts which he loved, and a potent influence in disseminating a sound understanding of them is of very great moment indeed."

353

It was in 1937 and 1938 that the estate of Joseph Pennell, thus bequeathed by him in 1926, was turned over to the Library of Congress, its income accruing in full to the Division of Fine Arts. The funds are dedicated to three purposes:—the purchase of Whistleriana, the purchase of prints made by Joseph Pennell, and the purchase of prints by artists of any nationality made within the last hundred years, with no stipulations as to the proportion of income to be devoted to each. Such fascinating items as Whistler's palette, with its ivory disc incised with the butterfly which was the artist's emblem; charming letters interspersed with clever little pen-and-ink sketches, and rare and beautiful prints have been added.

Various photographic deposits made from time to time in this division of the Library of Congress had given rise to an idea which was to develop into an important and interesting historical enterprise. A proposition for establishing at the Library of Congress a national repository for photographic negatives of early American architecture, to preserve and make available to students of history and others, pictorial records of our rapidly disappearing ancestral homes, was suggested to the Carnegie Corporation. On April 16, 1930, the Corporation responded with a grant for $5,000 for preliminary work in organizing a subdivision of the Fine Arts Division to be known as the Pictorial Archives of Early American Architecture. At the annual meeting of the American Institute of Architects held that May in Washington, official indorsement of the Institute was secured. National response to requests for negatives was extraordinary. At the close of Herbert Putnam's period of active service as Librarian, this collection consisted of more than 26,000 negatives; and drawings and negatives of the Historic American Buildings Survey, initiated by the National Park Service, were being added.

By 1901, about 200 readers were dropping in to the Periodical Room of the Library of Congress regularly to read the 3,000 newspapers and other serials that were then being placed on the racks, or to call for any one of the 4,000 additional serials from the adjoining stacks. In those early days the Library of Congress was subscribing to 823 of the 7,200 serials regularly received. Herbert Putnam listed at the time 2,612 as gifts of American publishers; 1,383 as copyright deposits; 1,981 received through the Smithsonian; and 426 from Federal departments and bureaus. Of the newspapers received, more than 400 were published in the United States and 150 in foreign countries. In custody of the Periodical Division were extensive files, the newspapers alone aggregating nearly 20,000 volumes, of all general periodicals.

When the collection was moved into the new building, these files were only in part bound, or in any kind of condition for sorting or placing on the shelves. Piled upon the floors, the newspapers had filled the aisles and alcoves of seven of nine extensive decks and the unbound mass could only be estimated by tons, occupying three rooms, piled upon the floor six feet deep, with only narrow aisles along the walls. It represented the accumulation of nearly half a century. Only four persons, under the organization of July 1, 1897, had been provided to deal with this appalling accumulation. A year after Herbert Putnam had taken over the Librarianship the force, increased to eleven for this purpose, had cleared for administrative uses every one of the three rooms and the two pavilions, had shelved some 50,000 bound volumes, had reduced appreciably the dimension of the unbound heaps and had proceeded in the direction of collation of individual sets after a rough classification and alphabetization.

Putnam gave constant attention to filling the gaps in sets, saw that volumes were made up for the binder and that, after January 22, 1900, the needs of the increasing number of users of current serials were attended to. In addition, early in 1900 the Library had found time to issue a *Check List of American Newspapers*—a work which has continued to this day. In the closing years of Putnam's librarianship about 170,000 separate periodical items were being received by this division and a thousand more new titles were being added annually. Some idea of the increased use of the files by the reading public may be gained from the fact that during 1937 alone more than 55,000 unbound periodicals, more than 157,000 unbound newspapers, and more than 45,000 bound volumes of newspapers were called for in the Periodical Reading Room, and 22,451 items were listed as "outgoing loans." At the close of this same year 916 newspapers were being regularly received, 777 of which were published in the United States. The Library was receiving 135 American second-file newspapers by gift in addition to thirty by way of copyright deposit. The material is in constant use by persons engaged in serious investigation and research, as well as by casual readers. Writers make free use of the files in compiling information for publication. Many notable accessions have accumulated, files of old and rare newspapers, ships' news-sheets, *Porcupines' Gazette*, *The Rush-Light*, Cobbett's political pamphlets, and other curious and valuable items.

Always concerned with increasing the usefulness of the Library's priceless stores so far as the people of the nation were concerned, Herbert Putnam had so far succeeded in developing his dream of service and "interpretation" of the collections during the years he headed the national institution, that in 1936 a special writer for the *Washington Sunday Post* was able to report:

No longer can the Library be considered solely or chiefly a legislative library, for in the logical and inevitable enlargement of usefulness it reaches out far beyond. In general relations with the outside world, in character and range and in service, it has become the national library of the United States. Not only is reference work done for readers within the Library, but many write in, as a result of which last year yielded over 3,000 typed pages of reading lists on about 2,500 subjects. In the same period over half a million were served in the building, young and old, of various races—residents and visitors. These readers consulted works on over 1,200 subjects. Nearly 1,200 serious investigators used the various collections, 463 of whom came from 124 important colleges and universities; 59 foundations, associations and learned societies sent 130 investigators. Every State and Territory was represented, while 24 foreign countries sent 72, China leading with 29. That the needs of these advanced students are filled is proved by their presence in increasing numbers. The total circulation exceeded 1,000,000 volumes.

Putnam realized, too, that while catalogues and bibliographies can go far toward interpreting materials, human guidance becomes necessary at a certain point. Incumbents of the "chairs" he had established were proving helpful guides and counselors to thousands of students and investigators as the mass of material grew under the dome of the Library.

Lyman Beecher Stowe marveled at the attention accorded the investigator. In 1937 he told this story in the *New York Times*:

Not long ago a student wrote to the superintendent of the Reading Room at the Library of Congress at Washington to say that he wanted to come to the Library and use it for two or three weeks going over material which he needed in connection with his writing and lecturing. He mentioned the subjects he wished to look up. When he reached the Library three or four days later he was shown into a little office furnished with chairs, a desk and bookshelves containing the books and magazines which he would be most likely to need. His name was even on the door. During his stay he not only was surrounded with the books and papers he needed but received kind and constant advice of experts as to their use.

When he mentioned this almost unbelievable service to friends their comments implied that he must have a "drag" with the Library of Congress. His "drag" consists in being on a list of students who requested the use of the collections and services of the library. To be eligible for this list one must be of reputable character and engaged in some serious study.

The Library of Congress had truly become by the last year of his active administration what Herbert Putnam then termed it: "An institution of learning—not a university, yet approximating the definition by President Lowell cited by Bliss Perry at the head of a chapter of his reminiscences: 'The best and most fruitful conception of a university or college is the ancient one of a society or guild of scholars associated together for preserving, imparting, increasing and enjoying knowledge.' "

But years pass and a man grows older, and Herbert Putnam was beginning to feel that forty years is a long span for continuous service. Only once in that time had he interrupted his faithful attendance upon the Library's daily demands. That had been from the autumn of 1917 to the autumn of 1919 while he had served as Director of the American Library Association War Service, which had undertaken to supply reading matter to American troops. Covering various cantonments in this country and training camps abroad, the service had maintained circulation among diminishing detachments following the armistice and had continued to maintain collections and reading rooms at Coblenz, at the "A.E.F. University" at Béaune, on the transports and even in such outlying posts as Vladivostok. The enterprise included numerous library buildings, an extensive personnel, more than 5,000,000 books and the expenditure of about $5,000,000. It had been directed from the main headquarters in the Library of Congress. Dr. Putnam had made various trips of inspection to the cantonments in the United States and in December, 1918, he had left for France to supervise remaining operations. These finally reduced themselves to the activities of the American Library at Paris. Typically, Herbert Putnam had refused to accept the Distinguished Service Medal which had been awarded him for this work on the ground that credit was due to the entire library organization.

Other honors had come to him during the years, however. He has received a long list of honorary degrees—Litt.D. from Bowdoin in 1898, Brown University in 1914, and Princeton University in 1933; LL.D. from Columbian—now George Washington—University in 1903, University of Illinois in 1903, University of Wisconsin in 1904, Yale in 1907, Williams in 1911, Harvard in 1928, and New York University in 1930. From 1902 to 1906 he was an Overseer of Harvard College.

In 1897, Dr. Putnam had been United States delegate to the International Library Conference in London; he was a member of the administrative board of the Congress of Arts and Sciences at the Louisiana Purchase Exposition in St. Louis in 1904; United States delegate to the Congrés International de Bibliographie in Paris in 1900, and to the World Congress of Libraries and Bibliography in Rome in 1929. At the celebration of the 500th anniversary of the birth of Johannes Gutenberg at Mainz in 1900 he represented the United States. Twice Herbert Putnam has served as President of the American Library Association. In 1928 he was decorated a Knight of the Royal Order of the Pole Star of Sweden, and in 1921 received the Roosevelt Distinguished Service Medal. These honors he accepted for himself only as the personification of his high office. He is a member of a long list of learned societies.

Herbert Putnam throughout his long career aided scholarship whenever an opportunity presented. Henry Folger, whose benefactions made possible the Folger Shakespeare Memorial Library across the street from the Library of Congress in Washington, always entertained a friendly spirit for the Congessional Library and faith in those responsible for its administration, as one clause of his will—not made public at the time of its reading —attested. This clause had contained the provision that in the event that Trustees of Amherst College should decline the responsibility of trusteeship for any reason in connection with the Shakespeare Library Mr. Folger was founding, the charge should be transferred to the University of Chicago; and if this university should fail to fulfil the trusteeship, responsibility for the maintenance of the library should be transferred to the Library of Congress.

At the time that Henry Folger had been looking about for a suitable site for the Shakespeare Library, the Librarian of Congress had begun negotiations for the purchase of certain plots along "Grant Row" between Second and Third and East Capitol Streets. To his surprise he discovered that much of this land had already been set aside for the purpose of erecting the Folger Shakespeare Library, whereupon he immediately withdrew negotiations for the Grant Row site and subsequently purchased, in the name of the Library of Congress, the adjoining plot, where the Annex now stands.

In many similar ways Herbert Putnam had endowed the office of Librarian of Congress with distinction in forty full years of active service; and by 1938 he was ready for less lively responsibilities. In a report to accompany "H. R. 8136" submitted in the House during the first session of the 75th Congress in 1937, Representative Keller, of the Library Committee, recommended for the Committee that Congress pass that bill which was "designed to provide for Librarians of Congress who have served thirty-six years or more a reward of long service helping them to experience the fullest and richest enjoyment of peace and security in old age that such service deserves."

On this occasion the Committee, through Representative Keller, expressed the opinion that "the services of Dr. Putnam to this country have certainly been equal to that of any general in the Army who has served the same number of years. He has built the world's greatest research library—our great National Library—which serves and is served by the world."

On June 20, 1938, an act "to create the office of Librarian Emeritus of the Library of Congress" received executive approval. The act read:

> That upon separation from the service, by resignation or otherwise, on or after July 1, after the approval of this Act, Herbert Putnam, the present Librarian of Congress, who has served in that office for thirty-nine years, shall become Librarian Emeritus, with such duties as the President of the United States may prescribe, and the President of the United States shall thereupon appoint his successor, by and with the advice and consent of the Senate. The said Herbert Putnam shall receive as Librarian Emeritus compensation at the rate of $5,000 per annum. Such salary shall be paid in equal monthly installments by the disbursing officer of the Library of Congress, and such sums as may be necessary to make such payments are hereby authorized to be appropriated.

Five days before the bill was finally approved, Herbert Putnam had addressed a letter to President Franklin Delano Roosevelt:

> DEAR MR. PRESIDENT:
> The attached bill (H. R. 10846), passed yesterday, is, as I think you have been assured, entirely acceptable to me. I hope you will approve it.
> In that case I shall be prepared "on or after July 1," to turn over the administrative duties to my successor as Librarian, and to facilitate his entrance upon them.

Should the selection of him require deliberation, I shall assume that I am to continue in them until notified that he is ready to take office. I shall then gladly shift to such duties as you may prescribe for me as "Librarian Emeritus."

With deep satisfaction that the choice of my successor rests with a President who can fully appreciate the requirements of the position under the recent evolution of the institution, believe me

Faithfully yours,

HERBERT PUTNAM

As he submitted his report for 1938, Herbert Putnam reminded the Congress, "My successor as Librarian not yet having been named, I am at the date of this report still exercising the functions of that office, though earnest for those which may be my privilege as Librarian Emeritus."

He was, however, to round out forty years of service as Librarian of Congress before giving up control to a younger man, and on the 5th of April, 1939, the occasion was commemorated by his colleagues and by the Associates of the Librarian's Round Table. At that time a letter of congratulation from the President of the United States was read by the Honorable Frederic A. Delano, as well as other congratulatory messages read by Dr. Waldo G. Leland. The President Emeritus of Williams College, Dr. Harry A. Garfield, and the Honorable Robert Luce, Representative in Congress from Massachusetts, made addresses of appreciation. In the Librarian's office was unveiled the portrait in bronze of the Librarian, executed by his daughter, Brenda Putnam—a National Academician and sculptor who had studied under Pratt, Fraser and Grafly. Presentation of the plaque to the Library of Congress was made by Dr. William Adams Slade, who for many devoted years of the Putnam administration had served as Chief Reference Librarian. Remarks were also made by the Superintendent of the Library building, William C. Bond, and by the retired chief of the Card Division, Charles Harris Hastings.

Two months later, on June 7, 1939, Archibald MacLeish was nominated Librarian of Congress by President Franklin Delano Roosevelt. On June 29th his appointment was confirmed by the United States Senate, and on October 1st he took office, and Herbert Putnam assumed his duties as Librarian of Congress Emeritus.

XVI

CONTROVERSY OVER A POET

*T*he gods choose our battlefield and in that arena we ply our talents. Probably no one was more surprised than the American poet, Archibald MacLeish—whose restless spirit, seeking expression, had sent him to Paris, driven him to Teheran, set his feet along the trails of ancient conquistadores—to learn that his main field of activity was thenceforth set for him in the Library of Congress in Washington.

In that curiously unobtrusive fashion in which fateful announcements seem so often to be made, the *New York Times* of June 7, 1939—leaving the "a" out of the poet's name—ran a tag line to a front-page story which had outlined at some length the President's intention of delaying his Western tour. Referring to the President, that concluding line stated: "Finally he decided to originate a bit of news and announced his selection of Archibald McLeish to be Librarian of Congress." It was an announcement destined to fall like a bombshell upon the sensitive ears of librarians in many quarters, reverberating with special distinctness in those circles where certain officials of the American Library Association waited and listened expectantly.

There is also every reason to believe that it set up more than one credulous or approving echo in the marble halls of that institution which, most nearly concerned, had exhibited for many weeks now the liveliest curiosity with respect to Dr. Putnam's possible successor.

President Roosevelt had given his own reasons for the choice he had made. The post demanded so many qualifications in one man, "there being so many parts to the profession, technical and otherwise." He had concluded, therefore, that technical men could be hired, and that the head of the great literary establishment should be a man universally known as a scholar. Such a man, he said, he had found in Archibald MacLeish, who, first educated in the law, and later achieving recognition as a leading poet and editor, would be known as "a gentleman and a scholar" in all nations.

The *New York Times* dismissed the most colorful of the charges leveled against MacLeish as casually as it deserved:

> The charge has already been made that Mr. MacLeish is tainted with economic heresy. The truth seems to be that, like most poets, he is not entirely satisfied with the world as it is.

A few days after Dr. Milton James Ferguson, then President of the American Library Association, and chief librarian of the Brooklyn Public Library, had predicted that librarians throughout the country would protest the nomination of Archibald Mac-Leish as Librarian of Congress because of his lack of technical training, Senator Tobey drew the attention of his colleagues in the Senate to the fact that Mr. Swanson though appointed Secretary of the Navy had never commanded a gunboat; Mr. Harry Woodring, Secretary of War, was no military expert, no expert in gunnery and no expert in aircraft defense; members of the Interstate Commerce Commission had not been chosen for their long experience in railroad operation; and the General Electric Company had not selected to head its great industrial organization a technical engineer with special knowledge of turbines and electrical apparatus, but Owen D. Young, "a man with no engineering training, but a man of outstanding ability as a lawyer and of great personal charm and high character."

Many librarians, despite the stand taken by the head of their organization, believed that the Librarian of Congress should possess qualifications that went far beyond an ability to catalogue, to classify, to balance a budget or to "hire and fire." On June 29th, Senator Tobey read impressive endorsements of the poet from the floor of the Senate.

The *New York Times* gave early and favorable recognition to the President's choice. Its editorial of June 8th stated:

> Archibald MacLeish, named by President Roosevelt to succeed the admired Dr. Herbert Putnam as Librarian of Congress, is not a professional librarian. He is a number of other things that should commend him to those who wish to see the great traditions of our national library carried forward. He is an eloquent and impassioned poet—certainly one of the two or three at the top of our American list. Unlike some poets, he has a brilliantly logical mind, which the Harvard Law School recognized twenty years ago by ranking him highest in its graduating class for "scholarship, conduct and character." He has been notably successful as a practising lawyer and as an editor. There is every reason to believe that he has both the vision and the executive ability to give continued life to an institution which deals not only with books but with all the arts. . . . So warm and generous a spirit, keenly sensitive to the finest cultural traditions, aflame with love of liberty, can hardly be a danger to the Library of Congress.

On the same day the *Baltimore Sun* and the *Boston Herald* had expressed hearty editorial approval. The *Sun* saw no reason why the appointee's lack of formal training in technical librarianship should constitute a handicap, for he was, after all, "a man of wide experience as well as a poet who stands in the front rank of contemporary writers." Unquestionably the Library of Congress had its share of experts and he would have the benefit of their advice. MacLeish, on the other hand, would bring to his work in the Library of Congress "not only the imagination which shows clearly in his poetry, the experimental temperament which marks his admirable poetic drama for the radio, but also the critical intelligence that informed his Turnbull lectures and the vital broad interest in American affairs which characterizes his writings from *Conquistador* to *Land of the Free*."

The high and special qualities which men of genuine creative powers possess, the *Sun* reminded its readers, "are likely to be of considerable value in any field of work." After all, it is to Anthony Panizzi, an Italian, friend of Foscolo and Mérimée, and student of poetry, that the British Museum owes much of its present-day greatness. And if nations have found that men of letters serve them well in diplomatic and governmental posts—and a long list of such men could be recalled, from Chaucer and Spenser, through Lowell and Irving, to Claudel and Ayala—there is certainly no reason to think that similar talents will not be "happily and beneficially employed in the great national storehouses of literature—as the cases of Coventry Patmore and Henry Francis Cary, in England, and of Charles Nodier and Remy de Gourmont, in France, suggest."

The *Boston Herald* predicted that the enthusiasm of Washington at the appointment would be duplicated "wherever Mr. MacLeish is known." The *Herald* summed up his accomplishments—"First man in his class at the Harvard Law School, and declined an appointment to the faculty . . . one of the most promising young lawyers in Boston when he left one of the leading law firms to give all his time to literature . . . as an editor of *Fortune*, a Pulitzer Prize winner in poetry, a writer of excellent prose, a man of affairs, an administrator, and, as the President characterized him, 'a gentleman and a scholar,' he deserves immediate, unanimous, hearty confirmation."

In contrast to these glowing tributes, the *New York Herald*

Tribune the following day referred editorially to MacLeish's appointment as "a shocking nomination"—one which appeared "more deplorable" the more it was considered:

"There is no question of Mr. MacLeish's high talents as a poet or the excellent quality of his mind," said the *Tribune*. What really mattered was "his complete lack of training for any library post." Here was an important and valuable profession; for two generations it had had its regular training schools. . . . It seemed to be the President's "easy notion" that Mr. MacLeish could hire these skilled and learned technicians to do his job for him. Such a suggestion the *Tribune* saw as "unsound" and "unfair"; to call such a conception shocking seemed to them "a calm and accurate statement." And in such large words as "outrage," "affront," "disheartening" and "dismaying," the editor registered his unqualified disapproval. Moreover he was "at a complete loss" to understand how President Roosevelt "could bring himself to make a purely personal appointment to a post of such distinction and special learning or how Mr. MacLeish could bring himself to accept a nomination for which he is so completely unequipped."

If the truth were known Archibald MacLeish was probably wondering just as hard as the *Tribune* how President Roosevelt had come to appoint him. For, as Senator Barkley had told the Senate on June 22nd, MacLeish had been as surprised as anyone else in the United States when the President advised him that he had his name under consideration, and "asked him to come down and talk the matter over," and Senator Barkley had probably also come as near to the reason for it as anyone when he said with Kentucky forthrightness:

I think what the President had in mind was not to obtain a cataloguer of books. The Library probably has all the cataloguers it needs. It was not the purpose merely to obtain even a man who knows what books ought to be added to the Library. Probably the experts in the

Library are as well qualified as any librarian could be to recommend additional literature to be added to the Library. It seems to me the President was in search of a man of well-rounded scholarship and experience, with a broad-minded attitude toward the problems of the American people; a man who not only could make the Library an institution or an instrument for the advancement of knowledge, but could make its facilities available to the American people, not only in the operation of their Government, but in their approach to social, economic, and political problems as well as literary and other problems which are supposed to be met by a great institution such as the Library of Congress.

MacLeish was busy at the time in a variety of interesting ways. He was curator of the Nieman Foundation for Journalists at Harvard. He was writing social-minded poems and radio dramas and making speeches in defense of freedom. Poet, lawyer, editor, journalist, he had filled and was filling a distinguished role in contemporary affairs and making some bitter comments upon contemporary life. He was forty-seven when President Roosevelt appointed him Librarian of Congress and he had already lived a number of lives, beginning, if we are to accept his own estimate, with the day he turned over the keys of his office to his partner in a Boston law firm and started off for Paris with his wife and children, to write "the kind of poetry I wanted to write, not the kind I was writing." This was in 1923. For five years he read and wrote in Paris and traveled in the near East with occasional summers spent in the Berkshires of his own land.

Before he returned to the United States in 1928 he had written *The Happy Marriage, The Pot of Earth, Nobodaddy,* and *Streets to the Moon.* The first volume, intensely subjective, was concerned with the poet's individual emotions or perplexities, tempered with his own humor, modified by his own perspective. *The Pot of Earth,* published a year later, returned for its theme to the common fund of human experience, as expressed in folklore. Far less personal in tone than its predecessor, it marked the trend of the poet's philosophy, which was later to identify the purely personal in human experience, the bewilderments of the individual soul with the experience of the race. In 1926 the volume of poems, *Streets to the Moon,* appeared, in which the poet used new devices, tried new effects and experimented with the sound of words. Social and psychological currents of thought were providing fresh subject matter for literature and writers generally were presenting it in untried forms, so that MacLeish did not stand alone in this era of technical experimentation.

One analyst sees the poetry of this period in MacLeish's development as no longer expressive of devastating despair, with a new note struck—"a note of dignity, of human inviolability in the face of overwhelming odds." The *Hamlet of A. MacLeish,* published in 1928—"that strange poem which expresses the extreme in self-probing"—concludes with acceptance of man's fate, of inevitability:

We must consent now as all men
Whose rage is out of them must do.

In his *American Letter,* which appeared in *New Found Land* in 1930, MacLeish wrote: "It is a strange thing—to be an American." It makes clear why the poet felt the imperative need to return to his own country to live:

This, this is our land, this is our people,
This that is neither a land nor a race. We must reap
The wind here in the grass for our soul's harvest:
Here we must eat our salt or our bones starve.
Here we must live or live only as shadows.

This urge to return to his native land after the years spent abroad and to learn more of its present traditions, and its ancient culture, had sent MacLeish to Mexico in 1929 to travel alone over the route Cortez had taken in the sixteenth century. The result of these journeyings was *Conquistador,* published in 1932, wherein with sensitivity to detail and great force of feeling, he recounted the conquest of the Spaniard Cortez as remembered by one of his soldiers, Bernal Diaz del Castillo; thus it differs as the reminiscences of an old man would differ from historical or scholarly accounts. The long narrative poem won for MacLeish the Pulitzer Prize in 1933; *Poetry* had already awarded him, in 1929, the John Reed Memorial Prize, but this subsequent honor brought with it greater publicity and prestige.

MacLeish, meanwhile, had become a contributing editor of *Fortune* magazine—an indication perhaps that the poet was no longer restricting himself to indefinite ideals but, as a participant in the confusing and busy activity of a realistic world, was now concerning himself with the objective facts of man's existence. There were other indications of the widening of his interests and perhaps of the realization that to be listened to by a small group of esthetes is not enough for a man desiring to interpret in universal terms the happenings in the world today. In February, 1937, he had begun a series of lectures on poetry as guest professor at Princeton University, and had conducted there a course in creative writing. His next volume of poems, *Frescoes for Mr. Rockefeller's City,* give evidence of this increased interest in the American scene and his more active participation in the life of America. Greater awareness of contemporary social and political agitations, of the parts played by labor and capital in the economic life of the nation and a growing conviction of America's great strength—"She's a tough land under the corn, mister"—were now replacing that introspective consideration of his own thoughts and feelings, that personal search after eternal verities that had marked MacLeish's earlier poetry. His volume, *Poems, 1924-1933,* indicates this awakened social consciousness, so definitely expressed in *1933*—his Harvard Phi Beta Kappa poem—when he wrote of "millions starving for corn with mountains of waste corn."

MacLeish continued to write poetry of increased distinction, of increased maturity, poetry instinct with feeling—like the lovely *The Woman on the Stairs* series, where the personal is yet universalized, or *Dover Beach*, whose theme is the passage of time and the advance of the younger generation.

In 1935, in an introduction to *Panic*—a play in verse—MacLeish had declared that art, by nature dynamic, must find methods suitable for the time for which it is intended. Thus his later writings *The Fall of the City* and *Air Raid* make use of the radio as a medium, for "over the radio verse has no visual presence to compete with. Only the ear is engaged and the ear is already half poet. It believes at once: creates and believes." In *The Fall of the City* MacLeish showed what may happen when people are obsessed by fear and yield supinely to defeat. In *Air Raid*, written during the summer of 1938, several weeks before the Czecho-Slovakian crisis, MacLeish proved strangely prophetic, for he depicted vividly and tensely situations that were later the fate of many of the cities and villages of Europe. In *Land of the Free* he employed another modern technique, illustrating a series of photographs by a poem, much as a moving picture is animated by its sound track. Poverty and exploitation of those who had believed that "all you needed for freedom was being American" is the theme of the pictures, and the need for overcoming social wrongs. In *America Was Promises*, published in 1939, America's development as the people's land of promise, is sketched. There is in it still the old quest for an ideal—"but now he seeks it not for himself, but for all Americans. He seeks it, furthermore, not in an abstract realm, but in the material, physical, economic world, in man's harmonious relation with his fellow man."

MacLeish has insisted always that poetry must concern itself

372

with the "common spiritual experience of man"; man must be restored to that position of dignity from which he has been dethroned by science, before poetry can be at its greatest, for "poetry like any other art," as he wrote in *An Anonymous Generation*, "can only reach its highest level in a universe of which man is the center." He believes that the failure of the world today is a failure of the spirit and that only poetry can be of service in this incapacity of the people to imagine, this impotence of the people to imagine and believe. For, of all those proud and clumsy instruments by which men explore this planet and themselves, only poetry creates the thing it seems; "only poetry moving among living men on the living earth, is capable of discovering that common world to which the minds of men do, inwardly, not knowing it, assent." Drawing the picture of "things that may possibly happen," it is a challenge to human possibility and "alone imagines, and imagining creates, the world that men can wish to live in and make true."

To bring this world about MacLeish holds in his poetry no brief for this political party or that. A poet, he insists in *Invocation to the Social Muse*, must not align himself with any faction. As an artist he has "no stake in the existing economic order,"— he is concerned only for the artist's freedom to pursue his art. "We cannot exist," he has written, "without that freedom to do our own work in our own way which is called, for lack of an accurate term, intellectual freedom."

It would seem that a concern for intellectual freedom would prove a very fine fulcrum from which to manipulate the affairs of the world's greatest library—and so, apparently, thought Congress.

Early in June Senator Barkley had sent a telegram to Archibald MacLeish, inviting him to appear at his convenience before

373

the Committee, so that—in the words of Barkley—"the committee might look him over and examine him, size him up and decide for itself whether he fitted into the position of Librarian of Congress." MacLeish came, saw and conquered.

Meanwhile members of the American Library Association had opened their attack. On June 13th they had asked the Senate to deny confirmation of the poet as Librarian of Congress because "he lacks the essential qualifications of a librarian." The request was made through Milton James Ferguson, President of the organization, in an open letter to President Roosevelt, Vice-President Garner, and the Senate. In it, after a bow in the direction of MacLeish's "ability and distinction as a man of letters," they stated, "We think that the confirmation of Archibald MacLeish as Librarian of Congress would be a calamity," and gave as their reasons his lack of technical training in the fields of personnel administration, financial administration, and general library administration; referring to such an appointment as "a denial of the value of professional training and experience."

Almost immediately protests and petitions began pouring in to the Committee and other Members of the Senate. The executive board of the staff association of the New York Public Library was prompt in offering congratulations to Archibald MacLeish in his appointment, and sent a telegram to the President endorsing his choice, and another to the Senate urging confirmation.

Also taking prompt issue with Dr. Ferguson, the Metropolitan Library Council of New York made public a statement approving the appointment:

> Since the Librarianship of Congress calls for unusual administrative force and not merely effective technical knowledge, the Metropolitan Library Council approves Archibald MacLeish for the post. It believes that the status of libraries and librarians will advance under the leadership of men of vision.

374

The question of MacLeish's appointment was duly reached on the Senate calendar in the regular order on the 21st of June, at which time Senator Austin of Vermont had requested that it "go over," it being then late in the day. The next day, following an inquiry of Senator Barbour, Senator Barkley reviewed the distinguished career of Archibald MacLeish. In his remarks he referred to the presence of the two members of the American Library Association before the Committee:

> . . . In the very beginning of their statements they said they had no charges to make; they acknowledged the scholarship, the ability, and the high character of Mr. MacLeish; but they did object to the appointment on the ground that they felt that a trained professional librarian should have been selected rather than somebody who was not.

When Senator Barbour of New Jersey, reiterating his former statement that the nominee had been recommended to him "very highly, especially by a close friend of mine whose opinion I esteem very greatly," rose to remind the Senate of the wisdom of discussing the charges made against the poet earlier in the House, Senator Maloney of Connecticut got to his feet. He said:

> I am very hopeful that the consideration of this nomination of a distinguished man will not be very long postponed. I respectfully warn the Members of the Senate of the great danger involved in charging Communism or some alien connection to a prominent American, or to any American . . . the danger I see in referring to a man such as Mr. MacLeish as a "fellow traveler of Communists" is that when the pagan philosophy of Communism does creep more forcibly toward us we will not recognize it, because of charges so frequently and so carelessly made about men of liberal mind and tolerant viewpoint. . . . We should not lend our positions or our forum to a lightly conceived charge against a brilliant and patriotic American, and a great soldier, as is Mr. MacLeish, by giving too sympathetic attention to thoughtless statements by careless men. . . . As I searched for information about Mr. MacLeish, and I

already knew much about him, my admiration increased. I honestly feel that one day we will all be proud of the selection.

Senator Barkley called to the attention of the Senate the fact that when Dr. Putnam had retired to become Librarian Emeritus, "many scholars and eminent men throughout the country very naturally had a right to, and did, aspire to the position." He had himself presented to the President the name of a distinguished man "and urged his appointment." The American Library Association as an organization had recommended to the President its secretary, and urged his appointment to the position. "The President," said Senator Barkley, "I think very properly, paid no attention to politics. I do not know what the political faith of Mr. MacLeish is. I do not know whether he is a Democrat or a Republican or whether he is an independent. I think he is liberal in his political views. So am I."

The appointment, continued Barkley, was not a political appointment. "It was based entirely upon scholarship and the attainments, the vision, and the general attitude of this man toward the functions of the great Library, not only as an agent of the Government of the United States and of Congress, but as an agent for the dissemination of knowledge and information, and for the utilization of the accumulated wisdom that we have been able to assemble in the Library of Congress for the benefit of the American people."

"Must we be confined in our selection," demanded Senator Borah, during the controversy, "to a person who actually has had library training when we find a person who is finely equipped in every other respect?"

At this point Senator Minton of Indiana quietly interposed: "I notice that the qualifications of the gentleman whom Mr. MacLeish is nominated to succeed, were at the time of his appointment much like those of Mr. MacLeish. When he was made Librarian, Dr. Putnam had been graduated from Harvard, attended Columbia Law School in 1883 and 1884, and was admitted to the bar in 1886. He practiced a little law, just as Mr. MacLeish did. Then he went out into another field, as librarian of an institution; came back to Boston and practiced law again, and then became librarian at Boston before coming to the Congressional Library. So his career was parallel to that of Mr. MacLeish, in the beginning, at least."

Senator Austin, still upholding the cause of the trained librarian, called the attention of the Senate to a letter written by Joseph L. Wheeler, Librarian of the Enoch Pratt Free Library in Baltimore, and published in the *Baltimore Sun*, wherein Wheeler had expressed the belief that "this unsound appointment will tend to disrupt the organization. A librarian's duties are essentially directive and administrative." The *Baltimore Sun* had itself answered Mr. Wheeler's communication with these questions and answers: "What is, after all, the secret of Mr. Wheeler's outstanding success? Is it his technical competence, the competence that comes with training? Only to a very small extent. The essence of Mr. Wheeler's contribution to the Baltimore Library is that he brought curiosity, energy, and especially imagination to his job. It was his imagination which was stirred by the comparative passivity of the library as it existed before he came here. It was the thought that the people of Baltimore were not using the resources they possessed. His great achievement has grown out of that thought."

Editorials for and against the appointment were impartially introduced into the discussion by Senator Austin, who declared that his desire was to "encourage the development of the profession of librarian, and I would not discourage it by going outside of the family of librarians—which is a very large family—to make a selection for one of the choicest and most important posts within our reach." "This," said Senator Austin, was their library, it was "particularly, primarily and foremost the Library of the Congress," and they wanted it led by "a man who will make it of the greatest utility to us as servants of all the people of the country." The nomination of Archibald MacLeish, he contended, would "fail to recognize the efforts of a half-century of development of a profession" and would be "a discouragement to those who have sought to elevate this profession. . . ."

At this point Senator Tobey rose "to speak in favor of the confirmation of the nomination of Archibald MacLeish." He had, he said, attended the hearings before the committee. It had not been his privilege to talk to Mr. MacLeish. He had read his writings. He had gone into the matter very thoroughly. He had tried to put himself in the position of a juryman, "to listen to all the evidence and then to act wisely, refusing to take any position in answer to correspondence until today." Senator Tobey faced his colleague: "I now say, sir, that I consider it both a duty and a privilege not only to vote for the nominee's confirmation, but to speak for him on the floor of this honorable body." The New Hampshire Senator then quoted the opinions, favorable to the appointment, of Louis Kirstein, the philanthropist and giver of libraries; of Alexander Laing, assistant librarian at Dartmouth College; of a New Hampshire State Senator; of the director of the library of the University of Chicago; and concluded with the unadorned assertion: "Mr. President, this man is a straight shooter, if I know one. He rings true. He is the kind of man I want to see placed in authority, a man fit to occupy the position as Librarian of Congress."

The Chairman of the Library Committee, Senator Barkley, then expressed the opinion that he believed there was no greater man in the field of library accomplishments and attainments than

Dr. Putnam, adding, "I believe that Mr. MacLeish will be a worthy successor to Dr. Putnam. Not only does he know books, not only does he know their contents, not only is he widely read in history, in philosophy, in poetry, and in economics, but, Mr. President, Mr. MacLeish is the sort of man whom any Member of the Senate might be glad to visit and sit down with after dinner or in the evening and discuss for an hour or two not only books, not only catalogues, not only library shelves, but discuss the economic, social and moral problems that confront a great nation of 130,000,000 people. That is the kind of man I should like to see at the head of the Library of Congress."

Senator Frazier put in a final word for the trained technical librarian, Senator Maloney for Mr. MacLeish, and a "yea and nay" vote was taken on the nomination. By thirteen yeas, against eight nays, Archibald MacLeish was confirmed to succeed Herbert Putnam as Librarian of Congress. One of the warmest tributes tendered him came from his predecessor: "There is first the Scot in him—shrewd, austere, exacting, but humorous. There is the poet in him—whose stuff is not made of mere dreams but of realities. . . . There is the humanist, keenly sympathetic to all that calls for social sympathy. The lawyer—trained to analysis through determination of exact issues. The soldier—pledged to duty under discipline. The athlete—pledged to fair play. And finally there's the orator—capable of vivid and forceful speech."

XVII

THE NEW LIBRARIAN

*A*rchibald MacLeish was brought
up to appreciate books. He was born May 7, 1892, in a wooden
château hanging above the waters of Lake Michigan at Glencoe,
Illinois. His father, a Scot born in Glasgow, had been one of
Chicago's early settlers and a successful merchant. His mother,
"entirely self-less and beloved" was the daughter of a Connecticut Congregational minister, and had once taught at Vassar College. Thus it was a Connecticut school to which her 'teen-age son
was sent to prepare for Yale.

Young MacLeish led an active undergraduate life at Yale,
playing football, water polo, swimming and diving, yet his scho-
lastic record brought him election to Phi Beta Kappa in his Junior
year. He was a member of the Elizabethan Club, of the Pundits,
and of the Senior society, Skull and Bones; and in his Senior year
was class poet and editor of the *Yale Literary Magazine*.

His literary career had begun early. In October, 1912, he had
written a story, *The Shears of Atropos*, for the *Literary Magazine*
and contributed regularly thereafter. *The Marshes* was the first
of his poems to appear, in December, 1912—

> *There it is the white tides sleep—*
> *Tides that serve the waning moon.*

Graduated from Yale in 1915 MacLeish looked back upon his
undergraduate days with the feeling that perhaps the facts and

380

figures he had accumulated had not been the most important part
of the experience:

> *A year or two, and grey Euripides,*
> *And Horace and a Lydia or so,*
> *And Euclid and the brush of Angelo,*
> *Darwin on man, Vergilius on bees,*
> *The nose and dialogues of Socrates,*
> *Don Quixote, Hudibras and Trinculo,*
> *How worlds are spawned and where the dead gods go,—*
> *All shall be shard of broken memories.*
>
> *And there shall linger other, magic things,—*
> *The fog that creeps in wanly from the sea,*
> *The rotten harbor smell, the mystery*
> *Of moonlit elms, the flash of pigeon wings,*
> *The sunny green, the old-world peace that clings*
> *About the college yard, where endlessly*
> *The dead go up and down. These things shall be*
> *Enchantment of our heart's rememberings.*
>
> *And these are more than memories of youth*
> *Which earth's four winds of pain shall blow away;*
> *These are youth's symbols of eternal truth,*
> *Symbols of dream and imagery and flame,*
> *Symbols of those same verities that play*
> *Bright through the crumbling gold of a great name.*

Although he chose law as his profession, MacLeish never liked
it. Notwithstanding, he led his class at Harvard Law School, and
in 1919 received his LL.B., his course having been interrupted by
enlistment in a United States hospital unit during the World War.
While still a student he had married, in 1916, Ada Hitchcock of
Farmington, Connecticut—a singer.

As a member of the Field Artillery, to which he was soon transferred, he saw active service in June and July 1918 at the front,

north of Meaux. Then he was ordered home to train recruits at Camp Meade. When demobilized he was Captain of Field Artillery. Of this experience he wrote later:—"It was neither heroic nor particularly hard, but it destroyed my brother, many of my friends, two years of my life." After the war MacLeish taught for a year at Harvard, and then practised law successfully for three years in Boston, or until that day in 1923 from which he dates his "real life," when, giving up the law he started with his family for Paris. There began for him his whole creative existence—that period which was so surprisingly interrupted by his appointment as Librarian of Congress.

The job that awaited Archibald MacLeish in Washington was a very different job to that which had confronted Herbert Putnam forty years earlier. Putnam had been faced then with the necessity of bringing to an organic state that great mass of unorganized material which had accumulated under Spofford. As a result, MacLeish found the work of amassing and "processing" accessions well under way when he assumed charge. He found, ready-made, well organized collections that compared very favorably with the most famous collections anywhere in the world. His job seemed to be one of putting this great cultural instrument to wider work, of finding new means by which it might enrich American life and the lives of Americans. He found ready at hand a limitless source of intellectual energy, the application of which challenged his industry and his inventiveness. He set to work, taking office on October 1, 1939.

The Library staff consisted of 1,200 employees when MacLeish took over. Even a superficial survey of the salary scale convinced him that mature men and women engaged in exacting scholarly labor in the Library service were underpaid and he called the attention of Congress not only to this fact but to the need for complete reclassification of their professional status. His own annual salary was that received for some years now by Herbert Putnam—$10,000. So successful was he in presenting the financial needs of the Library to Congress that in the winter of 1940 he was given an increase of $400,000 over the appropriation granted the Library the previous year, and authorization for fifty sorely-needed additional staff positions.

At the very beginning of his administration MacLeish had demonstrated his belief in the value of attaching young, energetic, scholarly and liberal-minded men to the Library staff, of infusing new administrative blood into its life-stream. First of his chief appointments had been that of Dr. Luther H. Evans, who, as organizer and first Director of the Historical Records Survey, had distinguished himself with the brilliance and magnitude of his operations in a practically untried field. Evans was a man whose outlook was similar to MacLeish's own—young, forward-looking, not afraid of unbroken trails. Like MacLeish, he had imagination, a fine appreciation of the Library's possibilities, and a high ideal for service. With his A.B. and A.M. from the University of Texas and his doctorate from Leland Stanford, Evans had, moreover, chosen political science and international relations for his field—a useful understanding in an institution which serves Congress. He had had wide experience, too, as a University professor at Leland Stanford, New York University, Dartmouth and Princeton.

MacLeish persuaded him to come to the Library of Congress as the Director of its Legislative Reference Service. The appointment, effective December 1, 1939, caused something of a stir in those quarters where administrative changes were being observed with curiosity and not always friendly interest; there was some criticism on the part of those who feared the "liberalism" of the new appointee; but there was more applause. When MacLeish followed this appointment with a second—naming Arthur A. Houghton, Jr., as Curator of the Rare Book Collection, the *New York Times* announced, with probably as great a show of glee as it ever permits itself:

> Among the minor shocks administered by the New Deal to a tradition-loving nation has been the minor revolution in the Library of Congress. . . . First, President Roosevelt appointed a young poet to be librarian, and within a year that poet, a modern of moderns, reached out and dragged into the whispering gallery of the Rare Book Division a mere youth of thirty-three, making him curator of that remarkable collection. Arthur A. Houghton, Jr., is undoubtedly the youngest man who has ever occupied that position, and he came to it, not from another library, not from a college professorship, but from a glass works, to which he still devotes about 50 percent of his time. It is proper to inquire, then, what sort of person is this curator and how Librarian Mac-Leish happened to appoint him.
>
> Mr. Houghton himself is too modest to shed any light on his appointment, but it so happens, according to others who ought to know, that he is probably the outstanding private collector of rare books in the United States and, in addition, an executive of unusual ability. . . . He is one of the Houghtons of Corning, and after he was graduated from Harvard in 1929, he went into the glass works in Corning as an apprentice, reporting for work at 6 A.M. and learning the business from the bottom up. . . . He is president of Steuben Glass, Inc. . . . Mr. Houghton virtually alone guided Steuben out of the doldrums into its present national and world position. . . . Librarian MacLeish casting about for an active man to take charge of the Rare Book Collection, decided that young Houghton was the man if he could get him. So MacLeish wrote him a letter, suggesting that "it might not be entirely out of the question for him to begin even at his age a progressive retirement from active business life and devote some of his abilities to public service. I put it on a purely patriotic basis, and, rather to my surprise, after some correspondence, he took to the idea with enthusiasm."

By this appointment Archibald MacLeish secured for the Library of Congress perhaps one of the best-informed men in the rare-book field in America today, one whose expressed ambition is "to do something toward making this collection a bit less of a museum"; who would like to see it made "as broadly available to bona-fide scholars as is consistent with the preservation of the books and manuscripts themselves."

Repercussions to these successive victories were generous and immediate. The *Washington Star* gave early recognition; on April 1, 1940, it published an editorial headed "Achievement":

When President Roosevelt last summer named the poet Archibald MacLeish of Connecticut to succeed Dr. Herbert Putnam as librarian of Congress, there was prompt and more or less violent objection to the nomination. It was argued that he was a radical amateur, altogether lacking in qualifications for the post to which he had been designated.

But those who knew Mr. MacLeish personally were not disturbed. True enough, he had contributed to "left wing" magazines and had attended no library school. But his friends realized that these were unimportant faults as compared with the endowment of intelligence, sincerity and earnestness which he possessed. They trusted his imagination and the vitality of his courageous spirit. Also, they had the wit to understand that he had marvelous powers of adjustment. He could meet the opposition on equal terms—and triumph over it. Senators who questioned him came away from the encounter anxious to vote for his confirmation. Members of the Library staff who had trembled in their boots in fear of his coming emerged from his office ashamed of their panic. Within a few weeks his bitterest foes found themselves applauding him.

Now after six months it is plain to everybody that Mr. MacLeish has justified the President's confidence and merited the public's respect. Whether or not he remains on the job indefinitely may not matter. If he left the Library today, his influence would remain a constructive force of durable value. He has set a pace which in itself is a fine achievement. The battle he has waged for necessary increased appropriations for the purchase of new books, repairing old volumes, bringing cataloguing up to date and especially for adequate salaries for scholars employed in the Library is but one incident in the story of his service. His

385

success in persuading fellow-idealists like Dr. Luther H. Evans and Arthur A. Houghton, Jr., to collaborate with him is further evidence of his genius for doing what needs to be done.

A little less than a year after he had named Evans Director of the Legislative Reference Service, MacLeish selected him for his Chief Assistant Librarian.

This post had fallen vacant at the death, on June 15, 1940, of Martin Arnold Roberts—one of the most devoted laborers who ever served the Library of Congress. Roberts had entered the service of the Copyright Office in the Library in 1903 and had made his way, rung by rung, up the administrative ladder. From Assistant Chief Clerkship of the Library he had been appointed Chief of its Division of Accessions in 1923. For a decade, from 1927 to 1937, he was Superintendent of the Reading Room. On September 17, 1937, Herbert Putnam had selected him as his Chief Assistant Librarian. From 1936 to the time of his death Martin Roberts had also directed the national service for the blind in the Library. Entire and single-minded in his devotion to its interests, he was a true example of a "career-man" in the Library's history. Archibald MacLeish wholeheartedly acknowledged his own indebtedness to him: "During the early months of my librarianship, he put his knowledge, his energy and his loyalty at my disposition with a generosity for which I can find no adequate words of appreciation."

When Luther Evans left the directorship of the Legislative Reference Service to succeed Martin Roberts as Chief Assistant Librarian, he had already completely reorganized that division and had rendered it of far more extensive service to Congress than it had formerly been.

Organized, as we have seen, in 1915, under an appropriation of $25,000 provided for in the bill of Senator La Follette of Wisconsin—the Legislative Reference Service in its first full year of operation, 1916, received and answered 756 Congressional inquiries. From then its service increased until a high record of 1,604 inquiries was reached in 1920; appropriations rose gradually from the initial $25,000 to $61,530 a year, with an average of around $39,000. In the four years immediately preceding Dr. Evans' appointment as Director, Congress was making increased use of the service, asking questions at the rate of 5,000 or so a year and appropriating an average of $98,000 for its maintenance.

Shortly after December, 1939, so great had the volume of business grown that Evans effected reorganization of its various sections charged with individual functions such as the digesting of bills, indexing of Federal and State legislation, and general or specialized research. Today, a monthly average of more than 1,500 research problems of Senators and Representatives cross the desk of the Inquiry Section, are assigned to and answered by a skilled staff of trained researchers, and returned to Members of Congress in the form requested. Inquiries, involved or simple, in the field of international affairs, sociology, American or European history, economics, military affairs, legal research, literature or the arts, are put to it by Congress, and its scholarly research and counsel are freely used by the White House, by Members of the Cabinet, the Supreme Court, and other high officials of the United States Government, and ambassadors and ministers of certain of the foreign countries, as well as by that body whose personal service it really represents, the United States Congress. Responsibility for all information, written or oral, that is dispensed to these distinguished inquirers in answer to the great bulk of the general research inquiries is vested in the Head of the Inquiry Section. The Director of Legislative Reference Service, with its Bill Digest, Federal Law, State Law, and reference units, and its section devoted to problems of national defense, is Dr.

Ernest S. Griffith, former dean of American University, appointed to succeed Dr. Evans at Evans' elevation to Chief Assistant Librarianship. Evans saw the demands placed upon this important division of the Library of Congress as growing out of the times. However far dictatorships might depart from the light of true learning, he reasoned, democracies are unable to function without libraries. And as the relations which lie at the base of the democratic way of life become increasingly complex and more difficult to comprehend and to regulate, "so does the literature of research and of controversy become more prodigious and unmanageable, and plain citizen and statesman alike more bewildered." In this predicament, said Evans, "they perforce turn to libraries, not only for reading matter, but for the intelligent counsel of those whose business it should be to possess knowledge and to impart it." It is his belief that it is to answer this demand, "or the part of it that comes from the Congress of the United States," that the Legislative Reference Service of the Library of Congress exists. The influence of his philosophy, the freshness and vigor of his viewpoints, served to vitalize this service during his brief tenure of office to an extent that marks its astonishing recent growth as a veritable personal achievement.

The appointment of Luther Evans to the second highest position in the Library of Congress, as Chief Assistant Librarian, was but one development of the Librarian's plans for administrative reorganization. Prior to his appointment, all chiefs or heads of divisions had reported directly to the Librarian of Congress. With the unprecedented growth of the Library and the extension of its services, Archibald MacLeish did not consider this feasible—or indeed any longer possible. One of his first acts as Librarian of Congress had been to enter upon as complete a survey of Library conditions as could be made. All phases of the administrative and technical work of the Library were made the object of study by various independent investigatory groups. Upon their findings and recommendations the Librarian of Congress based his plans for reorganization. During June and July of 1940, MacLeish created, with the issue of a series of General Orders, three major departments in the Library of Congress: the Administrative, the Processing, and the Reference. Director of the Administrative Department is Verner W. Clapp, as Administrative Assistant to the Librarian. Like Martin Roberts, Clapp is a Library "career man," with a long and distinguished record for service in the Library.

There are fused under his single direction all the "housekeeping services" of the Library, such primary functions as the Accounts Office, the Disbursing Office, the Mail and Delivery Service, the Office of the Secretary, the Office of the Superintendent of Library Buildings and Grounds, the Personnel Office and Supply Office.

Under the Processing Department, as the second major department, is centered over-all direction of all those technical divisions of the Library which are concerned with the operations by which books are prepared for the shelves. It has been active since September 1, 1940. Its first Director was L. Quincy Mumford, whose services, now terminated, were made available to the Library for a restricted period through the co-operation of H. M. Lydenberg, Director of the New York Public Library. Under this department are the Accessions Division, the Division of Descriptive Cataloguing, of Subject Cataloguing, of Catalogue Preparation and Maintenance, and the Card Division. All work of acquisition, cataloguing and card distribution are co-ordinated under this department head.

The Librarian of Congress sought to effect an early reform in the matter of speeding up the distribution of cards to other libraries by securing whenever possible copies of copyright books in advance of publication. About 12 percent of the copyright books, practically all important titles, are now prepublication copyright deposits, as a result of the co-operation of publishers. This has cut down the time required in preparing a library card from six to three weeks.

In addition to his duties as Chief Assistant Librarian, Dr. Luther H. Evans also serves as Director of the Reference Department—the Library's third major department. Under his general direction are the various reading rooms of the Library of Congress, the Rare Book Collection, the Union Catalogue, the Hispanic Foundation, the Photoduplication Service, Books for the Adult Blind, the Legislative Reference Service, the Library Fellowship, and the Divisions of Fine Arts, Periodicals, Documents, Smithsonian, Aeronautics, Manuscripts, Maps, Music, Slavic, and Semitic—each of which is separately administered by its own chief.

The highly specialized services of the Law Library and of the Copyright Office are not under the jurisdiction of any of the three new major departments. The Law Librarian, John T. Vance, and the Register of Copyrights, Clement Lincoln Bouvé, report directly to the Librarian. Under this simplified administrative plan, only five men report directly to the Librarian, whereas more than fifty were reporting to him when he took office.

In 1940 Archibald MacLeish had described the Library of Congress as "a People's Library of Reference." Congress, he said, had extended to the people not only the use of the collections but also "of the services of scholarship which had been created to make the collections more usefully available to the Congress," so that the Library had become, as well, a "reference library to the people." It is a fact, he believes, which most deeply characterizes the Library of Congress today and one which dictates its policy

390

as regards the maintenance and service of its collections. He has described it in this way:

> The Library of Congress is a people's library which provides to the people, through their representatives in Congress and their officers of government, as well as directly, the written record of their civilization. It is also, and at the same time, a reference library which provides scholarly facilities for the study of that record not to a limited number of selected scholars only, but to the Government, and to the people of the United States.

For these increased responsibilities Congress had already provided additional space and facilities. MacLeish derived immediate benefit from the increased space made available by the opening of the new Annex in the spring of 1939, and so was not hampered in plans for expansion as Putnam had been hampered in the closing years of his administration by the encroachment of the collections upon the little remaining available space of the old building. Moreover Congress, denying the greater part of an increase for 181 new positions requested by his predecessor, had placed direction of future expansion of facilities in his hands when the House Appropriations Committee had reported in the first session of the 76th Congress: "If a new Librarian is shortly to be appointed it seems only fair that any expansion of the Library which may be determined to be warranted should be left to his discretion. It is altogether possible that a change of administrative policy of the Library will accompany the change in administrative officers." Thus, while the Annex was practically completed at the close of the Putnam administration, it was destined to be fully occupied and in regular service in the early days of the administration of his successor; and to the discretion of that successor had likewise been left responsibility for staffing the new building.

In his first report to Congress, MacLeish had referred to the year which ended with June of 1939 as a notable year in the history of the Library, since during its course the Library occupied the new Annex, opened the Whittall Pavilion, and saw almost completed and dedicated the Hispanic Room, made possible by the co-operation of the Hispanic Society of America and its President, Archer M. Huntington.

The dedication of the Hispanic Room, on Columbus Day, 1939, was one of the new librarian's first official acts. The details of this beautiful room carry out faithfully the style of the *Siglo de Oro,* the sixteenth and seventeenth century taste of Spain and Portugal. An atmosphere of cloistered quiet and serenity pervades it. In its vaulted vestibule hangs a remarkable silver chandelier— an original example of the *mudéjar* style of Toledo. Armorial tapestries hang on the walls; the furniture is rich and distinctive. Special displays of rare maps, important documents and autographs, pamphlets, or early printed books, are arranged here in cases which line two walls. In this manner have been commemorated at suitable times the anniversary of some great event—such as the quartercentenary of Hernando de Soto's expedition from Cuba which culminated in the discovery of the Mississippi River, or the 400th anniversary of the printing of the first book in the Americas, in Mexico, in 1539. This latter exhibit traced the history of Mexican printing to the present day, showing the earliest examples that the Library of Congress possesses; the most significant books, beautifully printed or beautifully bound; and books of outstanding literary, social or historical value in rare editions, of the four subsequent centuries. Coincident with the international celebration of the 800th anniversary of Portuguese independence was presented an exhibit devoted to Portuguese printing in Portugal and its colonies.

From this exhibit vestibule opens the main reading room of Hispanic collections. Some 130 feet in length, it is decorated like

Reading Room in the Rare Book wing. *Below:* Entrance to the Hispanic Room

DONALD HOLMES

The Magna Carta in its temporary shrine in the Library, as it was on view until the
entry of the United States into the War

the vestibule, by a lofty frieze which records the names of great historic and literary figures of the different Hispanic countries— Cervantes and Camões, Magellan and Columbus, Loyola, El Cid, Lope de Vega, Calderon and Bolívar, with such great figures in Latin American letters as Gonsalves Dios, Bello, M. A. Caro, Sarmiento, Icazbalceta, Ricardo Palma, Rodó, Medina, Montalvo, Heredia, Darío.

Immediately adjacent to this gallery are the wood-paneled alcoves where any one of the 100,000 Hispanic volumes in adjoining stacks can be called for and studied in such seclusion and beauty as might have characterized the library of some seventeenth-century monastery.

A dado of soft blue tiles from Puebla in Mexico runs along the lower walls of the reading room. Gold brocade curtains the long windows and hangs at the entrances of the alcoves and the recesses of the wrought-iron balconies. The silver tone of the woodwork is complemented by the delicately colored leather of the chairs, and the soft woods of the reading tables. Two doors of Spanish design open into the administrative offices; a marble tablet commemorating the gift of the room hangs between them. The tablet is surmounted by a mural representation of the coat-of-arms of Columbus in the vivid blues and greens of old Mexican tiles. Adjacent individual studies are available for mature scholars or serious investigators pursuing special research.

Most striking feature of the room today is the decorative work on the walls of the foyer and vestibule by the famous Brazilian artist, Cândido Portinari, whose monumental murals were inaugurated on January 12, 1942, as the result of a project sponsored by the governments of Brazil and of the United States. Expressing common aspects of the history and culture of the other American republics, these murals represent, first, the discovery of the land; second, the great American theme of pioneering, the conquest of the forests and the dominion of the land; third, the teaching of the Indians by members of religious orders; and fourth, the mining of gold. Brilliant splashes of unrelated colors, superb draughtsmanship, strong masses of figures, rapid lines and staccato strokes combine in these murals curiously to excite the beholder and render unforgettable the high talents of the artist. He was one of the first to recognize the brilliance of American color and to use it in his paintings of life on the great *fazendas* of São Paulo, of coffee growers at their toil, Indians in the Amazon jungles, fishermen of Pernambuco, Negro dancers, and the hills of Río.

The Foundation was opened to readers on July 1, 1939, with Dr. David Rubio—who has been consultant in Hispanic Literature in the Library since 1931—as Curator of the Hispanic collections, and Dr. Lewis Hanke of Harvard University as Director of the Hispanic Foundation. Dr. Robert C. Smith of the School of Fine Arts of the University of Illinois subsequently joined the staff as Assistant Director.

The room was dedicated in the presence of a distinguished company which included high officials of the Government, and diplomats of the Latin-American countries. The Librarian of Congress designated the occasion as one "without precedent in the history of the Library of Congress, but not perhaps for the reason of which you think." It represented, he said, "the first time in the Library's history when the Librarian has opened a new building or a new division with a speech." The Library, he said, had moved across from the Capitol to the building in which they then stood, "to the accompaniment of an eloquent and admired silence." Forty years later it had "pushed its frontiers across the street to the Annex which can be seen from the windows without a single word." The difference, said MacLeish, was not only "a difference in librarians," one of whom being truly a librarian knew the golden value of silence, and the other of whom being a versifier suffered "from the itch which has always characterized my calling." The real explanation was that the times change as well as the men—that "there are times when a great institution can let stone and mortar speak for it. And there are other times when it must attempt to speak, however haltingly, for itself."

Once the value of the things of the spirit could be taken for granted. "Once it could be taken for granted anywhere in the civilized world that the free inquiry of the free spirit was essential to the dignified and noble life of man. Once it could be assumed as a matter of course that the work of artists, the work of poets, the work of scholars, was good and should be respected, and would be preserved. Now it is no longer possible to assume these things. Now—and it is still incredible to us that it should be true —now such an act of faith in the life of the human spirit as we perform here today, such an act of respect for the labor of poets and scholars and of love for that which they have made, cannot be taken for granted; cannot be left to speak for itself even in a room as beautiful, as eloquent as this. It is necessary to say what it is that we are doing and why it is that we are doing it. I for one am not proud of this necessity. I am not glad that it is necessary to speak."

What they were doing, said MacLeish, was dedicating a room and a division of the Library of Congress "which has been set apart for the preservation and the study and the honor of the literature and scholarship of those other republics which share with ours the word American; and which share with ours also the memories of human hope and human courage which that word evokes—evokes now as never before in the history of our hemisphere."

The reason for doing this was obvious. "We do it because this literature and this scholarship are worthy in themselves of the closest study and the most meticulous care and the greatest veneration; and because they, more than any other scholarship, help us in this Republic to understand the American past which is common to us all."

Man never was, and never can be such a philosophic abstraction as the thinkers of the nineteenth century supposed. Man is a creature living on this earth and the earth he lives on qualifies his life. America has shaped and qualified and redirected the lives of men living on her continents for four hundred years. "But we who are born in America and live our lives here have not very well understood our relations to these continents, nor our debt to them, nor in what way they have altered us and changed our bodies and our minds."

It is because we have turned, for the most part, to the literature and scholarship of Europe for instruction and for the interpretation of our world that we have not understood them. "We have found there great treasures, great wisdom, high instruction —but only rarely an interpretation of our own lives in terms of the earth we know. . . . We have looked at America with borrowed European eyes so long that we should hardly recognize our country if we saw it with our own. . . . But though it is inevitable that the great richness of our European past should impose its values upon our American present, it is not inevitable, and it is surely not desirable, that the great richness of our European past should exclude us from the richness of our own."

There has been accumulating on these continents from the beginning of the sixteenth century, the Librarian said, "a body of recorded American experience of the very greatest importance to anyone concerned to understand the American earth and the relation of that earth to the men who live upon it. Because this experience has been recorded in several languages and because it has been deposited in scattered places—places as far apart as

Santiago de Chile and Bogotá and Buenos Aires and Mexico City and New Orleans and St. Louis and Quebec—because, furthermore, it has been overlaid with the continuing importation of European literature and European thought—for all these reasons the recorded American experience has not influenced the common life of the Americas as it should have influenced it. It has not been useful to an understanding of the Americas as it should have been useful. . . . No man living in the United States can truly say he knows the Americas unless he has a knowledge of these things—a knowledge of this other American past, this older American past which shares with ours the unforgettable experience of the journey toward the West and the westward hope. What we are doing in this room, then, is to dedicate to the uses of the citizens of the United States, and to the uses of learners and readers everywhere, these records of the American experience. In this Hispanic Room of the Library students of the Americas may follow the great Iberian tradition which has populated with its ideas and its poetry by far the greater part of these two continents. Here they may read the rich and various works written in these continents in the Iberian tongues—the two great tongues which, with our own, have become the American language. Here, if our hopes are realized, Americans may some day find the greatest collection of Hispanic literature and scholarship ever gathered in one place.

"There are men in the world today—and many rather than few—who say that the proper study of mankind is not man but a particular kind of man. There are those who teach that the only cultural study proper to a great people is its own culture. There are those also who say that the only real brotherhood is that blood brotherhood for which so many wars have been fought and by which so many deaths are still justified. The dedication of this room and of this collection of books is a demonstration of the fact that these opinions are not valid in the Americas: that in the Americas, peopled by so many hopes, so many sufferings, so many races, the highest brotherhood is still the brotherhood of the human spirit and the true study is the study of the best. This is the belief of the people of this Republic expressed by the action of their national Library in the dedication of this room."

This message was significant far beyond the modest importance the Librarian of Congress had attached to it. It marked, in a way, the entrance of the Library of Congress into international relationships—establishing a spiritual fellowship with other countries beyond the deposit of duplicate cards with foreign libraries, or the pleasant exchange of documents. Here was welding of a strong bond, a plea for good-neighborliness, for mutual understanding between nations of a common heritage. It pledged the resources of the National Library of the United States to development of that better understanding.

Quietly but certainly it launched the Library of Congress upon a mission of international usefulness, and set a policy as much greater than any previous policy in its spiritual import as the writing of a book is to cataloguing it.

When the Librarian had stated that the Library "had pushed its frontiers across the street to the annex—without a single word," he spoke with literal exactness, for when that white marble structure at last stood ready for occupancy those divisions of the Library marked for removal to the new quarters picked up the tools of their trades and went, one by one, more or less quietly, across the street. The guards first, to protect the building and its contents; laborers and elevator operators to help move the divisions; and the charwomen for housekeeping. Then, in sequence out of the old building and into the new went the Card Division, the Copyright Office, the Classification Division, the Accessions Division, the Catalogue Division, the Photoduplication Service and its laboratory of microphotography, the Photostat Section, Periodicals represented by bound newspapers, the Smithsonian Division, the Building Division and the Reading Room Binding Section. The labor force assisted in transferring one million volumes of books, 90,000 volumes of bound newspapers, and more than 100,000,000 catalogue cards contained in 105,000 steel card-trays in steel cases.

The staff of the Government Printing Office took charge of the installation of the Printing and Binding Divisions.

David Chambers Mearns—another Library of Congress "career man," and one whom the Librarian of Congress has recently appointed to the even more responsible position of Chief Reference Librarian—was at the time of the transfer Superintendent of the Reading Rooms. His duty it was to make the reading rooms of the new Annex ready for the public and to superintend the tremendous task of installation of the public catalogue which duplicates that of the main Library, so that readers in either building may conveniently be served with any books on the Library's lists. On April 5th, after books had been transferred to the Annex building in sufficiently large numbers to make their use there desirable and profitable, the Annex Reading Rooms were opened to the public, with all the important reference books in place and the pneumatic book-conveyors between the main building and the Annex in operation.

The building which was being thus gradually placed in service had been designed by the firm of Pierson and Wilson of Washington, and Alexander G. Trowbridge, consulting architect, at the commission of David Lynn, Architect of the Capitol. Directly east of—that is directly behind—the main building, the Annex occupies all of two city squares, with the exception of that extreme northern part on which Herbert Putnam had relinquished option in order that the Folger Shakespeare Library might be built where it stands today. Directly north of the main building, across East Capitol Street, stands the new Supreme Court building—so the Annex, like its parent building, is in distinguished company on every hand.

Rectangular, its white Georgia marble surfaces unrelieved except for the slight projections which give them interest and the broad set-back of the fifth floor, with a lesser one above it, the building rises five storeys above the ground—a chaste, classically simple block of dazzling white marble. Its fifth floor is given over in its entirety to the use of readers and the investigators conducting research in the study rooms. Below this level the whole central core of the building is filled with bookstacks, with work space provided outside this central core or shelf space, to a width of thirty-five feet all around the building on the three lower floors, with the corresponding space on the fourth floor reserved for storage. The entire building covers somewhat over two acres of ground, and has twenty acres of floor space. While the main building has a capacity for about 5,000,000 volumes, the Annex will eventually shelve about 10,000,000.

The fifth floor, devoted entirely to the public as it is, has received the greatest attention in the matter of decoration and ornamental detail. A spacious lobby of gray-veined marble, its windows hung with velvet draperies, faces the spacious card-catalogue room which divides the reading rooms into separate north and south halves. The muted greens and silver of this lovely hall are so delicate that they create almost that hazy effect of color which is created by the underwater greens and grays of submarine grasses. In both North and South Reading Rooms these muted tones are accented by the colorful friezes that run along the top of the walls. In both rooms these murals are the work of Ezra Winter—an artist also responsible for the distinctive ceilings of the Supreme Court building. The panels in the North Reading Room picture the Canterbury Pilgrims on the way to the shrine of their saint. The mural on the north wall recalls that "Aprille with his shoures swoote" when "longen folk to go on pilgrimages." The theme for the lunette in the south wall is taken from the introductory verses of the Prologue of the Franklin's Tale:

> Thise olde Gentil Briton in his dayes
> Of divine aventures maden layes,
> Rymeyed in his firste Briton tonge;
> Whiche layes with his instruments they songe,
> Or elles redden hem, for his pleasance.

It pictures those ancient Britons, in a company of three, playing on their instruments and singing their lays.

Ezra Winter's murals also decorate the South Reading Room. Originally planned on a different theme, they were redesigned at the request of MacLeish and with the sympathetic consent of the Joint Committee on the Library, as a memorial to Thomas Jefferson. Drawing their theme from quotations from the writings of Jefferson, the paintings reflect his essential thought on Freedom, Labor, the Living Generation, Education, and Democratic Government. Prior to the execution of these murals there existed in the Library no impressive recognition of the fact that Jefferson was the spiritual begetter—as MacLeish puts it—of the Library. They now stand as an eloquent and noble acknowledgment of the debt owed by the Library of Congress to its true founder. The murals were dedicated in the "Thomas Jefferson Room" with impressive ceremonies on December 15, 1941, as part of the observance of the sesquicentennial of the adoption of the Bill of Rights. The Librarian of Congress on this occasion introduced the Honorable Francis Biddle, Attorney General of the United States, whose address preceded a concert given on the Stradivari instruments by the Budapest String Quartet.

Each of these reading rooms is approximately sixty by one hundred feet, with a capacity of several hundred readers, alcoves for reference books, rooms for special collections, and a reference and book-issuing desk. They are thirty-five feet high. They are furnished with long, broad study tables, well placed lamps and comfortable chairs for the readers, and are well ventilated.

The Science Reading Room, adjacent to the Smithsonian Division, opens from the Jefferson Room. It will also be decorated with murals by Ezra Winter, illustrating the history of science and technology.

On this same floor, arranged in two tiers around the periphery of the structure, are 172 private study rooms, each about eight by eleven feet in size, with outside light, and individually equipped for study or research with a desk and swivel chair, a reading lamp, ample bookshelves, a typewriter stand and chair and a small extra table. Each study room is air-conditioned and the occupant has independent control over heating and ventilation. Removable partitions make it possible to form larger units when additional space is desirable. These rooms are practically soundproof, and the wall panels are of a corklike substance which permits the hanging of maps, charts, graphs, or other media of research.

In this pleasant atmosphere of privacy and comfort, the investigator is privileged to make the fullest possible use of the resources of the Library of Congress. Books which he has selected from the catalogue are delivered to his room and picked up for return to distribution when he has finished with them. At his fingertips he has available the illimitable wealth of source material that this—the world's largest library, can provide. He can go to ancient manuscripts or books dating from the dawn of printing for his information or he can consult all the important newspapers and periodicals of America before they are a few hours old. In any branch of literature or the other arts, in any line of science he has available the thoughts, the findings and conclusions of great minds, the reports of the learned societies of all the world. In practically any subject which he elects to pursue he may enjoy the advice and counsel of experts, the co-operation of the Library's "consultants" or incumbents of its "chairs."

This all costs nothing . . . all that is required of an applicant for these privileges is a reputable character and a serious pursuit. Nowhere in any other country of the world are greater efforts made to advance the cause of scholarship or learning by making freely accessible to whoever requests it every available written record of the past. And nowhere in the world is that accomplished with a greater spirit of helpfulness, real interest, or more practical, willing service than in the national library of the American people.

Just how highly those same American people regard these opportunities for individual research is evident from the reports of Donald G. Patterson, in charge of the Library's Study Reference Service. There have been, he records, four stages in the development of these special research facilities at the Library of Congress. While students and scholars had always made extensive use of the Library's resources, it was not until early in the post World War period that the need for appropriately secluded quarters and special facilities for those engaged in mature and productive scholarship became acute. The demand and pressure grew, until Dr. F. W. Ashley, then Superintendent of the Reading Rooms, reported in 1922 that it had "never been so great as this year." At that time only a limited number of tables were available "for use of authors, scholars, and governmental researchers whose requirements for the successful prosecution of their studies are obviously greater than those of casual readers." About 160 of these more serious investigators had been accommodated from time to time "but at least as many more requests have had to be refused, deferred or partially met by inferior accommodations, because of lack of space."

Ashley called attention at the time to the fact that "the Library possesses no research room where really adequate accommodations can be provided for those who need to examine large numbers of books, to dictate, or to use typing machines. Such facilities of this sort as we have are scattered about the building among the book collections or on the main floor of the reading room. In only a very few of these places are the conditions for intensive study satisfactory."

The demand must have been great, for when the Study Room Reference Service was organized in 1927 there were already on file the names of more than a thousand investigators; it had only been possible to accommodate 160 annually of this number. With the completion of the northeast stack in 1927 additional accommodations became available around the periphery of one of the decks in this stack; a series of twenty-five study rooms, with outside light and natural ventilation, was built for investigators doing advanced work. On the deck above space was provided for tables and desks for the use of research workers or staff members. Thus the Study Room Reference Service opened with 25 study rooms and 100 study desks. For three years the Service had to function within this limited area, and in that period it accommodated 1,012 investigators, 145 of whom came from foreign countries. Of the 867 from the United States, 675 represented American universities, 95 governmental units, and 134 were from associations, foundations, and similar organizations. Still scholarship was not being adequately served, judging by increased requests for study facilities, and as early as 1928 Martin Roberts had foreseen the necessity of ultimately sacrificing even this table space to meet administrative expansion.

Congress came temporarily to the rescue by providing $387,000 to enlarge the east and southeast bookstacks to correspond with the enlarged northeast stacks. This practically doubled the number of study rooms and greatly increased the number of study tables, and added space for group research. The requirements of encroaching administrative activities made sharp inroads on these facilities, however, often depriving the Service of as many as a hundred study tables at a time, but despite these handicaps the Library of Congress accommodated, from 1930 to 1938, when the Annex made its encouraging contribution of space, 8,200 private investigators—7,641 from the United States and 559 from abroad. Of the Americans, 4,416 investigators represented American universities and colleges. With the opening of the Annex the 172 additional private study rooms became available to writers and scholars. Today the records show that citizens of practically every foreign country have made use of these facilities and men and women from every State in the United States; a great number of foreign universities, and practically every important university and college in this country have been represented; associations, foundations, and government departments; Congressional committees and Congressional secretaries, Senators and Representatives—all have occasion to be grateful for this special service. The list of published books which have been written or partially written, or for which research has been undertaken in the study rooms of the Library of Congress is a long list and impressive. Van Wyck Brooks's *On Literature Today*, Duncan Aikman's *The All-American Front*, Roger Burlingame's *Whittling Boy*, John Dos Passos' *The Ground We Stand On*, Edmund Burnett's *The Continental Congress*, Richard Aldington's *The Viking Book of Poetry*, Howard Kennedy Beale's *A*

History of Freedom of Teaching in American Schools, Stoyan Christowe's *The Lion of Yanina,* Elmer Ellis' *Mr. Dooley's America,* Holman Hamilton's *Zachary Taylor, Soldier of the Republic,* Herbert Agar's *Pursuit of Happiness,* Elizabeth Page's *The Tree of Liberty,* Frank Smith's *Thomas Paine, Liberator,* Jenny Ballou's *American Success Story,* Henry Pringle's *Life and Times of William Howard Taft*—to name at random but a handful of the more recent, grew out of research conducted wholly or in part in the study rooms of the Library of Congress, or were entirely written there. Today, encouraged by the expressed intention of the Librarian of Congress to extend to everyone who wants it the opportunity freely to use the Library's resources, writers and scholars everywhere are applying for study-room privileges. The numbers accommodated have swelled to thousands, and even this soon after the opening of the Library Annex, facilities are strained by the demand. But every applicant is given consideration, and no one is discouraged, for—as it has always been true, in the Library's history, or any other history, when the need is great, the means are in time forthcoming.

With occupation of the Annex came extension of another service of great value to contemporary researchers and to researchers yet to come, to the public at large, and to busy Members of Congress. This was the Photoduplication Service.

With the aid of the grant of the Rockefeller Foundation which established it on March 1, 1938, the Photoduplication Service of the Library had been enabled to purchase apparatus of the most advanced design and equipment for the development of an outstanding microphotographic laboratory in time for its installation in the Annex. The Service, with George Schwegmann Jr., as Director, was set up with two clerical assistants and four competent technicians under the immediate supervision of Donald C. Holmes, Chief Photographer.

For eleven months prior to moving to the modern, air-conditioned laboratories of the Annex, this Service had operated with such success that it was able to reproduce in answer to the demands of Congress, the Library and the public, more than 106,000 microfilm exposures—equivalent to nearly 200,000 pages, 31,000 photostat prints, 1,500 cut film negatives and 7,000 photographic-paper prints. This had been accomplished in spite of lack of adequate space and laboratory facilities in the old building. After only five months in their new quarters, production doubled what it had been for the same period the previous year. In the first year of operation photo copies were produced "in complete satisfaction of public demand," as the Director reported.

As soon as the American people became aware of the fact that there existed in their national library a service equipped to reproduce for them, at nominal cost, any item in the Library's collections, they were quick to take advantage of the opportunity. This documentary duplication opened up hitherto undreamed of possibilities for the citizen, the teacher, the student, the scholar, the writer. No longer was a journey to the Capital necessary for verification of a fact, reference to a source, or the securing of a document. In its first complete year of operation more than four thousand requests for photoduplication were received from correspondents in every State of the Union, from Canada and from many foreign countries. And the demands were as varied as the resources of the Library. They included requests for copies of the Declaration of Independence, of manuscripts, maps, pictures, newspapers, copyright records, and selected passages from books. An encouraging evidence of the value of the Service was the fact that a very large proportion of these orders came from scholars and business institutions in distant sections of the country, far from established cultural and library centers. As the Director reported, "Indeed, microphotography and other photographic processes enable the distant research worker to assemble in his own study, at modest cost, the wealth of not only one but of many libraries."

This service was contributing in another way—to the preservation of the sources of learning. One of the major problems of libraries has always been that of preserving the wood-pulp newspapers that accumulate in great quantities. Representing as they do the contemporary record of American civilization, these newspapers contain such invaluable research data that their permanent loss would constitute a national catastrophe. Because the collection of American newspapers in the Library of Congress is the largest and most important collection in existence, the Library was faced with the prime obligation of preserving these records from disintegration.

Before 1876, newspapers were printed on durable rag paper, but after this date practically all newspapers were printed on wood-pulp stock, which is affected by use and exposure. After fifteen years such paper becomes discolored; in twenty or twenty-five years it becomes brittle and begins to disintegrate. An idea of the importance of the problem may be gained from the fact that about 80 percent, or 60,000 volumes of the Library of Congress collections of American newspapers are printed on wood-pulp paper. Science, as it has so often done, came to the rescue. There was developed the microfilm technique of reproduction. The National Bureau of Standards estimates that the microfilm image can be made as lasting as the best quality of rag paper.

The Librarian of Congress, concerned with preservation of these valuable records, presented the problem to Congress. In 1939 that body provided the modest sum of one thousand dollars to be used experimentally in microfilming a portion of the Library's newspaper collection. There was chosen for this experiment the file of the *Washington Post*. Before Archibald Mac-

Leish had been a year in office, 125 rolls of microfilm, reproducing the *Washington Post* from 1877 to 1904 and the *Washington Weekly Post* from 1894 to 1900 had been made. The following year Congress granted a continuing appropriation of a thousand dollars and the sum was used to defray the cost of microfilming the *Evening Star* of Washington from 1853 to 1918 under the terms of an agreement to share the cost equally, made between that paper and the Library of Congress. Co-operative undertakings of this kind whereby other libraries may share the benefits, with the costs, of microfilm reproduction, are now being considered by the Librarian.

If by these increased means the Library of Congress was being brought to distant citizens of the Republic, those citizens were still coming in great throngs to visit the Library of Congress. In 1941 more than a million visitors crossed the threshold of the main building—an average of almost 3,000 people daily, and more than 130,000 visited the Annex across the way. Thousands of that million or more had come with one prime objective, to satisfy an old and cherished ambition—to see for themselves, in the original, the Declaration of Independence and the Constitution of their free land.

XVIII

"OF SUCH AS CANNOT DIE"

*I*f one ascends the grand staircase of the main floor of the Library of Congress and turns right across the spacious marble area of the second-floor exhibition hall, he will face that shrine which for many a traveler marks the end of a determined pilgrimage—the Shrine of the Declaration of Independence and of the Constitution of the United States.

Placed between two marble pillars topped with curled acanthus leaves, the repository resembles a marble altar, with a stone footstool set between the clawed feet of its pedestal, and tiny bronze eagles flanking the opened doors of the cabinet above. Designed by Francis H. Bacon, the shrine safeguards these precious documents from touch and from injurious light, without in any way obstructing one's view of them.

Inscribed on the wall panel above, between the pillars are these all-sufficient words:

THE
DECLARATION OF INDEPENDENCE
AND THE
CONSTITUTION OF THE
UNITED STATES OF AMERICA

These historical documents were installed in the Library on February 28, 1924, in the presence of President Coolidge, the Secretary of State, and a representative group from Congress. Not a single word was uttered on that occasion until the onlookers started to sing *America*. As Verner Clapp and David Mearns observed in recording the event, "The impression upon the audience proved the emotional potency of documents animate with a great tradition."

That the documents are now enshrined in the Library of Congress was due to Dr. Gaillard Hunt—in charge of the library and archives of the Department of State at the time, and to Secretary Charles Evans Hughes, who recommended to President Harding on September 29, 1921, that the originals of the Declaration of Independence and of the Constitution be transferred from the Department of State to the Library of Congress. The President, in directing the transfer, did so, he stated, "that they then might satisfy the laudable wish of patriotic Americans to have an opportunity to see the original fundamental documents upon which rest their independence and their government." Accordingly, in an act approved March 20, 1922, Congress appropriated "For providing a safe, permanent repository of appropriate design, within the Library of Congress building, for the original of the Declaration of Independence and the Constitution of the United States, $12,000 to be immediately available."

These documents had been closely guarded by every custodian in turn responsible for their safe keeping. Mearns and Clapp in their authentic account of the travels of the papers trace the Constitution from that historic first-floor chamber in the State House in Philadelphia, where, beautifully transcribed, it was first read aloud, to the marble shrine in the Library of Congress, step by step.

From the Philadelphia State House, Major William Jackson, Secretary of the Convention, carried the Constitution to the Continental Congress, which was sitting in New York, and there gave it into the keeping of the Secretary of Congress. Congress occupied quarters at the time on the east side of the second floor of

City Hall, at Wall and Nassau Streets—a location from which they moved temporarily to permit renovation of the building. This fact suggests that for a few months the document may have been transferred to another building. But the papers of the Continental Congress were back at the City Hall in 1789. While the new Government was launched, with the inauguration of President Washington, many government functions, until the organization of the executive branch, continued to be discharged by the old confederation. Thus the original of the Constitution remained in the custody of the Secretary of Congress, Charles Thomson, along with other records of the old Congress. On the 23rd of July, Thomson surrendered the documents to President Washington, who subsequently instructed him to deliver them to "Mr. Roger Alden, the late Deputy Secretary of Congress, who is requested to take charge of them until further directions shall be given." An act to provide for the safe-keeping of the papers, records and seal of the United States, was approved by Washington on September 15, 1789. This act created the Department of State and provided for a Secretary of State, who, among other duties, "shall forthwith after his appointment be entitled to have custody and charge . . . of all books, records and papers, remaining in the office of the late Secretary of the United States in Congress assembled."

As first Secretary of State appointed under this act, Thomas Jefferson would automatically have assumed immediate custody of the Constitution. However, he was on the way home from Paris at the time, and John Jay acted as Secretary of State until his return. As the Mearns and Clapp account points out, Jefferson arrived in New York on March 21, 1790, to take over next day the duties of office, so that "it may be presumed that on that day the primary responsibility for the custody of the Constitution devolved upon him." From that moment, although the removal

412

of the Government to Philadelphia and from Philadelphia to Washington and the later invasion of the Capital by the British made it necessary to carry the Constitution to many places, the original document never passed out of the custody of the Secretary of State, "was never put on exhibition, and suffered no deterioration."

By such devious routes it came eventually to the State, War and Navy Building in the Capital, and there it remained until Dr. Hunt suggested its removal to Secretary Hughes, who in turn recommended it to President Harding—at whose direction it was installed for all time in the Library of Congress, where, as the Librarian of Congress has said, it is "visible without formality to any visitor." Like the Gutenberg Bible, the Constitution and the Declaration of Independence have temporarily been removed, for the period of the war to a place of greater safety.

Similar precautions have been taken to protect another document of great historical value—the Lincoln Cathedral copy of Magna Carta, the Great Charter of England. Archibald MacLeish wrote in November, 1939:

> It is natural that men should value the original documents which guarantee their rights. The great Constitution and charters are not mere records of something already accomplished. They are themselves its accomplishment. It is for this reason that Englishmen, and those who have inherited the political institutions of the English, attach particular importance to the actual ink and parchment of the Great Charter of John. The original of the Great Charter is valued not because its terms are terms of present significance but because it is itself an action in the long struggle for liberty.
>
> Like certain feudal ruins, to which it is related in terms and time, its establishment was a limitation upon the absolute power of the King. It belongs, therefore, in the great sequence of such limitations. And since liberty is itself only the freedom which such limitations leave, it belongs in the great tradition of liberty.

The deposit of "such a document in such a place" was, as Archibald MacLeish stated when receiving it in the name of the American people, "an action full of meaning for our time." Its deposit in the library of the people's representatives in Congress, said MacLeish, "is a plain and intelligible statement of a plain intelligible fact—the fact, namely, that the institutions of representative government are the protectors, and the only possible protectors, of the charters of the people's rights. For generations past we have taught our children in this Republic that our institutions of representative government were dependent on our Constitutional charter for their existence. We have more recently learned, and now believe, that the opposite is also true: that without the institutions of representative government the charters of the people's rights cannot be saved.

"There are those in this country," said MacLeish, "as there are those in England, who have told us by direction and by indirection that we should abandon representative institutions. There are those who disparage the people's representatives in Congress and who lose no opportunity of publication or of public speech to explain that representative government is not efficient government in a complicated and industrialized society like our own. But though there is much talk there is little listening. For we have been brought to observe, in these last several years, that government by the people's representatives, whatever else it may or may not be, is the one government of which history has record under which the people's liberties have been secure."

The Great Charter was given into the custody of the Librarian of Congress on November 28, 1939, by the late Marquess of Lothian, then Ambassador from Great Britain. Justices of the United States Supreme Court were present, a few Members of Congress, some representatives of the diplomatic corps, and a crowd of spectators who had left the reading rooms to witness the ceremony.

The British Government, the British Ambassador said, did not want to incur the risk of sending the historic document across the ocean. It had been on exhibition in the British Pavilion at the New York World's Fair and his government had instructed him to ask the Library of Congress to keep it "until travel is safer."

The Marquess of Lothian had turned over the precious document with the words: "The principles which underlay Magna Carta are the ultimate foundations of your liberties no less than ours. Samuel Adams appealed to 'the rights of Magna Carta to which the Colonists, as free subjects, have undoubted claim.' It was in their name that your ancestors threw the tea into Boston harbor and rejected the claim of King George III to tax the Colonies for defense.

"It was in their name," he added, "that, after bitter sacrifices and frustration, they drew up that Constitution which Mr. Gladstone, one of the greatest champions of human freedom, described as 'the most wonderful work ever struck off at a given time by the brain and purpose of man.' "

After the Librarian had accepted the document and directed its installation in the imperial case which had been prepared for it and in which it had been exhibited at the New York Fair, he received the keys from the hands of officials.

"History," remarked the Librarian of Congress, "has many curious and circuitous passages—many winding stairways which return upon themselves—but none, I think, more curious than the turn of time which brings the Great Charter of the English to stand in the same house with the two great charters of American freedom. Thomas Jefferson, who was the true founder of the Library as well as the true author of the noblest of our charters, would have relished the encounter. But Thomas Jefferson would perhaps have relished it with a different understanding from our own. For Jefferson was a man who dared to think of history in timeless terms, and of the rights of men as rights which had existed, and which would exist, in every time and every country:—rights which nothing done by tyranny had ever yet destroyed or ever could. To Thomas Jefferson, the deposit, beside the Declaration of this Charter of the liberties of those from whom we won our independence, would not have seemed incongruous but just and fitting—an affirmation of the faith in which this nation was conceived."

This main second-floor hall of the Library of Congress contains many other interesting and significant exhibits, for, according to the times and the events, on the acquisition of valuable or historical collections, the contents of the exhibit cases are changed from time to time. Thus, there is a case devoted to such sentimental and personal items as Abraham Lincoln's inkwell, Mary Todd Lincoln's bespangled fan, the letter of condolence written to Mrs. Lincoln by Queen Victoria of England after the President's assassination, and other interesting "association" objects of Lincolniana.

Various and diverting have these exhibits been. There was, for example, the display of George Arents' unique collection of books, drawings and manuscripts relating to tobacco, which traced in rare and entertaining documents the origin of the "divine weed," the disputes that raged over its use, the history of its cultivation and the irresistible anecdotes to which its introduction gave rise, so that whether one agreed with Edmund Gardiner's estimate— proffered in 1610—"Here lieth he, had lived longer, if He had not choakt himself with a Tobacco whiff," or stood with Holyday in his assertion—made in 1618—

416

Earth ne'er did breed
Such a jovial weed,
Whereof to boast so proudly,

he was still in a way to derive satisfaction from the display.

Then there was the display of that provocative assortment of literary treasures that John Davis Batchelder had gathered in every corner of the world, pursued throughout years of travel, reading and study and finally gave to the Library of Congress— a collection of more than 1,500 books of all literatures and ages, manuscripts, fine bindings, illustrations and broadsides, every item distinguished for five intrinsic values—its fundamental value of subject matter, its printing—either a first edition or the work of some famous printer, its illustrations, its binding, and its association value. Rare and charming are the items characterized by this last value, for the autographs of the immortal Goethe, Gibbon, Pepys, Duse, Pavlova, and Newton are but a few of the illustrious signatures on the fly leaves of these books.

Especially alluring had been that case devoted to the Orientalia of the Batchelder collection, containing such fabulous curios as a prayer-wheel from Tibet, a wheel of jade inscribed with the emblems of Confucius, Persian and Sanskrit manuscripts, an Arab saddle-book and fan-books from Burma and Ceylon whose lacquered leaves, spreading like thin gold and crimson wings, recount in raised letters of red rich as mahogany some story of Buddha in Pali.

As Keeper of the Collections—a post to which he was appointed by Archibald MacLeish on July 1, 1941, after eighteen years' service in the Library—Alvin W. Kremer has general supervision of the Library's exhibitions, as well as heading the central agency having physical custody and care of all materials in all departments and divisions of the Library.

Another "career man" raised to a more responsible post by

the Librarian is Robert C. Gooch, who was appointed on July 1, 1941, Superintendent of the Reading Rooms with responsibility for the centralized supervision of all reading rooms. This post had fallen vacant by the promotion of David Mearns to the position of Reference Librarian of the Library of Congress.

MacLeish, if one may judge wisely after only two and one half years of service, seems to have set out to open, in every direction and so far as practicable, the immeasurable resources of the Library of Congress to Congress and to the American people. It was to be expected that a man of his natural abilities would accomplish far more than the efficient administration of an institution, and that the boundaries of usefulness of the Library, its importance and interests, and its value to Congress and to people everywhere, would be correspondingly extended.

From the floor of the House, Representative Plumley of Vermont said on March 13, 1940:

> I would like to make public acknowledgment of an error of judgment. I opposed the confirmation of Mr. MacLeish as Librarian of the Library of Congress, on the ground I thought we should have a man trained in library work. I wish now to acknowledge publicly, and as publicly as I protested his confirmation, that I made a mistake.

MacLeish's aim is to extend the Library's usefulness. In July, 1940, he established, with the aid of a generous grant from the Carnegie Corporation, a group of Fellowships of the Library of Congress, so that in time the collections might be surveyed for quality and a planned program of acquisitions be developed that would increase the Library's influence. These Fellows are young scholars who have finished their graduate work and have begun the practical specialization in their various fields which will enable them to criticize the Library's holdings with judgment and perspective. Appointments are for a year and on leave of absence from the faculties to which they belong. The first Fellows of the Library of Congress are Dr. Richard H. Heindel of the University of Pennsylvania, Dr. Edward P. Hutchinson of Harvard, Dr. Jerrold Orne of the University of Chicago, Dr. William E. Powers of Northwestern, and Mr. Francis J. Whitfield of Harvard. The special fields represented are modern European history, sociology, the influence of United States culture on foreign cultures, population studies, vital statistics, library science, history and culture of the Romance peoples, meteorology, climatology, geography, Slavic history and Slavic culture. Dr. R. D. Jameson is Administrator of Consultant Service.

The ultimate objectives of any library determine the program of acquisition, MacLeish realized, and so he appointed a Committee to determine what the Library's accession policy should be. Out of conferences based on their surveys and study, was evolved his "Statement of Objectives." Spofford, said MacLeish, had considered the library first as "a library for the use of a legislative body," and second, as "the library of the American people, supported and constantly enlarged by taxation." He did not "aim at the impossible goal of 'universal completeness.'"

Spofford's basic views had been accepted by Herbert Putnam, who, like Spofford, believed that while a library "universal in scope" was pleasing in idea, it was not practicable "unless you are sure of unlimited funds." Putnam had been of the opinion that the Library should, therefore, lay particular stress "on the material peculiarly appropriate to it under its title as a National Library"; nor should it duplicate the special collections of other libraries.

The Statement of Objectives submitted by MacLeish stemmed not only from these declarations but also from a consideration of the historical position of the Library and the nature of its development. The Library of Congress, he believes, "is, by creation and primary responsibility, the library of the elected representatives of the people of the United States." But "Congress long ago extended the use of its library to other officers and offices of the Federal Government and to the people themselves, placing at the disposition of the users not only the rich collections with which the Library was in time provided, but the skilled services of the scholars, the technicians, and the experts in various fields whose first duty was to make the collections serviceable to Congress. The Library of Congress thus became what Thomas Jefferson had once called it: 'the Library of the United States'—the library of the people's representatives in Congress, the library of the officers of their government and the library of the people themselves." Thus, said MacLeish, the fact that the Library of Congress today is really a "People's Library of Reference" will in the future dictate its policy as regards the maintenance and service of its collections.

Under this policy it is his intention to secure all bibliothecal materials in some useful form that are necessary to the Congress and the officers of government of the United States in the performance of their duties, and all books and other materials—in original or copy—which express and record the life and achievements of the people of the United States. These two "canons of selection" will control his choice of books; they must be satisfied first "both in order of time and in order of money," but they do not exhaust the book-buying interests of the Library.

"No people," the Librarian of Congress believes, "is isolated either in space or in time, and no civilization is autonomous. To understand their own records, the people of the United States must understand what went before and what exists elsewhere. The written records of European civilization are their concern as are also the records of Asiatic and African civilization and the records of the civilization of the Americas. The people of the

United States are a people of many pasts, being a people of many origins, and these pasts are a part of their common past." This determined the third canon of selection for the Library; to possess, in some useful form, the material parts of the records of other societies, past and present, and to accumulate, in original or in copy, full and representative collections of the written records of those societies and peoples whose experience is of most immediate concern to the people of the United States.

Two exceptions to this canon, said the Librarian, should be noted. First, the Library of Congress as the central United States depository for the publications of all foreign governments will attempt to secure all the official publications of all governments of the world. Second, the Library will not attempt to establish intensive collections which duplicate outstanding collections of other libraries in well-defined areas in which the Library of Congress is not strong.

The same considerations, or nearly so, will under MacLeish govern the policies of the Library of Congress as an agency of research and reference work. Unlike other reference libraries, whose main function is simply to secure, keep up to date and make reference material available to readers without responsibility for organization or preparation of the material for the reader's use, the Library of Congres exists primarily to serve the needs of Members of Congress and thereafter the needs of officers of government generally—and must often do reference work for them and at their direction, since few public men have time to search the collections for themselves. Thus the reference services of the Library of Congress, are, and must be, manned by trained research and reference workers able to consult the Library's collections on behalf of Members of the Congress and officers of government whose duties require recourse to those collections. "It is for this reason," states MacLeish, "that the Library of Congress maintains in its Reference Department, its Division of Documents, its Legislative Reference Service, its Law Library, and its special reference units, such as the Social Sciences Reference Room, the Division of Aeronautics, the Division of Orientalia, the Hispanic Foundation, the Division of Maps, of Manuscripts, etc., a large staff of persons trained in scholarly work. And it is this reason which determines the Library's reference research objectives."

Under this policy the Library undertakes for Members of Congress any and all research and reference projects bearing upon the Library's collections and required by Members in connection with the performance of their legislative duties. It undertakes for officers and departments of government research projects, appropriate to the Library, "which can be executed by reference to its collections, and which the staffs of offices and departments are unable to execute"—projects which are deferred, except in cases of emergency, to reference projects undertaken for Congress.

The reference staff and facilities of the Library of Congress are also available to members of the public, to universities, to learned societies and to other libraries requiring services "which the Library staff is equipped to give and which can be given without interference with services to the Congress and other agencies of the Federal Government."

In line with this objective of Archibald MacLeish to make the services of the Library of Congress as broadly useful as possible, the Union Catalogue is being extended so that, when completed, it will serve as a finding catalogue for books in any American library; its photoduplication service is being set up to supply scholars anywhere with copies of materials in the Library's collections; its Archive of American Folk-Song is preserving, and its Phonoduplication Service providing, copies of the folk-music of the country; its interlibrary loan service is providing books or photo copies from the Library's collections to scholars unable to consult them on the shelves; its Card Division is selling copies of its catalogue cards to other libraries at incalculable savings to them of time, staff, building-space and other costs; its co-operative catalogue service is giving comparable aid, and for these and many other services libraries, universities, private scholars, and the general public are grateful for the existence of the Library of Congress.

The Librarian is branching out as well, into untried fields of national service. Within the Library of Congress on January 1, 1941, he established the Radio Research Project. This project had originated when a grant from the Rockefeller Foundation in 1940 placed at the disposition of the Library the services of two Fellows in Radio Research, to survey its resources with special regard to service to educational broadcasting groups throughout the country—at least 1,200 in number. The first Fellows in Radio Research of the Library of Congress were Philip H. Cohen, a former production director of the Office of Education Radio Division and associate director of the New York University Radio Workshop, and Charles T. Harrell, Program Director of Station WLB, on leave from the University of Minnesota station.

While the survey of these Fellows was still under way, there were being installed in the Library, under the enthusiastic eye of its modern Librarian, three sound-proof studios and the most modern phonoduplication equipment procurable—financed by a generous grant from the Carnegie Corporation of New York. Shortly thereafter the Radio Research Project, with Philip Cohen as chief and Charles Harrell as program editor, became a full-fledged permanent division of the Library of Congress. Within a few weeks of its organization a staff of experienced radio script writers and technicians was assigned to the project to write scripts and for the production of transcribed programs for both experimental and broadcasting purposes.

First of these programs to be developed was "Books and the News"—a series of six five-minute programs, each of which analyzed a given news topic and outlined in connection, in brief form, a reading list prepared by bibliographers of the Library of Congress. In this series were presented: The Balkans, The Machine Tool Industry, Latin America, Aviation, The Far East, and Automotive Construction. In each program an unidentified commentator urged the radio audience to secure the books mentioned at his public library. In addition, the audience was invited to write to the Library of Congress and obtain a book list on the topic discussed. These programs were, late in 1941, in use in more than two hundred stations, and in every instance local libraries offered full co-operation. In many small communities of twenty thousand or less inhabitants, the program was the means of procuring for the public library regular fifteen-minute radio programs, of which the five-minute transcription of the Library of Congress was a part. Book lists were compiled in cooperation with Miss Florence Hellman, Chief Bibliographer of the Library of Congress.

Here was a literal bringing of the Library of Congress to the people. Requests began to stream into headquarters in Washington. "We want weekly book-reviews," said the American public.

Encouraged by this response the Radio Project of the Library developed a second series of programs. In 1928 Mrs. Alvin Afflick Parker, of Strafford, Pennsylvania—one of the Library's "Friends of Music"—had furnished the initial subscription toward a fund which enabled the Library to organize an Archive of American Folk-Song. Since then John A. Lomax, consultant and honorary curator of the Archive, accompanied at times by his son Alan and other members of the staff, have been collecting the folk-songs of the American people for permanent preservation. For more than thirty years the elder Lomax had been traveling across the American continent recording these songs of the people, songs sung on the job, at a frolic, or at the fireside of their own homes; taking the songs and stories down at first on the old-fashioned wax cylinders of a talking machine. In later years as funds were provided for the Library of Congress for the project, modern equipment made perfect transcriptions. Out of his journeyings in all sections of the country, Lomax had garnered over a period of years thousands of recorded songs, discovering such favorites as *Home on the Range, Goodbye, Old Paint,* and *Boll Weevil,* and enough material to publish one book of cowboy songs and another of American ballads and folk-songs.

Upon this rich store in the Library of Congress the Radio Project drew for its second series—"The Ballad Hunter"—of ten fifteen-minute programs. Transcriptions were prepared telling the stories of Lomax's song hunts, so that—probably for the first time in radio—the American people were able to hear true American folk-music sung by authentic singers. Distributed by the Federal Radio Education Committee of the United States Office of Education at cost to schools and libraries, and radio stations, as well as to individuals all over the United States, they are proving one effective means of "making available to Americans everywhere the resources of their national library." On May 18, 1941, was inaugurated under this project a series of broadcasts over a national hookup, written by Joseph Liss and Oscar Saul, which, under the name of "Hidden History" develops the thesis that history is found not only in books and manuscripts in public libraries but in the minds and memories of the people. The Project also advises libraries as to more effective utilization

425

of the radio, furnishes bibliographical material, and develops collaboration generally between the public library and radio.

Another departure from precedent early in the Librarianship of Archibald MacLeish was inauguration of a series, made possible by Mr. and Mrs. Eugene Meyer of Washington, in which such representative American poets as Robinson Jeffers, Carl Sandburg, Stephen Vincent Benét, and Robert Frost appeared, discussed their poems informally and read from their best-known works. This series, free to the public, and inaugurated under the direction of the Library's consultant in Poetry and Drama, Dr. Joseph Auslander, proved so popular as to gainsay the assertion that poetry has no place in the life of the ordinary citizen. Hundreds of inquiries are received annually by the Poetry Archives of the Library of Congress, and gifts of holographs and other items of interest to poetry lovers are being made in increasing numbers.

One such outstanding recent gift was that of Mrs. Matthew John Whittall—to whom the music-loving public is already so deeply indebted—of every early draft known to be extant, and many later drafts and fair copies, of the poems of A. E. Housman. This superb gift constitutes probably the only collection in the world of all the known original manuscripts—as distinguished from fair copies—of any poet of comparable stature. In addition, the gift includes first editions of *A Shropshire Lad*, *Last Poems*, and *The Collected Poems of A. E. Housman*.

Other notable gifts are those of Mr. and Mrs. Eugene Meyer of the Thoreau commonplace book, and Juanita Miller's gift of Joaquin Miller material. Many such rare and intimate papers of absorbing interest to lovers of poetry are available for study in the Library of Congress today.

From nine to ten million items are now at the service of the American people in the Library of Congress, including books and pamphlets and manuscripts that are of such a nature or worth they may be said to speak authentically for the dead past or the living present. Archibald MacLeish analyzed the collections at the time he became Librarian of Congress. He found the Library pre-eminent not only in American local history but in American history in general. He found it pre-eminent in bibliography and in library science, as well as in the publications and proceedings of learned societies; and in economics and the social and political sciences. It was, he said, "eminent" in medicine. Its collection of incunabula ranked second in size in the United States, totaling 4,438 volumes, and the Library had collected more than 1,350 English titles printed before 1640. Its newspaper collections are "in all probability the largest in the country," and include the country's largest collection of foreign newspapers, with English files running back to 1620, Italian to 1768, German to 1773, French to 1777, and Spanish to 1786. Its collection of eighteenth-century newspapers is notable, being one of the two largest in the United States. In American newspapers of the two succeeding centuries its collection is the largest in existence.

In documents, the Librarian of Congress could report: "The Library's holdings are now the largest in the country with the old weakness in State and municipal documents corrected and the problem of foreign documents boldly attacked." The collection of older foreign documents is probably the most extensive in existence "and increasing vigilance in pursuing the exchange of current publications—which the Library of Congress by law controls—keeps the collection as full and as complete as the means available permit." The active and imaginative co-operation in this regard of the Department of State MacLeish considers invaluable.

For purposes of popular reading, the general collection of books about art is unsurpassed. The collection of fine prints includes the best collection in the country of the works of Pennell and will in time provide a similar collection of the works of Whistler and other modern American artists. The Library's map collections contain the best existing collections of American maps, one of the best atlas collections in the world, and a noteworthy collection of manuscript maps of great historical and æsthetic interest.

Second only to the library of the Harvard Law School stands the Law Library, though special collections at Yale, Michigan, Columbia, and in the library of the Association of the Bar of the City of New York are superior to comparable collections in the Library of Congress; there is reason to believe, however, that the Law Library of Congress is superior to any other American library of law as a practical working library.

In Hispanic materials, largely in the Hispanic Foundation, the Library of Congress possesses an outstanding collection of books published since 1917, "for the purchase of which," as the Librarian of Congress points out, "Mr. Archer Huntington has made generous provision." Its collections of eighteenth-century Spanish literature, Portuguese history, Camões, natural science, Catalan books, and works on archæology and Indian linguistics are also well-rounded, while its collection of Spanish drama of the nineteenth century is practically complete.

In music, in which the Library was "weak" in 1900, it possesses unrivaled collections of musical publications of the last fifty years, the largest collection of opera libretti in the world. Its Archive of American Folk-Song, including 45,000 phonograph records with sixteen to twenty thousand songs, is pre-eminent, and its collection of original manuscripts of composers from Bach to modern manuscripts dedicated to the Library's great benefactress, Mrs. Elizabeth Sprague Coolidge, is "rich and varied." Many of its great scores of chamber music have been presented directly and by radio in programs made possible by Mrs. Coolidge and Mrs. Whittall.

In the field of aeronautics, the gift of the Guggenheim Fund has made the Library's collections pre-eminent in the history of aeronautics and practically complete in early American aeronautic literature, while its files of aeronautic periodicals and serial publications are the richest in the world.

In Orientalia the outstanding position of the Library is as well known as Dr. Walter T. Swingle's part in its development. The Chinese Collection, with more than 30,000 items, exclusive of 32,000 in collecteana, is the foremost in this country "and inferior only to the holdings of the two or three major libraries in the Far East." The Japanese collection, though not outstanding, is good, strengthened by a recent Congressional appropriation of $30,000 for purchases in both fields. In Semitic literature the Library has what is probably the finest collection of Hebraica in the world, and its Russian collections are outstanding.

The manuscript collections, though still concentrated in the American field and still strongest in eighteenth and nineteenth centuries—particularly the period from the Revolution to the drafting of the Constitution—have increased from some 26,000 pieces at the beginning of Herbert Putnam's administration to more than six million at the present time. Moreover, the photo-duplication project financed by the Rockefeller Foundation, and the establishment of the Wilbur Fund have enabled the Library to obtain an unparalleled collection of transcripts and photocopies of materials relating to America in the archives of Great Britain, France, Spain, Mexico, Canada, and other countries. The Library's holdings of the papers of the Presidents, recently enriched by Mrs. Woodrow Wilson's gift of the Wilson papers, and the deposit, by members of President Taft's family, of the Taft papers, is by far the greatest collection of such papers in existence.

"But if the Library of Congress is a far greater library today than it was in 1900," Archibald MacLeish finds it "still a library of many and serious imperfections." He would fill in the gaps in the Italian and Spanish files of foreign newspapers, he would build up a better collection of books on art for reference purposes for the benefit of serious scholars. He would strengthen its Hispanic collections by the addition of books in Spanish-American history, in languages and literature, particularly prior to 1917. He would add monographs, treaties and encyclopedias of the sixteenth to the eighteenth centuries to its science collections, as well as collected sets of the works of scientists and scholars of that period. He would strengthen the Semitic collections by adding Arabica and building up its Yiddish periodicals, files and collection of Judaica. The Slavic holdings he would strengthen with additions in the Polish, Ukrainian and other Slavic languages. And he would make more distinguished the Library's manuscript collection by increasing its holdings in American literary and scientific and social manuscripts.

But the most serious present weakness in the Library of Congress collections, he considers to be "in those general non-American fields in which separate divisions or deposits, like the Hispanic Foundation or the Division of Orientalia, have not been provided. . . . in these fields, which include the principal European literatures, books are not added by copyright, gifts have not been frequent and recommendations for purchase have been largely left to impulse or chance." He would like, too, to add not only to the specific fields of European literature and social science, but "general history, education, modern anthropology, and technology."

These are the problems which the present Librarian of Congress is attacking with an engaging enthusiasm. "Nothing is more difficult for the beginning librarian," he wrote in June,

430

1940, "than to discover in what profession he is engaged. Certain professions define themselves. Others are defined by those who practice them. The librarian's profession is of neither nature. A librarian is so called not for what he does, as the farmer who farms or the lawyer who laws, but from the place in which he does it. And the definitions of the librarians, though they are eloquent in describing the librarian's perfections, are reticent in saying what the librarian's perfections are for. . . . Even modern librarians write as though the profession of the librarian had been defined when the scholarly and linguistic achievements of the perhaps ideal librarian have been described."

Everyone who may be said to know Archibald MacLeish—either by a study of his writings or by contact with the man himself—accepts as a foregone conclusion the high purpose he brings to his post. They expected of him that, respecting and appreciating the technical aspects of the profession, he would yet not see the cataloguing of a card, the compilation of an estimate, the tidy arrangement of rows of books on rows of shelves as the beginning and end of the librarian's responsibility. It is the spiritual quality that MacLeish stresses in everything he touches.

The librarian is more than the keeper of a physical book, a "sort of check boy in the parcel room of culture" whose duty is "to receive the priceless packages confided to him by the past and to redeliver them to the future against the proper stub." Such a librarian need only be "reliable, orderly, industrious, and clever"; he need only devise "infallible and complicated ticket systems to find the parcels on the shelves"; he need only guard the wrappers from "the risks of time and theft and matches and men's thumbs," and be "courteous, and patient with the claimants." For the rest, such a librarian has no duty but to wait. "If no one comes, if no one questions, he can wait."

But the librarian, to MacLeish, is custodian of the "intellectual

431

book" as well as of the physical book. This intellectual book is not "a ticketed parcel which can be preserved by keeping it from the mice and mildew on a shelf." The intellectual book "is an imagined object in the mind which can be preserved only by pre-serving the mind's perception of its presence." Nor is the intel-lectual book a deposit of the past which the future has a right to call and claim—it is rather "a construction of the spirit, and the constructions of the spirit exist in one time only—in that continuing and endless present which is now."

Thus, contends MacLeish, the profession of the librarian is not and can not be the "neutral, passive, negative profession of the guardian and fiduciary, but must become instead the affirma-tive and advocating profession of the attorney for a cause. For the intellectual book is the word. And the keepers of the word, whether they so choose or not, must be its partisans and advo-cates."

Which of these two meanings of the book is to be taken? Both, says MacLeish, are held. But "the librarian who asserts that the sole and single strength of his profession in a distracted world is its disinterested objectivity, meaning its negative and custodial detachment from the dangers which beset the world, thinks of the book necessarily as a physical object on his shelves for which, in its intellectual aspects, he accepts no share of risk or credit. The library trustee or the moralizing editor who demands of li-brarians that they stick to the job of pasting on the labels and handing out the loans accepts, but with less honesty, the same assumption—less honesty because he speaks, not from love of the librarian's profession, but from hatred of the Word."

Here is a philosophy, which, held by a Librarian of Congress will make the Library of Congress in time the greatest, instead of the biggest, library in the world.

It is not a philosophy which MacLeish forces upon librarians

432

or upon anybody. A man, he says, can choose only for himself. But there are, notwithstanding, certain considerations which "even a novice among librarians may propose." The chief of these is the nature of the times in which men live. A generation ago "the word, the life of the mind, the monuments of unaging intellect," were not under attack. All civilized nations, all governments in power agreed "that the cultural tradition was a common treasure, that truth was an end to be sought equally for all men, and that the greatest glory and final justification of human life was the creativeness of the human spirit." But in the world in which we live it "is no longer agreed by all governments and citizens that truth is the final measure of men's acts and that the lie is shameful."

Granted, says MacLeish, "that it was not only possible but desirable for the librarian to think of his profession in negative and custodial terms in the quiet generations when the burning of books was a medieval memory," is it still possible for librarians to think of their profession in these passive terms in a time "in which the burning of the books is a present fact abroad and a present possibility at home?"

Here is no impractical idealist speaking. MacLeish had already made preparations to protect with certainty every book of value in the Library of Congress should the need for such protection ever rise in the United States. For days volunteer workers in the Library of Congress, after their own day's work was done, labored until ten at night, selecting books for special care in case of national emergency, marking and labeling them, trundling them in and out of decks to the typists who compiled long lists for use at any moment of threatened emergency. He has made provision for deposit of the books in his trust where no harm can come to them, though the venerable building itself be selected as the special target of the bombs of those who, more than they fear any other vital force, fear the free mind of man.

In his *American Cause* Archibald MacLeish gave the reason for this hatred of the free mind. It stems from the realization that it is unconquerable . . . "the cause of the creative human spirit—the cause no enemy has ever overcome. Or ever will."

Bulwer-Lytton once termed books the "movers of the world." George Crabbe referred to libraries as "the tombs of such as cannot die." Walt Whitman recognized the immortal nature of books, their magic power to quicken at the touch of a reader:

> *Camerado, this is no book,*
> *Who touches this touches a man. . . .*
> *It is I you hold and who holds you,*
> *I spring from the pages into your arms.*

This is because man fights in vain against the truth and nobility of a sincere book. No reader can come unaffected from the reading of a good book, whether he will or no. Samuel Johnson spoke often of this secret influence on the understanding, of our inability to obliterate ideas at our pleasure: "He that reads books of science, though without any desire fixed of improvement, will grow more knowing; he that entertains himself with moral or religious treatises, will imperceptibly advance in goodness; the ideas which are often referred to the mind will at last find a lucky moment when it is disposed to receive them."

Archibald MacLeish, in his capacity as Librarian of Congress, is offering books as ideas to the mind of the American people without formality. The authority of art and learning, he tells the people, "rests on knowledge of the arts and learnings. Only by affirmation, only by exhibiting to the people the nobility and beauty of their intellectual inheritance, can that inheritance be made secure."

434

He is sure that one-half of a librarian's assignment is getting books for readers, the other half, is getting readers for books.

Times change and with them a librarian's responsibilities. It was a brilliant and stupendous job Herbert Putnam accomplished of building out of chaos a rich and orderly library and of developing it to a deserved position of fame and prestige. Much more is demanded of the present Librarian of Congress. The Librarian of Congress today must be capable of ardor and rage and jubilance and fury, as well as of the quiet pursuit of a well-ordered routine. His spirit must burn with indignation at the mutilators of books, their dismemberment of the written word. His imagination must be fired with high purposes of a patriotic, as well as a literary service. No one has said it more perfectly than MacLeish himself:

> Against those who would destroy the tradition he must bring the force of tradition. Against those who would mutilate the monuments he must bring the beauty of the monuments. Against those who would limit the freedom of the inquiring mind he must bring the marvels of the mind's discoveries.

This is necessary today in order that every succeeding generation of Americans may experience what Carl Sandburg has termed the peace of great books. Thomas Jefferson wrote that the earth belongs always to the living generation. MacLeish believes that the same is true of the past—it also belongs always to the living generation, and the true task of the librarian is to make the title good in truth as well as theory—to make the ownership bear fruit.

INDEX

437

INDEX

439

Divisions (Cont.)
  Orientalia, 315, 316
  Periodicals, 190, 313, 390
  Photoduplication, 345, 347
  Prints, 311, 351, 352
  Radio Research, 423, 424
  Semitica, 340, 341, 390
  Slavic, 390
  Subject Cataloguing, 389
Documents, 146, 147, 151-153, 184-186, 303, 304, 307, 347, 349-351, 390, 427
Dodge, William de Leftwich, 256
Donations, 314
Donoghue, John, 251
Dougherty, Joseph, 112
Dozzi, M., 251
Drama Consultant (Auslander), 426
Dresden library, 168
Duane, William, 39, 55
Duckworth, L. G., 197
Dupontes, Signor, collection, 148, 149
Durazzo collection, 184

Early purchases, 38, 39
Eastburn, J. & Co., 143
Economics consultant, 318
Edinburgh Review, 191
Eliot's inscriptions, 251
Endowments, 318, 322, 323, 325, 329, 332, 333, 339, 340, 345, 347, 351, 353, 354, 406, 424
Enoch Pratt Free Library, 377
Establishment of Library of Congress (Act of 1800), 34
Essex Register, 105
Esty, Alexander, 224
Evans, Dr. Luther H., 383, 386, 388, 390
Evans, Thomas, 34
Everett, Edward, 89, 144, 145, 148, 154, 155, 167, 318
Ewing, George W., 53
Exchanges, International, 185, 208, 303, 307, 329, 350
Exhibits, 416, 417
Expansion of Library, 211-216, 222, 229, 230, 343, 344, 347, 391

Federalist, Washington, 47
Federal Law Section, Leg. Ref. Serv., 387
Fellowship, Library, 390, 418, 419
Ferguson, Dr. Milton James, 365, 374
Fess, Senator Simeon D., 328
Fine Arts, chair of, 352
Fine Arts Division, 347, 390
Fines, 63, 64
Fires, 75, 154, 155, 170, 174, 175
First Collections, 24, 25
First Library of Congress, 23-25
Flanagan, John, 251, 252
Fletcher, William I., 234

Folger, Henry, 340, 359
Folk-song, Archive of American, 422, 424
Force, Peter, 165, 200, 204, 205, 304, 343
Ford, Worthington, 283, 343
Foreign libraries, 168, 215, 238, 262, 305, 346
Franklin, Benjamin, 26-29
Frazier, Senator, 379
French, Daniel C., 251
Fromentin, Eligius, 116-118, 132
Frost, J. T., 71, 72, 77, 78
Fung, Dr. Hing Kwai, 316

Gales, Joseph, 47-49, 104
Garfield, Dr. Harry A., 362
Garfield, Henry, 266
Garnsey, Elmer, 256
Gerry, Elbridge, 31, 32
Gerry report, 32, 33
Gleig, George Robert, 74, 75
Goldsborough, Robert, 117
Gooch, Robert C., 418
Göttingen library, 149, 168
Government Document Bibliography, 350
"Grant Row," 326, 360
Great Charter of England, 413, 414, 415, 416
Green, Bernard R., 226, 234, 264
Greenwood, G. M., 265
Griffith, Dr. Ernest S., 387, 388
Guggenheim fund, 325
Guide to Memoria of the Republics of Central America and of the Antilles, 350
Guide to Publications of Government of Mexico, 350
Gutenberg Bible, 326, 327

Halstead, Murat, 266
Hanke, Dr. Lewis, 394
Harnden Express, 191
Harned, Thomas B., 344
Harisse, Henry, collection, 337
Harper's Bazaar, 294
Harrell, Charles T., 423
Harris, Dr. W. T., 234
Hartley correspondence, 188
Harvard Library, 149, 285
Hastings, Charles Harris, 363
Hayes, Rutherford P., 234
Hearings of 1896, 234-242, 300, 301
Hebraica, 342
Heindel, Dr. Richard H., 419
Hewitt, Abram S., 307
"Hidden History," radio program, 425
Hinman, Charles W., 191
Hispanic Foundation, 259, 340, 390, 392-394, 428
Hispanic Literature Consultant, 318, 319, 339, 340
Hispanic Society of America, 339

INDEX

Historic American Buildings Survey, 354
Historical American libraries, 283-295
Historical Records Survey, 383
Holland, Dr. Leicester B., 352
Holmes, Donald C., 406
Holmes, Justice Oliver Wendell, 324
Hopkinson, Joseph, 117
Houdini, Harry, 324, 325
Houghton, Arthur A., 384, 386
House Reading Room, 257
House Resolution, 8136, 360, 361
Hubbard, Gardiner Greene, bequest, 333, 351
Hughes, Charles Evans, 411
Hume, E. J., 161, 191
Hunt, Lieut. Edward B., 189
Hunt, Dr. Gaillard, 411
Hummel, A. W., 317
Hunter, William, 117
Huntington, Archer M., 339
Hutchinson, Dr. Edward P., 419

Incunabula, 204, 230, 306, 307, 324, 327, 329, 338
Independent Gazetteer, 47
Inquiry Section, Legis. Ref. Serv., 387
Interlibrary Loan Service, 239, 329
International Exchanges, 185, 186, 208, 303, 307, 329, 350
International Law Consultant, 319
Invasion of Capitol by British, 75, 85-87
Investigation, Spofford shortages, 219, 220
New building, 225
Investigators, Service for, 357, 358, 402-404
Islamic Art Consultant, 319

Jameson, Dr. R. D., 419
Japanese collection, 324, 429
Japanese Law Consultant, 319
Jay, John, 412
Jefferson library, 93-103, 105, 106, 108, 113-116, 126, 150, 151, 175, 343
Jefferson murals (Winter), 401
Jefferson Room, 400-402
Jefferson, Thomas, 52, 53, 55, 57, 58, 60, 88, 93, 94, 97-103, 109, 112, 113, 115, 126, 150, 151, 435
Jewett, C. C., 202
Johnston collection, 352
Judaica, 340-343
Junto Club, 27, 28

Kaas, Huitfeld, 324
Keeper of the Collections, 417
Keller, Kent, Representative, 360
Kennedy, Julia, 136
King, Cyrus, 103
King, Josias Wilson, 50
Kirstein, Louis, 378
Knapp, Samuel, 167
Kremer, Alvin W., 417

La Follette, Senator Robert, 321, 386
Laing, Alexander, 378
Lamar, L. Q. C., 224
Langley, S. P., 234
Latter Day Luminary, 165
Latrobe, Benjamin Henry, 82, 122
Law, International, Consultant in, 319
Law, Japanese, Consultant in, 319
Law Library, 131, 134, 136, 144, 146, 153, 184, 185, 301, 303, 308, 311, 313, 329, 330, 390, 428
Law, Roman, Consultant in, 319
Law, Thomas, 84
Legislative Reference Service, 257, 319, 321, 330, 383, 386, 387, 390
Leipzig library, 168
Leland, Dr. Waldo G., 362
Lenox, James, 188
Lewis, Joseph, 98
Librarian, Chief Assistant, 386, 388
Librarian, Chief Reference, 399
Librarian Emeritus, 361, 362, 364
Librarians of Congress:
1. (John Beckley), 45
2. (Patrick Magruder), 61
3. (George Watterston), 48, 88, 89, 90, 108, 112, 113, 116, 126, 130, 131, 135, 136, 151, 152, 156
4. (John Silva Meehan), 161, 164, 165, 169
5. (J. G. Stephenson), 164, 193, 197, 198
6. (A. R. Spofford), 191, 197, 198, 199, 200, 202, 203, 208, 209, 210, 214, 215, 216, 217, 218, 219, 220, 224, 228, 230, 232, 233, 238, 242, 245, 264
7. (John Russell Young), 219, 220, 232, 242, 243, 244, 245, 259, 260, 261, 262, 263, 264, 299, 301
8. (Putnam, Dr. Herbert), 199, 220, 221, 222, 228, 230, 234, 239, 240, 266, 279, 280, 281, 282, 296, 303, 305, 306, 307, 309, 311, 312, 314, 315, 316, 320, 322, 336, 337, 338, 339, 340, 353, 354, 358, 359, 360, 361, 362, 377
Powers, 132, 235, 272
Requisites of, 241
Salaries, 45, 129, 156, 191, 314, 383
Service "rewards," 360
Librarian's profession, 430-434
Librarians, recommendations of, 234-242, 267-276, 280
Librarian's room, 254, 255
Librarian's Round Table, 362
Librarian's Testimony, 1896, 234-242
Librarians, training of, 290, 296
Librarianship, contestants for:
William Duane, 39
John McDonald, 39
at death of Young, 265, 266
Librarianship, press comments, 267-276, 280

444